POWER
AND

POWER
AND

The Female in Iberian
Families, Societies, and Cultures

ANN M. PESCATELLO

Contributions in Intercultural
and Comparative Studies, Number 1

GREENWOOD PRESS
Westport, Connecticut
London, England

HQ
1166
.P 47
1976

Library of Congress Cataloging in Publication Data

Pescatello, Ann.
  Power and pawn.

  (Contributions in intercultural and comparative studies;
no. 1)
  Bibliography: p.
  Includes index.
  1. Women—History. 2. Women—Social conditions.
3. National characteristics, Spanish. 4. National characteristics, Portuguese. I. Title.
HQ1166.P47   301.41'2'09   75-35352
ISBN 0-8371-8583-1

Library of Congress Catalog Card Number: 75-35352
ISBN: 0-8371-8583-1

First published in 1976

Greenwood Press, a division of Williamhouse-Regency Inc.
51 Riverside Avenue, Westport, Connecticut 06880

Printed in the United States of America

IN APPRECIATION
for the
FAMILY throughout history, everywhere,
because it made my study possible
and
IN MEMORIAM
for my mother, a lovely lady whom I loved,
who also made this study happen

CONTENTS

SERIES FOREWORD

Formed in 1974, the Council on Intercultural and Comparative Studies is a nonprofit academic organization dedicated to the dissemination of scholarship of the highest quality. The Intercultural and Comparative Studies Series presents distinguished works in four categories: history, anthropology, ethnomusicology, and linguistics. A fifth category, special series, includes works of merit not within the domains of the four more specialized categories.

The council is especially interested in sponsoring studies of subcultures within our society and of cultures other than our own. The council also encourages interdisciplinary or multidisciplinary works that reflect the latest scholarly trends. With this series, we hope to present comparative, cross-cultural, and innovative studies that will be of value to scholars and general readers alike.

PREFACE

Study of the female seems to have opened a Pandora's box of social, economic, and political ills as well as a new area of scholarship. More than a decade ago and long before it became academically fashionable, I began dispassionately collecting information, asking questions, and formulating hypotheses about females in the "developing areas." I continued this process for more than ten years as a corollary to research on immigrants, blacks, families, and peasant groups. During that time I lived, worked, taught, and undertook research in Latin America, Asia, Africa, the Middle East, Australia, and Europe, particularly Iberia.

My dispassionate approach began to dissipate as I became aware of some basic realities of discrimination and prejudice that seemed to make irreconcilable the worlds of female and male. I did not presume to put these materials together until Sheldon Meyer of the Oxford University Press prodded me to make available a scholarly tome on the female. I began work on the project, but with a strange enthusiasm. I felt that a book should be written but was not certain that I should do it and subject myself to the epithet "woman's liberationist."

My fears since have been dispelled. I believe that scholarly investigations of the historical world of women are long overdue. And they are long overdue from women. I do *not* endorse the idea that only women should write women's history (nor do I believe in that argument vis à vis any group). But United States scholars have been unable to escape our own culture's ideological biases and have failed to develop theoretical constructs that consider women as social actors. Women have different viewpoints, different emphases that derive not only from basic differences inherent to any individual but also from the particular environments in which they have been raised, educated, socialized, and have worked. Within that context this book reflects my own interpretations of ideas and events in the history of some of the world's women.

The methods as well as the theories and contents also reflect my own sui generis disposition as an "ethnohistorian." By original training an historian, from the beginning I have found the environment of traditional historical scholarship far too narrow and conservative in its all-important function of dealing with the record of human events and processes. Since then, I have labored diligently in several disciplinary fields, finding anthropology the most congenial of them for the historical dimensions of my subject matter. In addition to history and anthropology, other disciplines and approaches, such as linguistics, ethnomusicology, historical sociology, archaeology and art history, mythology, folklore, oral tradition, and literature, all have been of immense utility in formulating an approach to historical processes. In particular, I owe much to Johann Huizinga's view that historians and anthropologists are spiritual cousins; personally, I owe much to Richard Morse, who has boldly and often alone labored to raise the imagination of historians; and I owe much to the work of Bernard Cohn, historian and anthropologist. This book does not represent, nor does it demonstrate a consummated marriage in disciplinary methods discussed above, but it does presage my direction for the future.

In the past few years books have proliferated as publishers have heeded the needs and demands of intellectual curiosity about the female. But the overwhelming majority of those volumes have been anthologies of essays trying to speak to a common theme or collections of readings that generally concern only the woman's movement. Furthermore, almost all discuss the United States female, whose history is as different from the history of other women in the world as is the history of the United States different from that of other cultures. To my knowledge there is no scholarly study that attempts to synthesize, to summarize, to describe, and to interpret the female's historical experience either in individual cultures or in the general historical perspective. It seems obvious that such studies are needed.

To make my contribution to the larger study of women in history I have chosen to focus on the cultures and areas of the world I know best as a student of history: the worlds of and colonized by the Iberians, the peoples of present-day Spain and Portugal. In addition to contributing to an understanding of women in Iberian cultures, I hope that an investigation of the lifeways of women in Iberian cultures will offer new insights into Iberian history and will provide a mirror for study of other cultures, including our own.

The title of this work speaks to a dual interpretation, a polarization of views, each of which reflects theses of woman's place in history. One theory conceives of the female as the wellspring of power and wielder of influence in all areas of activity in her society. The other interpretation suggests that the female always has been a pawn in a world dominated by males. This duality has much to do with concepts of power and authority, for, in the end, the crux of the female "problem"–spreading worldwide in ever-widening concentric circles from its Anglo-American core–is in determining and attempting to reallocate on an egalitarian basis spheres of influence, power, and authority between female and male. In this I follow Weber's classic distinction between power and authority (Weber, 1947:152-3, 324-63 passim). In simple terms *power* is the ability of a person to carry out his or her will, despite resistance and regardless of whether that individual has the culturally ascribed right to do so. *Authority* is the ability of a person to have his or her will as a culturally legitimized and sanctioned right, and it is exercised through a hierarchical chain of command and control. The extent to which power may override authority might have something to do with the extent to which informal or unassigned power may be exerted by an individual and the strategies employed in exerting that power. *Influence,* which is a major form of persuasion, is a concept crucial to understanding the types of strategies employed in this process (see also Smith, 1960:18-20; Lamphere, 1974: 98-100; Parsons, 1963a:232-62; 1963b:37-62).

It seemed to me that the only way to end emotional polemics of this conceptual polarization of woman as power or pawn was to undertake a rational study of each area of female activity in society by seeking answers to such questions as: How has woman been regarded by each group and each stratum of society? What have been her legal, civic, and political responsibilities and rights? Where has she fit into the schema of miscegenation and marriage? What has been her position in social and economic activities, her influence on cultural and artistic life, on customs and tradition, in family and society? To what extent have societies been male dominated? Are male activities always considered more important and given more value and authority than are female activities? And, perhaps most importantly, to what extent have women acquired and used power, authority, and influence in these many Iberian cultures and societies?

This book is explicitly cross-cultural and multidisciplinary; it is implicitly comparative in approach, method, and content. It attempts to answer these questions both as a summary of what is known of women in Iberian families and societies in particular and as a contribution to a synthesis of female history in general. This book is about Iberian females–

in Europe, Asia, Africa, and America—and about females of those Asian, African, and Amerindian cultures with whom the Iberians came in contact and on whom they left their imprint, either in shadow or in substance. In order to arrive at an understanding of contemporary female life through an examination of females in Iberian cultures, it is necessary to discuss the place of women in the world view of all cultures involved. The results of the clash of world views as they relate to females also can tell us something about the general processes of assimilation and acculturation, about colonizers and colonized, and about what is general and what is particular to human societies.

Woman's sphere of influence has been accepted as the "private" arena of family and household, or domestic sphere, while man's has been "public" or societal activities. Although this book was not conceived as a study of family per se, in the thinking and writing it became clear that the female must be studied in the context of family and household, of family activity outside of the household, and, finally, in interaction with other societal institutions. One of the many things that has become clear to me in reanalysis of females, children, and families is that "family" is a complex and multifaceted concept. "Family" is, in fact, much more than a co-relative of terms such as "marriage," "kinship," "household," "nuclear," "joint," "patriarchal," and the like. "Family" is a complex of processes and arrangements, each different in its own right, its differences determined both by internal and external mechanisms and milieux. So, too, is "household" not a thing but a process. Household is just one component of family structure, but it is an important measure of family and can indicate important social relationships. Two basic concepts used with family and household are "nuclear" and "extended." A nuclear household consists of parents, children, and grandparents; an extended household is the nuclear group and any extra nonnuclear kin; an augmented household is a nuclear group plus extra non-kin. It really makes a difference as to who goes with whom and what, and there is an implicit relationship between ownership of agricultural property and an extended family (Daniel Scott Smith, lectures, 1974).

In addition to family conceptualized as cyclical processes and varying arrangements, we also must deal with concepts of society and culture, for females and families should be studied within the societal and cultural contexts and also within the context of public or male spheres of influence. M. G. Smith, whom I follow here, has defined as *societies* territorially distinct units having their own governmental institutions. The core of a *culture* is its institutional system, and each institution involves set forms of activity, grouping, rules, ideas, and values. The total system of institutions embraces three interdependent systems of action, ideas and values, and social relations, i.e., "the institutional system that forms the cultural core defines the social structure and value system of any given population" (Smith, 1965: 62-3, 71). For Smith "culture concept is normally wider than that of society since it includes conventions, languages, and technology," but there can be "two or more culturally distinct groups within a single society," and these would vary independently in their limits and their relations (Smith, 1965: 64-5). The institutions of a people's culture form the matrix of their social structure so that in order to define the social structure we must analyze the institutional system. To define a system of social value or action we must identify and analyze the institutional framework. If a population shared or shares a single set of institutions it will be culturally and socially homogeneous; if it also is politically distinct it will also form a homogeneous society (Smith, 1965: 63). By Smith's definition, for Iberia the basic institutional system forming the cultural core has been the "family."

A final note. This undertaking admittedly is presumptuous in its temporal or its spatial dimensions. It has been hazardous because sources are scattered and often polemical. My methodological and materials routes often have had to be ad hoc. But it is a beginning for study of half the world's historical population. Perhaps it is appropriate to begin here in the new age of discoveries, of space and, hopefully, of humanity.

ACKNOWLEDGMENTS

This book is a very personal experience for me although many persons have helped bring it to fruition. It is impossible to thank all the people who have been part of it, but there are some whom I must single out—first and foremost my parents, who raised me "liberated" and in whose home inferiority as a word or in practice was unknown. Friends and colleagues at stages along the way helped finalize the shape of this book. Several of my mentor-friends at the University of California, Los Angeles—Robert N. Burr, Earl T. Glauert, and Stanley Wolpert, for all of whom at some time or other I was a research assistant—always encouraged me, at a time when female graduate students were few and far between, and they gave me support and the benefit of their vast store of knowledge. In particular, the substantive manuscript and other materials on Padre Feijoo and the Iberian Enlightenment, that were part of Earl Glauert's collection, were useful to me, particularly for Chapter 7. In that regard, so too were my conversations with Kenneth Maxwell, now at Princeton University, helpful on matters of Spanish, Portuguese, and Latin American Enlightenment periods.

Members of my honors seminars and several graduate students at Washington University, St. Louis, and several classes at Florida Interna-

tional University, Miami, contributed much to the theory and content of
the project. In particular I single out Joanna Rosenthal-Mendelsohn, whose
thesis and with whom conversations on her thesis were helpful, and Joan
Przeworski and Anne Crabb, with whom in conversations I was able to
clarify controversial points of historiography on women. My research assistants at Washington University, James Wilson, now at Cornell University,
and Donald Douglas, now at the University of Texas at Austin, were of
immense help in the hunting, gathering, and organizing processes. Countless workers and officials in dozens of archives, libraries, and other institutions that provided me places in which to work and guided me to sources,
in Asia, Africa, the Middle East, Australia, Southeast Asia, Latin America,
Europe, and the United States, were really the bricks and mortar of this
study. Without them, there would have been but wisps of dreams.

Charlotte Peskind at Washington University typed and retyped the
early drafts, sometimes from almost illegible copy.

Several fortuitous events along the way aided this study. First, my
tenure as chairman of Latin American studies at Washington University
and later my positions as director of Latin American studies and dean of
the Center of International Affairs at Florida International University gave
me access to invaluable contacts throughout the Iberian world, many of
whom patiently answered my questions and occasionally argued a different case, but almost invariably aided in my ironing out problems and
paradoxes. Then, the world of scholarship on the female opened immensely
through two events. The panel "Female and Male in Latin America" (which
later became the basis for a successful collection of essays), of which I was
the coordinator and chairwoman, was a keystone of the Third Biennial
Latin American Studies Association meeting in Austin, Texas, in December
1971. And then, in the same month, in the first session ever devoted to
Latin American women at the annual meeting of the American Historical
Association in New York (which I organized and participated in) new
methods, research, and theories regarding the female were presented.

There are innumerable friends and colleagues who made my research
in Latin America, Iberia, and Africa particularly rewarding. To list them
all here would be to reproduce a mini-catalogue of scholars and citizenry.
However, I should make some special mention regarding impressions and
observations from fieldwork and oral history interviews conducted during
1964-1965 and 1968-1969 in South Asia. Entree into villages in northwestern and northern India was made possible by several Indian friends
and scholars: American anthropologist Jack Marshall; ethnomusicologist
Bonnie C. Wade; and the late Dr. Panduroga Pissurlencar, Dr. V. Gune,
and historian Michael Pearson, who provided archival and other invaluable
documentary information.

I have benefited from the advice and criticisms of colleagues in many
disciplines, among them Lewis Hanke, Richard Greenleaf, James Lockhart,

Stanley Hilton, Henry Landsberger, Thomas Skidmore, Thomas McGann, Thomas Glick, Robert Nachman, Dauril Alden, Barbara and Stanley Stein, Rebecca Bergstresser, Bonnie C. Wade, Louise Lamphere, Shirley Harkess, Cornelia Flora, Ivan Schulman, Joseph Schraibman, Martin Needler, John P. Harrison, Howard Kaminsky, Joyce and Brian Peterson, John Murrin, Richard Walter, Rosalind Mael, and E. Bradford Burns. In particular, I owe immeasurable thanks to Professors Lois Weinman and Francis A. Dutra, both of whom read the manuscript in its entirety, gave sound suggestions and criticisms, and were helpful with materials on Hispanic and Lusitanian cultures. Professor Dutra was additionally helpful on sources, directions, and other areas of polish, and we had many discussions, in person and by correspondence, on points in the manuscript.

My work on families, households, kinship, and related processes have benefited from (and hopefully are reflected here) my teachers in the Newberry Library Family History Institute, especially Daniel Scott Smith and Richard Jensen. To them and to their 1974 summer program I owe much.

All of these people, and many more, along the way have helped a great deal with the conceptualizations and content of the volume. Whatever shortcomings and other deficiencies of a pioneering study it may have, these failures are solely my own.

I have one final and irrepayable debt—as always, to Clem. With all my being.

Ann M. Pescatello
1975

POWER
AND
PAWN

1 THE FEMALE IN THE IBERIAN WORLD IN HISTORICAL PERSPECTIVE

In order to know where we are going, we need to know where we have been. Where we are going seems to be determined by changes in the woman's movement and may have its roots and validity in the peculiarities of the Anglo-American past. But will all cultures choose "liberation" options? The end results of this book might help us to answer that question for women in cultures influenced or shaped by Iberians. If they choose the same options, then perhaps we can generalize about values shared across cultures. If they choose different options, then a different set of generalizations may be valid.

Where we have been is intimately linked with the family, the major institution of societies. But in almost all cultures, family has been an institution different from the one with which middle-class, Anglo-American suburbanites are most familiar. Historians have said that women have no history. In the sense of how history has been written, for the most part in terms of powerful, visible individuals, then that is a fair assessment. But if historians were to shift their inquiries to the broader canvas of groups in society, then inevitably they must focus on that most powerful of all groups, the family, and its most important member, the female. And that is where we have been.

3

THE FEMALE IN WESTERN AND
NONWESTERN THOUGHT

Seeking answers to contemporary problems in historical ideas and institutions is a chicken-and-egg approach since it is difficult to discern whether institutions arise from theoretical concepts or whether ideas define a de facto situation. In searching for historical roots of woman's position in societies, I have encountered variant attitudes that developed separately from our own European tradition yet ultimately were absorbed into modern European social thought.

A growing school of Latin American theory contends that *latinas* always have been rulers of their destiny and are perpetuators of a cult of feminine spiritual superiority that has its basis in the riverine civilizations of the East and is expressed through "the feminine principle of life" (Acworth, 1965: 13-30 passim; James, 1965; Neumann, 1955; Stevens, 1973). Probably derivative from early man's awe at woman's ability to produce a live being within her body, its earliest expression is in art, particularly the "pregnant" Gravettian figures produced by Paleolithic painters. Archaeological evidence suggests southern Russia's Caspian Sea area as sources of the mother goddess cult that spread into the Tigrus, Euphrates, and Indus valleys as well as into Crete and the Aegean area.

From Mesopotamia to the eastern and northern Mediterranean the goddess figure spread. She appeared alone in archaeological and mythological evidence until the third to second millennium B.C. Then consciousness of male individuality appeared and the "unmarried mother" emerged, accompanied by a young male seen either as her son, her consort, or both. The prototype for an Iberian *mater dolorosa* developed in that Mesopotamian culture: the grieving mother whose young "god" is depicted as suffering, dying, and being carried to the underworld, and sequentially is linked into a regular cycle of changing seasons. From Crete the mother goddess cult spread throughout southwestern Europe, Italy, and Iberia. Supremacy of the female figure evolved in response to conceptions of what a "real" woman should be: semidivine, morally untouchable, and spiritually superior, in contrast to the unalterable imperfection of men.[1]

Almost all cultures maintain a matriarchal ideology that in the beginning women possessed all cult secrets and all sacred objects and that men later stole them (Eliade, 1965: 50). Cultures in America, Asia, and Africa with whom Iberians came into contact had their own corpus of myths as to the "prehistorical" place of woman in the cosmology of mankind. In many sections of South America myths recount female rule over land and men in prehistory, which suddenly is reversed by male discovery of female sources of power. A clear example of the transition from chaos (female) to order (male) is the Juraparí myth and rite.

Jurupari, depicted as the offspring of a virgin birth or as the son of the Sun, is made the vehicle through which the cosmic order becomes established. His laws are the laws of a tribal system that upholds a sacred convention wherein a separate set of values is maintained for men and for women. The laws stipulate that women are excluded from participation in important social and religious events because all females fall short of perfection as defined by the Sun Father and his earthly protagonist, Jurupari. Sexual differences, defined by and legislated in myth, are demonstrated in ceremony. To preserve these sexual distinctions in social life, supernatural sanctions are invoked. . . . Everywhere women find themselves restricted in their actions and subordinated to rules set by men. This pattern of male dominance and female subordination is a consistent theme surfacing over and over again in South American myth and ceremony. (Bamberger, 1974: 275-6.)

In South and East Asia there were similar myths heralding the rule of women and then their downfall. In India, motherland of the South Asia tradition, the myth pattern is documented by archaeology and oral tradition. In mother goddess fertility rites and worship practices similar to those in the Mediterranean and West Asia (Middle East), there is an association of mother goddess worship with the bull in all these ancient agricultural communities. A tantalizing suggestion has been made concerning the decline of mother goddess cults in that she was likely the divinity of the people, while upper classes preferred a god (Basham, 1959: 13-14, 22). By 2000 B.C. or later gods appeared more frequently, particularly for society's males and frequently formed permanent attachments outside and who, in his most important aspect of fertility deity, is known as "Lord of the Beasts," perhaps an indication of the rising influence of pastoral communities (Basham, 1959: 23). Thereafter, especially after the arrival of the Aryans, from about 1500 B.C. few goddesses appear, an indication of their decline in public influence.

In China, too, the motherland of the East Asia tradition, archaeological and mythological records delineate the shift from a matriarchal to a patriarchal society divided into tribal and clan units. The ultimate triumph of patriarchy and patriliny made "of Chinese women as so many uterine pawns in a male system. The Confucian [551-479 B.C.] values dominating Chinese social behavior (from that of the emperor to that of the poorest farm laborer) certainly codified such attitudes" (Wolf, 1974: 159).

Throughout Africa and Oceania the corpus of myths is similar. Exemplary of the shift of females from believed superiority to inferiority is the initiation address in several African societies: "Until now, you have been in the darkness of childhood; you were like women and you knew nothing!" (Eliade, 1965: 25). In almost all the myths, in oral tradition, art forms, and archaeological remains, scant as some may be, the belief is inherent and implies a shift from what had been prehistory and chaos to history and order,

> What we have is a break . . . with the world of childhood—which is at once the maternal and female world and the child's state of irresponsibility and happiness, of ignorance and asexuality. . . . The maternal universe was that of the profane world. The universe that the novices now enter is that of the sacred world. (Eliade, 1965: 8, 9.)

Although the presence and belief in a pancontinental corpus of myths that chronicled the shift from matriarchy and female superiority to patriarchy and male superiority imply utility in the amalgamation of donor and recipient cultures, primary Western attitudes regarding females were forged in the Judaeo-Christian tradition. In the Middle East, woman's status had been high, but in the millennium before Christianity it had begun to decline because Judaism had developed into a monotheistic religious system that expunged feminine influence. The Jews argued that goddess figures were inventions of their enemies and thus sought sustenance in a patriarchal, nationalistic, divine leader. Hebraic peoples began to place honor on women through motherhood, by encouraging early marriage, and by expecting love and fidelity from both husband and wife. But precepts of sacred law excluded females from ritual observances, except those within the home.

Another body of thought paralleling the rise of monotheistic Judaism developed in Hellenic Greece where patriarchy had become firmly entrenched, exploration of the intellect had become a pinion of society, and "man" was considered "the measure of all things." Variations existed in ancient Greece but the philosophical strain that Westerners suckled was nurtured in Athenian soil. Athens' citizens belonged to *phratries,* family groups connected by blood, in which they shared rights and privileges, but since this city-state harbored a sizable foreign community and since its citizenry wished to preserve purity of phratries, seclusion of their women became common.

As patriarchal superseded matriarchal influence, any Athenian wife was legally barred from her husband's household and remained under protection of her male kin. From childhood she was trained for an early marriage and for duties as wife and mother. Conversely, non-Athenian women could not marry a citizen but did provide female companionship for society's males and frequently formed permanent attachments outside matrimonial bonds. These *hetaerae* had no legal rights although many were learned women whose functions were to be physical and philosophical companions to their male sponsors. Hence Hellenic Greece affords a preview of Iberia's dichotomous behavioral patterns harmoniously existent within one society. Wives were true servants of society, preserving purity of bloodlines and dignity of male patriarchy, a sacred vessel to be excluded from mundane corruptions. Less "fortunate" women who could never share in Greek patrimony could be exposed to life, perform as priestesses, as philosophical companions, as powerful possessors and purveyors of the supernatural.

Rome, which was to shape so much of the institutional and intellectual life of Christian Europe, displayed yet another concept of woman shaped through time. Writings on the Roman female usually ennobled her as a figure of dignity, a concept highly honed and prized in Iberia. Republican Roman women were in tutelage to fathers and husbands, but during the transition to imperial rule numerous laws liberated the female, endowed her with much freedom and, especially in the halcyon days of empire, tolerated in her a laxity in moral behavior. Nonetheless, certain measures of acceptable standards were enforced. Chastity and purity were considered prime attribues for a marriageable daughter or patrician's wife. It was accepted that woman would preserve her honor and virtue as a civic duty and that males would honor that duty. Vestal virgins enjoyed a special place of reverence in Rome. The point to be stressed here is that these attitudes and patterns in Hebrew, Greek, and Roman life seem more the purview of the privileged classes than of peasants and proletariat.

FEMALES AND FAMILIES IN THE MEDIEVAL WEST

Although changes in institutions and thought were constant with the evolution of Western civilization, some very basic and fundamental shifts occurred sometime between the end of antiquity and late medieval times, shifts not only in the general order of Western institutions and thought but shifts that delineated more clearly than in the past differences among various Western societies. It is important to discuss here some basic patterns of development in institutions and ideas that have molded and characterized mainstream Western European cultures, since it is these cultures' values and concepts by which we measure other cultures.

"In societies of all types, the family is the fundamental multipurpose organization for many of the principal life functions of the individual and of society . . . the whole society begins with the family" (Mandelbaum, 1972: I, 33). Rankings in society "refer back to ways in which people handle their domestic affairs" (Wolf, 1966: 8). When we speak of family we refer to tremendous variations in that institution. Biologically, family constants are rooted in all parent/child, husband/wife, sibling/sibling relationships. In family as social processes and arrangements, the cycle of family development is replenished through marriage and mating, through establishment of households, and through social kin relationships. Symbolically, family is defined by a complex imagery agreed upon by social groups. In modern Western culture "family" means the nuclear or companionship family, which did not appear until about the fifteenth century and reached full flower in the eighteenth. The companionship or "conjugal" family is best typified by the relative exclusion of a wide range of "affinal" and blood relatives from its everyday affairs and no great extension of kin networks (Goode, 1963: 8). Prior to that the so-called medieval family had been the basis of social structure.[2] This "premodern" institution had functioned primarily as a transmitter of property, life, and legal names. Excessively communal and polygamous, it existed essentially as a polymorphous unit of relatives, friends, and servants who shared the same house and often the same rooms and beds, enjoying a high degree of unconcerned promiscuity. Individuals in such medieval units apparently brought a different set of expectations to marriage, which was regarded as perfunctory in human relationships.

Peasants and nonaristocratic rural freemen families apparently were able to function within a social, economic, and political framework in village communities aided by their seigneurs' usurpation of public authority. Peasants lived a free and flexible life, as intimate with friends and neighbors as with any biological or marital kin. Almost any freeman could live in whatever independent fashion desired, and husbands and wives managed their own properties, transacting business individually without interference.

There is evidence that an extraordinary mobility characterized medieval society from the eleventh century, accompanied by increased responsibilities for women of privileged classes. The Crusades, beginning in 1095, were a dominant force for change for the twelfth and thirteenth centuries and since males were absent on these military expeditions, rural family power and influence shifted to women who became de facto, if not de jure rulers of castles and kingdoms (Herlihy, 1962: 89-120 passim, and medieval troubador literature). In the cities budding urban life and mercantile activities, especially among wealthy merchant classes in the Italian city-states, relied on managerial skills and commercial expertise of women (Villani, 1823: 184).

Many of these women were literate, for not only were they active in mundane mercantile and other affairs of society, but they also were prominent in the arts. In the eleventh and twelfth centuries, Europe's aristocratic classes fashioned a relatively sophisticated and cultured style of court life, supposedly beginning first in southern France and spreading rapidly through Europe. Accompanying the prominence of the Crusades was a concentration on standards of chivalry in war and concepts of love as an extension of Christian grace through which one is saved. Preoccupation with the arts of war and love, considered to be the two major human activities, caused the two to become closely intertwined in an intricate code of court behavior. Chivalry in war was valued as highly as "pure love" between man and woman. Capellanus relates that true love could not exist even in marriage, that this love for man and woman was unrelated even to procreation and, indeed, courtly lovers rejected marriage as the acme of life (Capellanus, 1941: 171). Poets, writers, troubadors, artists, and others celebrated these ideals in art forms, focusing on women as the catalyst for and revered element in the new courtly life. Women seemed to be much in favor, if not in power.

Parallel to chivalric traditions exaggerated by two centuries of Christian wars was a reform movement pervasive of Western European ecclesiastical life. Begun by Pope Gregory VII (1073-1085) it carefully whittled away indirect avenues of female influence as well as such direct sources as a married clergy and the double monastery (Southern, 1970: 309-10). The Gregorian reforms seem to mark the watershed of feminine influence; thereafter women were excluded from the religious elite and, gradually, from other power groups in society. The Church "banned women from holy orders and considered their entrance into the sanctuary a profanation; women could not preach, nor could they attend the cathedral schools or the universities that succeeded them...." (Russell, 1971: 281). An unfortunate side effect of such exclusion was that reform leaders developed a hostility toward women that radiated from sacred to secular institutions.

Another effect from the eleventh century was changes in medieval piety induced by an exaggerated veneration of Mary, the Virgin. While veneration of the virgin and reverence for Mary, Mother of God, had existed in Christian mythology it was not until the twelfth century that her cult took hold. Some literature, documents, art, and other sources speculate that Marian worship developed as a result of Western contact with the Middle East during the Crusades.[3] Others suggest more specifically that "at the same time as courtly love, veneration of the Virgin Mary developed, placing one woman closer to God than any other human being save Christ himself" (Russell, 1971: 281). Thus historians have some paradoxes to deal with. On the one hand, war and other secular activities provided times and places for women to exert power and authority. On the other hand, religious reaction to these activities created an alien and hostile environment for females who wished to further enhance their public influence. These changes in concepts of piety, ideals, and morality were accompanied by more secular and material ones. Medieval life was dynamic and flexible. Changes in the Christian ethos were accompanied by developments in nation-states from the tenth century, the growth of cities from the eleventh century, and the birth of bourgeois "capitalism." Economically it was a time of growth of corporations of which the Church was the largest with its extensive endowments, tax benefits, and contribu-

tions from the faithful. From the later twelfth century, concomitant with
a growth in urban centers, was a growth in population, especially in
textile towns, and in new social groups and new working classes. This,
too, was accompanied by a new social consciousness symbolized by
hospitals, orphanages, misericordias, poor houses, and the like, attended
to and supported by women (Herlihy, 1967: 286). In political terms
secular power was challenging the power of the Church and, intellectually,
the later thirteenth and fourteenth centuries were frameworks for anti-
Aristotelian and anti-Ockham philosophies.

From the fourteenth century the "modern" family emerges from the
shadowy pages of legend and legal history. A "slow and steady deteriora-
tion of the wife's position in the household continues" and "she loses
the right to take the place of the husband in his absence or insanity"
(Petiot, 1955: passim). Furthermore, more control came to be exerted
by society over marriages of young men and women, possibly as a measure
to check a population growth too rapid to be accommodated by existing
resources. The shift from male to female dowry not only was complete
but also had foisted a larger burden on girls than it had imposed on men
previously. Requirements for dowry had become such that less fortunate
families had to send their dowryless daughters to convents although they,
too, demanded contributions to accept young women. Shortly, convents
also proved inadequate to handle the increasing number of unmarried or
unmarriageable girls who populated Europe by the end of the Crusades.

If an excess male population could be controlled by war no similar external mechanism for societal balance existed where women outnumbered
men. Thus society had to provide internal controls in the form of intellectual doctrines and institutional programs fashioned by an alliance of
sacred and secular decision makers. Reduction of an excess female population by natural processes, as in death in childbirth, probably worked
only when the sexes were in balance or when men outnumbered women
but were themselves kept in check and balance as victims of population
control by military means.

THE RENAISSANCE, THE REFORMATION,
AND THE AGE OF RECONNAISANCE

The Renaissance and especially the Reformation injected new ideas
into daily life, ideas that were responsible both for severe shifts in the
structure and functions of family and for differences that would develop
among various European ethnic groups, best symbolized by the "Anglo"
and "Latin" culture groups. The Reformation diffused ideas of individualism, liberty, egalitarianism, antitraditionalism, and other personal freeedoms,
which, in the protesting nations, were translated to the family. This is
significant to our understanding of the female in history since her role and

rights seemed more egalitarian and free in catholic medieval society where lines of class, sex, and color appear less clearly defined than they became in protestant modern society. According to some scholars the crucial change for family and female occurred with the emergence of the child as an individual entity. Prior to Renaissance and Reformation influence, children were relatively unimportant in themselves, although they existed in such numbers that at an early age they could be apprenticed out of the family. In medieval society childhood was "a great arena of free expression and spontaneity," in which "people let the young grow up as they pleased" (Ariès, 1962: 261ff., 369ff.). The idea of "childhood" as we in modern society conceive it did not exist in medieval Europe and emerged only when the family underwent transition, when sentiment and blood became increasingly important.

Longevity must also be considered. Women probably enjoyed more freedoms when life spans for both sexes were short. Similarly, children were not singled out as distinctive units because medieval society did not exhibit the enormous span in age groups or generations that we now enjoy. Hence, within narrowly circumscribed life expectations the notion of "child," either in mental or physical terms, was not necessary. But Protestantism, especially Puritanism, enforced new notions inclining family life to center around the child with primary obligations of families to train and nurture children, and Puritans had the narrowest definitions of kinship (Smith, 1974), Thus an apprenticeship system was gradually replaced by "coddling" and later formal education, and one in which women were increasingly confined to home.[4]

Coeval with changes regarding children were continuing alterations in secular and sacred concepts of marriage. In lay terms medieval marriage was simply a business contract, exchanged at the doors of the church, not within the church (Ariès, 1962: 356). In fact, the main function of any Church legitimization of a marriage was to legalize the transfer or retention of property and names, usually a concern only of the propertied in the society. By the sixteenth century, however, the Church had begun to enforce the necessity of sanctification of an institution so closely linked with the flesh as was family. The Council of Trent was responsible for giving the Church greater control over marriage. Before Trent marriages could be performed and contracted validly by the parties themselves. After Trent no marriage was considered valid unless performed by an ordained priest.[5] It also has been suggested that this sixteenth-century increase in Church control may have coincided with rises in marriage age.

Sacramental marriage now paralleled the religious rehabilitation of the layman and rise of northern European common piety, results of the Reformation and Counter-Reformation. Simultaneously, sixteenth-century married woman was placed under legal disabilities. She could perform no

action without authority of either her husband or the law, a development
that strengthened the powers of husbands and was reinforced through
European royal legislation.[6]

In addition there seem to have been profound demographic changes,
both in population supply and in relationships that developed as a result of
demographic changes. Scholars just now are beginning to tackle this
problem so there is not much that can concretely be said. Braudel has
investigated what he calls a biological revolution in the Mediterranean
world, which he contends was the basis for all other revolutions that
were to follow. This revolution saw the population of the Mediterranean
world rise from thirty-five to sixty or seventy million people in the sixteenth century (Braudel, 1973). The reasons for and overall effects of
this numerical change are yet to be determined but obviously raise questions
of a social, political, and economic nature. How did this tremendous
growth in population affect or stimulate the outward expansion of the
Iberian states? How did it affect changes in the living and laboring patterns of the Mediterranean and other Europeans? How did it affect family,
children, and females?

Scholars of the northern European perimeters have also been tackling
the problem of demographic supply and shifting social patterns. One
expert has demonstrated that the emerging pattern of European marriage,
characterized by later marriage and substantial increases in numbers of
bachelors and spinsters, dates from the late fifteenth and sixteenth centuries.[7] Another has determined that the sixteenth century profoundly
affected Western European family patterns, the causes for which are as
yet poorly understood (Noonan, 1968: 480-1). These changes possibly
"laid a social basis for . . . crystalization of the nuclear family . . . marriage by choice (and not by arrangement) found among Lutheran and
Puritans alike."[8]

The implications of later marriage and of the substantial increase
in numbers of people who never married are revolutionary for social
and economic reasons. What do you do with a growing female population,
one that in places outnumbers its male folk and that does not marry?
Western European society had been accustomed to marrying 95 percent
of its women; now it found itself with as much as a 20 percent supply of
unmarried females. This pool of spinsters (and widows who did not
remarry) posed an economic burden and a social threat to established
family patterns. Possibly in the transition period of society's attempt to
adjust from old to new family patterns, attitudes toward women would
change. Since "the structure of the society was so completely geared to
the family . . . persons without families were automatically peculiar, un-
protected," out of the purview of male control (Midelfort, 1972: 185).
In medieval cultures the larger family had provided refuge for dependent
peoples, particularly widows and unmarried daughters. But with growth of
the concept of individualism and other societal changes, the concept of

caring for oneself became rooted in Anglo-European lore as did the corollary that the unfortunate were responsible for their own misfortunes. To summarize, in premodern European society the extended family, including the conjugal cell, had been the major institution performing all operating functions of society. By the sixteenth century, however, the "modern" family was well on its way to assuming a position in society as merely one of several institutions performing more specialized functions that the family previously had monopolized. This new conception—or rather reemergence—of a "companionship family" in the sixteenth and seventeenth centuries was based on a unit of parents and children. Sociability, which had been a touchstone of medieval life, gradually declined. As family life became more child oriented, privacy and our modern type of domesticity increased so that by early eighteenth century the family had gradually shed its public character and donned the cloak of privacy. Family had pushed society from its doors.

Ironically, the age of the individual created some paradoxes. Individualism had enjoyed relatively free expression in the age of medieval sociability. Now social changes had created cravings for group identity, and individuals were submerged in a smaller family unit, with woman more secluded than she had been. In order to protect the fragile bounds of the unit, all members had to relegate their identities to the authority of a father figure. New rules of morality applied, and family members withdrew from the promiscuous pleasures of the old sociability. This was the case especially among a growing middle class, since nobility was free to do as it wished and the masses remained indifferent to these pressures of group behavior.

Familial changes are delineated in several ways. In architecture, houses were altered externally and internally. The recognizably modern house came to be the norm, its design a series of rooms that opened onto corridors and allowed separation, for the first time, between servants and family. Friends and peripheral relatives were no longer acceptable guests since houses lacked facilities to service them. This spatial characteristic of change was best expressed socially by an expanding middle class in cities, towns, and even villages and among whom the conjugal family assumed the norm. Old casual social relations were channeled into formal visiting patterns and the home now assumed accoutrements of comfort and isolation.

Individual relationships within the family also changed. In addition to and by virtue of estrangement of servants from family circles and with more emphasis on prerogatives of the child, the situation of the wife and mother was drastically altered. As parents became more preoccupied with their children, the role of the mother became more circumscribed. Since her husband earned *outside* the home, children's health and welfare became almost exclusively the wife's purview and increasingly limited her external social activities. These changes were basically characteristics of development of an urban, middling sector of society, the

bourgeoisie, although many of its precepts were to gradually contaminate
other strata of society.

According to Ariès, when the old polymorphous social body in which
all had lived in proximity to each other was broken up into big groups,
called classes, and small groups, called families, the middle class was the
first to withdraw from the old society and to begin the process of
physical segregation, which ultimately and clearly divided society into
separate and strictly regulated compartments (Ariès, 1962: 356). If
you apply Parsons' and Smelser's model of structural differentiation, the
segregation of traditional society into "modern" families and classes
also demonstrates the passing of functions. The traditional family had
been responsible for economic, social, political, educational, juridical,
and other obligations that became infused into other societal groups
and institutions. What modern marriage partners subsumed were the
physiological and psychological joys of parenthood and "companionship,"
as replacement for the broader sociability of premodern society (Parsons,
1955; Smelser, 1959: 2).

NOTES

1. Sources for this discussion are Hebrew, Greek, and early Christian
literary and archaeological sources and oral history interviews in the
Middle East, India, Greece, Italy, and Iberia.
    2. An excellent review of literature on children is in Singer, 1961: 9-90.
For models of structural differentiation for families, see Parsons, 1955,
and Smelser, 1959; also Ariès, 1962, and Hunt, 1970. See Burgess
and Locke, 1953, for the discussion of "companionship marriage" as a
modern institution.
    3. The eminent art historian Kenneth Clarke devoted a segment of
his *Civilization* series to examining this cult development through art.
    4. Three concepts for childhood emerged, according to Ariès, 1962:
132. "Coddling" emerged in the sixteenth century and was practiced
by women. Education, the second concept, emerged at the same time and
was the purview of churchmen. The third, dating from the eighteenth
century, was a concern for hygiene and physical health. Laslett suggests,
from evidence for England, that the world of the child as distinct from
adults seems no older than the Victorian age (1965: 105). MacFarlane
suggests a compromise, leaning toward Ariès's view (1970).
    5. See Noonan, 1968: 468, for a fuller discussion of canon law.
    6. Law and codes, civil and canon, abound with this in Europe.
    7. Hajnal, 1965. Also, for supporting views Wrigley, 1966; Spengler,
1968; Van der Walle, 1968; Demeny, 1968; Daedalus, 1968: vol. 97.
    8. Midelfort, 1972: 184. Ariès, 1962: 69-75, 403-4; and Morgan, 1944,
chap. 2-3, especially beyond New England.

2 IBERIA: FRONTIERS, FIDALGOS, FAMILIES, AND FEMALES

Women . . . have been and are the repositories of the essential virtues of the race and the transmitters of its moral vitality across all the infinite accidents of our history. (Marañon on El Duque de Olivares' ancestors in Moreau de Justo, 1945: 30.)

CONQUISTADORES AND MERCHANTMEN: THE FRONTIERS IN PRECOLUMBIAN IBERIA

Iberian traditions have been different from the mainstream Western European heritage, and these differences have been manifested in the colonizing experience of European empires. The Iberians dominated the first phase of European overseas expansion. The rapidity, immensity, and wide-ranging effects of Iberian imperial development in the sixteenth century were the product of two traditions: the Iberian one of conquest and lordship and the Mediterranean one of mercantile capitalism (Johnson, 1970: 4-5). Within the first heritage were "The Great Tradition," or legal concepts and administrative institutions of Crown over colonies, and "The Little Tradition," which reflected the mores and folkways of the ordinary citizenry (Redfield, 1956: 49-50). The Mediterranean element derived from seamanship and navigation of Normans and Italians, the Crusades, northern trading city-states, and the manpower, money, and materiel of

Italian cities that ultimately gave impetus to the commercial "houses" of the Iberian empire. Iberian and Mediterranean heritages melded together at a crucial time in the history of the peninsula—in 1492 at the closing of the Hispanic frontier (Wolf, 1964: 158).

In an attempt to explain the growth, size, and impulse of the Iberian empires, historians and other scholars have developed several theories. Braudel's, which is most appealing, places major emphasis on the enormous demographic expansion of the Mediterranean world in the sixteenth century (Braudel, 1973). Verlinden has described the Iberian empires more as mercantile structures developed to supply goods to growing external markets rather than as the later European empires geared to industrial capitalism. He suggests that in character and in structure they resembled the earlier Mediterranean empires of the eleventh and twelfth centuries, the great trading states of northern Italy that had developed with the Crusades (Verlinden, 1951: 219-36 passim). Whatever the motivation or complexion, Iberian empires were in ways sui generis creations, for they also had characteristics that had developed during centuries of reconquest: land conquest and dominance of military lords.

Although both mercantile and military traditions developed together, forged in an environment of Christian conquest of the infidel, particular conditions in the peninsula made some areas more receptive to one tradition than to the other. The mercantile tradition became more important for Portugal and the Spanish northeast, while the reconquest tradition dominated Castile and central Iberia.

The mercantile tradition had developed under the aegis of Normans and Italians who began their thrust into markets and sea-lanes dominated by Islamic cultures. Northern Europeans, falling back on their traditions, chose to establish fiefdoms and principalities in the Holy Land. Italians, on the other hand, chose to take their reward for outfitting ships and underwriting expeditions in forms of commercial privileges and trading posts (factories) that were established in each newly conquered area. The Italians created agencies to oversee functions of these posts, and Verlinden has suggested that they were models for the houses of trade established by Iberians (Verlinden, 1954: 20). Furthermore, the Italians developed a shopping list of commodities to be bought and sold in their new markets, commodities later familiar in the Atlantic trade: sugar, slaves, and precious metals, particularly the gold craved by a bullion-starved Europe. The format the Italians established was simple but successful. In response to demands for sugar, they developed cane fields and encouraged some northern European knights to grow sugar on their estates in the Holy Land. Later, with the growth of political instability in Middle Eastern areas, the Italians shifted their production centers to the Atlantic islands. This increasing production required labor, which was supplied by the extension of slave systems, first in the Mediterranean, then on the islands, finally from Africa.

The reconquest tradition, which ultimately became the dominant Iberian tradition, produced culture heroes like the Cid, advanced chivalric notions of courtly love, glorified codes of honor and fidelity. In theory, all reconquered lands belonged to the ruler who, to secure settlement, granted parcels to lesser authorities, such as military orders, archbishoprics, and municipal councils. Lands given to municipalities were then subdivided into four sectors: one for ruler, one for church, one for lay and ecclesiastical officials, and one for general settlement (Johnson, 1970: 6-8 passim). In some ways reminiscent of old Roman practices, general settlement gave lands to those who had participated in reconquest, based on status; better lands were distributed to cavalry, smaller plots to infantry. The old Roman and Moorish systems of latifundia were preserved primarily for demographic and environmental reasons: the population was too sparse to occupy all available lands and the general condition of the land made it unfeasible to split into small plots. Those who did not acquire land moved to the cities, thus establishing a feature of Iberian overseas occupation: growth of large cities in the middle of sparsely populated agricultural or pastoral areas (Johnson, 1970: 6-8). The function of Iberian cities was quite different from those urban centers that the English and Dutch established in America.[2]

In addition to land settlement patterns, other characteristics developed from the reconquest tradition. The presence of a constant, such as the frontier, promising quick spoils in land and riches influenced attitudes against "honest" or manual labor and toward easy rewards. Furthermore, constant warfare necessitated a centralized leadership and thus mitigated the tendency in central Iberia, particularly Castile, to develop a decentralized society or feudal traditions of local rights and responsibilities that tended to characterize other Western European cultures. Also, the nomadic nature of the reconquest discouraged development of an urban bourgeoisie. Towns and cities that developed in newly reconquered lands tended to be religious or military centers and not commercial outposts. Furthermore, many reconquest areas became converted to ranching and other pastoral activities, and the growth of a lucrative wool industry further enforced a cultural ethos radically different from the mercantile one (Johnson, 1970: 9-11). The emergence of the Iberian "nation-states" and particularly of their far-flung empires must be viewed within the context of the development and interaction of these two traditions.

The Iberian peninsula today refers to nation-states of Spain and Portugal, but at the age of reconnaisance there were several Spains and more than one Portugal divided by differences of language, geography, economy, and society, for reasons of conflicting traditions. At the time of America's discovery, the peninsula sheltered thriving ports and commercial centers selling wools to England or Flanders and iron and grain to the Muslims, harbored adventurers who were seizing slaves from Africa, and attracted citizenry who were sponsoring raids on Saracen cities.

Profit, proselytization and, perhaps most important, an incipient national ego eager to test ideals nurtured in medieval soil, motivated them. Chivalry, courage, individualism, and a desire to dominate the future were pinions of empire. While the city-states of Iberia shared these ideals, they also recognized and emphasized the differences that made them Castile, Aragon, Catalonia, Andalusia, Extremadura, Galicia, Portugal and the Algarve.

Present-day Portugal (Portugal, the Algarve, and part of Galicia) had enjoyed relatively consistent maritime contact with Europe, a relationship that continued with establishment of *Terra Portucalense* about 1095 A.D. under Henry of Burgundy. Portugal developed its own fair and market system, and its cities supplied crusaders with provisions after the fall of Lisbon in 1147, which marked the effective end of Islamic penetration in Portugal. Under King Dinis (1279-1325) commerce and agriculture benefited, privileges were extended, new charters granted, and foreign commerce encouraged, which, in turn, introduced new classes into the society. Italian influence increased on the sea-lanes, in trading centers, and in Portugal where Genoa and Venice encouraged new kinds of merchants and mobilization of a nation. Portugal's landed nobility was much involved with marketing the production of its estates, and the king also exerted a strong influence on economic contacts. Thus that country embarked on more commercial ventures. By the end of the fourteenth century Portugal had a new economic and social structure: nobles, clergy, agricultural, and rural interests were pressed by civil, secular, commercial, and urban elements. The latter groups dominated port cities, supported the new house of Avis, and fed an incipient nationalism that was to move Portugal beyond the realm of commercial interest, into the arena of national aggrandizement (Diffie, 1963: passim).

In regions that today compose the Spanish nation, the Iberian and Mediterranean strains were converging, reflecting themselves in different degrees in the diverse territories as variations of the Castilian and Aragonese prototypes. Castilians were heirs to seven and a half centuries of sporadic yet persistent thrusts against Moorish intruders. Rather than religious motivation, which later was used to rationalize the reconquest, Iberian drives were determined by demographic density, by economic and other needs, but "principally by a hunger for land and booty" (Johnson, 1970: 5). This process honed certain chivalric notions such as the belief that individual valor's reward was wealth and honor, while a nation gained riches by warfare. Thus the military might of Castile pushed the expansionist ethic and created a moving frontier. Across dry plateaux, across lands of peasant soldier-cultivators whose rewards for military service were freedom and land, moved herds of cattle and sheep, the latter to supply the lucrative wool trade. In the wake of the drive against the infidel emerged the sheep and wool industry.

In Iberia sheepherding had been a major activity since early times.

Sixth- and seventh-century Gothic codes regulated long-range transhumant flock movements, the establishment of sheep walks, rules that
separated the transhumant herder from the villager, branding, and other
activities. Near the end of the reconquest, with the increasing unification
and pacification of great areas of Castile and Andalusia, an atmosphere
was created for movement of huge flocks with safety along sheep walks
that extended from northern mountains (summer pasturage) to southern
tablelands (winter forage).

The basis for Iberia's wool industry was the merino sheep, which,
by early medieval time, had become the most important strain of sheep,
superior for its wool. In Spain's broad central plateaux of Castile, particularly northern old Castile and León, merino herding had long been a
major operation. To control this industry there were established throughout
plateaux areas numerous local self-regulating *mestas,* or guilds of herders.
Women were voting members of local mestas, which were forerunners of
the powerful royal mesta (Freeman, 1970: 189 n.6). In 1273 Castilian
sheepherders were incorporated by formal charter into the mesta, and
by early sixteenth century this corporation wielded enormous power.
Through its influence Spain maintained a monopoly on wool in international markers until the early eighteenth century when merino sheep were
introduced into northern Europe (Klein, 1920: passim).

The Mediterranean mercantile ethic that had taken root in Portugal
found its most receptive Spanish environment in Catalonia-Aragon. Here
commercial exchange, industrial expansion, and capital accumulation
were controlled by an urban bourgeoisie sufficiently powerful to resist
Castilian aristocrats. Unlike Castile, eastern Spain boasted both a free
peasantry that had already achieved charters of self-rule and a proletariat
in Catalonia's incipient industries. At the moment of frontier closure
Catalonia and Castile clashed, for the urban merchant-entrepreneurs
wanted capital investment in industry and reduced aristocratic privileges.

Was this within their grasp when Columbus discovered for Castile
a land that promised easy wealth, abundant labor, and vast estates? It
is only exercise to predict other historical conclusions. What we do know
is that Iberians followed the Columbuses, da Gamas, and Magellans and
transplanted to Asia, Africa, and America ideals and institutions that
took root but that seemed to flower best in American soil.

In the Spanish schema fidalgos and frontiers assumed new importance
as the centralized Castilian kingdom asserted authority over its decentralized Aragonese competitor and translated the Iberian strain of
military conquest into empire. Colonial cities were not commercial
centers but military-religious towns. Social and economic groups transplanted their agropastoral occupations and ethos. And the Castilians
developed a theory of "just conquest" drawn from medieval Catholic
tradition and Hispanic precedents.

The Portuguese, on the other hand, geographically oriented to the sea, had already established a merchant-maritime reputation. Lisbon was a great metropolis and trading center, and Portugal early had embarked on a program of maritime expansion in search of products salable in its markets. Portugal's policy was establishment of trading posts in areas requiring minimum employment of manpower and maximum utilization of sea-lanes, not military conquest but peaceful profit, not a puritanical ethos but an expanding economy.

IBERIA: FROM THE RENAISSANCE TO THE ENLIGHTENMENT

In these varying Iberian traditions, what of the woman? Many scholars have emphasized the impact of Moorish civilization on Iberian society, especially attitudes that seemed to regard females as inferior. From the Moors, Iberian upper classes supposedly inherited and continued the custom of keeping their females secluded. In home life women were restricted from appearing at windows, squatted on cushions instead of sitting on chairs, and in all areas of Spain except the north and northwest remained semiveiled. Even more than those prohibitions, Iberians exhibited a paradox in behavior also supposedly Moorish in origin. On the one hand males considered females inferior, yet they were excessively gallant and protective of women (Elliott, 1966: 305).

There is an important qualification to Islamic impact on Iberian attitudes. Carriers of Islam never really effectively occupied more than one-third of the peninsula, their center of endurance primarily in south-central and southern Spain, *Al-Andalus*. Consequently we must look for other reasons, and one that equaled and perhaps overshadowed supposed Moorish influence was the turbulent and uncertain conditions of life in medieval Iberia that prompted an elaborate protective system that segregated women and ultimately hardened into a style of life. In Iberia chivalric pride, honor, and chastity flowered, and rules of behavior were established that set standards of personal dignity, self-sacrifice in ideal pursuits, and disdain for material values. In this respect Iberia reflected western European currents.

Spain

Spanish proverbs are rife with directives on divisions of female-male responsibilities in upper-class society, directives that hardened into tradition from medieval through Renaissance times (Correas, 1924: passim). On the other hand women of lower classes were less bound by strictures of proper behavior, able to engage in numerous occupations and "improper" activities, and relatively dominant within their own households. A sizable number of females, especially in Seville and Lisbon, were domestic slaves who directed household activities, nursed children, and prepared foodstuffs for sale in markets. Sixteenth- to eighteenth-century plays emphasize the intimacy between female slaves and their mistresses, in which capacity servant girls were confidantes or love brokers for their secluded and idle Iberian ladies (Pike, 1967: passim).

Spanish society from the Renaissance to the Enlightenment was a hierarchical one in which privileges and responsibilities of classes were recognized in law and custom. The hierarchy consisted of three estates—nobility, clergy, and commoners, the last group totaling seven-eighths of the population. Numerous proportions among these groups varied in different geographic areas. For example, Santander and Asturias counted about 50 percent of its population as noble, while Andalusia claimed less than 1 percent of noble birth (Domínguez Ortiz, 1971:113-5).

Nobility owned much of the country's wealth in land, often as recipients of encomiendas for their position in military orders. Encomiendas also were granted to women and children as rewards for services rendered by their families.[3] However, in both Spain and Portugal these comanderies were granted to women only as administrators, especially when male children inherited the commandery on their fathers' death. There was a growing tendency in the seventeenth and eighteenth and possibly even the sixteenth centuries to award these commanderies for the duration of only three lifetimes. Also, the commander did not own the land itself but only enjoyed its use along with various dues and other perquisites, because the land was not alienated by the military orders (Dutra, 1973; Wright, 1963).

While land was most important, those who were unable to acquire it were honored with the habit of the military order and though this carried no real economic significance it meant much social prestige and bargaining power. A man who obtained a habit for his future son-in-law "could be sure of having his choice of suitors without having to provide an enormous dowry" (Domínguez Ortiz, 1971: 117-8). This was so because the habit in the military order *was* the dowry or at least a great part of it. In the seventeenth and eighteenth centuries both the Spanish and Portuguese Crowns awarded habits as dowries to those who would marry daughters of fathers who had been killed in military action or who had served the Crown well and honorably. Soon services of uncles and brothers were also being used to obtain dowries of military order habits (Dutra, 1973).

Women who did not marry entered nunneries, of which there were relatively few. By the early 1600s monasteries and convents enjoyed a new attention from a public that had begun neglecting churches. But by the middle of that depression century monastic orders had been greatly restricted by royal decree. The most severely affected were nunneries that depended on dowries of its female entrants. Mendicant houses for women (811) were only half the number for men (1,608) by 1700, a situation that, incidentally, had reversed itself by the twentieth century (Domínguez Ortiz, 1971:125.).

More than 80 percent of Hapsburg Spanish society resided in villages, on farmsteads, or in small towns but we know very little of their lives and must glean our information on that society from the elite (Dominguez Ortiz, 1971: 148). Authority was vested in seigneury lords whose "feudal" powers were expressed less in political terms and more by enormous economic and social influence. They supported fairs and free markets and generally conducted affairs in a manner reminiscent of French feudalism. The remainder of the population was clustered in larger urban centers, particularly in the north and northwest. Despite their parasitic reliance on the countryside, medieval and Renaissance urban nuclei enjoyed a supremacy over their rural neighbors that was supported by legal measures. During the seventeenth century rural-urban relationships had new tensions and a reversal of reliance. Countrysides began to rely on larger towns, a pattern that in the latter half of the seventeenth century, coincided with the diminution of inland Spanish population by plagues, famine, migrations, expulsions, and wars.[4]

The sixteenth and seventeenth centuries—the period known as the Hapsburg empire in Spain—are crucial to an understanding of later developments in overseas territories and elaboration of the two traditions in Iberian imperial rule. In 1500 the population of the Spains was some seven million, of which 6.63 million comprised the artisan-laborer-peasant classes. Spain's population jumped to 7.5 million by 1540 and to around 8.5 million in the 1590s (Payne, 1973: 268-9). These figures support Braudel's contention about bases for overseas expansion and the imperial ethic.

On the eve of Empire the two major Christian kingdoms of Spain, Castile and Aragon, had been united by the marriage of Isabella and Ferdinand in 1469. Aragon's medieval history had been diametrically opposite the Castilian experience. Long before the Castilians had succeeded in expelling the Moors from central and southern Spain, the Aragonese had completed their reconquest and had begun building a new state. Aragon consisted of the kingdoms of Valencia, Aragon, and the principality of Catalonia, each with its own institutions. The Catalans were the most important segment of this federation and had a commercial-maritime empire that extended from northeastern Iberia and the Balearics to Greece. Furthermore, their institutions were based on mutual obligation contracts that extended even to the relationship between ruler and subject. The thirteenth and fourteenth centuries were the apogee of the Catalan-Aragonese "empire," for in the fifteenth century Catalonia underwent severe economic, social, and political crises, from which it did not begin to recover until the early sixteenth century.[5]

The newly revived Catalonia, and therefore the crown of Aragon, from the sixteenth and throughout the next few centuries retained its commercial, cosmopolitan, and Mediterranean outlook. But the fifteenth-century decline had cost Aragon dearly, for Castile had managed to assume control of policies and profits from overseas endeavors, thus relegating Aragon to a junior partnership. Catalonia of the sixteenth through nineteenth centuries was an overwhelmingly agrarian society. Most towns were predominantly extensions of the rural areas rather than "urban" centers. Catalonia's countryside in broad relief can be seen as one of isolated farmsteads worked by a class of peasant farmers that was "the backbone of Catalan society from the end of the fifteenth century almost to the present day; and more than anything else it was responsible for the fundamental stability of Catalan rural life in the sixteenth and seventeenth centuries" (Elliott, 1963: 29).

From 1486 to 1520 legislation and kingly charters guaranteed certain guidelines for development so that from the early sixteenth century Catalonia's rural society became basically hierarchical in nature: nobles-bourgeoisie-absentee landowners; peasants with sizable properties; poor peasants in a tenant-farmer relationship; and rural landless laborers. For those who held property Catalonian customs allowed it to be passed on by both women and men. An example of this procedure is a mid-seventeenth century Catalonian house inherited by a woman and having remained in the family through centuries, although passing on occasion through heiresses whose husbands took the woman's family name on marriage (Elliott, 1963: 31).

The basic and most important institution in Catalonia, as in all Iberian life, was the family. "Catalan society was ordered within the framework of the family and the community, and it is the marriage contract which can tell us most about the basic element in society . . . the family" (Eliott, 1963: 34). The family decided the participants in marriage and negotiated the dowry; then the man was allowed to visit the bride-to-be, "to kiss and to touch her" (Elliott, 1963: 35). The marriage contract designated the properties and dower rights of male and female.

Terms of property also emphasize family as the primary social unit to which all individual interests were subordinate. There was only one heir, usually the eldest son, but *always* a son in whom was vested family powers and properties. The heir could not possess his estate until his father's death, and often his mother would retain control of the estate until she died. If there were no male heirs, then property was inherited by a daughter who, Elliott has suggested "was as typical a figure in Catalan life as the *hereu* [male heir]" (1963: 37). She inherited the entire estate, and her parents ensured its proper transfer.

The influence of Catalan and, generally, the northeastern sector of Spain, continued to reinforce its particular patterns of economy and society in such a way as to create inevitable and constant conflict with the metropolitan center in Madrid. The origins of such discontent, which endured throughout the sixteenth to twentieth centuries and culminated in the Civil War, had its roots in the northeast and in northern mining and agricultural communities of Asturias and Galicia. Northerners who migrated to parts of the Spanish empire took with them their customs and patterns of family and society, seeking to preserve them in the face of edicts and practices of their imperial Castilian overlords.

Castile was a pastoral and nomadic, military, and religious society organized for wars and crusades. That pattern and a lucrative wool trade that dominated its economy had encouraged the growth of a strong urban society. New riches and new ideas developed, and with the end of the reconquest Castile was politically and economically ready for new frontiers.

It is said that the energy and enthusiasm of Castile made it possible to discover and to conquer new lands, while the techniques of government and administration of Aragon allowed the organization and survival of a Spanish world empire. But despite the revival of Catalan and utilization of its institutions for empire building, Castile became the dominant partner in this process. Castile's population was 6.5 million to the crown of Aragon's 1 million or so in the early part of the sixteenth century (Ruiz Almansa, 1943: 120). More importantly, as a result of the reconquest, the energies of Castile's vested interests were too dissipated to counter the increasing power of monarchy. Unlike the shared mutual contract of obligation between ruler and subject in Aragon, the Castilian monarchy was energetically absolute. Castilian laws provided that newly conquered and otherwise acquired lands would become the property of Castile and not be shared with the Aragonese. Castile's larger population, military supremacy, near-absolute monarchy, and monopoly of trade with the Americas assured its dominance as the premier Spanish kingdom of the Hapsburgs.

As a result of its trade monopoly, the major city of Castile and the Spains became Andalusian Seville. Its population grew enormously after the 1540s, leveling off after the 1580s and declining after the plague of 1599-1601. From about 55,000 inhabitants in 1534, of which there were 6,568 householders and 2,365 widows—a substantial ratio in the population—by 1588 Seville counted more than 100,000 people (Pike, 1972: 10-19 passim). City boundaries pushed outward so that by the end of the sixteenth and early seventeenth centuries the areas of greatest growth were in parishes peripheral to the city: the poorer masses in northern suburbs, the wealthier in southern suburbs (Pike, 1972: 17).

Seville is the city for which we have the most detailed accounts of Spanish urban female social and economic life commensurate with its importance in Hapsburg Spain. Seville became a rich, severely changed cosmopolitan international port rather than simply an Andalusian urban center. Among the upper classes shifts occurred particularly with the move of landed nobility into the ranks of urban merchants. It became

routine for noblemen to wed daughters of newly wealthy merchantmen.
Similarly, new nobility married their daughters to wealthy merchants,
particularly as a means of replenishing coffers and maintaining the family
in a style to which it had become accustomed (Pike, 1972: 22, 26).
A fixed element in Iberian life was the religious world. Restrictions
on nunneries and the general dearth of mendicant houses throughout
Spain in the latter part of the sixteenth century did not seem to severely
affect Seville, which, in 1579, had nineteen female and nineteen male
religious houses (Pike, 1972: 64). Practically all female orders were
cloistered or not actively involved in social welfare, educative, or medical
activities. Indeed, those functions were almost unknown to nuns at that
time, possibly because of the influence of some aristocratic women who
belonged to the nunneries. Convents were supported by rents or dowries
that women had to pay to enter. Since they did not provide common
services and therefore received much less official support than priests' or
brothers' homes, they had more limited sources for recruitment than did
male religious orders (Pike, 1972: 65).

Most female and male orders were comprised from all strata of society.
In the early sixteenth century a sizable proportion of religious came from
the urban artisan class, many *conversos*. But as the century wore on more
of the wealthy and titled joined the regular clergy, especially female orders.
By the early seventeenth century the composition of female religious
orders was largely from the growing newer and wealthy classes, and women
entered convents with large dowries and a retinue of personal servants and
slaves (Pike, 1972: 69-70 passim).

Information about women in other activities is scarce. Among the elites
and professional classes, there were no women lawyers, doctors, professors,
notaries, or merchants. Occasionally women took over management of
an estate or a business but usually on a caretaker basis. But because family
was the basis of business organization and all else, women enjoyed more
de facto power and influence. They became the transmitters, through
marital alliances, of business and professional connections and practices.

It is difficult to determine the situation of the lower classes. Manual
labor was not considered desirable by Spaniards during this time period,
probably a carryover of attitudes from the reconquest tradition in an area
of Spain, Andalusia, that had been the last to come under Christian aegis.
The ideal seemed to be not to do what one did well with a sense of pride
in one's work, but to aspire to the relatively easily obtainable status of
noble and merchant. I have found no evidence of women in the crafts
and skilled trades guilds. The main work of women seemed domestic
services.

Among the poorest groups in Hapsburg Spain—Moriscos, slaves, and
freemen—women often outnumbered men in urban census rolls. In

Seville's 1580 census, females outnumbered males among the free Moriscos, but among slaves males outnumbered females. Married females between the ages of twenty and forty were married to males in the forty to sixty age group. Widowers were uncommon but widows with small children figured prominently in the rolls, probably because of the discrepancy in ages between husbands and wives (Pike, 1972: 156-7 passim). Among Morisco slaves, or *esclavos blancos*, females outnumbered male. Most Morisco slaves in Seville were women between the ages of twenty and forty; in Seville in 1589, 283 of 381 were female (Pike, 1972: 172). But the overwhelming majority of slaves were black, or *Negroes*, as they were called. In the cities, Seville and Lisbon in particular, most were women who were employed in domestic services as cooks, maids, nursemaids, laundresses, and attendants.

Among those not engaged in "useful" occupations the main activity was prostitution. Brothels were recognized and licensed by cities, care was taken to assure that women who entered were commoners, more than twelve years of age, no longer virgins, either orphaned or abandoned, and in good health, all regulations to protect women from being forced into prostitution. The officially sanctioned public brothels employed a doctor to tend to the women's health, just as a doctor was officially assigned to the female prison population (Pike, 1972: 83). Although mulattas and married women were prohibited by law from working in brothels, many did. Careful regulations applied only so far. By early seventeenth century Seville recorded some 3,000 prostitutes, most of whom were streetwalkers, many of whom had been expelled from brothels because of poor health (Pike, 1972: 204-11 passim).

Through seventeenth-century economic depressions and revival of Iberian fortunes during the eighteenth century, economic and social class patterns, forged in reconquest and reinforced during Hapsburg Spain, did not change significantly. Among working classes women were still employed for the most part in domestic activities and very few females of other groups were visible in public activities. Personal accounts of seventeenth-century Spanish and Portuguese life are very uninformative about females. They note that in wealthy homes there were dozens of female servants. They discuss the dress, figure, and face of the upper-class woman and suggest that these women did nothing but visit with each other, talk incessantly, and finger their rosary beads. In all, from travel accounts, memoirs, plays, and novels we have the idea of a life of hard work for poorer women and a sequestered and boring existence for women of the upper classes.[6]

The description that follows encapsulates much of what we know about seventeenth-century Iberian urban women of all but the poorest classes:

They . . . are generally pleasant . . . seldom laugh, and never aloud,
but [are] the most witty in repartees and stories and notions in the
world. They sing, but not well. . . . They play of all kinds of instruments likewise, and dance with castanetas very well. They work little,
but rarely well, especially in monasteries. They all paint white and red,
from the Queen to the cobbler's wife, old and young, widows excepted,
which never go out of close mourning, nor wear gloves, nor show their
hair after their husband's death, and seldom marry. They are the
finest shaped women in the world, not tall; their hair and teeth are
most delicate. They seldom have many children. (Fanshawe, 1907 ed.:
167-8.)

There were some who gave different descriptions. Most tracts unfavorable
to upper-class Iberian women seem to be of the eighteenth century and, in
particular, of Spain. This observer noted that "none of them dance, or
sing, or play upon some instrument, or like to walk or play at cards—one
thing they do to admiration . . . is continually to demand favours for themselves, their friends, and their servants [and to be] altogether unwilling to
work" (Ursins, 1826: III, 441-2).

Our sketchy source materials show that seventeenth- and eighteenth-
century working-class women served as ushers in legitimate theaters, received
no salaries, and had to depend on tips (*Memorial literario*, March 1788: 423).
A familiar urban street sight was women hawkers of oranges, limes, and
hazelnuts. In addition, they served as go-betweens with messages from young
gallants to ladies in their carriages. Male and female beggars were also common sights (Cruz, 1765: 252ff.).

Among Spanish public officials, it seems that on the death of lesser
ministers and similar functionaries, widows enjoyed the emoluments of
their deceased's office. A widow could use it as a pensioner or she could
auction it off to the highest bidder (AHN, *Libros*, 1778: folios 285-9).

Paralleling shifts in population and the rural-urban ambient were changes
in socioreligious affairs, one area of which concerned family matters, especially marriage. Previously the Church had recognized marriages that
merely entailed consent by the couple before witnesses and without sacramental blessings. These marriages were common until the Council of
Trent declared them unlawful. Thereafter, the Church pressured to bring
an orthodox routine to the sacrament of marriage.

The life of females from Hapsburg through eighteenth-century Bourbon Spain seemed determined largely by their sex. Among upper-class
urban girls certain proprieties were observed. If any education were given
it was usually within the home, but for the most part formal, classic education was not provided for girls (Dalrymple, 1777: 72). Many daughters
were sent to convents, others were placed in private schools for "moral"

education, the effectiveness of which is questioned by the fact that girls
seemed to have much freedom to go to the public square, to sing and
dance in public, and to roam the marketplace (Cruz, 1775: II, 157). Girls
educated in their homes were trained in traditional household tasks,
Christian dogma, and embroidery. If they had private teachers girls would
also learn French and Italian; reading, writing, and arithmetic; singing,
dancing, and drawing (Cruz, n.d.: I, 370; *Diario de Madrid*, 18 January
1800).

In 1783 King Charles III ordered the establishment of thirty-two free
schools for girls in Madrid and urged that other Spanish cities follow
this pattern. These schools basically were to provide the same education
as was offered in convents, private schools, or by private tutorials in
homes, and all had the same aim: To prepare girls for duties they would
subsume when married (*Memorial literario,* January 1788: 132; Cruz,
1764: I, 167). Several trade or vocational schools also were opened to
train girls for textile work. Meanwhile, by the late eighteenth and early
nineteenth century middle- and upper-class women began formation of
clubs to promote education and charitable programs.

Any "decent" young city girl could not attend popular masquerades
or other social events by herself, although she could go with a man to
these affairs providing her mother was also present. Many women married
in order to escape the grasp of parents, for, once married, women could
go anywhere or receive anyone in their homes (Cruz, n.d.: *El sastre,* II, 391).

Observers of the Spanish scene from about mid-eighteenth century
noted a decline in the spirit of gravity, sobriety, and propriety that had
characterized seventeenth-century social life, resulting in "husbands [re-
laxing] their vigilance; women, becoming more refined, more accessible,
gained in freedom" (Kany, 1932: 173). The eighteenth century belonged
to the Bourbon dynasty, which attempted Gallicization of Spain's economic and administrative machinery and influenced social and cultural
patterns. Through a growing middle class was channeled elegant and
frivolous behavior, one manifestation of which was a female character, the
petimetra, a fashionable coquette who led changes in fashion, of clothes
and manners, who freely attended theaters and churches, and made unescorted promenades; she was the "modern girl" (Cruz, 1779: I, 342). She
and her male counterpart consciously imitated French fashions in matters
of food, furniture, apparel, manners, and education, learning foreign
languages, and becoming facile in salon behavior and verse.

Women of the upper classes who desired male companionship found it
in *abates* (religious brothers) who were tutors and musicians in wealthy
families. They and doctors were favorites of Spain's wealthy housewives,
and it was said that both "practically lived night and day in the [drawing
rooms]" (Torres y Villaroel, 1794-1799: II, 168; Quijano, 1785: 149).
Another ladies' companion, mainly in Madrid, was the *cortejo,* a gallant

and an extremely important social figure. Foreign observers noted that
"each lady of fashion had at least one cortejo," and so widespread was
this amorous fad that sources suggest that even wives in poorer classes had
these paramours (Dalrymple, 1777: 45; AHN, 1778: legajo 4482, 19; Cruz,
1767: I, 489). The cortejo was exploited by his mistress, was always at
her beck and call, and, in some senses, was a slave to her in "his soul, his
life, his person, and his goods" (Cruz, 1773: I, 412-5). Husbands apparently tolerated this; some travelers suggested that many a cortejo
was the husband's intimate friend and that "there were no other people
in Europe [than in Spain] among whom fewer jealous husbands existed"
(Bourgoing, 1789: II, 189; Cruz, n.d. *niñería*: I, 480; *Memorial literario,*
September 1787: 178).

At parties women seldom danced with their husbands, and often husbands were not even invited to these *tertulias*. Women seemed to have
their own lovers or escorts, a practice their husbands seemingly accepted
(Kany, 1932: chap. 10). Some women held card-playing tertulias for
profit. They were fond of theater, also. There was a place, the *cazuela*
(stewpan), reserved for women. Although supposedly only for middle- and
lower-class women, upper classes used it also. They would go to the
cazuela once the theater had dimmed to gossip, or whatever, and were
not recognizable since they wore veils (Clarke, 1763: 103). Men were
forbidden by law to sit in the ladies' section or even to stand near the
woman's entrance to the theater (*Nova Recop.*, book 7, xxxiii, 9). The
general conclusion that can be drawn is that while public activities were
not supposed to be the bailiwick of upper-strata Spanish women, within
the more private confines of their kinship or friendship circle they enjoyed freedom and mobility.

Spanish society in the latter half of the eighteenth century reflected
the organic weakness of social and other institutions. Harbingers of the
modernizing age were struggling with traditional influences. In general
the social atmosphere was permissive and there seemed a neglect of socio-
sexual codes of honor. Women seem to have become more refined, more
accessible. There seems to have been a growing disinclination to marriage
among the upper classes, men doing so only at an advanced age, partly
to marry widows with substantial pensions.[7]

In eighteenth-century Spain one would question the element of promiscuity and the number of illegitimate births as a result of illicit alliances.
There are no data on that, but there is some information on letters of
legitimacy (proof that one was of "pure" Spanish or Portuguese Christian
lineage). It seems that they were very popular. They were important as
much for the nobility and other elites as for the guilds. In Spain this was
true especially as a result of the Bourbon kings' attempt to remove any
stigma attached to manual labor. In 1703 Philip V required every merchant
and artisan to be enrolled in his respective guild and to contribute to the

treasury.[8] In order to belong to a major guild, a man had to be a Christian
of pure descent; therefore letters of legitimacy were crucial. This applied
only to men; no women were allowed membership.

Lower-class women were frequently outside their homes, working as
domestics and wet nurses, for seldom did upper-class females nurse their
children. There existed a hierarchy among female servants in a wealthy
household. The more privileged were the lady's maid and the manager
of the household, both of whom held the other servants, male and female
alike, in disdain. Young women from provincial towns or countryside
were eager to migrate to major urban centers. Among these females the
master of the household often found a willing sex partner to whom he would
pay extra salary or bestow gifts (Cruz, *Saientes* I: 417, 472; Cruz, 1772:
II, 238).

Economic, political, social and other changes affected Spain throughout
eighteenth-century Bourbon rule. One of the most significant was demographic. Spain's population, which by the late sixteenth century had increased enormously consonant with the general population rise in the
Mediterranean world, over the next two centuries experienced severe drops
in population. These resulted from catastrophic plagues of 1598-1602
and 1649-1652, the expulsion of Moriscos in 1609, emigration to the
Americas and other Spanish territories, poor harvests, and famines. From
8.5 million in the 1590s, Spain's population fell to 7.5 million in 1717,
and although by 1768 it was recorded at 9.3 million the latter figure's
rise, relative to the previous two centuries, indicates that the revival was
not commensurate with the previous loss in population (Livi-Bacci, 1968:
524). From 1768 to 1900 Spain's population doubled to 18.6 million while,
simultaneously, apparently because of the spread of birth-control practices, fertility rates were reduced (Livi-Bacci, 1968: 525). It can be seen
as a prelude to the growing practice of later marriages and smaller families
that seem a feature of modern Spain.

Portugal

Spain's peninsula neighbor and sharer in overseas empire development
is the nation-state of Portugal. While the countries share many traditions
and basic values, there are pronounced differences determined in part by
geography, language, social and economic development, and early history.
Portugal, unlike Spain, was a sparsely populated Atlantic state whose
economy, social values, and general pattern of daily existence was much
closer to that of its Mediterranean cousins than to its northern neighbors.
At the time of overseas expansion, about 1 million to 1.5 million people
occupied this western sector of the Iberian peninsula in a "class" hierarchy
of nobility, clergy, and commoners, all agricultural and rural oriented.
Like their Spanish relatives the nobles and clergy were divided into
several subclasses, each differentiated by codes of behavior, responsibilities,
and rights, but all privy to certain perquisites, economic and other, that

maintained their superiority over the masses. But pressures exerted by the rise of bourgeois groups after the fourteenth century encouraged stricter attitudes among the upper class toward bourgeois "upstarts" who might infringe upon such privileges as *Limpieza de sangre.*[9]

Geohistorically, if Spain has many faces, Portugal has at least a Janus countenance. The north, cleaved by mountains and valleys, colder, wetter, and more humid than the south, has been more isolated and prone to regionalism than has southern Portugal. The north has supported pockets of dense population living in scattered settlements and a predominantly agricultural economy. The south is a land of wide, undulating plains, much easier to negotiate than the northern hills and valleys and therefore an area in which transportation and communications have been relatively easy. The configuration of the land, its pastoral economy, and its sparse population have made the area traditionally prone to the invasion of men and ideas.

The dominant alien influences in Portugal were Romans and Moslems. Romans established administrative units and a macroregional economic system, introduced their language, agriculture, and other land-developing techniques, and "originated the fragmentation of land holdings in the north . . . and their concentration in the south" (Oliveira Marques, 1971: 6) Islamic influence was less pervasive, in part because "from the eighth century to the thirteenth" the Portuguese tried, eventually with success, to obliterate it (Oliveira Marques, 1971: 6). Nonetheless influence of the various Islamic cultures in Portugal has been substantial in language, scientific and technological development, the arts, and behavior patterns.

By late medieval times the configuration of Portugal's population indicated that in northern sectors, above the Tagus River, "almost no cities existed, and even the villages were small and poorly kept. The large nuclei of inhabitants were found in the south" (Oliveira Marques, 1971: 7). In rural areas, "Here and there . . . [was] a clump of houses, a center surrounded by cleared fields which sustained its population," while in more densely populated areas "one would find a more dispersed settlement, in even smaller hamlets and little farms" (Oliveira Marques, 1971: 7). Communications and transportation were difficult and fostered independence and localism.

Portugal's chief economic products were wine, olives, and grains, and on the coast salt and fish. The growth of commerce, foreign and domestic, encouraged development of trade fairs and some stimulation of a money economy. Within this process of economic growth and its concomitant state formation rose new groups, in particular the bourgeoisie. A set of panels reproduced in a text supposedly are representative of all groups in late fifteenth-century Portugal. Of the sixty figures in the panels I count only three women: two older and one younger, all wearing hat veils and none seemingly of any rank importance (Oliveira Marques, 1971: 10-13).

Architecture styles and dwelling types differed from region to region
depending on the climate and on materials available. In the north all
classes lived in homes made of granite. In the south the lower classes
lived in brick or mud and plaster houses, while the upper class had
homes made of limestone. In the country a peasant's home usually was
a single room. Women and children slept there while men slept in the
hayloft. In the cities were two types of homes. The Muslim type followed
the same principles for building as the Roman house but there were some
exceptions.

> The greater intimacy of Moslem family life and the circumspection
> imposed upon women obliged certain special practices unknown in
> the Roman home . . . the entrance hall and access to the inner patio
> were cut with bends in order to forestall indiscreet glances of passers-
> by. . . . Great use was made of the . . . Moorish balcony totally enclosed
> by a wooden grating. (Oliveira Marques, 1971: 99.)

By this manner girls could look out on the world without being ogled by
passersby looking in.

From medieval times through the Renaissance Portugal harbored
flourishing urban centers and a tradition of seigneury derived from the
Romans. [10] As in the Spains the center of seigneury influence was the
country estate from which the noble class provided protection, supported
fairs and markets, and afforded amusements for themselves and commoners
alike. People not resident in rural areas lived in regional towns that relied
on the countryside for their sustenance. In areas where reconquest battles
had occurred, rural estates became fortresses, cities were contained within
defensible walls, and much effort was exerted to concentrate blocks of
population in urban areas, a pattern followed in the Spains.

Population had much effect on Portuguese social patterns in these
centuries. Longevity spans were forty to forty-five years for those who
survived infancy. There was a high rate of infant mortality, and geneaologi-
cal records indicate that in an average household approximately two
children became adults, although in many homes only one survived (*Livro
de Linhagens,* 1856: I). The additional factor of the death of many women
in childbirth reduced the proportion of females of childbearing age and
probably contributed to a situation in which population levels were barely
maintained. These statistics are mostly for upper classes, particularly the
nobility, but it should not be assumed that women in these classes had a
lower death rate than women from lower strata. Conditions, particularly
in the countryside, probably did not differ significantly among classes,
for childbirth was a process of unsanitary conditions and ignorant practices for any women.[11] Another factor that probably contributed to a
mother's death in childbirth was the practice of prompting premature
birth and the application of abortive techniques. Both these practices

were known and applied among all classes, and they were considered justified when a mother's life was in danger (Oliveira Marques, 1971: 151).

In sexual relationships and marriage matters vis à vis family, certain distinctions existed between classes. Sexual activity was a matter of class and was overseen by churchmen. The Church prohibited sexual relations during menstruation, after pregnancy was verified, and after birth until the mother was "purified" (Oliveira Marques, 1971: 173).

Lower-class females appear to have had more freedom than their upper-class counterparts (Oliveira Marques, 1971: 157). Aristocratic love had more complex expression and seemed not so free. Love was often equated with duty, especially in later medieval times. Yet "carnal unions before marriage were not unusual," and extramarital affairs were common, "the frequency of adultery [requiring] the drafting of more severe laws" (Oliveira Marques, 1971: 160-1).

The sexual mores of the day were closely linked to marriage practices. Most upper-class marriages were arranged between parents, often as early as the birth of their children. The usual pattern was marriage of boys fourteen to sixteen years to girls twelve to fourteen years, although it was not uncommon to betroth teenage girls to old (forty years) men.[12] Under this kind of regimen infidelity in marriage was common. Tremendous differences existed between the socio-moral ideal and actual practice, but there is little evidence to suggest that wayward wives paid for any blemish to their husband's honor. Illegitimate children were common, but since privileged classes could afford letters of legitimacy, concubinage and other amorous excursions were the accepted course of events.[13] Reliance on letters of legitimacy continued to be popular throughout the following centuries, both in Portugal and Spain and their overseas territories.[14]

The frequent traveling done by nobles until the sixteenth century contributed to another common practice—seduction of lower-class women by nobles who lodged in their homes. Apparently traveling nobles even perpetrated their desires on nuns in convents, and sources frequently mention such "outrages."

Libertine sexual practices were not exclusive to nobles. Clerics commonly took mistresses, had children, and provided them with luxuries. Many women apparently preferred this type of union to formal marriage since they could more easily indulge their fancies as mistresses to priests than as wives to commoners. Nuns and abbesses, as well as priests and high-ranking religious officials, petitioned for letters of legitimacy for their children. This behavior persisted in contravention of both Church law, which excommunicated sinners, and civil law, which punished bigamy with death and exiled any man who committed adultery with a married woman, confiscating his property if a noble or condemning him to death if a commoner (Baquero Moreno, 1961: 156-61; Santos Cruz, 1841: 394-7). These codes were less applicable to the lower classes.

After the fifteenth century, throughout the peninsula seigneury influence expanded, and with it came adjustments in social convention. While marriage had been considered the ultimate social arrangement it was not until the Council of Trent (1563) that strict sacramental monogamy assumed canonical importance. In Iberia the Roman custom of consent between partners under oath but without witnesses or canonical blessing had been a common form of matrimony, as had Roman customs of separation and divorce, but by the end of the sixteenth century in Portugal and Spain these practices had become less respectable among the upper strata of society.

This simple exchange of vows remained popular among poorer classes. Ordinary citizens were unable to pay a priest to solemnize the oath or to provide food and drink for feasting guests. More importantly, since property was divided in legal marriage, the commoner could not afford to pay a notary to draw up property contracts and, most likely, there was little property to be divided so there was no need for an official (Herculano, 1907: 36ff., 49-50). Also, one of the main objectives in medieval marriage was the transfer of property, and because lower classes had little, there was no need for legal union.

In Portuguese law there was equal participation in property. The woman had the right to dispose of her own belongings, including paraphernalia that she brought to her marriage, wedding presents, and most importantly any inheritance that she received (Paulo Merea, 1913: II, 4-8). She had equal participation in the administration of the property, in its inheritance, and in transferring it directly to heirs (Paulo Merêa, 1913: II, 4-8).

Any woman wed in church, and that was usually a woman of the upper classes, wore a veil on her head, "a very old ritual contemporary with early Christianity." The exchange of rings after the blessings was the Spanish variation of the symbol of dowry, which, in German law, the husband presented to his wife.

> The earnest money, or dowry, paid by the husband to his wife signified the purchase of her body. This Germanic practice, contrary to the Roman custom of the endowment of the woman by her father, was in effect in Portugal during almost the entire Middle Ages, particularly since it was reinforced by an identical Moslem rite. (Oliveira Marques, 1971: 166.)

The custom that became common was the parents giving the bride to the groom. If the bride had been wed previously or was a widow "there was no feast nor should there have been, because she was a widow" (Oliveira Marques, 1971: 168). Presumably that attitude had something to do with the early church fathers' belief that a woman who was a widow should mourn the loss of her virginity more than the loss of her husband.

In general the prevalence among the upper classes of Germanic customs in the north and similar Islamic customs in the south proscribed certain female rights and responsibilities. Customs of different regions caused diversity in marital rites to be sure, but some moral guidelines were held in common. Among nobility chivalry persisted, but enactment of strong legislation to prevent adultery would suggest that among these groups "licentious" behavior persisted (Oliveira Marques, 1971: 160-1). Consent marriage remained quite popular and also was not infrequent among the clergy. Even during the fifteenth, sixteenth, and seventeenth centuries when forbidden by the Church, it occurred between noble man and woman. But for the most part it was the form of marriage for the lower classes. Consent marriage for the lower classes and church marriage for the upper classes became the rule for Iberia after Trent.

As the growth of estates, proliferation of property, and other wealth resulting from overseas adventures made it increasingly necessary to ensure proper legal inheritance and its administration, class marital differences hardened. Among the upper classes it remained common when making political alliances to give towns as dowries. One such dowry comprised the towns of Soria, Almazán, Atienza, and Molina, which were given to Catalina, daughter of the Duke of Lancaster, who was to marry Don Enrique, son of Juan I of Castile. If Enrique died before the age of fourteen, Catalina had to marry his younger brother Fernando as part of the dowry bargain (Russell, 1955: 506, 507). A more important example was the Braganza gift of Bombay and other overseas areas to Charles II as dowry for his marriage to the Portuguese princess Catherine.

Under this more sanctimonious regimen of marriage, temptations for infidelity were many. But sexual mores increasingly became linked to proper marriage, and adultery increasingly was frowned upon. Any husband who was "sinned against" by his wife was completely justified, by custom and law, to kill his wife for any supposed insult. Mistresses of clergy and married men, if discovered, were excommunicated from the Church along with their lovers. Twelfth-century civil law, which stayed on the books, even put clerical mistresses in jail. By the late thirteenth century, rulings prohibited mistresses at courts and forbade married men to give them legacies or gifts. Conversely, any man who "deflowered a virgin" or slept with a widow had to marry her. A tool to keep the aristocracy in check was confiscation of the property of a nobleman and death to any other male who committed adultery with a married woman (Oliveira Marques, 1971: 177).

In cases of rape, although women were vindicated, they had to endure a barbaric ritual to acquire vindication. They had to go immediately to the public square and cry out loudly enough for the public to hear exactly what had happened in detail. The man was severely fined (Oliveira Marques, 1971: 178). The process for a woman was humiliating and little different from the trauma endured by today's rape victims. While the man was merely fined she publicly had proclaimed herself to be in unpurified condition.

The major form of sexual "deviation" was prostitution, which was accepted at all levels of society, even though Renaissance-Reformation moralizing fervor had caused regulation and segregation of prostitutes. As early as the mid-fourteenth and fifteenth century, royal ordinances required prostitutes (and Jews) to wear signs labeling themselves (Santos Cruz, 1841: 395-7; Oliveira Marques, 1971: 179). Prostitution was commonplace and tolerated, and the right of husbands to sleep with prostitues was recognized by the king. In mid-fifteenth century Evora, for example, it was acknowledged that "honorable men come to this city and lodge at the inns and desire to sleep with single concubines, and send to the brothel for them" (Pereira, 1885-1891: II, 53). Some pimps belonged to the squire class. But a common class of pimps, *tafuis* (dandies), kept their mistresses in prostitution,

> placing them in the inns to publicly sleep with the travelers, taking for themselves everything the girls earned . . . if they . . . do not earn enough . . . they take the girls to the villages and cities of which they hear greater fame, for there they earn more and . . . put them in the public brothels. (Oliveira Marques, 1971: 180.)

Laws against prostitution were on the books. Pimps and procurresses were flogged the first time they were caught, publicly proclaimed so, expelled from the area, and lost their properties to the king. Repeaters usually received the death penalty (Oliveira Marques, 1971: 178). How closely the letter of the law was followed we do not know, but the profession seems to have flourished and to have been condoned by public officials.

Indeed, so vital was prostitution that there developed a hierarchical system of categorizing prostitutes, not unlike our modern-day system. In Portugal, in keeping with the hierarchical nature of the society, prostitutes were graded. The most sophisticated were, perhaps, *mulheres de segre* (women of the world), followed in descending order by *mancebas* (concubines) or mistresses, *meretrizes* (common harlots), and *soldadeiras* (hired servants), women who accompanied jesters by singing and dancing and who were of similar lower- to lower-middle social status as jesters.

Professional male pimps have remained to the present day keeping women in prostitution and living from their income. Madames do not seem to have been so common earlier as they later became, exploiting other women.

Outside the realm of socio-sexual activities among the lower classes females contributed their share to economic activities. The majority of the Portuguese population was engaged in agriculture on lands that were not theirs and/or for which they paid an annual fixed rent or *emphyteusis* (lease-contract). In addition, serfs, tenant farmers, landowning peasants and, occasionally, knight-villeins were subject to corvée tribute (Oliveira Marques, 1971: 184). Women always had worked in the fields, but during the reconquest when every able-bodied man was required for military expeditions all fieldwork had been left to women. It was the right as well as the duty for common people to work, said Portuguese law. In the countryside activities of sowing, harvesting, cutting grass, and feeding animals, iconography of the time show women side by side or slightly behind their menfolk, but both doing common work. Women also worked the vineyards, a major export income source.

Urban manual professions were ranged in hierarchical strata of eighteen groups. Women were in the fourteenth level as street vendors, the fifteenth as bakers, and the sixteenth as fishwives (Pereira, 1885-1891: II, 159-61). In general, women made and sold bread and baked goods, sold fruits, vegetables, and herbs, helped in various trades, and served as street cleaners, ragpickers, and garbage collectors (Oliveira Marques, 1971: 202-3).

Since medieval times in Portugal's cities, females have worked in all capacities of domestic service and have continued in other activities. They have worked alongside their husbands in tile manufactures, often composing a majority of workers (Oliveira Marques, 1971: 27). Throughout Portugal, public washerwomen are still seen at the town center's well. Around the 1550s Lisbon alone counted 3,500 laundresses. After the late fifteenth century, slave women were also recorded in the same activities (Ibid.: 137-8).

Women workers were denied membership in various brotherhoods, guilds, and unions and were paid far less than were men. In tilemaking men drew two and one-half times the wages of women for the same number of hours, while in baking women worked five times the number of hours as did men but received only twice the wages (Oliveira Marques, 1971: tables 198-201). Women laundresses, assistants in trades, food sellers, and street vendors were excluded from artisan classification. Until the twentieth century women were rarely included in the ranks of intelligentsia or commerce or public officialdom.

Although basic institutions and behavior patterns that had become fixed by events such as Trent, the Reformation, and the Counter-Reformation guided Portugal through to the twentieth century, some other changes that occurred affected women. As in the rest of Europe, the cult of the Virgin and Marian devotion had grown rapidly after the thirteenth century. By the sixteenth century, veneration of Mary and the concept of virginity became fixed in attitudes (which have remained constant until recent decades; now, it seems, the attitudes are finally breaking down). The veneration and ennobling of the pure female has been reinforced in Portuguese song and text through the centuries. And, curiously, the shift of nunneries toward good works and welfare in the seventeenth through nineteenth centuries reinforced the idea.

From the eleventh through the fifteenth centuries changes in sports, amusements, and entertainments have permitted women greater public participation in them. There has been, since the sixteenth century, an increase in the types of activities that male and female can do together, albeit chaperoned. These changes occurred in Portugal much later than in the rest of Europe and especially among the upper classes. Among the lower classes gaming was popular and medieval casinos and cabarets contained many women. These amusements continued to flourish after the Renaissance and through the Enlightenment period. And in cities one can always find women in numbers in bawdy houses.

Music and dance have always been popular and all celebrations are based on and utilize them. João II issued a decree in late medieval times "that from all the Moorish quarters of the Kingdom all the men and women who knew how to dance, play instruments, and sing must come to the celebrations . . . beautiful girls who know well how to dance and sing should come" (Oliveira Marques, 1971: 258).

Late medieval times through the Enlightenment frame the time period that, theoretically and practically, influenced the definitive shape of later Iberian societies and their overseas territories. Characteristics developed during that time frame define social and family structure and the position of women in contemporary Iberian societies. From the late eighteenth and early nineteenth centuries Iberians lost hegemony over most of their lucrative empire. Still, Iberian mother cultures in the last century and a half have profided their ex-colonies a sentimental referent to abjure or emulate.

IBERIA IN THE NINETEENTH AND TWENTIETH CENTURIES: AFTER THE LOSS OF AMERICA

There is little improvement for this time frame in information about the classes that are fundamental to the development of any society, the working classes. A major distinction is operative among them: proletariat "families" were much more loosely structured and relatively unstable while peasant families were tightly knit and loyal to their own and their villages. Nonetheless lower-class urban groups and peasants and rural workers exhibit similar attitudes regarding public activities for women, for the need to work together mitigates severe restrictions on female behavior.

Lower-class women have comprised the majority of Iberia's female population. They belong to farming or pastoral families in the countryside or to artisan, laborer, shopkeeper, and service families in the cities. Legally their rights have been as circumscribed as for all classes of women, but in practice they have enjoyed relative mobility since their tasks often take them out of their homes to help husbands to supplement meager family incomes. Women perform almost any type of menial public job available: field worker, factory laborer, preparer of foodstuffs, domestic servant (usually prior to marriage), and public-service jobs, especially in post offices and primary schools. The life of lower-class woman has been hard, her diet meager, and her monetary resources inadequate to purchase decent food and clothing, to light or heat her small home, or to supply sanitary facilities. Working women have been poorly paid—only one-third a man's salary—and there have been few possibilities for advancement, even in jobs created by the state in which, incidentally, women are quite prominent. Since World War II there has been noticeable growth in the percentage of women workers among lower classes, particularly in labor sectors and public works that used to be male preserves. Lower-class women assume the monetary and administrative obligations of their family. Only within the household itself does labor divide according to sex. Lower-class women, rural and urban, have retained prerogatives generated by shared responsibilities.[15]

Sex mores of the rural peasant and urban proletariat were almost diametrically opposed to those of middle- and upper-class groups. Working women were far removed from upper-class ideals of fidelity and female chastity. They worked at jobs in which they were in constant contact with men, thus, in theory, enjoying more "sexual" freedom. In rural agricultural areas courtship traditionally remained tied to varieties and phases of work that the affianced would undertake together, tasks such as building a stone house or preparing crop plots. Furthermore, rural men and women could meet and woo before informing their families. Premarital sex was common in the countryside and persisted despite prohibitions by the Roman Catholic Church.[16] In an area of supposedly Moorish influence, Portugal's Alentejo, peasants traditionally have never attached any value to virginity. In fact, it has been the rule that men and women live together in consensual unions. If they have children they might have a civil marriage, although usually relatively later in life (Cunha Gonçalves, 1922: 57).

In Spain women have been prominent in labor activities, particularly since the turn-of-the-century conflicts between Spain's center and the Catalonian triangle. In the northeast, in Catalonia and its major city of Barcelona, socioeconomic and "nationalistic" agitation culminated in the tragic week, during which a workers' strike was brutally suppressed. In 1905 Barcelona's labor force, industrial and commercial, comprised 155,828 workers, of whom 35,333 were women and 8,796 were girls. By far the majority were textile workers—in toto, some 27,098 women and 4,516 girls (Ullman, 1968: 69). Women began work in the factories at twelve or fourteen years of age and continued to work after they were married, primarily because their husbands' salaries were too low. "Usually illiterate, cut off from the traditional Spanish pattern of churchgoing and intense family life these women sought social identification in labor unions or in women's affiliates of the Radical Party" (Ullman, 1968: 232-3). A typical product of this environment and one of the more prominent participants in the tragic week was twenty-eight-year-old Juana Ardiaca, "separated from her husband and working in a factory to support her child and her parents. She joined the *Damas Radicales* because she wanted the health insurance that they had promised but could not finance" (Ullman, 1968: 232-3).

A substantial number of working-class women, "primarily machinery operators employed in textile factories," were incorporated into the Radical party of Catalan. They were "tough, semiliterate women who could not vote," but were "an important sector of the labor force. . . . Women attracted the sympathies of the general public" during any mob action (Ullman, 1968: 91-2). In the highly politicized atmosphere of the northeast there was plenty of need and opportunity for female agitation. There were two groups of women revolutionaries, the Damas Radicales and the *Damas Rojas,* the latter of whom wanted civil marriages and funerals and who wished to remove the influence of the Roman Catholic Church.

This seemed a prelude to female participation in the Spanish Civil War. "Women played as great a part as they had done in the early days of the war" throughout the entire 1936-1939 conflict (Thomas, 1965: 409). In demonstrations they appealed for all able-bodied men to go to the front and a woman's batallion even fought before the Segovia bridge for the Republicans. Women also participated for the Falangists.

> A decree of 7 October (1937) obliged all fit women between the ages of 17 and 35 who were not occupied by their families, other war work, or hospital duties to undertake some kind of social service. . . . A certificate of social service became essential to secure any employment for Spanish women. (Thomas, 1965: 616.)

As a result of the Civil War and for other reasons after the ensconcement of Franco, changes have occurred in urban areas. In cultural and intellectual development Spain has produced a number of prominent women writers, among them the Duchess of Medina Sidonia and the internationally famous novelist, Ana Maria Matute. More and more women filter into public life. The marriage rate is lower and the average age of marriage is later than anywhere else in Western Europe except Ireland. Birth rates are higher among the upper classes than among urban lower and middle classes. Bourgeois life, which has become increasingly attractive to Spaniards, requires greater capital outlay, so single women and men work and save to savor it. For married couples, it has become increasingly common for both to work outside the home.

Urban upper-class Iberian women's behavior had been strictly regulated in the nineteenth century. Portuguese women veiled and concealed them-

selves and did not descend from their carriages in public. Their existence
has been described as one resembling that of "Circassian harem inmates"
(Moigénie, 1924: 246). Now upper-class women enjoy the material advantages that money allows. Younger wealthy women use their leisure time
for clubs, shopping, and travel.

In Spanish cities now, women of all classes are becoming more independent, although their societal role is supposedly determined by the
official term *sus labores* (housewife). Unmarried girls are chaperoned
until they are eighteen or so. Thereafter they are allowed in public with
girl friends of similar age and status whose families are known to their
parents. Freedom of action for girls varies according to their family's
position, and generally greater freedom now is allowed daughters of
upper-class families due to factors such as university attendance, travel
and study abroad, and the opening up to women of the professions and
other occupations.

Women have entered the professions gradually, but today they still
comprise only a fraction of Spain's lawyers, doctors, and the like, although
many more than in the United States. About one in every seven women in
Madrid is employed, and in the last thirty years or so women's wages have
risen much faster than have men's (Kenny, 1966:161, 197).

Although prostitution was officially outlawed in 1956, professionals
and brothels abound in the cities, catering to male prerogatives of extramarital or double-standard sexuality. Nonetheless, marriage is the ideal
for most Spanish and, true to tradition, the "honest female" is accorded
chivalrous attention while the prostitute or mistress is treated as a woman
of impropriety.

Social, economic, and political patterns really began to change for the
Portuguese people after the end of a civil war in 1834. Ultimately, more
changes followed when the Liberal parliamentary monarchy, which had
assumed power at that time, was replaced in 1910 by a parliamentary
republic and then by the *Estado Novo* (New State) in 1926. In Spain the
seemingly enduring republic was not established until 1931 and then, in
1939, was replaced by the Falangist government of Franco.

Legislative changes that were in effect after the establishment of the
republic in Portugal really benefit more urban women, especially those
in a position to take advantage of legal opportunities. According to the
1911 census "women were in a backward condition; their rate of illiteracy (for those over seven) was 77.4 per cent" (Oliveira Marques,
1972: 134-5). There was, at the time, only a small group of well-educated
women who actively worked to improve the civil and political rights
of Portugal's women. The Republican League of the Portuguese Women,
founded in 1909, played an active and influential role in these activities
despite the fact that its membership was only 500 in 1910. But it
agitated for and won reforms. The government, in an act of 3 November
1910, allowed divorce for all couples and "considered husband and wife

as equal in respect to the causes and results of divorce" (Oliveira Marques, 1972: 134-5). In 1910 civil marriage was made compulsory for all, and equal rights in marriage was made compulsory for all, and equal rights in marriage were given to both male and female. In 1911 the first woman university professor, Carolina Michaelis de Vasconcelos, was appointed. But the vote was not given to women until 1931, and then with restrictions (Oliveira Marques, 1972: 135).

Land is the key to Iberian life. In Portugal land use and land ownership underwent change, altering the social, political, and other relationships integral to it. The Liberal parliamentary monarchy's legislation on land changed the system of entailment and allowed for its equal division between female and male heirs. This relationship between land and society had enormous implications for today's Portuguese females.

Because marriage is the key to keeping property and passing it on, since the mid-nineteenth century land reforms there has been an almost total absence of anything other than intragroup marriage in Portuguese rural society. This is reinforced by segregation of boys and girls and adolescents according to class status in villages and towns.[17] Although marriage has, in the past few decades, become more a matter of free choice between young men and women, patterns of expected traditional behavior still endure. During the *namoro* (period of betrothment) the girl's responsibilities are more weighty than the boy's. Any improper behavior on her part, even talking to men unrelated to her, is sufficient for ending the relationship. In theory, sexual intercourse before marriage is taboo, although in practice it seems to have become more common among the more "respectable" classes in the countryside, and definitely in the cities. But the rule of thumb is that a father will pass on his virgin daughter to her betrothed, and the daughter's virginity reflects both the father's honor and his bond in the passing of property.

> A woman who has been *cevada* (... "used by a pig") is defiled and will not be acceptable to another man if he is to keep his ideal self respect. [Yet] defloration of the woman one marries ... either before or after marriage ... is a basic assumption. (Cutileiro, 1971: 96.)

Marriage also reflects the persistence of some basic attitudes about woman's and man's honor and shame. A woman should marry to remove herself as a burden of expenditure from her father's household. A man must marry because he then attains full manhood as the "full trustee of a woman's honour, and her behaviour is intimately tied up with his reputation and the fate of their family.... They are protecting the good name of the community against the dangers implicit in the sexuality of its women." (Cutileiro, 1971: 102).

The two major pillars of family in contemporary Iberian rural societies are maintenance of material circumstances and morality of family members. The first is the responsibility of the man, the second of the woman. For the man to fail in taking the responsibility of providing for his family is a serious shame for him as an individual and for his family. But for a woman to fail to protect her family's morality is the most serious transgression of all. If a wife commits adultery she "has destroyed the viability of her family by destroying the main moral assumption on which it was based and must therefore disappear" (Cutileiro, 1971: 142). Portuguese criminal law still provides a very mild punishment for a husband who kills his wife and her lover if they are caught.

In practice, wives of poorer families more often deviate from this ideal and with fewer and less harsh repercussions. It is almost as if society expects it and therefore has a built-in condonation of immoral behavior. Among the poorest, the peasant and laboring families, particularly those who work on large estates, there is a type of acceptance of adultery that "has become institutionalized as a means of securing patronage benefits" (Cutileiro, 1971: 144). In fact, husbands often suggest and usually condone wives' giving of themselves to the landowner, for, among other things, it is a guarantee to the economy of the worker's family as well as a form of protection.

In a sense, morality and material well-being are complementary values. There is more tolerance for, or at least a clearer ingestion by society of the shame of poorer families whose women help maintain the material through laxness in morality. There is no tolerance for a wealthy woman who engages in misbehavior for she destroys the well-being of her family. In essence, poverty makes it more difficult for women to lead an honorable life, honorable in the sense of upper-class values that presume to hold the general society together.

Other than their importance in transmittal of property and maintenance of the material and moral bases of the family, what other roles do Iberian women play in rural areas? Wives of the working classes are not nearly so secluded as are upper-class women and are, in fact, very different from the supposed ideal of a wife. The architectural layout of homes of poorer and wealthier classes gives a clue to the public involvement of females. In wealthy homes the kitchen is in the rear of the house and the husband's office in the front. Thus if a woman wanted to leave her house or engage in public activities she would have to pass under the eye of her husband. In homes belonging to the poor the kitchen opens to the outside, allowing for immediate entry of the female into street activity. Homes emphasize the seclusion of wealthy women and the sociability of poor ones.

Whitewashing of houses, as anyone who has driven through the Iberian countrysides can attest, traditionally has been woman's work. White symbolizes purity and the home is woman's purview; the connection is clear. Also, women are not supposed to whitewash during menstruation.

The public role of the rural wife has been one of subordination, which is so marked by public ceremonies. When a woman dies church bells toll twice and not thrice, as for a man. When a couple leaves the house, the wife must walk a few steps behind her husband. If someone is invited to their home, the wife eats at a separate table and after the menfolk.

In practice, however, things are quite different. A man cannot interfere with his wife's domain, but she can and does in his. "The legal dispositions which make the husband the head of the family . . . elector . . . source of power and authority, conceal the fact that . . . the wife has extensive power and authority herself," the case for all except the wealthiest and most status-conscious classes (Cutileiro, 1971: 104). Among the masses, women manage the budget and the household, and if needed will work the fields to earn extra money. If husbands work away from home, returning only on weekends or less often, wives assume even more responsibilities, including banking and negotiating with public authorities. These women have important contacts with the outside world. Often they maintain a client-patron relationship with wealthy women, especially if they have worked for them prior to marriage. They serve to inform the secluded upper-class women of events in the outside world, provide other services, advise them of the availability of servants, and supply them with gossip. In return, wealthy women provide a form of protection, gifts of money, and intercession with hospitals and with other public authorities (Cutileiro, 1971: 105-6).

Women and their role in kinship relationships differ from area to area. In Old and New Castile great reliance on kin relationships seems the norm (Pitt-Rivers, 1961; Kenny, 1966; Lisón-Tolosana, 1966; Freeman, 1970; and Cutileiro, 1971, for similarities and differences). In areas of western Spain, Andalusia, and southern and central Portugal, outside of the nuclear family little attention, except in ritual times, is paid to the more extensive family and kin ties (all the above and OHI, 1968, 1973). Although kinship in all these regions does retain one of the general characteristics of kinship, an identification with "family," it has little affinity with other general characteristics, such as reciprocal and exclusive rights. This seems especially so in central and southern Portugal.

The main cross-kin relationship that persists in areas of Iberia where kinship seems to have faltered is a network of feminine ties. This is true partly because the female is considered the continuity figure in all relationships. In each family unique relationships are formed by each person with the mother. In southern and central Portugal whenever a woman has children by different fathers, the children "remain more united throughout life than the children of a common father and different mothers" (Cutileiro, 1971: 113). Overall, the entirety of family life "is conditioned by the operations of feminine networks—determined, persist, and manipulated by women, and men have little to say. . . . These networks form the only operative groupings based on kinship" (Cutileiro, 1971: 127).

In addition to family kinship ties, neighborhood and village relations basically are feminine ones. Women are the constant in all of these areas. Based in mother-daughter, sister-sister ties, especially among all but the wealthiest classes, women's relationships often are ones of mutual aid and also of a type of overseeing of others' activities. For the common citizen, the outdoors—and, in particular, the street on which they live—is the living room. Women sit on the steps to sew, to watch their children, to chat with their neighbors, to watch every movement that occurs within their view. It is their "duty" to hear about everything that is not within their immediate earshot or eyesight. Information is exchanged at public places such as the markets, the laundry, the shops, during visits, and at church. The information then travels through these feminine networks, socially or biologically kin, to other neighborhoods and villages. Women provide a major communications network for a still largely illiterate sector of the population.

The public purview of the educated woman and the freer female of the upper classes is limited to what she has been trained for and the extent to which she is allowed mobility. The major public positions that women can occupy are in teaching, law, and medicine. Traditionally, teachers have played a major role in Iberian life. In Portugal, in particular, under both monarchical and Republican rule, they have played key roles in local and provincial administrative posts and today hold political office. Since the republic many women have become teachers. They acquire substantial prestige from this. But they are also somewhat secluded because they are removed from their village network sources by occupying such a superior position. At the same time usually they are excluded from political and administrative positions (Cutileiro, 1971: 197; OHI, 1968, 1973).

There are some conclusions that can be drawn here that encompass the Iberian peninsula and almost all societies whose culture focus is less within the purview of modernizing, urbanizing, industrializing Western European societies. Females seem to cross kin, neighbor, and village lines quite easily, particularly in rural areas. Indeed, in some areas this is helped by the extensive practice of exogamy. In northern Castile, for example, almost all village wives come from different villages. Also, throughout Iberia older daughters of large families are sent to work for other families in neighboring villages or large towns. One reason for this is the various ladies' circles (for example, the spinning circles), especially of northwestern Spain.

Also, although a woman's husband is, in law, the administrator of the home, in practice the female makes crucial decisions. She can involve herself in activities where he cannot do the same. She may have as much property as (if not more than) her husband, and by Spanish and Portuguese law, she retains veto power over its use and disposal (Freeman, 1970: 194). Contrary to public roles, man and woman share management of family and household and are nearly equal in all enterprises. "The near equality of male and female statuses is closely related to the ideal of household autonomy and to the crucial importance in the social structure of the householder, male or female, married or single" (Freeman, 1970: 195).

Theoretically, when a woman marries she passes from the legal tutelage of her father to that of her husband and only as a widow does she acquire legal status as head of the family. In practice, that is not the case. Although the male in law is the executor of the estate, it is the woman who handles the routine of running the household and overseeing the functions of society's most important unit. This is so for almost all groups except the very wealthiest, in which case the woman seldom has anything to do with external authorities or with budget and similar activities (Cutileiro, 1971: 107-8). In law, however, as far as inheritance is concerned, women of any class enjoy the same rights in both Spain and Portugal: equal rights of inheritance. In custom, practices do differ, particularly in rural areas (Freeman, 1970: 72).

In the Iberian peninsula there seem to be two separate and distinct female traditions, but they are distinctions of class, more than of the separate national cultures. What is common to Portugal appears common to Spain and, indeed, can be recognized in cultures with similar patterns of value, attitude, behavior, and socioeconomic composition. To be sure there are numerous variations on the theme, but it would be safer to say that what is common to pastoral areas in Spain is common to pastoral areas in Portugal, ad infinitum with specific differences for each. But the underlying basis for difference lies in the socioeconomic differences between groups in society, their functions, their roles, the dimensions of the expression of behavior that they are allowed. This dichotomy between classes has been perpetuated partly because Iberia was the progenitor of these characteristics and partly because it found comparable characteristics in other societies.

NOTES

1. *Fidalgo* (Spanish: *hidalgo*), literally, "the son of someone," presumably of importance. More commonly used to identify men from a petty nobility stratum of Iberian society.

2. For excellent urban history materials, see the numerous works of Richard Morse.

3. At this time an encomienda consisted of a town with some land attached and whose residents depended on a *comendador* to whom they paid dues (Domínguez Ortiz, 1971: 117).

4. For some revisions and specific studies of population shifts and declines, see Phillips, 1972.

5. Elliott, 1963 passim, for an overview of this situation. Also see Nadal and Giralt, 1960: 117, for figures on Catalonia's problems. Between

1347 and 1497 Catalonia lost 37 percent or about 300,000 of its population due to plague and famine.

6. As good examples of seventeenth-century descriptions of female life, see Letter VIII, 1679 in D'Aulnoy, 1691: 179-214.

7. Larruga, 1793: I, 12. In 1787, one-eighth of all males about fifty years of age had never wed. Livi-Bacci, 1968: 533.

8. *Nova Recop.*, Book 8, iii, 5. A full list of minor guilds is given in AHN Libros, 1766: folio 110.

9. Literally, "purity of blood," but more specifically it defined one's line according to "class" and place of birth. An Iberian refinement of a transplanted Roman precept.

10. Southern Portugal had more urban areas. In 1527, it had twenty-five towns with more than 2,000 people each, while northern Portugal had only eight towns of comparable size (Ribeiro, n.d.: I, 576).

11. An example of how not to presume living standards is that in medieval Portugal poor peoples' diet consisted of vegetables and fruits because they could not afford the starchy and fatty diets of the rich.

12. There seems a consistency in time to people of the upper classes marrying later in life, increasingly later from the sixteenth through late eighteenth centuries, and many did not marry at all. See Kamen, 1971: 13, 19, for statistics.

13. Baquero Moreno, 1961: 207-10. Whether records were kept better or this situation was the case, in fact a marked increase in illegitimate births is indicated from the late fourteenth century.

14. As examples, the thousands of petitions for *Gracias al Sacar* documents, letters indicating a person's lineage. In colonial Latin America they legitimized race and color.

15. See Nunes Pereira Neto, 1968: 20-1, 44, 55, 63, 67, for Portugal. My notes confirm this for Spain (OHI, 1960, 1967-1968, 1973).

16. The *Constituições Episcopais* of the Church, although insistent, has never been able to eradicate the customary practice of sexual intercourse between engaged couples.

17. My research confirms this in both Spain and Portugal, agricultural and pastoral areas, also.

3 IBERIA IN ASIA: AN EXPERIMENT IN INTERCULTURAL LIVING

INDIGENOUS CULTURES AND
THE CONTACT SETTING

During Europe's late-medieval, early-Renaissance period a spirit of new and zealous curiosity existed in which men sought knowledge and questioned scientific truths. This time was the age of reconnaisance, "the early process of discovery," which began independently of the Renaissance "with medieval motives and assumptions" (Parry, 1963: 52). Technical developments in navigation, changes in monetary systems and, especially in Iberian "nations," a residue of crusading fervor prompted Europeans to cast their ambitious eyes across uncharted oceans to lands of fabled wealth. The Italian city-states were the successful emulative model for all Mediterranean countries, from Egypt to Portugal. Once the Iberians, and particularly the Portuguese, perfected their sea-legs, expeditions from various Portuguese ports sailed for Asia and Africa, testing new navigational and shipbuilding techniques and, occasionally, carrying persons imbued with proselytizing fervor. The Portuguese were the first "modern" men to venture extensively into the unknown, and throughout most of the fifteenth century Lusitania's hardy sailors and ships plied oceans and seas for their king and their God.

The rise of Iberian states, the ultimate shifts and amalgamations that transformed them into the two imperial powers of Portugal and Spain, was allied to changing balances in world political and economic power. From about the mid-fifteenth to the late seventeenth century the basically agrarian societies of western Europe had been mobilized into national military machines and had developed new organizational skills, managerial techniques, financial and technical resources, state administration, and ideological and legal theories to underwrite those changes. A restless, awakened congeries of ethnic regions, western Europeans still battled one another, but they also began turning their gunsights outward, their appetites whetted by crusading ventures in the East. Determined to thrust into alien lands, they contracted alliances among each other in order to ensure each state's imperial hegemony over newly claimed territories. Motivations were many: the continuing crusading zeal, desire for fame and riches, scientific and humanistic curiosity, political and economic power or, as in Castile's case, the need to find ample lands with which to reward military heroes of the reconquest.

Although the Spanish were early in Asia, with the exception of the Philippines they quickly turned almost all their energies to the Americas. It was the Portuguese who persisted in the East, believing the Orient to be the greatest source of quick wealth, fame, and power. During the sixteenth century they settled strategic Asian areas, India first, Timor last.

Relatively little is known of the indigenous societies among whom the Iberians settled permanently in the island areas of India (Goa, Daman, Diu), China (Macao), Indonesia (Timor), and the Philippines. To understand Iberia in Asian cultures and to determine how much influence and or syncretism between cultures occurred, it is necessary to examine areas of permanent settlement on the eve of the encounter of cultures.

The various ethnic groups of Portuguese India, China, and Indonesia and the Spanish Philippines shared much in common that we could designate as Asian, not that there is anything identifiable specifically as pan-*Asian* but because local economies, societies, and politics of these peoples possessed characteristics similar both in philosophy and operation. The major sectors of Iberian influence in the East were South and Southeast Asia. The Portuguese had commercial arrangements with Japan, Malaysia, Siam, Pegu, Ceylon, Madras, and Bengal, but their first permanent settlement was along India's Malabar coast, in the western Ghats north from Bombay south to the Mandovi River. This region was inhabited by Konkan peoples.[1] The Portuguese, sailing under Vasco da Gama, first reached the Malabar coast in 1498. Geographically, Portuguese India consisted of sections of land—Goa, Daman, Diu, and the "New Territories"—but administratively the *Estado da India* meant Portuguese political, military, commercial, cultural, and religious hegemony everywhere in the world east of Africa's Cape of Good Hope.[2]

Precontact Indian societies were, and remain, predominantly agrarian, the framework of their social structure based on caste, kinship, and village organization.[3] The patrilineal, joint family has been the Indian ideal and under this form of social organization land and other major economic assets are jointly owned by the family with the oldest *man* directing production and consumption (Mandelbaum, 1948: 123-39; Kapadia, 1958, 1959, 1966; Schneider and Gough, 1961; Karvé, 1953; Mayer, 1952; Srinivas, 1962; Dube, 1955; Marriott, 1955, 1960; *Salsete,* passim, for general discussion of Indian family and kinship structure). Ideally this Indian family included a man, his sons, grandsons, wives, and daughters. It also might encompass a few adult women who resided in their parental home.[4] Sanctions were imposed on parents who failed to arrange for their daughters' marriages during preadolescence.

The ideal of female life in India seems to follow

a rule of Indian manners that they [women] should pass unnoticed and unremarked, even in the household of a friend. . . . [They should have] . . . contentment with their own womanhood, faith in religion, and the natural hope of life. An unremitting devotion and an unfailing tenderness, that is the Indian woman's service in the world. (Rothfeld, 1928: 13, 14, and 1-14 passim, on Indian conceptualization of women).

It has been woman's responsibility to run households, handle budgets, supervise cattle and agriculture, do manual field labor, spin, weave, and make rope. Bearing children, particularly a son, immediately heightens a woman's status.

It has been suggested that religious changes and the introduction of non-Aryan wives were responsible for shifts in historical attitudes regarding women. Hinduism as we know it today passed from an "aristocratic" religion of Brahmans through orthodox and heterodox reactions of Upanishadic, Buddhist, and Jainist beliefs and, reformulated with popular indigenous cults, became a type of devotional "system."[5] These shifts appear in texts. Earlier Brahmanic scriptures (*Vedas, Brahmanas, Upanishads*) differed from later Hindu scriptures (*Epics, Puranas,* Sacred Law, hymns). Hindu scriptures "were available to all, even men of low caste and to women" (Basham, 1959: 299). Furthermore, the *Vedas,* the earliest Sanskritic texts, did not endorse practices or beliefs discriminatory to women. Women in Vedic times (1500-300 B.C.) seemed to have exerted power in and outside the household, and also to be educated (Altekar, 1956: 343ff.). The *Aitareya Brahmana* says that wife is the companion friend of a man, but she must be true to her husband in her marriage vows, lead the life of an ideal, and try her utmost to promote her husband's happiness (VII, 3, 13 in Altekar, 1956: 97, 98; the *Mahabharata,* I:73, 374; XII: 20, 144).

In the Sutra and Epic periods (600-300 B.C. to 100-200 A.D.) woman's position changed more. The wifely ideal was a negation of her personality. Wives did not have a controlling voice in affairs because there were evils inherent in the female character, especially in sexual matters, for "there is nothing more heinous than a woman" (*Manusamhita,* 1933:V:147; IX: 5, 6, 11, 75. Manu's opinions were supported by Epic and Purana writers whose writings are gems of discriminatory insights. *Yaj navalkya smrti,* 1926; *Mahabharata,* 1834: I, IV, V, XI-XIIIff.).

In the *Dharma sutras* wifely duties are described in detail. A woman must always remain dependent on males throughout her life, her husband in betrothal arrangements receiving authority from her father to dominate her. Protection, or seclusion of the woman according to sacred texts, is to preserve purity of offspring. From the "theological" view, the female came to be seen as of the same status as a *Sudra.* Female infanticide increased, the marital age for women was lowered, female participation in religious duties curtailed, and the *sati* custom became increasingly common.[6] It was not until the thirteenth- to sixteenth-century revival movements that equality between woman and man was shown to derive from ideals expressed in the *Bhagavadgita,* which preached redemption through *bhakti* (fervent, emotional devotion) and devotion to a personal god, for both women and Sudras. Ironically, the later revivalists, especially the most famous bhakti saint-singer Kabir, found females an obstruction to spiritual realization and considered woman "a hellish well" (Desai, 1936: 40ff.)

Certain other changes occurred. Women of any status in society within any family relationship were, and are, by Hindu law entitled to maintenance by male relatives. The chief law book, the *Mitakshana* (twelfth century) emphasized that each male was entitled to an equal share of family property. Generally, women could neither hold nor inherit property. They had no other rights than maintenance by their menfolk vis à vis family property (Mandelbaum, 1972: I, 35). This law was enforced particularly during British rule, although critics claim that British courts made rigid and inflexible for much of India what had previously been dynamic (Kapadia, 1958: 250-1). Actually, only in some areas, have there been regional variations in law, such as the *Dayabhaya* code of Bengal (Mandelbaum, 1972: I, 36). There was more flexibility in territories under Portuguese control because in the twin process of trying to preserve Indian laws yet insert their own, the practice allowed for adaptions. Portuguese law gave male and female equal sharing in property.

It was a telling characteristic of Indian society that men always referred first to a woman's physical attributes or beauty. These were the characteristics most highly regarded and sought after. These idealized male notions of a civilized woman, of a beautiful, accomplished companion, closely resembled the Aspasias or Phrynes of classical Greece.

Prostitution and polygamy were two sexually acceptable situations for women. Prostitutes were both ornaments in festivities and gifts for special guests. The female has been given as a gift, for sacrifice, to repay a debt. She has been used either as slave woman, daughter, or wife to satisfy the sexual needs of guests according to the *Mahabharata,* "woman is a chattel" (IV:26, 32, 68, 72, in Meyer, 1953:507). She has been a booty of war, used as currency, lent and exchanged by her husband under legal authority, for woman was considered property to be taken or given at whim, to be bought or sold. If she were an unfaithful wife, because she was property and because adultery was considered a crime against property, she could be punished by her husband (VIII: 371, etc., quoted in Meyer, 1953: 521). Woman was an object of the senses, an instrument for pleasure and merely one among many physical necessities of life, such as a chair, food, or a house. If she should die it would be unsuitable for her husband, even unworthy for him, to show public expressions of grief (Meyer, 1953: 531).

Polygamy was perfectly legitimate for men but illegal for women who were considered the essence of all evil, full of falsehood and trickery (Meyer, 1953: 471). Polygamy was well established in certain sections of society. While it was accepted that men should and could have several wives, it was a grievous insult to a woman's husband and family should she maintain any other extramarital arrangement, including adultery (Altekar; 1956:105, from the *Mahabharata* I:36, 169; and *Taittiriya Samhita* VI:3, 4, 6).

Neither the Moslems, the Portuguese, nor the British, for all of whom inequality between the sexes was accepted practice, did much to improve the lot of Indian women. India's first sustained contacts with Europeans were with Portuguese. Less than two decades after da Gama's arrival Goa had become Portugal's headquarters in the Orient (1510). Malacca was secured the following year. In 1515 the Portuguese seized Hormuz in the Persian Gulf, and Portugal reigned supreme in both naval and commercial ventures, contributing to the legend of the "Portuguese century." The Portuguese were able to preserve their presence in the East and to maintain mastery of the Indian Ocean for lack of any strong Asian naval power.

Portugal's adventures elsewhere in the East were less extensive than in India and hardly enduring, with the exception of two island enclaves of China and Indonesia. Portugal's easternmost colony, Macao, perches on a rock peninsula in the Heung Shan District of Kwong Tung (Canton) province in southeastern China, some eighty-eight miles south of Canton city.[7] The Portuguese had been permitted to form a settlement in Macao in 1557 in return for their aid in expelling pirates, but it was not until 1887 that China formally ratified a treaty of perpetual occupation by Portugal of Macao and its dependencies (Boxer, 1948: 8). When Portuguese trade routes with the East had stabilized, Goa was the initiatory point and Macao the entrepôt for boarding raw and finished silks and disposing of silver bullion. Until the cession of Hong Kong to Great Britain in 1842 Macao was the main depot for trade through Canton with the mainland. The first half of the nineteenth century appears to have been Macao's heyday since foreign merchants were allowed to spend only a short time in Canton and then were obliged to go to the Portuguese possession. Trade patterns shifted to Hong Kong during the last century, and Macao has since become a resort.

Unlike our rich storehouse of information for India, we know relatively little about the indigenous peoples who occupied Macao peninsula prior to Portuguese penetration. We are informed that women in these groups were kept in almost total seclusion and that outside of the family confines they engaged in relatively little decision making concerning their roles in society or economic tasks. They had little choice in marriage, which they usually entered by the age of twelve (Franco, 1897: 140ff.). For the most part, these were peoples from China's southern districts of Canton and Fukien provinces whose people were farmers and fishermen. Allocation of duties and rights was established according to their specific needs.

The other area of Portuguese permanent settlement in the East was Indonesia. Earliest records available for Timor, thirteenth- and fourteenth-century Javanese and Chinese manuscripts, refer to the island as a source of sandalwood, a basic commodity in Asian trade. These sources noted that Timorese peoples lived and worked hard under extremely harsh physical conditions and social handicaps resulting from an excessively humid climate that limits human activity and from the land and labor structure. Despite the involvement of the Spanish, Portuguese, Dutch, and English little substantive information is available on the development of Timor to the present.

What has conditioned Timorese development more than anything else is its geoecological situation. The island is affected by the monsoon climate of the Indonesian archipelago and climatic conditions that create the dry areas of coastal Australia. This makes Timor the only area of Indonesia subject to tropical cyclones and its people victims of flood, drought, and famine. All human activity has revolved around accommodation to those factors.

The population of Timor at time of contact indicates that Timor was a racial transition zone of Indonesian-Malay and Melanesian, but today there are only two major population groupings: the Belunese, the younger ethnic group in the East, and the Timorese or older Atoni, in the mountainous center and west of Indonesian Timor. The Belunese, the more populous people, settled in Portuguese Timor and, unlike the Melanesian Atoni, live under a matrilineal system in which polygamy is practiced. The Belunese, although racially complex, have the more recent Indonesian-Malay influence rather than older Melanesian characteristics of other Indonesians.

The arrival of the Iberians in Timor is linked to the lucrative trade in sandalwood, a commodity coveted by Chinese and Indians for religious ceremonies and by Iberians for medicinal purposes. From about the mid-sixteenth century the Portuguese began making annual voyages to Timor, and in 1566 Dominicans settled the area by constructing a stone fort at Solor where there soon grew a settlement of mixed bloods (Topasses), offspring of Portuguese from Malacca and Macao and Indonesian women (Boxer, 1948: 174-5). The Portuguese showed little interest in Timor until the eighteenth century, and until that time major control or influence in the island remained the purview of the Topasses.

Portugal reluctantly shared Asian waters with a cousin state. The Castilian eye took into its sweep one-half of the world, ceded it by the 1494 Treaty of Tordesillas. Spain was in America, Africa, and Asia, and by the Treaty of Sarragosa (1529) centered its interests on the Philippines.[9]

Portuguese expansion into the Far East had initially tempted the Spanish there as well. Discovery of the Moluccas (Spice Islands) and the Portuguese navigator Magellan's prodding of Spain's emperor Charles V to dispute Portugal's claim to those islands resulted in increased Spanish interest in the Philippines. By 1512 the island of Mindanao had been discovered by Magellan's friend Francisco Serrão, the first European to set foot on the Philippines, but Charles V, impressed by the East's gold, ginger, cloves, and other spices, was convinced to press his claims to the Moluccas. Yet in 1529, after several years of litigation, the loss of expeditions, difficulties of navigation, the persistence of the Portuguese, and other problems, Charles sold his claim to the Moluccas and shifted attention to the Pacific archipelago stretching from the Celebes to Papua.

From 1529 until Legaspi landed on Cebu in 1565, Spanish squadrons were sent to the Philippines, and in 1542 a special expedition was dispatched from Mexico for the purposes of discovery, conquest, and colonization of these islands. This project established the feasibility of using Mexico as a starting point for annexing the Asian islands to Spanish America. The actual conquest and colonization of Spanish Asia began with the expedition of Miguel Legaspi from Navidad, New Spain, in November 1564, his arrival in Cebu noted as April 27, 1565. He was carrying out Spanish objectives that were to secure a share in the lucrative spice trade, heretofore a Portuguese monopoly; establish direct contacts with China and Japan for commercial and missionary purposes; launch the famed trade venture of the Manila galleons; and convert the inhabitants of the archipelago to Catholicism (Phelan; 1967: 7).

The types of societies the Spanish encountered in that polyglot of cultures we call the Philippines shared striking similarities. Peoples of Negrito and later Malay stock occupied the Malayan islands until about 2000 to 1500 B.C. when migrations from southern and Indo-China joined the indigenous races. In the Christian era both Indian and Arab merchants traded and occasionally intermarried. By the fourteenth century Islam had filtered through the Sulus and Mindanao and had touched as far north as Manila. By the sixteenth century, however, non-Islamic Malays occupied most of the archipelago. Only in the southern islands had Islamic influence remained substantially strong enough to keep the Christians at bay for two and a half centuries. The Spanish concentrated on the central and northern islands only superficially touched by Islam and thus more accessible to foreigners. These islands were characterized by political decentralization, geographical particularism, and social groupings of small kinship units (*baranguays*) independent of and hostile to each other and under the rule of individual chieftains (Phelan, 1967: 9). In Many ways they resembled the civil fissures so common to the Castilians and other Spanish cultures, and they made widescale resistance to the Hispanic conquistadores nearly impossible.

Despite political decentralization and linguistic diversities the cultures of Philippine provinces had similar social organizations in which all activity revolved around the joint and nuclear families.[10] Women in these pre-Hispanic societies were negotiable items in a marriage that would consolidate kinship and property ties. The groom paid either a "bride-price" or "bride service," premarital sexual relations were the norm, and the apparent authenticity of Philippine marriages was dependent on a woman's ability to bear children. Since polygamy was not widespread the woman's failure to produce a child was one of the more common grounds for divorce, which, although infrequent, was socially acceptable in indigenous societies.

Pre-Hispanic Philippine economy was essentially an agrarian one based on cultivation of root crops and rice, with fowl, fish, and swine raising supplementary activities. Women performed all barnyard tasks and traditional domestic duties. The division of labor and value of the female were intertwined. Individual children of a free man and dependent woman were half-free and half-dependent or the children were divided, half of them free and the other half dependent, and this was the manner in which their labor services were designated. The Spanish utilized both preconquest Tagalog systems and land and labor patterns developed in their island encomiendas.

THE HISTORICAL MILIEUX: SOCIAL, ECONOMIC, AND POLITICAL ACTIVITIES OF THE IBERO-ASIANS

Although the Iberians, and later other Europeans, occupied themselves primarily with economic profits from their Asian affiliates, they also involved themselves with Asian females. Iberian women were less likely to travel or to survive in tropical climes; consequently Iberian male adventurers, explorers, colonizers, and officials, looking both for political alliances and sexual companionship, sought out local women. Despite royal decrees to Iberian men to marry only women from the "best" class, this was not always easy to do. Europeans in Asian societies remained ignorant of cultural customs of Hindu, Buddhist, or Muslim, most of which forbid marriage outside of one's particular group. "With the possible exception of some Japanese and Chinese Buddhists, any Asian woman who married outside her race, her caste or her religion, forfeited all claim to the respect and consideration of her family and compatriots" (Boxer, 1965: 223). Iberian males in Asia associated with women of slave, lower-class, or Eurasian origin, and very few were able to break the boundaries of indigenous cultural restrictions regarding upper-class women. Between Iberians and the Asian cultures with whom they intermingled there developed an Ibero-Asian culture, one perpetuated by lower-class females.

We know little about the Indian masses with whom the Portuguese initially made contact, for they were most concerned with ruling groups and the Brahman class.[11] Among the peoples on the Malabar coast it seems that the system of marriage, inheritance, and succession followed Hindu traditions. Among the upper and ruling classes, men took as their mates women of good families, built them homes, and gave them allowances so that they could live independently. Children inherited no more than was due them according to their mother's rank, and among the kings' sons the inheritance of the kingship "usually devolves on the sons of their sisters, who are usually the mistresses of Brahmins" (Lach, 1968: 355, n. 116).

This type of matrilineal descent system often meant that kings' sisters never married in the contemporary Western sense. Rather they had an arrangement with males from a Brahman group. Sisters and nieces of these rulers were financially and residentially independent. Upon reaching puberty each was deflowered in a ceremony by a young noble, after which each could do whatever she wished in setting up more permanent relationships with any man she chose (Lach, 1968: 356).

Other rights and expectations of females were even less generous. Among the *Nambutiri,* the predominant Brahman caste on the Malabar coast, any unfaithful wife, whether upper or lower class, was poisoned to death (Lach, 1968: 361).

Among the *Kshatriya* (warrior) class, the *Nayar* caste was predominant on the Malabar coast. Nayar males were "not permitted to marry, rear families, or control property" because it might interfere with their duty (Lach, 1968:363). Instead they practiced a type of polygyny "cohabitate with the same woman at certain specific times which all Nayars members of the group . . . (*taravad*) have agreed upon" (Lach, 1968: 363). The taravad was, in fact, a polygynous group in which one woman serviced all the males in a carefully proscribed and rotated basis. Nayar women were free to take Brahman men as lovers, and the same process of puberty rites was followed among the Nayars as among the Nambutiri.

It seems that the practices of rulers of the *Vaisya* class were different from those of the Nayar and Nambutiri. Each man had and could take only one wife, and only her children inherited. Vaisya wives could never remarry even if widowed at a young age although their husbands could. This, too, was the case with the Sudra class. Among the "untouchables," however, "their women openly earn their living with their bodies . . . their women 'sleep with anyone soever' " (Lach, 1968:366-7).

Further north up the Malabar coast into the central area of Goa, Kanara women seemed somewhat different from the other coastal women. At all levels they were willing and, apparently, allowed by custom and law to form alliances with or to marry foreign men. When the Portuguese arrived this factor stood the Europeans in good stead and was further encouraged by the Portuguese policy of giving municipal subsidies to newlyweds.

Many men who already had wives at home made secret marriages in India. Native wives of upper-class Portuguese usually were kept indoors, jealously guarded by their husbands, but kept in finery. It seems, however, that female adultery was common, wives often drugging their husbands to get away. "Conjugal fidelity . . . is conspicuous in Goa by its absence" (Lach, 1968: 483). In Goa, also, there was an entire street inhabited by and named for Portuguese prostitutes who worked it (Lach, 1968: 445). The Asian and European twain had met!

It is conjecture that in the sixteenth and seventeenth centuries there were never more than 7,000 able-bodied Portuguese men serving the Estado da India at any one time.[12] Portuguese males who went to Asia did so in the service of either Crown or Church; they contributed to widespread miscegenation since there were probably no more than a dozen white women for every ship carrying 600 to 800 Portuguese males. Although more white women left Portugal than has heretofore been realized, very few of them seem to have survived the journey or rigors of childbearing in alien lands.[13]

Alfonso de Albuquerque had encouraged his men to marry widows and daughters, "white and beautiful," of the Muslim defenders of Goa but had wanted these marriages to be only with Aryans converted to Christianity and not with the "black women" of Malabar (Boxer, 1963: 65). Portuguese males usually married Asians and Eurasians when they could no longer resist pressures to cease living in concubinage and give up their harem households of female domestic servants.

The key to colonizing successes was the female. Albuquerque, his administrators, the military, and missionaries all favored utilizing the female to expand the population and to solidify the colonial structure.

One official stated that one married man was worth ten bachelors (Boxer, 1969: 59).

The treatment of females in Portuguese Asia, from Goa east to other Portuguese spheres of influence in Bengal, Orissa, Siam, Pegu, China, and Malacca, came under the scrutiny of Church and Crown officials. In a letter of 5 December 1550 to Ignatius Loyola, the Jesuit Nicolas Lancilotto noted that

> the sin of licentiousness is so widespread. . . . There are innumerable Portuguese who buy droves of girls and sleep with all of them, and subsequently sell them. There are innumerable married settlers who keep four, eight, or ten female slaves and sleep with all of them. . . . There was one man in Malacca who had twenty-four women of various races, all of whom were his slaves. . . . Men, as soon as they can afford to buy a female slave almost always use her as a girl-friend. (Silva Rego, 1947: VII, 32-8.)

Unfortunately, most issue from unions of Portuguese men and slave women seldom were allowed to acquire an education or fortunate enough to find families to care for them. Life became increasingly difficult for illegitimate female offspring once the Portuguese caste system took effect and melded with the Indian class structure, although it was much easier for a legitimate mixed-blood heiress to find a husband than it was for a full-blooded Asian woman.

The vicissitudes of conquest and colonization seem to have deposited an excess supply of women, many widows and children, in Portuguese Asian territories. Macao was called a "city of women" and the same appears true for Cochin and Ceylon, since more than 10,000 white women, homeless and without husbands, were cited as resident there in the last decades of the seventeenth century (Ribeiro, 1685: III, cap. 3, 8).

One group of women safe from the clutches of concubinage and marriage resided at the Convent of Santa Monica. Since many of the lesser gentry were unable to provide marriage dowries for their many daughters, the traditional reliance on convents to accommodate unmarried women of noble birth was begun in Goa. Originally, the Convent of Santa Monica was chartered for 100 females with an additional 120 servants and slaves and a dowry that fluctuated over the years (Boxer, 1965: 37-8). Gradually the number of girls in the convent grew, and the municipal council complained that not only were there more than 100 nuns in the convent but also that nearly all the wealthy heiresses and unmarried women of Portuguese Asia wished to be admitted, thus depriving the ordinary citizenry, fidalgos, and soldiers of suitable wives. Further, the convent was accused by the council of accepting only wealthy unwed women and widows, of rejecting poor, deserving applicants, and of possessing enormous wealth in real estate and other properties (Boxer, 1965: 37-8).

In these and other accusations the relationship between convent and council bears a strikingly close relationship to the situation at Macao and elsewhere in Portuguese colonial society. In an additional outburst the councillors claimed that the convent now stipulated dowries of a much higher figure than initially had been quoted and that it carried on commercial transactions with its accumulated capital in competition with merchant-citizens of Goa, whom it was ruining. In retort, the nuns were supported by the Augustinian friars who served as their counsel and who, by the end of the seventeenth century, noted that although the councillors continued their opposition to Santa Monica, they were still anxious to place their unmarried daughters in convents.

A large number of female slaves was necessary to the existence of Portuguese India. Nuns and families, from the highest to the lowliest ranks, kept a large contingent of slaves. The convent kept several hundred. An unmarried European or Eurasian artisan would have between fifteen or twenty female slaves; a mulatto blacksmith was cited for keeping twenty-six women and girls; while a typical citizen of Goa who might serve in official capacities could have more than eighty-five, a lawyer more than sixty, and rich women more than 300 (Santa Maria, n.d.:263, 358-9; Sousa, 1710: I, 739-40; Boxer, 1965: 39). While Boxer correctly notes that large slave households were a requisite for status and prestige and a feature of Portuguese colonial society from Maranhão to Macao, there are other reasons that enforce the tradition of acquiring slaves. A very important one is the Indian varna system with its countless jatis, still operative in India, and which, by its very nature, allows for a large slave population in households and on estates. These are an inherent feature of the Indian scene and a tradition to which the Europeans easily became inured.

Through the centuries, Albuquerque's policy of intermarriage to create a class of *casados* that would stabilize the Portuguese position in India was resisted by upper classes and castes, especially the Brahman and so-called *Chardos,* a jati of Christianized Sudras, and also by the Portuguese authorities who did not endorse marriage of Portuguese men with low-caste women. Some efforts were made in 1644, again in 1684, and later in 1745 to have Christian Brahman widows marry white Portuguese males, the majority of whom were convicts and exiles drafted for colonial service, but this, also, was resisted by both Brahman families and Portuguese males, who preferred to live in concubinage with slave girls (Pissurlencar, 1957: V, 293-5). By the eighteenth century Portuguese men were forming permanent liaisons with dancing girls (*Bailadeiras* or *Nautch*-girls). Most such alliances were childless since the women practiced birth control or abortion (Boxer, 1961: 83-105).

Women became a pawn of yet another group. The ambition of most *mestiço* (mixed-blood) parents was to encourage a marital alliance between daughters and *reinos* (European-born Portuguese); if this was unsuccessful, they settled for a marriage with *criollos* (local-born Portuguese) or mestiços (Boxer and Azevedo, 1960: 39-40). Females were the most salable item in a society whose psyche was suspended between the different but highly stratified class and caste systems of a Christian Portugal and a Hindu India. The Indo-Portuguese, much as the Anglo-Indian, were bound to certain caste and class restrictions, and the female was the element necessary to preserve one's mestiço position, either by marrying one's own or marrying up.

The structure of the marriageable mestiço class disintegrated and further added to the concubinage, prostitution, and enslavement of less fortunate females. Loss of the fertile northern provinces and Baçaim, in the 1737 to 1740 Maratha wars, thus the loss of income from landed estates there; manumission of Hindus in Portuguese Indian territories in the early nineteenth century; the 1871 disbanding of the largely mestiço-officered Indo-Portuguese population; the traffic, both internal and external, in female domestics—these and more contributed to the decline of status for women of the lower and middle sectors of society. Antagonisms grew, and by late nineteenth century such conflict had developed between the Goans (Canarims) and the Indo-Portuguese that the Goan newspaper, *O Ultramar,* with the basest insult, claimed that the daughters of Indo-Portuguese ultimately would be wet nurses for the Canarim (Boxer, 1963: 80).

Eighteenth- and nineteenth-century Portuguese Indian society can be somewhat reconstructed from archival and family records. In many ways Portuguese and western Indian societies were extremely complementary. The two most important criteria for determining place in family, and consequently in the larger society, were age and sex. And when there was a dispute between an older woman and a younger man, the sex was decisive.

Portuguese India had escaped the establishment of a system of socially defined avoidance of men and an expression of deference toward them by women, called purdah; it was common in north India and other areas in which Islam was pervasive. In purdah, originally a Persian institution, women were isolated from all but a handful of people outside their kin group. In practice it was an ideal that relatively few could afford, but the principle came to affect much of Islamic-influenced India. This was not the case in Portuguese India, where there was more opportunity for women to move outside the household.

In land and labor some rules of class are determinants of social position. For Portuguese India, historically and to present times, the relative socioeconomic positions of groups were major criteria for determining female roles.[14]

Women seem to have been much more independent economically and socially in Portuguese India. They were self-sufficient, earned wages, and were able to make decisions about their own lives. Their position in family, kin, and village groups was not one of seclusion or submission, and certainly this seemed so for the lower classes.

Perhaps some explicit generalizations could be made on the basis of impressions from various data. Women were more likely to be independent as individuals the less their social and economic standing was tied to maintaining an ideal of the larger society. If, as it seems, the family was the vestibule of reputation and virtue for Portuguese and Indian societies and if a man's reputation were linked to that, the closer one was to the ideal the more dependent the woman seems to have been. These ideals seem more closely adhered to among the upper strata and family relationships and male-female roles in them more closely defined. As definers of the ideals of their society, the elites must be practitioners of those ideals. But families without land and without a stake in their society's future, thus removed from vested interests, defined their ideals in forms suitable to their conduct of life. This seems especially true in Portuguese India from the beginning of contact.

Another complementary feature of Indian and Portuguese societies that has been mutually reinforceable was, and is, the strong mother-son relationship. In Hindu Indian, Christian Portuguese, and Portuguese Indian societies it has been the central family relationship, particularly for the lower socio-economic groups (Cutileiro, 1971:112; Hsu, 1963: 48-52.

There were probably no white women among the original Portuguese settlers of Macao in 1555-1557. The first colonizers did not take women from the Chinese population of Heungsan; rather, they lived with Japanese, Malay, Indonesian, and Indian women, many of whom were slaves to the Chinese. Some Africans, Timorese slaves, and other women from other racial and ethnic groups were imported for domestic service or prostitution.

By 1582-1583 at least, the Portuguese had begun to marry Chinese women, of whom it was said they are "naturally reserved, honest, humble, submissive to their husbands, hard workers and house proud. . . . The Portuguese of Macao marry with them more willingly than with Portuguese women because of the many virtues which adorn the former" (Pastells, 1927: III, lv-lix. This was praise from the Jesuit Alonso Sánchez, reporting in his *Tratado* and *Apuntamiento* to Philip II in 1588). It is probable that these respectable Chinese women were daughters of Christianized Chinese settled at Macao, for mainland Chinese women "are so retired that the Portuguese never see them" claimed the chronicler António Bocarro in 1635 (Boxer, 1942: 38). Nearly a century after Portuguese settlement in Macao, famous traveler Peter Mundy noted there was "by report but one woman in this town that was born in Portugal; their wives either Chinesas or of that race heretofore married to Portugals" (Boxer, 1942: 64).

The female situation in Macao was an even more unusual one relative to most Iberian colonial outsposts. Seventeenth- and eighteenth-century records of various Macaense municipal institutions note that the shortage of qualified male persons to serve on boards and in official capacities was because of population decline caused largely by a vast surplus of females and dearth of males. Macao was "a city of women"; by the end of the seventeenth century of "one hundred fifty Portuguese families, and a total of 19,500 Christian souls, 16,000 of them were women" (Joseph de Jesus Maria, OFM, and Francisco de Sousa, SJ, in Boxer, 1965: 63; Hamilton, 1930: II, 116, on surplus of women in Macao).

The excess of females was a result of several factors, one being that the prevalent cultural bias against girl children prompted Chinese mothers to leave their unwanted infant daughters at the foundling hospital. Subsequently, the hospital was unable to accommodate the excessive numbers and parceled the foundlings out to poor foster mothers to whom they paid small monthly stipends for seven years. Thereafter, the girls were left on their own. Foster mothers sent their daughters out to beg; often girls became involved in prostitution, "obliged by sheer necessity to surrender themselves to Chinese, to foreigners, and to everyone else" (Boxer, 1965: 63; Soares, 1950: 340; de Sousa, 1710: II, 374)—this despite sixteenth-century ecclesiastical injunctions that prohibited any female slave *under* fifty years of age to peddle herself or her master's wares in the streets or to sleep away from his house (Boxer, 1948: 228).

The heavy admix of Chinese blood in the Macaense population resulted from considerable intercourse between Portuguese and Eurasian residents with their *muitsai,* the unwanted Chinese female children who were sold by their parents into domestic service for a fixed number of years, usually forty, or for the duration of their life (Boxer, 1965: 66). The practice of selling such girls to the inhabitants of Macao began at an early date in Portuguese settlements and continued for more than two centuries, despite the constant protestations and prohibitions by both Portuguese and Chinese authorities.

As in most forms of female slavery, young Chinese girls, mainly from Kwangtung province, were kidnapped or sold by parents as unwanted daughters. Buyers were often Chinese pimps who, in turn, sold the girls to Portuguese. These young females in Macao joined Indian, Indonesian, Timorese, and Japanese also brought to Macao and bought by the Portuguese for prostitution purposes. A Dutch traveler noted:

The women slaves . . . never go abroad but only at such times, or to Church on festivall days behind their [palanquins] upon which days they advertise their lovers, and leave their Mistresses in the Churches, or slip into some shoppe or corner, which they have readie at their fingers' endes, where their lovers meet them, and there in haste they have a sport, which done they leave each other; and if she chance to have a Portingal man for a lover, she is so proud that she thinketh no woman comparable unto her, and among themselves will bragge thereof. (Linschoten, 1622.)

A Portuguese naval officer in Macao in 1776 had observed that upper-class women were virtuous but lazy;

> the common women who are either ransomed Chinese girls (*muitsai*) or else the daughters of female slaves, as they have not the stimulus of honor but are likewise dominated by idleness, are easily debauched, particularly by foreigners, on account of the money and clothes which the latter give them. (Soares, 1950: 231-2.)

Female life in Macao left much to be desired. The women, who comprised much of the population, appear to have been ill treated and exploited. Some Portuguese women encouraged their husbands to cohabit with female slaves while other less laconic wives had their slave girls murdered (Boxer, 1948: 227ff.). Many mothers forced their female slaves to yield to their sons, yet slave women of the household usually had total responsibility for raising European children. Female slaves suffered severely both from their working conditions and from plague and epidemics that decimated the slums (Boxer: 1948: 227 ff.). Economic conditions throughout East Asia continued to force parents to sell their daughters and other female family members, many Macaense, into slavery. Some of these slave girls were exported to the East while others were shipped from Macao via Goa for sale in the Portuguese African settlements along the Zambezi River. For example, the carrack *Santa Catarina,* captured by the Dutch in February 1603, carried more than 100 women, both Eurasians and other mixed bloods, and the majority of both were slaves bound from Macao to Malacca (Boxer, 1963: 59 n.15). Furthermore, Timorese, Indian, and other slave girls were brought in great numbers to the Macaense city and were abandoned to a life of prostitution, a situation so serious that by 1747 it had contributed to a population in which females outnumbered males ten to one (Boxer, 1948: 238ff.).

The situation for other females in Macao was not paradisiacal either especially, as the poet Bocage noted in 1789, the lives of those "virtuous nuns in a den," the inmates of the convent of the Poor Clares (Boxer, 1965: 64). The order had been founded in 1633 and initially supported and protected by the senate from income from a 1 percent surtax on certain commodities. In 1692 the senate changed the arrangement whereby they would pay 1 percent promptly, in exchange for which the convent would receive one daughter without dowry from a citizen (Boxer, 1965: 64ff.). The number of nuns was limited to forty and preference always was given to daughters of *moradores* (heads of households) serving on the Câmara (city council).[15]

But, throughout the decades, numerous problems appeared, such as the one noted by the senate's complaint in 1746 that convents took all of the local rich girls with dowries, thus making it impossible for eligible bachelors to find suitable wives. The senate also complained that while nuns practiced an unrestricted business in lending money to Armenian, Spanish, French, and other traders, they refused to lend any money to the senate, pleading poverty (Boxer, 1965: 64ff. passim).

The relatively urban setting of Goa and Macao differed sharply from the rural setting and ethnic populatioñs among whom the Portuguese settled in Indonesia. The lack of Portuguese interest in Timor until the eighteenth century allowed those Indonesian peoples fairly unrestricted practice of their local traditions, which has contributed to the relative lack of Portuguese influence today. Agriculture and cultivation attuned to seasonal and climatic shifts has been the economic basis for all Timorese groups. The dry season was the most productive, being the time for salt making, beeswax collecting, felling of sandalwood trees, building houses, moving cattle, harvesting, and festivals.

Females of Portuguese Timor carried the heaviest labor burdens in their society. Harvesting was woman's work as was foodstuff preparation, planting, collecting savatu tree leaves, and grinding grains. Women did heavy hauling of water and materials necessary to their work, while traditionally men were responsible for lighter work loads. Females also were potters and weavers.

Climate dictated the economic cycle and social life of the Timorese. At the end of the rainy season the chief crop, maize, was harvested and, festivities inaugurating the "social season" for rites of passage and other ceremonies followed. Music has been an integral part of socioreligious events, and women have the important responsibility for beating out drum rhythms for both ceremonial and regular village events.

In general, though, despite their intensive and important labor and economic responsibilities, the social position of pre-Portuguese Timorese women was one of social inferiority, which was perpetuated for several centuries after Portuguese contact. Among some of the indicators of inferior position were the socioreligious festivities. Despite their honored role in drumming women were required to walk several paces behind their menfolk and, during festivals, usually were not permitted to dance with their men. Polygamy and child marriage were common, but the bride price was not. Even in death social positions have been honored. Portuguese Timorese men and women traditionally have been buried in different sectors, and the women's sections were often much poorer and much more overgrown with weeds than were the men's plots (King, 1963: 184). During the harvest, traditionally only children, women, and water buffalos eat the first ears of corn since it is considered a sign of shame to do so; men have not been allowed to participate in the activity (Ormeling, 1957: 111).

Apparently women from various Indonesian islands were greatly admired and preferred as concubines by the Portuguese and other Europeans and comprised a sizable number of the slaves transported throughout the East. Almost every ship to Java carried tens, sometimes hundreds, of Timorese females.[16] In fact, the majority of slaves for Java were from Timor, Buton, Celebes, and Bali, and slavery was an important commercial activity for indigenous and European traders (Boxer, 1965: 240 n.8). Indonesian women bore children of Portuguese, Dutch, English, and other Europeans, and offspring of these relationships increased the population of Topasses (Boxer, 1947: 1). In Timor, as elsewhere in the Portuguese empire, the universal practice of slavery was a companion to the widescale prostitution of female slaves despite protestation of Crown and clergy against such activities.

Timor was as burdened as other parts of the empire with a large surplus of women, usually "widows" and girl orphans, partially due to consistently high male mortality from armed conflicts. Surplus women and female orphans did not always fare well, especially if they were Topasses, because of the numerous incidents between Portuguese and Dutch and between Europeans and Indonesians. In one particular conflict of 1668, the "Black Portuguese" (Topasses) killed 200 inhabitants in a raid at Pulo Kisser, and most of the victims were women and children (Boxer, 1947: 11).

Among ruling groups in Timorese society, marriage of a daughter or sister was part of the indigenous political pattern of establishing alliances. Any raja who gave a female of his family in marriage could be approached for aid, and that made him a powerful person since the person able to give help is considered superior and must be paid tribute. However, such customs and rules traditionally were ignored, even throughout the eighteenth century, by the two most powerful Topasses families, the De Hornays and the Da Costas. Although they married princesses they refused to subordinate themselves to rajas, thus causing resentment and often military trouble (Schulte Nordholt, 1971: 174-5). Often the victims of conflict were women and children—not those of the ruling classes into which the Portuguese and Topasses had married but those of the lower classes. When the Portuguese governor evacuated Lifao in 1769 and transferred Portuguese Timor's headquarters from that town to the present capital, Dili, the majority of 1,200 evacuees were women and girls (Boxer, 1969: 60).

Through the eighteenth century Portuguese sailed from Timor to other islands in the archipelago, establishing their political and commercial influence. In addition to the lucrative sandalwood, gold, and beeswax trade the thriving commerce in female slaves between Portuguese Timor and Batavia, Manila, Macao, and the like continued. This traffic remained a principle source of income for the island (Murias, 1943: 192-232 passim; Boletin FUP: XIX, 390ff., 616, 774; Leitão, 1948: 173-83 passim; AM: II, 353-5). In another aspect of the trade, Portuguese women and Topasses played a far different role from their unfortunate concubine cousins. Widows and orphans could invest and participate in the sandalwood trade from Timor to Macao under a system of *bagues* (tickets of ownership) and *pautas* (sealed lists) (Boxer, 1965: 59).

As elsewhere in Portuguese (but not Spanish) imperial settlements, transshipping of peninsula women to Timor was discouraged with the exception of the "orphans of the king," orphan girls of marriageable age who were sent regularly from Lisbon at Crown expense. This was consonant with Portuguese policy either to marry their own or those women of the local upper classes. Many female "orphans" were either too old or too ugly to find husbands on their own in Portugal and therefore were willing to be provided with dowries, which, in such forms as minor government posts or commercial advantages, would be available to any man seeking a wife (Silva Correia, 1943-1958: passim). These women fared no better than their counterparts elsewhere in tropical empires; a majority of them either died or miscarried in childbirth.

Church and Crown joined in an attempt to protect rights and safeguard their Christianized female population. Although the Church could gain enormous economic advantages from the inheritance of widows and although the clergy seemed more concerned with women of their own ethnic or religious purview, nonetheless the Church made sincere efforts to protect poorer and indigenous women and orphaned girls.

While Portugal continued to exert its influence throughout the East, the Spanish settled into full colonization of the Philippines. The *indio* (pre-twentieth-century term for Filipino) and Spanish populations of the sixteenth-century islands were too small to undertake extensive agricultural development; thus the encomienda was utilized. It closely resembled the preconquest Tagalog institution whereby dependent groups delivered shares of their produce to baranguay chiefs; hence there was little early disruption in land and labor patterns. Also, the Spanish system of *repartimiento* closely resembled local forms whereby dependents performed a set amount of labor service for local chiefs and nobles.

As in America, the Philippine encomienda declined early. Basic differences in land control were evident in the Iberian concept of private ownership of "fee simple" land as opposed to the indio idea of common ownership and usufruct. The gradual acceptance, or implementation, of the Hispanic system by indio chiefs and officials, which after 1898 was reinforced by North American values concerning land, changed the land patterns, eventually creating a landless tenant farmer population in the Philippine countryside.

Sex roles were simple in the new land system. In labor distribution females did not pay tribute but, like their counterparts in the New World, provided service as field workers, domestic servants, or other designated female roles. When the encomienda system was liquidated, the Crown substituted free labor, which it paid, primarily to Manila whose suburbs had to provide free domestic female service for the convents.

It is impossible to say whether women in pre-Hispanic society enjoyed positions different from pre-Columbian Amerindian women. Socially, there was some separation of the sexes; during Tagalog rituals women were often separated from the men in ceremonies and drank separately from them as well. On the other hand members of a professional priestly class who performed ritual sacrifices were usually elderly women, and the few men involved in priestly practices of this nature were usually transvestities. Once the Spanish had infiltrated indio society there was, because of the scarcity of peninsula women, a substantial amount of intermixing between the conquerors and conquered. There is some evidence that Philippine parents encouraged their daughters to have intercourse with the Spanish clergy since any children would be well provided for by the priests (Phelan, 1967: 39).

Institutions, the Church in particular, showed different concerns for women and tried to impose the standard enacted in Pope Paul III's bull of 1537, which declared that the oldest wife or first-married woman of a man was his legitimate wife, a situation that ultimately proved unworkable in the Philippines. Catholics also objected to the "bride price" or "bride service" as a form of selling daughters. Despite the tradition of arranged marriages, Church doctrine applied in Spain and the Philippines left the ultimate choice to the couple. Perhaps as much as they abhorred the practice of bartering girls to the highest bidder, the Church also was disturbed by premarital sex, a feature of Tagalog society.

The small number of military and administrative personnel, lack of a mining industry, and the absence of a substantively exploitative labor system made the character of Philippine colonization fundamentally different from that of Spanish America. The small Spanish colony of merchants, soldiers, administrators, and clergy clustered mainly in Manila. In Manila, miscegenation was a common occurrence although Filipino women were more often mistresses than wives to the Spanish.

In addition to local women, there were foreign communities whose females were important to development of a mesticized Hispanic society, the most important of whom were the Chinese (Wickberg, 1965: passim on Chinese influence). Peoples from the Chinese mainland had enjoyed commercial contacts with the Philippine islands for several centuries prior to the arrival of Iberians, but after the 1560s China merchants, who recognized new and expansive opportunities, settled in Manila and by 1603 comprised 20,000 of the population (Wickberg, 1965: 5-6). There was considerable mixing, and by the eighteenth century a sizable Chinese-mestizo population had developed, primarily in Manila (Wickberg, 1964: 62-100 passim). Life was not always tranquil for the Chinese. Subject to high taxation and occasional violent attacks for their exclusivity and economic success, they withdrew even more into their urban ghetto in Manila and then were officially excluded from living in the provinces. Nonetheless, intermarriage did not decline. Rather, the Chinese mestizo population growth approximated the regular rate, and "throughout the nineteenth century, the most dynamic element in Philippine society was the Chinese mestizo, . . . about six per cent of the total population [of 5.5 million]" (Wickberg, 1965: 41, 134).

The sex ratio in the Chinese communities always had been balanced in favor of men, for in the early centuries an almost total absence of Chinese women had facilitated Chinese-indio intercourse and intermarriage, a pattern that continued into the nineteenth century. Evidence of this pattern is found, for example, in the 1870 census data, which showed only 193 women of a "pure" Chinese ancestry among the Chinese population of 23,000. In 1886 the numbers had advanced only one, to 194 females, of whom 191 were resident in Manila, of 66,000 Chinese. By 1903 these figures had increased to only 517 "pure" Chinese women in a community totaling 41,035 (Wickberg, 1965: 174).

Most of these Chinese women were less than fourteen years old and had been imported or smuggled in from China for older Chinese men to use as either servants or concubines. The almost complete absence of other females from the mainland naturally encouraged the continuation of miscegenation between Chinese males and indios or Spanish. These sexual differences, in addition to the assimilative elements within indio societies and the consequent voluntary or involuntary mixing, served to encourage the dispersion of Hispanicized ideas throughout the island because Hispanic values were to be emulated.

Miscegenation was one thing; marriage quite another to the Spaniards, since marrying out of one's culture restricted entree to social and economic opportunities available only to "pure" members of the conquest society. To settle this matter and attempt to redress demographic imbalance, Spain had attempted to enforce the order for officials to take their families with them and to give monetary incentives for this purpose throughout colonial rule. In the early seventeenth century *boletas* (tickets of ownership) of trading licenses were issued to widows who had followed their husbands to the Philippines or who had remarried in the islands (Schurz, 1959: 161ff.). The more than two centuries of these practices were recognized by a law of 1769 in the "custom" of giving trading licenses to widows and orphans. Merchants were not pleased with the issuance of boletas to women, but it had become such standard practice that the regulations of 1734 confirmed that principle and added the right of "poor and widows" to sell them. A report of Justice González Carbajal in 1783 noted that of the 150 members of the original *consulado* with privileges of shipping on the galleon, fifty-six commissioned their own trading operation on a percentage basis and of them eight, or 13.5 percent, were women. The aggregate working capital at that time was about 2.56

million pesos, and it appears that Manila widows were prime beneficiaries, a fact confirmed in all the commerce ordinances through the eighteenth century. In 1783 there were 412 Spanish widows in Manila's population of 2,000, and each widow received from one-half to two tickets. This would indicate that widows held a relatively significant amount of economic power.

On the other hand the Church did its best to remove Spanish women in the Philippines from economic or social involvements. In 1621 a convent of the Poor Clares was established in Manila, much to the chagrin of eligible Spanish gallants (Quesada, 1717; Concepción, 1788-1792: V, 9-17). Within a few years, twenty-two young, aristocratic girls, half of Manila's maritally eligible female population, had joined the convent taking with them, to the Church's pleasure, large dowries. The Spanish hierarchy declined the demurers of Manila's males and supported the subsidization of ecclesiastical organizations with the same charitable impulse with which it granted trading licenses to widows and orphans. In conjunction with this activity the Church actively encouraged the *obras pias* (charitable institutions conducted by regular clergy) to perform such services for the community as provisioning dowers for poor girls, educating female orphans, giving relief to widows, poor women, and inmates of prisons, and supporting hospitals and cemeteries.

From late seventeenth until late nineteenth century, certain practices had taken root representing a relatively symbiotic relationship between Spanish and local traditions. The baranguay remained the basic political and administrative unit. In 1786 it was modified for the last time into the form it retained until 1898. This meant that the *cabezas* (Hispanicized datu) retained their basic function as tribute collectors. Instead of inheriting their posts they were to be elected by community leaders for a minimum of three years. The cabeza-datu had all the privileges that accrued to hereditary leaders. No cabeza-datu was a female, and the community leaders who elected the cabeza-datu were all male.

The baranguay was the smallest administrative unit but others also were modified in the eighteenth and nineteenth centuries. The most important local unit was the *pueblo de Indios,* forerunner of the *municipio,* which had attached to it outlying districts, various little villages or hamlets (*sitios*), each with less than ten families. Thus a fairly consistent pattern of political and administrative units was maintained through to the twentieth century (Phelan, 1967: 123-5). Again, women and girls had no part in political and administrative control, for to both local and Spanish peoples that was a male role.

Change of rule in Spain from Hapsburg to Bourbon did not significantly affect females in the Philippines. Religious reforms mostly affected the male community. After the expulsion of the Jesuits in 1767, posts and perquisites that previously had belonged to Jesuits were given to Philippine priests. There was intense reaction to them because they were poorly trained, kept mistresses, and otherwise misbehaved to the dismay of Spanish upper-class society.

In land and labor practices large-scale latifundia did not reach significant proportions in the Philippines until the nineteenth century (Phelan, 1967: 116). Two Spanish concepts introduced into the Philippines were that land was a source of wealth and that individuals, and not just groups, could own land. Pre-Hispanic attitudes regarding land was that it was held in title by the communal baranguay and used by the entire community, male and female (Phelan, 1967: 117). The Spanish attitudes caught on in the seventeenth century and by the nineteenth were widespread. However, the bulk of all cultivated lands belonged to Filipinos and not to Spanish or other foreigners. Although the Roman Catholic Church was the largest single landowner, as of 1768 it owned only twenty estates, representing a very small ratio of land in Tagalog areas (Phelan, 1967: 118). In management and inheritance of these lands, the Spanish system of dower and inheritance was modified, partly to suit local tradition, which gave women more of a voice in administration and certainly in inheritance. In fact, both administration and inheritance reinforced each other.

Demographic, ecological, economic, and social factors encouraged a relatively more flexible and tolerable relationship between Spanish and indio in the Philippines, in comparison with the Hispanic-American experience. Throughout Spanish rule, well into the nineteenth century, the lack of a specifically defined Philippine national identity and consciousness encouraged continued homogenization of society. This influenced roles women were to play in the twentieth century. Spaniards Christianized various pagan ethnic groups and Hispanicized fragmented individual tribes by creating a centralized political, economic, and religious structure. They were careful not to destroy local values and found it more advantageous to work through customary networks and to exercise order through local kin control.

In other respects Spanish influence prevailed. Basic institutions were considered king's property and offices were bought and sold within Hispanic custom, a policy prevalent throughout the empire (Parry, 1953: passim). Also, Spanish imperial concerns were more urban in nature, and Manila became and remained the major center of European influence upon its acquisition of a royal charter in 1574. Spanish urban planning and traditional charters decided the municipal organization of the city, although suburban settlements, each self-contained urban units, grew up separate from the city's center. This pattern of local administration and decentralized functioning, which has continued into the twentieth century, owes much to the local traditions of baranguay-pueblo de indios-sitio (Wernstedt and Spencer, 1967: chaps. 4, 5). This development also influenced patterns of female participation in contemporary Philippine life.

CONTEMPORARY SCENES: IBERIAN
HERITAGE AND ASIAN VALUES

The preceding sections have delineated Iberian penetration into several Asian cultures and have suggested Iberian potential staying power in Asia. We shall examine contemporary Ibero-Asia to determine where Iberian values have melded with, superseded, or abdicated to host Asian value systems.

In 1961 the state of Portuguese India was incorporated into the nation of India. India, the world's second most populous nation and area of the most enduring Portuguese influence in Asia, had 226 million males to 213 million females in 1961. Since 1901 there has been a continuing increase in the male population. The south and the eastern states of Orissa and Bihar are fairly evenly proportioned, but northern and western India show fewer women than men, a fact also evident in major urban centers such as Bombay and Calcutta, with 633 and 612 females per 1,000 males, respectively. This population disproportion probably is due to the high ratio of male immigration to urban areas (Bombay and Calcutta are the two most populous cities in India). Female life expectancy is less than males from birth to age seventy but, ironically, in a population that seldom reaches the eighth decade, women outnumber men after seventy.

There are several reasons for the variance in longevity and expectancy statistics. Both Hindu and Muslim societies consider females less useful, thus less desirable, than males, so girls are not given equal treatment in health and welfare. Unsanitary conditions cause the death in childbirth of many women, particularly in urban areas. Also, girls still are married in their early teens, but since this is not officially acceptable, male household heads do not report these girls, "out of shame" (AHI, 1971: 92-3, 96).

Attitudes and involvement of Indian women outside their homes still are traditional in some respects. More women have been migrating to cities in order to find work, but many still consider their most important function in life to be childbearing, an attitude that has thwarted government attempts at population control. Nonetheless, India's government has planned a series of measures, which, although antithetical to traditional attitudes, should provide more safeguards for females. Parliament plans to legalize abortions, in the face of more than 4 million illegal abortions performed annually, mostly by unqualified individuals, and to raise the minimum legal marriage age for girls from fifteen to eighteen (AHI, 1971:101-2).

Information for Portuguese India is not so readily available as it is for India as a whole. During the same census period Goa, Daman, and Diu claimed a total population of 388, 654 Hindus, 230,997 Catholics, and 14,716 Muslims, while of that population of 626,667 there were 894 females for every 1,000 males (Hindustani Yearbook, 1970: II, 51-2).

Within general Indian culture, women have contributed in several
spheres of public life despite traditional opposition to their involvement
outside their homes. In the arts females always have played important
roles. For example, they have an almost exclusive hold over the artisan
craft of floor design known as *alpanas,* and they continue to be prominent in Indian music and dance performance. Until modern times the
only exponents of the south Indian dance form of *Bharata Natyam* were
female temple dancers (*devadasis*). Classical Sanskrit treatises carefully
delineated the importance of females in art forms, dividing dance movements into male and female forms, which were adhered to strictly
until recently by all dance forms except *Kathak.* The latter dance, in
its more vulgar performance, became known as the *nautch,* and it was
associated with "notorious" women, particularly brothel women of
northern India (AHI, 1971:264-7).

In the general social order, Indian values stress that the individual,
either male or female, is bound first to family and then to friends and
groups, such as caste and village. Kin ties are valued and act as law in rural
areas. Those are the major units of society, stressing a primary emphasis
on group collectivity in Indian society, in which the individual is secondary.
Wealth and fame are for household, not personal, glory. Marriage dis-
charges are a social duty; sex is not for pleasure but for reproduction to
propitiate the gods and to propagate family line; an individual's position
is inherited, not achieved; and duties rather than rights of an individual
are emphasized (AHI, 1971: 322-5). Most all of these contrast somewhat to
the values of Iberian society, although many other values are related in
belief and customary adherence.

Fairly recently it had been thought that the joint family was breaking
up and that the nuclear family was becoming the most common social
unit. Studies made since the early 1960s have shown that although
the nuclear family is still the core family unit, the extended family is
still the most characteristic social unit of India's 568,878 villages, containing 82 percent of its population; it is quite common in towns and
cities.[17] This is also so in areas of Portuguese influence, and in many
instances, Indian and Iberian social values have intermeshed. Mobility,
land reform, industrialization, internal migration, and other events by
the 1970s were making inroads into the larger kin group. But family
remains the essential social unit. More than 90 percent of Indian, and
almost all Hindu and Muslim, marriages are still family arranged, although
this situation is much less pronounced among Christian groups, including
Goan Catholics.

Education is helping to change this, especially in the middle and upper
classes. Educated wives, more and more a status symbol for middle-class
males, are reluctant to follow traditional patterns of family rule enforced
by illiterate mothers-in-law. "Modern" concepts of divorce, remarriage

for divorcees and widows, later marriage for daughters, and relaxation of formal restrictions on female activities coexist with traditional restrictions on divorce, belief in early marriages, and upper-class family customs of keeping daughters and women at home as a measure of economic status (AHI, 1971: 169-71). In Portuguese India most of the "modern" concepts, except divorce and remarriage, have made significant inroads.

Within the Portuguese Indian family, power traditionally is dispersed. In extended families the senior male is head of the household while one woman, usually the wife of the senior male, controls all the women of that family and manages all domestic affairs. She has authority over all her children, male and female, and controls the keys to the family's grain stores. Men of the household often are reluctant to interfere with her decisions and most other women cannot, so she often is considered to be more of a tyrant than any male head (AHI, 1971: 172). Females in Christian families, perhaps influenced by Iberian values, especially among middle and upper classes, seem not so possessed of extensive household and other powers as are their Hindu, and some Muslim, counterparts.

Marriage for all Hindus is a religious duty, with certain prescribed patterns of behavior for both sexes. Hindu girls from childhood are trained to respect a husband as a god, to perform religious rites, and to bear him children. All of this supposedly brings the male more honor and changes the wife's status, for "in traditional family and society the woman can find recognition or prestige only as the mother of a son" (AHI, 1970: 175-6, 179). This pattern of Hindu marriage holds true for Goa, and the persistence of this socioreligious attitude indicates that Iberian marital values had little reception in traditional Hindu households.

Among middle- and upper-class Muslims and among upper-class Hindus in northern India and former Portuguese India, the practice of *purdah* is still widespread. But lower-class Hindu and Muslim males either cannot or will not confine their wives because the labor and services those women perform outside their homes are necessary to their family's survival (AHI, 1970: 176-7). In southern and western parts of India, where Muslim influence was negligible, there is a lack of even the mildest forms of purdah. In these cultures there is little social segregation between male and female in a family. Thus, fewer restrictions apply to women in areas where Western Christian influence and pre-Muslim, early Hindu observances exist. This is so especially among Goan lower classes.

Other special female-male relationships develop within traditional contexts. A mother serves and dominates her sons, and after a son's marriage his first duty is to his mother, not to his wife. On the other hand close sentimental attachments, love and indulgence often develop between men and their daughters to the extent that, until puberty, girls can accompany their fathers to adult male gatherings (AHI, 1970: 179). Hindu women view their lives within the context of their existence in a household as daughter, mother, matriarch. As an infant a girl receives less attention in ritual celebration than does her brother. If she remains unmarried for longer than three years after she becomes eligible to be a bride, she is an undesirable in her household.

On the other hand, in Portuguese India, Christian Goan and mestiço women adhere to a view of themselves within the Iberian context. Similar emotions exist between mother and son, father and daughter but, in general, women of upper- and middle-class even quasitraditional Goan families seem to have more public visibility than their non-Christian Goan counterparts. Among the lower classes, however, regardless of the religion or culture, fewer restrictions are applied.

As with family and society quantifiable economic data are less available for Portuguese India than for India overall. As of 1967 in a total labor force of 220 million or 42.6 percent of the population, women constituted 35 percent or 75 million, 80 percent of whom were employed in agriculture with their husbands or other male members of their households. Nearly 1 million were in manufacturing, half of that in industries, mostly textiles or food production. Females also comprised 40 percent of the labor force on coffee plantations, 25 percent on rubber plantations, and 18 percent in mining (AHI, 1970: 102-3, 109). Wages for women were 40 percent less than they were for men in paid agricultural jobs. In India, caste as well as class structure must be accounted for in determining "sex discrimination." Also, women and children are willing to work for lower wages, which probably accounts, in part, for their substantial percentage of the work force and low wages in general (AHI, 1970: 580).

In Goa, Daman, and Dui of an estimated population of 760,000, as of July 1969, there were 1,070 female per 1,000 males. Most were engaged in agricultural production, primarily horticulture, on cultivable lands known as *comunidades* (*Times of India,* 1969: 337-9). These are survivals from Portuguese rule and include lands that are owned and worked by villages and that have been incorporated as agricultural cooperatives within community development block schemes. The population also works in manganese and iron ore mining and in the few cottage or small-scale industries in Goa (*Times of India,* 1969: 337-9). Figures for women in various economic activities were not available to me for Goa, but my interviews and observations indicated that agricultural involvement of women there is commensurate with the pattern in India's general population. More women of Portuguese India's upper and middle classes are employed in bureaucratic or clerical posts, more than is the case for their Hindu sisters. How much this is due to Portuguese Christian European ideology or to modern Bombay and Parsi cosmopolitan influence is difficult to determine. Whichever, Goanese females of these classes seem to be as involved in public activities as their western Indian counterparts, and both are more active than women in the Indian nation as a whole.

In civic and political rights India's government has modified or eliminated certain practices considered discriminatory to women, practices
such as bigamy, child marriage, lack of property rights, prohibition of
divorce, or remarriage of widows. Prime Minister Indira Gandhi has supported measures for improvement of women's status, and in January
1969 the national government established a national committee on the
status of women to examine sex discrimination and the workings of
constitutional and administrative provisions on education, employment,
and social status of women (AHI, 1970: 171).

Adherence to these provisions differs according to religio-cultural
groups. The Hindu Marriage Act of the Hindu Code (1955) prohibits
polygamy and allows intercaste marriage and divorce by either sex,
remarriage, and provisions of alimony to the divorced mate of either
sex who does not remarry. Divorce is much more acceptable among
lower class and caste groups since economic and social considerations
are less important than they are for upper-class and caste groups. Similarly,
remarriage is more common for lower-class widows, especially for young
women and among all classes of urban families. The family of a widow's
husband still has the right to keep her children, which helps to explain
the frequency of widow remarriage to a dead husband's brother (AHI,
1970: 187). Muslim, Parsi, and Christian marriage customs and inheritance rights are protected by special laws. The Special Marriage Act (1954)
permits marriage between faiths while Muslims are still permitted four
wives, although in 1968 only 5 percent of the Muslim males could afford
more than one (AHI, 1970: 174-5). Portuguese Catholic belief prohibits
divorce and remarriage by a divorced person, and although it is allowed
now by Indian civil law few Goans take advantage of their new rights.

Also under the Hindu Succession Act (1956) and other acts, full
equality is extended to both sexes on rights and obligations, particularly
as they affect woman's inheritance rights. Despite this egalitarianism,
laws sympathetic to females, particularly in marriage and inheritance among
Hindus, are often violated, especially in rural areas. Women's organizations,
growing in strength had, by late 1960s, issued strong complaints regarding
violations of government laws. The major problem with enforcement of
such measures, among Hindus especially, is that many social laws have a
religious basis, and since interference with religious tenets is taboo, not
all castes or other groups can be forced to adhere to this "secular law"
(AHI, 1970: 175).

One avenue likely to bring about widescale change for females is education, and India's government has undertaken a massive program that
would guarantee free, compulsory education through age fourteen within
a decade. Meanwhile, girls' education has grown at a faster rate than has
boy's. In 1961 some 59 percent of primary school children were female.
The major reason for such an upswing is that girls' education has to catch
up with boys'. In secondary schools in 1968 girls comprised about 30

percent of the 7 million children attending, while in universities some
1.92 million students were enrolled in 1968-1969, of whom less than a
fifth were women (AHI, 1970: 224-30).

Despite what may seem depressing totals, in view of the overwhelmingly
rural nature of Indian society as well as the definite male orientation of
the values and institutions of that society, these percentages for females
in education are impressive. On the other hand, growth in female education coexists with a female illiteracy rate that, in the 1960s "was nearly
three times that of males," although that should be measured in light of
the fact that in 1891 female illiteracy was twenty-one times that of
males (AHI, 1970: 243).

Indians admit an enduring prejudice against educating females. This
attitude surprisingly is strong among the upper strata where female literacy
rates are highest but among whom traditional attitudes are also strongest.
The highest female literacy rates among upper-caste Hindus and Muslims
are comparable to the rates among such minority groups as Parsis, Jains,
and Christians. Although the Indian government claims that Portuguese
colonial rule stifled educational opportunities, for Goans it appears that
the Iberian rulers created schools and educational opportunities of a
nature equal to or better than general Indian programs for their children.
Further, it is a quibbling argument to determine who has done more or
less, especially when the argument occurs between two cultural systems
in which the concept of hierarchical priority guarantees preferences for
peoples of the upper classes, for male rather female. However, I was told
by Goans, Christian and Hindu alike, that under the Portuguese, life
was freer and educational opportunities were as good as, if not better than,
at present, which may have been so for "pro-Portuguese" elites.

In former Portuguese India, although in the process of change, attitudes of both cultures remain consistent with both the Indian and Portuguese past. Aspects of family life that were always important to the
group, ceremonies in particular, remain more popular with and within
the purview of women than men, although there is a trend not only away
from female participation but also away from the ceremonies themselves.
Another fixity in Indo-Portuguese culture that remains strong but that
also is changing is the dichotomous position that woman has held in
family ideology. A worship of "mother" and idealization of "pure, noble
womanhood" remains strong and pervasive although belief in it, especially
on the part of Indo-Portuguese women, is changing; they are now articulating
a desire to fulfill roles that previously were the purview of men (Cormack,
1953, 1961; Ghurye, 1957; Srinivas, 1962, for discussions of class, caste,
and female participation).

Elsewhere in India, but to a far lesser extent in Goa, perhaps because
of the unique Luso-Catholic influence, malfunctions are occurring in
society. The joint family, if not breaking up, is at least reformulating
itself, especially in the cities, and there is much anomie, increased destitu-

tion of women, prostitution, and female participation in crime. Hindu-Muslim families are paying more attention to the education and future of their daughters and to marital choices for them in order to decrease what seems to have become a rather common practice of girls committing suicide rather than marry older men, or wives choosing suicide as an escape from husbands they do not desire, practices uncommon in Portuguese India. It is difficult to say whether suicide rates have risen or whether information-gathering techniques have improved.

Traditionally, then, while woman has been accorded a high place, in the *Vedas* even an "equal" one, within the bounds of family she has not enjoyed similar status in the larger society within which her family functions. Now women are being exposed to a competitive society and want to be an intellectual and social companion, not a drudge. In female-male relations her role and attitudes toward herself are affected by such dualities as India's belief that woman's ability to procreate is something for which she should feel and be highly honored, while on the other hand considering the sex act as a bestial necessity of life. It has been said that the Indian woman has enjoyed "individuality" but not "individualism," which, to a lesser extent, is true of Indo-Portuguese as well.

Two axioms seem true for both societies. One seems to be that the female is highly regarded in the family but not in society, that as she ventures more to the world outside her village and city walls she will begin to realize the conflicts between the security of tradition and the uncertainties of modernization. The other axiom seems to indicate more similarities of behavior among diverse groups within classes and castes. Cultural ideals are less adumbrated among lower- than among upper-class groups, and some generalizations on values seem more applicable across classes than across cultures. In the future it seems that India and Portuguese India offer more opportunities among upper classes or groups favoring less traditional and more " modern" values than it does for females of lower strata to assume power roles in society.

Portuguese China and Indonesia never have approached the importance of India in Portugal's colonial scheme and are not indicative of trends in intercultural relationships in the way India can be. Macao today boasts about 500,000 people and still survives as a colony of Portugal, although its obvious accommodations with the Chinese mainland give it a surrealistic tinge, the quality of toy life. My most recent excursion to Macao made me aware that many customs concerning women are still intact. Upper-class Macaense-Chinese families strive to ensure that their daughters will be first wives in a household. Marriage arrangements allow for the fact that they are for the perpetuation of the custom of a wealthy man, or any male for that matter, taking as many wives as he can afford. Among lower-class Macaense a heavy traffic is still carried on from Hong Kong and other areas of Asia in female slavery, prostitution, and concubinage.

Prostitution and employment in Macao's gambling dens are not the only occupations of Macao's working-class women. Poor women work alongside their menfolk in agricultural and fishing activities, while among middle groups many clerical and bureaucratic posts are filled by females. Data on education, employment, wages, and social services are difficult to acquire for Macao and are based on my observations and interviews. These indicate a mobile, relatively urban, and certainly far more cosmopolitan atmosphere than either India or Timor. Catholicism and Portuguese values remain strongest among families of "pure" Portuguese or mestiço blood who are trying to preserve the values of their Iberian heritage and among whom females are likely to exercise more freedom or social involvement than do their Iberian sisters. Perhaps this results from the syndrome of overemulation of European values. If puritanism exists—and it does not pervade the society as it does in India—it is as likely a result of proximity to mainland China as it is to any conservative strains of Iberian Catholicism. The same may be true in socioeconomic matters. It is difficult to determine how much the visibility of women in these areas is due to traditional Chinese cultural influence, to Portuguese emulation, or to the egalitarian ideas of contemporary China where women are active in all public sectors.

Macao seems quite different from rural, ramshackle agrarian Portuguese Indonesia, a colonial society outside international networks and relationships. Half of Timor, the largest of the Lesser Sunda islands, continues to be a Portuguese possession, having formed part of Portuguese India until 1864, then governed from Macao until 1896 when the then governor, José Celestino da Silva, crowned himself king of Timor. Now rule is back in the hands of Portuguese colonial administrators.[18]

Problems plague Portuguese Timor. Considerable taxation has encouraged emigration from Portuguese Timor to other areas of Indonesia. Women are a large part of this group since, by traditional law, they must go with their husbands, having little standing in law without their husbands.

Life for Timorese women is at variance with expectancies for her Portuguese cousins. In studies of women past childbearing age, the average Timorese female bore 5 to 5.8 children, of which 4 to 4.3 lived. However, these studies are difficult to use in assessing the impact of such information on the society, since most women do not know even their approximate age and life expectancies for the general population are not very high (Ormeling, 1957: 184). Venereal and other diseases have decimated the female and child populations today, a factor that defies the still common practice of Timorese males having more than one wife (Ormeling, 1957: 181).

Among nonagrarian groups, those who live in the towns are closer to Portuguese influence. Females are not very prominent in bureaucratic posts and those who are usually are mestiços or "pure" Portuguese. Inadequacies in educational and other public facilities for the general

population affect females to a greater extent only when they cross attitudes prevalent in the local society, which do not encourage female
participation. Whatever forms of inequality occur in the countryside are
the result of indigenous values, such as the fact that women and men
seem to share in festivals as part of society's insistence on complete
community participation.

It becomes clearer that generalization about the extent of Portuguese
influence on its Asian colonies has much to do with the basic values
of "class" of its own as well as the local societies. The sector where
Iberian values seem most pervasive in colonial cultures are among upper
and middle groups. Their aspirations and a deep-seated inferiority as
creoles cause an exaggeration of cultural imitation of the European parent
culture, as they perceive their parent culture. It is most evident in urban
areas. In such societies women often fare better than their counterparts in
the metropolitan control culture, perhaps because Europeans seemed
inclined to allow their females more mobility abroad than at home because
of limited human resources and other such colonial rationalizations.

The three areas of Portuguese Asia have been quite distinct from
Spanish Asia. Portuguese Asian cultures have been more alien intrusions
on still-functioning local cultures, whereas in the Philippines Hispanic
and indigenous cultures reached a process of accommodation and
assimilation. Texts, oral traditions of Philippine ethnic groups, and recent
scholarly studies offer an intensive view in time perspective of the changes
and continuities that have characterized Hispanicized societies of the
Philippines. The major tribal or ethnic groups in the islands are Visayan,
Tagalog, Ilocano, Bical, Panyasinan, and Pampangan, which together comprise 88 percent of the Philippine population. These six major tribes, or
ethnolinguistic groups, are lowland or Christian and are commonly called
Filipino because they have discernible similarities.

At the end of Spanish rule (1898) Filipino society had become a
"bilateral kinship system" with apparently no theoretical limit, either in
blood or marital relationships, as to who were kinsmen. Probably no more
than three generations lived together under one roof. Marriage was primarily an alliance of two "descent groups" or units composed of three
generations of relatives arranged by parents and regulated by Church law.
All property brought to the marriage was kept separate although income
from it was common. That nuclear family of three generations was the
strongest single unit in society and the only loyalty-commanding unit,
strengthened by the fact that allies were incorporated into it by *compadrazgo* (ritual co-parenthood).

There seems to have been a considerable degree of equality between
husband and wife as noted by the acceptance of both maternal and
paternal kinsmen, with descent traced through both sides of the line.
In theory illegitimate children had no right to inheritances. All legitimate

children were entitled to inherit property from both mother and father. In practice, one-third is divided equally among all children, legitimate and illegitimate, and the surviving spouse.

Although authority in the house theoretically was the purview of the father, in fact the mother held household power. Practical evidence of her influence is her control of much of the activity and all of the expenditures of her home, for "in no other part of the Orient have women relatively so much freedom or do they play so large a part in the control of the family or in social and even industrial affairs" (Leroy, 1906: 49).

A classic nineteenth-century Tagalog story, *Urbana at Felisa,* provides much information concerning Tagalog society. Ideals of female-male behavior seem not necessarily to have been practiced. According to custom women's duty was to care for their home under their husband's authority. They should never leave their home without his permission and must observe their husband's wishes unless they were "not right." It was the "not right" that apparently gave Tagalog women their escape clause to manage their lives and those of their families fairly much as they wished.

Among upper-class families, particularly those of the towns, "woman is not infrequently the business head of the family and . . . is as a rule consulted on all important business as well as family matters" (Leroy, 1906: 80). Among the masses "in addition to the proportion of women who are the chief or only supporters of the family, there is a much larger proportion who merely help toward the support of the families," by working in fields and at domestic services (Leroy, 1906: 81).

The financial power that women enjoyed must have been slight compensation, particularly among the upper classes, for their acceptance of the querida system. This system of maintaining mistresses seems to have been a fact of Philippine life. Extra wives and mistresses were an accepted part of indigenous social life and fairly commonplace among the Spanish. It has been said that the existence, or perhaps persistence, of the querida system indicated a tension within the all-important family system. However, it seems that the secondary wife or concubine, a prestige symbol even in pre-Spanish times, was desired by wives for their husbands as much as husbands themselves desired it.

In Philippine society of the 1970s, more than 30 million strong, the family is still the most stable unit and all socio-economic-political ties revolve around it. The monogamous nuclear unit remains the most important cell of this society, while the extended family, next in importance, thrives in urban areas or sections where there exists more economic security (Lynch, 1959: 48-51). There seems to be less economic dependence among urban than among rural families and city children seem to be more independent than their rural siblings. Fewer marriages, in fact very few, are arranged by families, and girls seem to have as much freedom as boys to choose their mates.

Although the social and familial structure sanctions male authority, Filipinos accord "high status and legal equality" to their women whose roles are "seen to be complementary rather than subordinate, to the male roles" (AHP, 1969: 89). Equality within marital bounds is supported by a civil code that makes no distinction between husband and wife in person, follows customary patterns, and allows children to exercise traditional rights of inheritance from both parents (Carroll, 1965: 77, chaps. 5, 7; Lynch, 1959: 48-51; Fox, 1956: passim). Wife and husband share authority, duties, and responsibilities, and the woman also assumes control over religious and economic obligations in her home.

The family is still child oriented although both parents retain strict authority over their offspring. The eldest child, either female or male, also serves the same authoritative function. The position of daughters within the Philippine family is demonstrated by the fact that until a few generations ago, when marriages were still arranged, future sons-in-law were required to live in the house of their fiancée and to work for her parents, this practice only occasionally substituted for by a male dowry. Today, that practice is carried on in the tradition that in marriage it is the man and his family who are responsible for both the ceremony and the feast (AHP, 1969: 96).

Formal authority of males, as represented by the father in the family economic sphere, is ameliorated by his dependence on his wife. In household duties there are no customary restrictions against men performing any tasks that, in most societies, are considered to be the female's. Men often cook, market, care for the house, and do other household tasks whenever wives or older children cannot or will not. This is particularly true in rural areas, and since the Philippines are predominantly rural this is rather common. Only in church going do men not subsume their wives' roles, although in the Philippines attendance of women at religious services is not so much excessive religious zeal but a spirit of family representation.

The official pose of male "superiority" is represented partially by the continuation of the querida system. The husband's maintenance of a mistress is much an accepted fact of modern Philippine life. There is widespread expectation that married men who are separated from their wives for a long period of time, six or more months, naturally must seek a sexual outlet. Prevalence of the reverse pattern, although not an accepted tradition, is frequent.

In the public economic sphere Filipinas seem to share with men a more equal influence than do most other Asian women. Although they comprise only a third of the nation's labor force, women outnumber men in the professions, especially medicine and education, and also outnumber men as administrators, executives, and managers (AHP, 1969: 293). One of the reasons for this is the dominant influence of family in employment practices in which merit is not nearly so important for advancement as are kin connections. This combination of nepotism and paternalism also is a major factor mitigating the development of organized labor in the Philippines.

In 1965 some 35 percent or 10.54 million Filipinos of a population of more than 30 million were employed, comprising some 48 percent of the adult male and 23 percent of the adult female population (AHP, 1969: 294). About 3.6 percent of the labor force—199,000 women and 178,000 men—were active in professional, technical, and related occupations. Of administrative, executive, and managerial personnel women comprised 198,000 and men 175,000. On the other hand, only 95,000 clerical workers were women and in the total labor force there were only 3.385 million women to 7.16 million men (AHP, 1969: 295). The past published census showed this to be greatly misproportionate to the population as a whole in which males were only 1 percent more in the nation and in greater Manila although the city itself boats 3.5 percent more females, an indication that women from rural and other urban areas freely migrate to Manila for work (AHP, 1969: 22).

Formal education during Spanish rule was generally for Spaniards and in Spanish. By the nineteenth century girls' schools had been established but primarily to prepare them for marriage and children. The educational decree of 1863, applicable throughout Spanish possessions, established free and compulsory education for all children from seven to twelve, and education is still highly regarded by Filipinos as a means of advancement. Poor parents will send their brightest child to school, and he or she then is expected to help educate his or her siblings. Among teachers there supposedly is no discrimination between female and male, and all are required to pass the same examination. There is no differentiation in salaries between rural and urban, married or single, female or male, and women are given paid maternity leave (AHP, 1969: 131).

In labor women and minors are accorded special protection by the constitution, although domestic servants and other family employees are not protected by official eight-hour days and forty-eight-hour weeks. Women are not allowed to work night shifts anywhere, although women in health and welfare supervisory posts are exempt from such restrictions-protections. In addition, maternity and postparturition leaves of fourteen weeks (six before, eight after) at a minimum of 60 percent regular wages is required, and employers also are bound to furnish nursery facilities with a registered nurse or midwife whenever fourteen or more women are employed (AHP, 1969: 297). These rigid requirements also work to a woman's disadvantage. Employers tend to be discouraged from hiring women because of the expense, and women eager to work are willing to be hired at wages lower than is lawful (AHP, 1969: 297).

The Philippine civil code forbids divorce, a Catholic stricture contrary to traditional indigenous practice, although it now allows separation for concubinage practice by a husband, adultery by a wife, or attempted murder by either party (AHP, 1969: 97). However, red tape and social sanctions, especially among the upper classes, discourage separation, and it is more common for men, and occasionally women, simply to leave their old household and establish another, illegal one. Marriage custom and legal code require that any property a wife brings to her marriage remains hers, and this reinforces the tendency to equality within the family.

Political activities have been the public area of least involvement by Filipinas. Many experts believe that the reactivation of pre-Spanish traditions combined with American theory tends now to encourage more equal roles for women in public affairs. Although in politics wives actively support their husbands, and women have held all major political offices except the presidency and vice-presidency, their influence is not commensurate with their other public activities. Yet, it is more than for most other Asian women at all political levels.

This lowland, Christian, Filipino culture, which is predominant in the Philippines, is one in which women share and often control wealth, power, and authority, particularly at upper-class urban levels. Filipino culture is one in which prestige has been associated with possession of wealth, education, service to the community, and power, much of which women enjoy. This is the result, I believe, of persistence of indigenous values, the relatively comfortable amalgamation of Hispanic and indio cultural values and attitudes and the careful Hispanicization of the Philippines; it demonstrates, as perhaps no where else in the Iberian world, processes of acculturation and interaction productive of a new culture, a synthesis of traditional lifeways within the context of a modernizing nation. Women and men share equal power, authority, and influence, in theory and practice, more than almost anywhere else in Iberian and Asian cultures.

NOTES

NOTE: To facilitate typesetting, Indian diacritical marks have been eliminated throughout the book.

1. "Konkan" is possibly Dravidian (pre-Aryan). Written Konkani history begins in the seventh century A.D. with arrival of the Bani-Israil and Parsis from Persia (Pissurlencar, OHI: 1969).

2. Materials for the following discussion, unless noted otherwise, are from the following archival collections of the AHEI: *Acordãos* 1-6 (1535-1793); *Assentos da Câmara* 1-4 (1572-1615); *Assentos do Conselho*

de Estado (1629-1676); *Cartas Patentes Alvarás* 1-267 (1596-1601);
Livros da Damão 1-70 (1770-1885); *Livros de Diu* 1-49 (1698-1870);
Livro das Monções 1-224 (1583-1850). Other observations are the result
of my field work and interviews throughout South and Southeast Asia.

3. A useful definition for family structure is one derived from schools
of Hindu law that identify family as "joint," a patrilocal extended one
consisting of two or more patrilineally related nuclear families living
in one household, employing one hearth, and sharing property. Males
are co-owners of family property at birth; women's rights are obscure,
although they are allowed property inheritance under certain conditions.
From all Hindu law codes; see also Orenstein, 1965: 35, and Aiyar,
1950: 48-9, 58, 600-30, 647-8.

4. Only a few areas have radically different kinship systems based on
matrilineal descent, one being Kerala state in southwestern India, and
its dominant peoples, the Nayars.

5. The earlier Brahmanic "religion" had been one closely restricted
to male elites, specifically priests.

6. Altekar, 1956: 354-5. *Sati* is known to us as a widow's self-crema-
tion but it actually refers to a "virtuous woman" and has been applied
erroneously by Europeans to the practice of widow burning. Indians
consider widow burning a virtuous act.

7. Materials for the following discussion, unless noted otherwise, are
from the *Arquivo Senado da Macao* general collection; the *AHEI,* Lisboa:
the *Filmoteca Ultramarina Portuguese, Livros de Macau,* 6-64A (1747-
1830), passim; and *AHEI, Assentos da Camara* 1-4 (1572-1615), passim.
Other information is based on my observations and interviews in Macao.

8. The following discussion is based on King, 1963, Ormeling, 1956,
Felgas, 1956, miscellaneous *caixas, maços,* and codices for Timor and
Portugal Overseas in the (*AHU*) *Arquivo Historico Ultramarino* (Lisboa),
and the (*ANTT*) *Arquivo Nacional Torre do Tombo* (Lisboa); *AHEI,
Provisões* (1533-1821), *fichas* 1-73, *gaveta* 3, *divisão* 3; Leitao, 1948;
Luna de Oliveira, s.d.).

9. Materials that form the basis for discussion on the Philippines are
available in Phelan, 1955; Wickberg, 1955; Blair and Robertson, 1903-
1909; *AGI,* Seville, and *Real Academia de Historia,* Madrid. The most
important Philippine collection in Madrid is in the *AHN* and the most
comprehensive collection for the nineteenth century is in Madrid's
Museo y Biblioteca del Ultramar. Also useful were three collections of
the *ARSI* for early Philippine history: the *Jesuitica* collection; *AGI*
documents on microfilm; and the *Fondo Gesuitico al Gesu di Roma,*
all for 1581-1767. Unfortunately, the extremely valuable eighteenth-
and nineteenth-century documents in the very fine Philippine National
Archives have been moved several times, as have the Philippine sources
in the *AGN,* Mexico City, which are considerable for the eighteenth

century. The remainder of information is based on my Philippine field interviews.

10. See Phelan, 1967, chapter 2 for specifics. The major source for preconquest societies is Plasencia's ms. in Santa Inés, 1892).

11. There have been four classes—not classes in our Western sense of the term but a division of society according to those who function within it. The Brahman, or priestly, class has been the highest, followed by the Kshatriya, or warrior class, who also usually were the rulers. Third in rank have been the Vaisya, or merchant class, and fourth were the Sudra, the unskilled, semiskilled, artisan, and peasant peoples. Within this range of classes, or varnas, as the Indians designate them, are thousands and thousands of jatis and subjatis, which we refer to as castes or subcastes. Jatis usually were ascribed on the basis of functions in society so that, for example, there could be someone from the Sudra varna (i.e., working class) who belonged to the laundryman jati. Intricate rules are applicable for social, marital, and other inter- and intra-class and caste relationships. Today, it seems even more confused to Westerners because it is possible for someone to be of the Brahman varna and also of a very low (economic) jati. Each jati, incidentally, carries a specific name. "Untouchables," or *harijans*, lay outside the pale of the varna-jati system. See Basham, 1959, for an excellent elaboration.

12. Boxer, 1969: 19-20. Sixteenth-century Portugal had about one million people. It seems unlikely that any more than 10,000 Portuguese males were in an empire that stretched from South America to the Spice Islands. About 6,000 to 7,000 were in the *Estado da India,* the rest in Africa, Morocco, and Brazil. Of the few women who left Portugal, most went to Brazil.

13. Silva Correira, 1943-1958: III, 50ff. He calculates that about 80,000 Portuguese women went to India from 1500 to 1700. Boxer, 1963: 59 n.15, refutes this and says that even 8,000 would be generous and 800 nearer the mark in estimate.

14. See Gough (1956) and her other studies on the *Adi Dravida* (original Dravidians), Cohn (1961) on the Chamars (leather workers, mostly landless laborers). Other such works, and my own work in the Salsete records for eighteenth through twentieth century, point to the following patterns.

15. *Livro de Termos dos Conselhos Gerais,* 1685-1709: fl. 51v in the Arquivo Senado do Macau, has the document, in toto.

16. For documents on the sale, export, and import of female slaves see the Dutch *Daghregisters* (annual reports) of the Dutch Indonesian government for totals on annual trade.

17. AHI, 1971: 41, 169. The controversy on this is influenced by University of Chicago sociologists-anthropologists.

18. HMSO, 80, Timor, for information on the island.

4 PORTUGUESE AFRICA: IBERIA'S "BLACK MOTHER"

AFRICAN COMMERCE AND IBERIAN COLONIES

Iberians had enjoyed a certain familiarity with the continent to its south. Centuries of physical interaction with Moorish peoples from Africa's northern peripheries, exchanges of ideas, and dissemination of oral traditions made Africa, as a concept and as a place, available to the Iberian imagination and interests. Iberians in Africa had two major purposes: commerce and, later, colonization.

In 1415 Portugal won a smashing victory over Moorish forces at Ceuta, a major Moroccan port. That successful military excursion was applauded and financed by Portuguese merchants anxious to obtain direct access to sub-Saharan gold and grains, rather than to deal through middlemen of desert caravans and Moroccan cities. Within a few years Prince Henry (the Navigator) had initiated a program of exploration designed to secure a sea route to the Indies. His program sent Portuguese sailors and navigators east through the Indian Ocean, west across the Atlantic, and south touching at Porto Santo (1418), Madeira (1419), the Canaries (1425), Cape Bojador (1434), Cape Blanc, and Arguin Island (1443), and doubling Cape Verde (1445). By 1448 Portuguese had ventured 300 miles farther south of the

Cape Verde Islands. Henry received from his regent brother Pedro a complete monopoly over trade and discovery for all areas south of Cape Bojador and soon a flourishing commerce was under way in numerous products, including human captives.

For four centuries—from the mid-fifteenth to the mid-nineteenth—Iberians and other Europeans trafficked in raw material commodities, the most infamous being their trade in slaves. Many of the countries of Latin America and, in the early centuries of overseas expansion, Iberia itself used Africans as servants and slaves; thus it will be useful to have an understanding of the types of economies, polities, and societies from which America's blacks draw their heritage.

Africans had developed sophisticated social, political, economic, and belief systems. From African archaeological, artisitic, folkloric and oral traditions, and travel accounts that date back more than two millennia, ancient Middle Eastern, European, and Asian chronicles, we know that several African empires, military and commercial "states," in the East, North, Center, South, and West had passed through cycles of influence and decline.[1] Their names conjure up remembrances of glory and splendor: the rich kingdoms of Mali, Songhai, and Ghana; the fabled trading cities of Timbuktu and Kano; the luxury of courts and ceremonies. For at least a half-millennium before the arrival of Europeans, Africans had well-organized and lucrative trades in sale, gold, and slaves, particularly along the western Sudanic areas and the Sahara to North African cultures. They also had developed an excellent middleman system that would serve them well in dealings with Europeans.

Many of the "states" had various forms of domestic, urban, plantation, and ritual slavery. Scholars representing polar viewpoints regarding the origins and development of slavery in recent publications have agreed upon the existence and extent of these systems of slavery and also their comparability to almost all known Western systems of slavery prior to the development of seventeenth-century New World plantation societies.[2]

Europeans came to Africa initially to trade, with little thought to establish colonies there. Indeed, the Portuguese, who had so wisely taken note of their miniscule population of 1 million when they established their elaborate system of fortresses and factories along Asian sea-lanes, were not looking for empire in Africa. They were seeking manpower, gold bullion, and other trading commodities to feed into their own rapidly expanding urban societies. After 1444, when the first known shipload of Africans was taken in a commercial transaction between Africans and Europeans, that slave trade persisted through several centuries and affected almost all areas of sub-Saharan Africa.

Most of these African societies shared basically similar world views and institutional structures, albeit each had its particular patterns of behavior and lifeways. Despite prolonged contact of Africa with the West, very little Western influence penetrated, for until the nineteenth century African and foreign contact occurred only at the coast, with the exception of the Portuguese, and then primarily in areas designated for trade by Africans.[3] Even after the middle of the nineteenth century, when other European powers began their "scramble for Africa," most of the changes affected only elites in contact with Europeans. European antiassimilation policy gave some guarantees to preservation of African tradition. The areas discussed below were the areas from which the Iberian colonies in America were supplied with labor. These African cultures are important to our story because they bequeathed heritages and traditions to Ibero-America.

The African Cultures of Iberian Commerce

The Africans with whom Portuguese and Spanish maintained extensive commercial connections between mid-fifteenth and mid-nineteenth century had sophisticated societies, economies, and polities. Within their complex systems of kinship and marriage Africans have recognized numerous types of marital relationships and families, such as the "elementary," "biological," or "compound." Further, they have defined differences between "parental" families and "households."[4]

The peoples of Portuguese East Africa maintained family cohesion through the mother's lineage, and all female members of a man's mother's lineage in her own and succeeding generations were his "mothers." In this principle of unity of lineage, the mother's lineage was a single united group, all the women of the lineage were "mothers" to the men, and the males in these tribal clusters maintained their closest connections with males of their mother's groups.[5]

In Portuguese trading areas of Central Africa most of the lineage descent and succession were matrilineal, and in many villages the female as head of the family was the outstanding personage. In these matriarchal societies of the western or lower Congo, property, houses, and lands passed through females.

Although Central Africa was a major supplier of slaves, the most important area was coastal and Sudanic West Africa, the culture area of Sudanic-Negro ethnolinguistic groups.[6] West African societies shared similar values and systems. West Africa, generally speaking, is a happy example of the exercise of both power and authority by women in social, economic, and political systems. Common to West African societies have been a major economic role for women; strong emphasis on mother and child, and sibling bonds; and culturally and individually accepted concepts of woman as a strong, resourceful and central personage in family and society.

In Dahomey females provided services vital to the functioning of the polity at the local and, especially, at the state level to a degree carried on in few other communities. Dahomean women were drawn into public life at its highest levels. Their excellence in administration has been attributed to a shared duality that was a pervasive feature of Dahomean culture (Polanyi, 1966: 56-7). In addition, women controlled the selling of foodstuffs in producers' organizations and in the *sodudo,* or selling societies. They procured their produce from specialized farms and also determined the daily prices in larger markets. For sale in smaller markets women obtained surpluses from their husband's village plots or from their field compounds (Polanyi, 1966: 76-88 for materials gathered by Herskovits, 1938). This female control over marketplace production and distribution has been a central feature of Afro-Latin, particularly Afro-Brazilian, cultures.

Among the Yoruba of present-day western Nigeria, commerce was carried on by women. Yoruba women were autonomous economically and had a high degree of mobility. Yoruba women have trade guilds, and their role as independent market leaders has been highly institutionalized. These economic institutions are powerful and their leaders play a major role in politics. Females also had various roles of prime importance in palaces, were priestesses in charge of palace shrines, and were "mothers" of cult organizations in the town with "little mothers" to assist them. These female-directed activities still have their counterparts in the *maes dos santos* and *filhas dos santos* of Afro-Brazilian cults.[7]

The Ibo (Igbo) of southeastern Nigeria have a social organization that, historically, has been fragmented. The Ibo comprise hundreds of relatively independent social units, each one linked not politically but socially by the Ibo system of exogamy. Ibo women have played a significant role in the economic and family life of the society, but they usually wielded their power in an unobtrusive way. Woman was food producer and crop owner, and in time of war it was her function to override the male fighting machine and to make peace (Green, 1964: 169ff.; Harris, n.d.: #5). Because of her high social position in her husband's as well as her own village, she always has been the link in intervillage communication.

Prominence of females also has been in evidence among the kingdoms of the Cameroons. Among the Kom of West Cameroon women were responsible for most of the agriculture, but the king had extensive rights over females in social situations. He could marry or dispose of women to others; his wives and retainers could select and use women from all sectors of the population, and commoners were expected to send a daughter or son to the palace (Forde and Kaberry, 1969: 143).

Among Akan-speaking peoples of southern Ghana, especially the Ashanti and Fante peoples, the dominant principle of social organization was matrilineal descent, and even a matrilineal descendant of an alien or slave women was a member by birthright in the lineage.[8] The Ewes in Ghana and Togoland, the Gege peoples of Dahomey, the states of Oyo (Yoruba), Benin, and Akan, all centered in West Africa around the Guinea forest, were similar in cultural traditions and organizations. Whether they were matriarchal or patriarchal, matrilineal or patrilineal, the roles and

functions of females bore remarkably similar characteristics in the
economy, polity, and culture of West African societies.

The Sudanese states constantly were in contact with the Muslims.
The Hausa, whose main source of wealth was agriculture, also had a
successful trade in slaves. The role of women was not static in these
societies before, during, or after the Islamic encounter. Some females
enjoyed wide jurisdiction. The power of women was extensive. An example is given of a deceased ruler's sister who in a succession dispute
took over the throne and held it for seven years before relinquishing it
to her son.[9] In some Hausa kingdoms, as with the Maradi, the queen
mother presided over all marriages and kinship ceremonials. For females of the royal lineage she was the official head and patron of local prostitutes and devotees of the pre-Islamic cult of spirit worship.
Although she had no direct role in the council of state, she enjoyed
enormous economic power through her slaves, from market vendors,
and annual taxes from prostitutes and cult specialists (Forde and Kaberry, 1969:108). On the other hand, the ordinary woman undertook
the usual field tasks. In wars she was responsible for supplying and
carrying all ordnance materials and foodstuffs.

Throughout western and Sudanic Africa, the economic and social importance of women has been significant. That queens appear so frequently
in scholarly literature on Africa suggests that they exerted persistent
political power as well. Even in the heavier centuries of the Atlantic
slave trade, the late seventeenth and eighteenth centuries, women had
powerful positions. "Angonna . . . is . . . governed by a Woman. . . . This
Governess is so wise, that to keep the Government entirely in her hands,
she lives unmarried. But . . . she generally buys a brisk, jolly Slave, with
whom she diverts herself" (Bosman, 1705: 63).

Women enjoyed high office for centuries in West African societies as
lineage heads, chiefs, and heads of secret societies. Being a mother was
an important self-image for an African woman *not* because of maternal
fulfillment but because it symbolized the transition from childhood to
adulthood. In West African societies, a woman who bore children had
shown that she was strong and capable of political leadership.

Sub-Saharan western, Sudanic, central, and eastern Africa served the
Iberians for centuries in commercial relationships and provided substantial
entrepôts for gold, grains, laborers, and technological information. But
the Spanish and Portuguese eventually sought imperial aggrandizement
and colonies to provide them a geopolitical base of operation. On the one
hand Portugal rationalized its permanence in Africa as a strategic necessity to protect the sea-lanes between Asia and America. On the other hand,
Africa had become the source of a lucrative trade that the Portuguese were
unwilling to share with European powers, especially the Dutch and English,
who had begun systematic harassment of Portugal's possessions from the
early seventeenth century.

Common Generalities of the African Past
with American Civilizations and
Continuities in African Traditions

What characteristics and values did these African societies contribute to American civilization? And what of the women? Despite variations in religions, technologies, and social and economic systems in regional and ethnic sub-Saharan Africa, certain generalizations can be made about elements of familial and societal unity based on geography and history. Differences can be viewed as gradations of change from one group to another. Recent scholarship has demonstrated similarities in language, agricultural and technological techniques, family patterns, and women's roles concomitant with shared characteristics of "matrilineal belt societies" of Africa (see note 6 below).

A basic characteristic in almost all African societies has been veneration and respect for a mother by her children, especially her sons. Perhaps this has resulted from polygynous relationships within these societies, since many African children have grown up in polygynous households. Another characteristic seemingly common to most African societies is that the bride is not responsible for a dowry; rather, it is the man who must pay a bride's price or service. Still a third area of commonality has been the considerable political power and prestige enjoyed by queen consorts or great queens in both matrilineal and patrilineal societies. Another identifiable characteristic has been a tribal or ethnic concern about legal possession of children that often dismisses the factor of biological parenthood but that also is concerned with legitimacy of descent.

Probably polygyny has been more an ideal than a reality. Polygyny implies prestige since it is associated with wealth and nobility. It has been an operative principle in nearly 90 percent of the African societies under examination.[10] Marriages generally were arranged by tribal elders although "romantic love" seems to have played a larger part in traditional African families than has been admitted, and romances often could be carried on without consideration of permanent marital attachment. Child betrothal seems to have been relatively common in numerous societies but has lost favor now that young African males and females increasingly demand freedom of choice in familial and social behavior.

Girls married young. When they did not they were likely to be supervised until wed. If a girl became pregnant a marriage usually was arranged quickly; in some areas the responsible young man could be held to account by marriage.

Changes have occurred in relationships between wives and their in-laws. Because of the ease and safety of travel, most women who remain in villages while their husbands seek work in the cities are less liable to control of either his or her relative. In addition, African women have been moving to the city, often without their husbands, exploiting new economic opportunities open to them and, in areas such as Freetown, seem to migrate in the same if not higher numbers than men. Female mobility lessens her subjugation by members of her family, but it also lessens her reliance on them, or rather lessens the chances of her obtaining aid or support should it be needed from her or her husband's kin. Similarly, since many African urban males cannot ensure adequate or constant support, the African woman must rely on courts, authorities, and, increasingly, voluntary associations that seem to have developed among urban African women.

The ideal and often the practice of polygyny in traditional society has carried over into urban areas. A man with a legal wife is free, under law, to set up a household with another or others, commonly known as "outside wives." However, there is another tradition of having only one wife. In urban areas the trend is strong, especially among educated and upwardly mobile Africans, to have only one marriage partner.

Changes in the role of women, structure of family, and opportunities in society are closely related to the degree of modernization and industrialization. Changes are most obvious among the upper classes, especially educated and urban women and men. Most educated African women are employed outside their homes. For example, in Lagos nine out of ten African wives work and, retaining African rural customs, their profit is their own to spend as they wish (Morris, 1963: 53ff.).

Other changes occurring concern patterns of inheritance and widow remarriage. In traditional families inheritance was a form of security for a widow. Furthermore, since woman's fertility was highly valued in African societies, a widow's remarriage was accepted and even desired. Now there seems to be gradual disappearance of widow inheritance as well as increased female mobility and choice in decisions on remarriage.

One of the more remarkable points of continuity has been the role of markets.

One outstanding fact concerning West African markets is that most of the trading is carried on by women, whose economic position in the culture is a very favorable one. What women produce is theirs, to be disposed of as they wish, and the proceeds cannot be alienated by father, husband, or son. (Herskovits, 1971: 25.)

The distribution mechanisms of the market are extremely complex. Women act as buyers of produce at wholesale centers and then resell their goods at a profit in retail centers. This central economic institution and its functions traditionally have been the purview of women throughout almost all of Africa. I have seen this procedure thriving in both Bantu and Sudanic ethnolinguistic areas, in Congo and Zaire, in Senegal, among tribes of southern, central, and eastern Africa, and in areas of present-day Nigeria, Ghana, and Liberia.

These are some of the changes and main continuities in the cultures with whom Iberians engaged in commercial ventures. These are evident in contemporary Africa, and the configurations identified above are evident in Afro-Ibero-American cultures. Their impact in American cultures will be addressed subsequently.

The African Cultures of Iberian Colonization

THE ISLANDS

The first areas of Iberian settlement were the upper West African islands of Cape Verde, São Tomé, Príncipe, the coastal section of what is today Ghana and then was known as São Jorge da Mina, and Fernando Po. The archipelago of Cape Verde was settled in 1462, its ten islands divided into captaincies. The first settlement was Santiago Island, which had been split into two captaincies. Most of the original peoples of the islands, it is assumed, were brought from the Guinea coast. The earliest Portuguese came from the southern Algarve and northern Minho districts and were soon joined by Jews fleeing European persecution, by native Madeiran islanders, and by Africans brought as slaves from Portuguese Guinea to work the plantations (Almeida, 1966: 141).

São Tomé was given as a donatary grant in 1485 and settled in that year. Thereafter it played a major role in the lucrative slave trade between Kongo and Portugal, Africa and America. Africans were brought as slaves from Ghana, Benin, Gabon, the Kongo and, later, from Angola, so there has been a substantial diffusion of African ethnic characteristics in this area. An added element in the early years of São Tomé's occupation was a few thousand children of Jewish descent who had been taken from their parents at about eight years of age and shipped to Africa as part of an experiment in Christianization. Those 30 percent who survived the misadventure were assimilated into the African population (Tenreiro, 1961: 68).

The most populous of Portugal's western island possessions was Guiné, which lies between present-day Senegal and Guinée and comprises a landmass, an archipelago, and several coastal islands. Most of Guiné's indigenous peoples were Senegambian Sudanic-Negro ethnolinguistic groups: the Balanta, Fula, Manjaco, Malinke, Papel, and Brame. These peoples had been pushed into the unhealthy coastal areas by intruding Malinke (Mandingo). Military disruptions caused disintegration of these peoples, fighting among themselves, isolation into separate strategic villages, and a ripe source for slavers (Abshire and Samuels, 1969: 112).

Very little is known of the activities, organization, and overall structure of these island societies until the late nineteenth-century European "scramble for Africa." More scholarly data are available on the three Portuguese mainland areas of Kongo, Angola, and Mozambique.

THE MAINLAND

The Kongo Experiment. In late 1482 and early 1483 a Portuguese seaman, Diogo Cão, discovered the mouth of the Congo River (called Zaire by the Portuguese) and established contact in that area with the Manikongo, the major chieftain. Cão initiated a promising experiment in diplomacy and alliance that preceded later Portuguese domination east and west of Kongo. Unlike the Sudanic-Negro peoples of western Africa who were Portugal's trading partners, the inhabitants of permanent Portuguese settlements were of the Bantu ethnolinguistic family.

The Bantu peoples of Congo, Angola, and Mozambique are considered to have migrated from West Africa's forests sometime in the latter half of the first Christian century. The migration prompted by population explosion was aided by their technique of shifting cultivation of food crops. The sheer size of these agricultural populations and their political organizations enabled them to push south relentlessly and eventually to replace the original inhabitants, the hunting and gathering Bushmen and Hottentots. Arabic sources for East Africa show the Bantu had already settled at Sofala, south of Beira, Mozambique, by the end of the first century A.D. Later migrations brought Bantu pastoral groups down from northern sub-Saharan Africa. By the sixteenth century Bantu peoples had spread throughout central and southern Africa and today occupy about a third of the entire continent (AHMoz, 1969: 24-5).

Agricultural Bantus, unlike their pastoral cousins, were distinguished by smaller, more cohesive units under strong chieftains, which underwent constant regeneration. Pastoral Bantu groups comprised larger units and contained aggressive military organizations that helped maintain a status quo.

The kingdom of Kongo stretched along the coast from the Cuanza River south of Luanda to Loango some 600 miles north of the Congo's mouth. Most peoples of the savanna of West-Central Africa, are matrilineal in succession, prestige, status, and descent, and matrilineage is an important factor in rules for residence and marriage. When the Portuguese arrived the Kongo's political base was localized matrilineage villages. However, the keystone of the structure was the king. Until at least late sixteenth century the organization of Kongo society appears similar to that of other African states.[11]

The ultimately unsuccessful Portuguese experiment on the southern bank of the Congo consisted of a diplomatic alliance based on a scheme to establish a Christian European cultural pattern and simple economic agreements. Since the nature of the relationship was not one of military conquest, commercial exploitation, or colonization, the Portuguese were able to establish an initial friendly relationship with West-Central African peoples.[12] From initial encounters in the 1480s until firm establishment of Portuguese interest groups by the early 1500s, relationships were compatible and cooperative.

Several white women were sent out to teach African females basic domestic functions as performed in Portugal. Orfas del Rei from Portugal and even Indo-Portuguese and Macaense females were brought to Portuguese territories in Africa for purposes of cementing relationships. However, miscegenation without marriage became prevalent. Portuguese males also had a concubinage relationship with African women.

There probably never were more than 200 white men in the Kongo experiment even up to the late 1540s, but the majority of Portuguese, clergy or colonist, mated freely with Congolese women, and a considerable mulatto community developed at São Salvador in the heart of the Congo. Once the Portuguese returned home, their children were left in the care of their African mothers and became agents in the slave trade, lesser members of the clergy, or colonial functionaries (Duffy, 1959: 5-23).

The Kongo experiment was not destined to become a permanent part of the Portuguese imperial scheme. Except as an entrepôt for slaves and missionaries, it was eclipsed gradually by Angola in the last quarter of the sixteenth century. Despite the creation of São Salvador as a city and a bishopric of Kongo and Angola in 1596, within twenty years most traces of Christian life had disappeared. By 1690 São Salvador was a deserted city, and in Stanley's 1874-1879 explorations there was no trace of Portugal to be found, other than biraciality. Portuguese claims to influence rested solely on the African female and her key role in the process of assimilation.

Portugal's African West. Earlier Portuguese interest in West Africa had been concentrated from Morocco as far south as São Jorge da Mina on the Guinea coast, where trade consisted of slaves, gold, and ivory (Lopes, 1924; Menezes, 1732; Ricard, 1955; Cenival and Ricard, 1934-1953). Some Portuguese traders, exiles, and adventurers settled in African villages and mixed freely with the female populations. A Jesuit described "the Joloff women, they are very good-natured and extremely fond of the Portuguese nation," and often were the secret source of revelation of African plots against the Portuguese (Boxer, 1963:10).

Mina Negresses also were favorites of the Portuguese. There was extensive miscegenation, but because the Mina practiced abortion and infanticide mulatto children were less numerous on the lower Guinea Gold Coast (Brásio, 1952-:III, 90; Blake, 1942, passim, for Portuguese in lower Guinea). Travelers noted uninhibited sexual relations between black and white. But one observed a phenomenon opposite from that observed by the Jesuits, in that "the women of Benin behave themselves very obligingly to all; but more especially to the Europeans, except the Portuguese which they don't like very well" (Bosman, 1705: 430-1).

To São Tomé Island off the West African coast were deported "criminals, convicts," and forcibly baptized Jewish children. An observer of this deportee population in 1506 noted, "Few of the women bore children

of the white men; very many more bore children of the Negroes, while
the Negresses bore children of the white men" (Ryder, 1959: I, 298n.;
Ryder, 1958: passim). The Crown provided all unmarried men with a
Negress for breeding purposes. A sixteenth-century Portuguese pilot noted:

> They all have wives and children, and some of the children who are
> born there are as white as ours. It sometimes happens that, when the
> wife of a merchant dies, he takes a Negress, and this is an accepted
> practice, as the Negro population is both intelligent and rich.
> (Boxer, 1959: 15.)

These relations of the Portuguese with peoples of present-day Ghana,
Senegambia, and Dahomey were an important initiatory chapter in the
Portuguese expansion in West Africa. They moved on Angola with very
different motives.

Initial impetus to shift permanent attention from Kongo to Angola
derived from Lisbon's concern over two events. One was seemingly
endemic warfare among Kongolese groups vying for power in an expanded
commercial-political arena. The other was incursions of Jaga tribes into
Kongo territory and the consequent need for Portugal to make good its
alliance with the Kongolese. The king, or Ngola, of the state tributary to
the Manikongo's kingdom, the Mbbundu kingdom of Ndongo, sought to
take advantage of Jaga attacks on Kongo by declaring his independence,
dealing with slavers from São Tomé, and seeking direct ties with Portugal.

The Ngola's efforts to secure direct Portuguese alliances met with
success in 1575. Queen Mother Catarina lay the foundations for settlement of Angola by appointing a governor of a donatory grant consisting
of 140 miles of coastline and by sending 400 settlers. But relations
between the Portuguese and the Ngola quickly deteriorated. The Ngola
had acquired power and influence through his dealings with São Tomé's
slave traders and balked at any attempts at external controls of his kingdom. For nearly three centuries thereafter, Angola was a land of conflicts,
military expeditions, and a thriving slave trade.

Despite Angola's initial development as an adjunct of and alternative
to Kongo and despite the persistence of conflicts, settlements began.
By 1576 Luanda had been founded, and by 1600 Angola had emerged
as the most important of Portugal's African possessions (Duffy, 1959:
49-78 passim). Initially granted as a *donataria,* a proprietary captaincy,
of Angola in 1571 to Paulo Dias de Novais, a grandson of the explorer
Bartolomeu Dias, Luanda became part of the colonial government in
1592, three years after Dias' death. Trading syndicates for European
goods, export of slaves, and expeditions in search of silver and souls were
part of the colonial picture. In the mid-1590s Luanda's population was
increased by twelve female immigrants from royal orphanages. They by

themselves did not alter the social patterns of the town, but, combined with slave and free African women and Portuguese males, a new society emerged.

Some African women involved in Portuguese affairs were powerful and prominent in their own societies and played significant roles in some chapters of African history. Queen Nzinga is an example. The sister of the king of Dongo, she arrived in Luanda in 1622 at the head of an embassy and a year later was baptized as Dona Ana de Sousa. In the following year she poisoned her brother for breaking their treaty with the Portuguese, declared herself queen, allied with the Jaga tribesmen, and warred against the Portuguese until a treaty was signed with the latter in 1636. Several years later she allied with the Dutch and was defeated in the 1645 conflicts between Dutch and Portuguese, but she continued to rule for several years thereafter (Duffy, 1959: 64). Other African and mulatto women became mistresses or wives of Portuguese administrators in Angola, campaign veterans who commanded fortresses, were municipal council members, and landholders.

If no more than twenty or thirty Portuguese women traveled annually to Goa, even fewer went to Portuguese Africa. Men from garrison soldiers to upper-class Europeans mixed with black women and fathered a population of mulattoes (Cadornega, 1940-1942: I, 210, III, 30). Almost all prominent Portuguese intermixed with mulatto daughters of earlier settlers, female slaves, or free concubines. Neither ancestry nor class seemed to matter in choice of "legal" wife. By the eighteenth century women were being married by men who wished to serve as city councillors in Luanda. In lieu of qualified individuals the council might have to take men "who were married three days before the elections, and to girls who were not daughters of respectable citizens" (Boxer, 1965: 116). This was due to the extreme shortage of white women in Luanda and Benguela, for few women went to Luanda and none to Benguela from late sixteenth to late eighteenth century.

A Capuchin friar estimated that by the turn of the seventeenth century 40,000 blacks, 4,000 whites, and 6,000 mulattoes lived in Luanda, Angola's major town (Boxer, 1963: 38-9). In 1665, 132 of Angola's 326 moradores lived in Luanda. Thus, much extant information on Portuguese West African urban life and society relates to Luanda, with little available about the interior. Despite citizen protestation of poverty and inability to pay taxes, Luanda in the final decades of the seventeenth century apparently was a thriving seaport. The "principal citizens and ancient moradores of some hundred households," mostly white men from Portugal, had filled the city with prosperity, families, and sumptuous buildings (Cadornega, 1940-1942: III, 5-44 passim).

The soldier-chronicler Cadornega, resident of Angola from 1639 to 1685, noted that other moradores "helped to increase the population with

many young people, especially women and girls, who live longer in this
kingdom since they are not exposed to the calamities of the sun and the
rigors of the backlands" (Cadornega, 1940-1942: III, 5-44 passim). He
also noted that black women mated with whites in unofficial unions that
gave rise to a large mulatto population. The crown regularly had sent out
small groups of women, either orphans or rehabilitated prostitutes, but
apparently at that time they were too few to matter (A de A, 14 August
1614: ser 1: IV, 111).

A report to the contrary noted that Luanda's municipal council asked
the Crown in 1664 not to send any more white females to their city
since, as a result of manpower losses in the Dutch war (1641-1648), there
was an extreme surplus of marriageable females in the colony.[13] Most reports agree, however, that the supply of white women was insufficient and
that most inhabitants "had accommodated themselves with mulatas,
daughters of worthy men and conquerors who had begotten them on
either their female slaves or on free Negro women" (Boxer, 1965:. 129 n.28).

The city was provisioned by a wide variety of imported and domestic
goods, the distribution of which was governed by *quintandeiras*, female
sellers, in the marketplace. This role of woman as both producer and
provisioner seemed a main feature of Portuguese African life. It carried
into Brazilian society as well, for Angolan women were part of the slave
shipments from Angola to Brazil.

The position of women and the interrelationship of Portuguese colonies
is evident in deportation and importation processes. In the eighteenth
century, shipments of women into Africa were made not in the context of
commercial exchange but as a punitive measure. Women were deported
or, in many cases, were responsible for deportation of males from Brazil
and Portugal to Angola. Registry books of the senate in Luanda for the
first half of the eighteenth century include women, such as one Luiza da
Fonseca, convicted for theft in Oporto (1715); Maria, female slave in
Oporto, banished to Benguela for procuring (1734); Maria Gomes Pimental,
a colored woman from Minas Gerais, sent to Angola for complicity in
her husband's murder (1841); Joana de Salazar, gypsy widow from Campo
Maior, her ten-year old daughter, and her five-year old daughter, per-
petually banished to Angola (1741). No reason was given for the last of
that list, but it is likely that she was banished because she was a gypsy.
The same reason would apply to another inhabitant of the same town, the
gypsy widow Maria da Encarnação (1741), and from Moura, Maria de Vargas,
a gypsy, was sent to Angola with her husband and children for the crime of
theft (1743).[14] There was a strong probability that these women were
deported precisely because they were gypsies. King João waged a bitter and
ruthless campaign against the gypsy population of Portugal during the first
half of the eighteenth century.

Portugal's East: The African Part of the Estado da India. Portugal's in-
trusion in eastern Africa began in Ethiopia with its search for Prester

John, the supposedly Christian ruler of Ethiopia.[15] From the fifteenth century several missions left Portugal for Ethiopia and for avenues to the East Indies. The first expedition reached Mozambique (1487-1489) under de Covilha. The more enduring Portuguese relationship in East Africa stemmed from attempts to build a commercial empire, a dream that gained permanence with Dias' circling of the Cape (1497), da Gama's voyage to India (1498), and Cabral's landing at Mozambique Island and Kilwa (1500). Although contact with Mozambique proper came later than with West Africa, Mozambique remained a consistently settled area under European aegis longer than any other European settlement south of the Sahara.

Trading hegemony of the East African coast belonged to Arab-Moors. The Portuguese Crown commissioned da Gama and several other expeditions to East Africa. By 1505 Portugal had acquired possession of or trading perquisites with the several Arabic posts of Kilwa, Malindi, Sofala, Zanzibar, Mafia, Pemba, Brava, Mozambique Island, and Mombasa. During the next several years the Portuguese sent out navies, soldiers, and traders to break the Moorish hegemony and establish its own.

From 1510 until 1600 the Lusitanians were supreme from Sofala in the south (Mozambique) to Mogadiscio in the north (Somaliland) (Gray, 1959: 117-8; Strandes, 1961: passim; Boxer and Azevedo, 1960). A captaincy of the viceroyalty of India was established at Sofala, and all commercial interests were directed to Asia. By the last half of the six-teenth century male military, missionaries, and merchants maintained the Portuguese presence in coastal entrepôts, military garrisons, and markets. A certain amount of miscegenation occurred with resultant cultural ex-change all along coastal areas. However, neither native Portuguese nor mulattoes ever completely controlled or settled the coast, and during the sixteenth century there were probably never more than 1,000 Portuguese residents in East Africa (Gray, 1947: 17, 20).

The entire seventeenth century was speckled with internal rebellions and external assaults by both Africans and Arabs. Within that time span Portuguese influence waned in most East African city-states. Mozambique was a different story, and because of its harbor it remained a haven for ships from Goa to Lisbon.[16] The Portuguese initially were interested in promotion and protection of commerce and trading routes in the Indian Ocean, for their economic, political, and geographic orientation was toward India and the East. At least from the beginning of their direct rule in Mozambique in 1507, and for nearly 200 years thereafter, the Portuguese were in political and commercial conflict with the Arab city-states in East Africa, for that island was both the center of Portuguese authority in southeastern Africa and a bastion of a Lusitanian mercantile empire.

By mid-sixteenth century the Portuguese also had directed their attention to the establishment of Luso-African trading colonies along the

Zambezi, won the river ports of Sena and Tete from the Arabs, located and exploited the mines of Monomotapa, and made appropriations of large tracts of African lands. By 1700 Lusitanian lust for metals, particularly the gold and silver mines of Manica, helped destroy Monomotapa (Mwanamutapa), the kingdom in which the mines were located.[17]

Some Portuguese married African women through whom they earned recognition as headmen or chiefs, and came to rule vast areas of the interior (Abraham, 1961: 218-20). On these estates, or *prazos,* the settlers coerced and exploited the native population for plantation labor.[18] The prazo plays an important part in the story of females in Mozambique.

The prazo originated in the late sixteenth century when individual Portuguese soldiers and merchants infiltrated the interior up the Zambesi and found an African society somewhat similar to the semifeudal one of their own country. With their African wives, their newly acquired languages, small personal armies, and their allegiance to the monomotapa (ruling chief), they were recognized by the Portuguese government in rights and privileges as a way to extend imperial influence in the interiors. The Crown divided the area into the captaincy of Rivers of Sena and to some distinguished subjects issued *prazos da coroa* (crown grants) similar to the donataria agricultural settlement system in Brazil. The grants were hereditary, and legally they were land leases for three generations only. But throughout the course of Portuguese African history, the concessions often passed into the hands of speculators. The prazo originally was granted to a European female married to a European settler, who were to occupy and cultivate the lands, passing them on through their daughters or granddaughters. It had its origin in a mix of the donatary system and the Portuguese Indian practice of granting dowries in land to males who married widows or orphaned daughters of Crown officials.[19]

By the latter part of the seventeenth century many of the prazeros were mulatto, so Lisbon devised a scheme whereby inheritance of the prazo would pass to the eldest daughter to be retained by her only if she married a Portuguese born in Portugal. Among the white and half-caste women who became wealthy landowners and slaveowners in the Portuguese colonies were these heiresses or *donas de Zambesia* and the *donas de Ibo* of the Querimba Islands, entrepôts for the gold, ivory, and slave trades with East African territories. Theoretically, although prazos were to be held by white women married to white men in female descent for three generations, the laws seldom were observed, and most prazos came into the possession of mulattas and their mulatto children (Boxer, 1969: 60).

The prazos, as initially founded by whites, mulattoes, or Goans who became completely integrated into the Bantu tribal system, carried omnipotence in economic, political, and social affairs; thus, the heiresses wielded significant power in these interior areas. Despite the lack of white

Portuguese males and the resultant intermarriage of prazeiras with mulattoes or Indo-Portuguese, the donas de Zambesia maintained an important role in the colony until the abolition of the prazo system in the nineteenth century.

Declining commercial fortunes and loss of Crown interests made the remainder of the seventeenth and most of eighteenth century Mozambique's history one of missionary enterprise and wide-ranging explorations into the interior. Until the early nineteenth century Portuguese tenure in East Africa was one of constant conflict with the Nguni Zulu and poor relations with Bantu groups in the interior. The Portuguese had little real control over their prazeiros, who collected head taxes on Africans and used forced labor, and were constantly harassed by both hostile Europeans and by Africans.

Portugal's African Colonies and the Slave Trade

From the sixteenth through most of the nineteenth century Portuguese African territories were entrepôts for a massive and lucrative trade in slaves, a trade in which moral strictures bothered neither seller nor buyer, whether Arab, African, European, animist, Christian, Jew, or Muslim. Perhaps as many as 20 million Africans were transferred to Asia and America; nearly 10 million went to America.[20]

The enslavement process and sexual selection in Africa had a particular pattern. After the initial acquisition of a salable supply of Africans, the sexes usually were separated from each other. Females were lodged in the courtyards of forts and castles or were marshalled in warehouses. In general they received more careful treatment since they were desired for domestic service, some selective fieldwork, and breeding. Even on ships women were separated from men and boys, although ship's officers had the right to any female (Crowder, 1966: 75).

It is an assumption, as yet unsupported by quantitative data analysis, that the number of women carried as slaves may have been somewhat greater than previously had been assumed. Especially near the end of the trade the idea of natural reproduction of slaves found support.[21] This might mean that a fairly stable male-female ratio existed in many areas of the Americas under circumstances that allowed for the voluntary reproduction of children. Females as brood animals would have guaranteed an expanding slave labor population.

On the other hand we know that certain areas of the Americas did not receive or retain sufficient numbers of females so that "involuntary" breeding of children was an aspect of plantation life. In certain areas and in particular time periods in Brazil, female slaves were given their freedom on the production of six, eight, or ten children. The United States had its regions and times for slave breeding as did several Caribbean areas. In Barbados, as time passed "the sex ratio lowered toward an equality of

men to women," thus indicating that in areas where there was a decline
in the number of deaths over births the presence of more females made
this possible (Curtin, 1969: 60).

Ironically, despite the obvious advantages of having female slaves for
domestic servants, or for fieldservice, or for brood mare, prices for females
reflect the unequal regard in which she was held by her Arabic or European
buyers and her African sellers. For example, in the slave port of Bonny,
the rate of exchange in the latter half of the seventeenth century was
thirteen iron bars for a male slave and nine for a female, while in the
first decade of the eighteenth century the price was twelve bars for a
male and still only nine for a female (Barbot, 1744-1746: V, 459; Jones,
1958: passim).

Portuguese Africa remained essentially a commodity export economy
and society in which the slave element was a prime ingredient of empire.
Defenders of Portuguese custom have pointed to missions and miscegenation as twin successes. Yet miscegenation surely implied the exploitation
of African women as concubines, wives, and laborers. When by 1845 the
slave trade finally was suppressed in Angola, followed by the 1850 abolition of the slave trade to Brazil, Portugal's African territories settled into
somnolescence.

THE REMAINS OF EMPIRE: COLONIAL
SETTLEMENTS IN THE NINETEENTH
AND TWENTIETH CENTURIES

With the exception of the slave trade, Portugal had neglected Africa in
favor of its American interests. For more than three centuries Portuguese
Africa had been an amalgamation of areas under direct military-civil
government, commercial concessions belonging to companies or individuals,
or native protectorates. Portuguese West Africa, particularly Angola,
practically was an economic dependency of Brazil, while until mid-
eighteenth century all of Portuguese East Africa was under the authority
of Portuguese India's viceroy.

In 1822 Brazil achieved its independence and triggered a series of
changes throughout the Portuguese empire. Africa assumed a new importance in Lusitanian imperial designs. On the heels of Brazilian independence, Mozambique was designated an overseas province, which, with
the exception of 1930-1951 when it was a "colony," it remained until
1974. In 1823 Angola's special relationship with Brazil was ended when
the Portuguese military intervened on Benguela's vote to join Brazil in
confederation. Brazil's separation from mother culture provoked nationalist
sentiment among Portugal's intelligentsia and encouraged a new "colonial"
ideology: Angola would be the new Brazil, Africa would assure Portugal's
stature in the world.

In addition to political disintegration in the Iberian peninsula, nine-teenth-century European imperial acquisitiveness and humanitarian idealism contributed to instability and uncertainty of Portuguese rule in Africa. Furthermore, pressures to end the slave trade and slavery were becoming effective and undermining Angola's economy, unrest in the interior was rising, and European nations were baying hungrily at Portu-guese Africa.

Political and economic problems, conflict with prazeiros until 1888, poor trade, and climate had discouraged European settlement in Mozambique. Most of the towns were on the coast or along the Zambezi River and, generally, until the end of the nineteenth century the Bantu and Portu-guese populations went their own separate ways. In 1891 Mozambique officially was proclaimed Portuguese East Africa under a royal commis-sioner which, after 1898, sat at Lourenço Marques. It was not until after World War I that Mozambique began to provide facilities to attract European Colonization.

Until the twentieth century most Portuguese "settlers" in Africa were *degregados,* convicts in effect, sometimes accompanied by their "wives" who generally were orphanage or reformatory girls whom they married on embarkation from Europe. The difficulties of persuading Portuguese males to migrate was multiplied "a thousand times" with the Portuguese woman (Duffy, 1959: 80ff.). Initial attempts of the Portuguese, with the shipment of twelve women to Angola in 1595, had been followed by such sporadic efforts as the shipment of thirteen prostitutes into Mozambique in 1782, accompaniment of governors by their wives in 1610 and then not again until the last quarter of the nineteenth century, or the occasional shipment of orphans. In 1810 a traveler noted that there were few European women on the Zambezi, most of them pipe-smoking, sallow, thin, slovenly; many had died in childbirth (Salt, 1816: 45). Mozambique remained practically devoid of European women, and only two were noted in Lourenço Marques in 1887. The contemporary phe-nomenon of a stable white population and a noticeable European female population were yet to come.

Meanwhile Goanese and other Indo-Portuguese came to trade or fight in Mozambique, often wed African women, and became associated with the prazos so that by the nineteenth century, most prazeiros, through marriage, were partly Indo-Portuguese.[22] An example of this phenomenon is the Cruz dynasty whose founder, Nicolau Pascoal da Cruz, either an Indo- or Siamese-Portuguese, settled in the Zambezi as sergeant of an Indian *sepoy* (soldier) company, married the half-caste Luisa da Costa, proprietress of several large prazos, and expanded the boundaries of his wife's prazos into Massangano, the largest estate in Mozambique. Daughters of the line, duly baptized, were the means by which the estates at first were expanded and power solidified. Thereafter, they disintegrated, but despite their decline and penuriousness, the Cruz family name endured until 1887 when the last family survivors were lost in a Zambezi war campaign.

The Portuguese continued the plan of passage of prazos to the eldest daughter on conditions that she marry a Portuguese and that grants of prazos be made as dowries to orphan girls. But the disease environment, harder work than what they were accustomed to, and other harsh conditions made these tribal plantations fatal to European women, and official suggestions to improve their situations included enforcement of inheritance laws. However, if no daughters were available, the land could be granted to a poor Portuguese male on the condition that he marry an African women within one year (Vasconcellos e Cirne, 1890: 26-7). In an effort to revitalize the prazo system in the last decades of the nineteenth century, the Portuguese established concessionary companies that they hoped would be successful enough to encourage settlement of European families.

The same problems of colonization and settlement plagued Angola, which, far more than Mozambique, had suffered severe disruptions because of the slave trade. Most European inhabitants lived in the interior either at military stockades or on landed "estates" used to supply them with slaves. For nearly four centuries, until 1900, colonization was nearly impossible, and the only two occupation centers were Luanda and Benguela, coastal cities that owed their existence to the slave trade. Luanda was somewhat more than an entrepôt for slaves and the provincial capital, for it was the only "white" city south of the Sahara. Despite the decay in which nineteenth-century travelers found it, Luanda still reigned as "the only city in Africa" (Kingsley, 1899: 284), in European terms, of course. In 1799 population in the interior numbered only seventy-eight whites, including five women; Benguela by 1845 had 600 houses and 2,418 people, of whom 2,200 were African, half of whom were slaves, 179 mulattoes, thirty-eight white men, and one white woman (*Annaes Maritimos e Coloniaes*, 1844-1846: 161; Duffy, 1959: 96; Hammond, 1966: 39). Even in 1902 there were scarcely more than a hundred white women in Luanda, all but eight of whom were wives of criminals deported to Angola. Most Portuguese males married African women or mulattoes and lived with their families and slaves in their own tribal-rural areas, concerned very little for the development of any urbanized communities.

After some decades of intermittent attempts by Portugal to establish permanent settlements, the colonies eased their own patterns of slow but steady growth. After the establishment of the *Estado Novo* (New State) begun in Portugal in 1926 by Antonio Salazar, a more concerted effort was made, and the government encouraged Portuguese women to accompany their husbands to Africa.

The European population in Angola in 1960 was approximately 172,529 white and 53,932 mestiços of a total of 4.83 million. Mozambique counted some 97,300 white, 31,500 mestiços, and 19,300 Asians of a total 6.58 million. Mestiços, or persons officially categorized as having at least one of four grandparents from a race different from others—usually a European father or grandfather—comprised only 0.5 percent of the population. This is a different perspective on the supposedly widespread miscegenation but one explained by the fact that Africans and Europeans settled in different areas so as to discourage contact. Africans lived in northern and southern coastal areas, dwelling primarily in the country in villages and hamlets of related kin groups with relatively fixed ethnic populations. Most Europeans, despite government encouragement to go to agricultural areas, settled in urban areas. Tensions have risen because more Africans have been moving to cities and settling in crowded suburbs, particularly around Lourenço Marques and Beira.

There were 109 women for every 100 men in the 1960 census in Mozambique. The ratio for Africans alone was 110 women for every 100 men due to the migration of African males, particularly those between twenty and fourty-four years of age, to mines and other jobs in South Africa and Rhodesia. In areas where urbanization, commercial farming, and general economic development were highest, men outnumbered women, overwhelmingly so among Europeans, Chinese, and Indians, most of whom had migrated without their families. Among Europeans in 1960 there were 100 men to 81 women; for Chinese 100 to 85; and for Indians 100 to 76; while in the mestiço population women were 102 to 100 men (*Recenseamento geral. Portugal,* 1964: 9ff.; *Anuario Estatístico. Moçambique,* 1964: 30-43; AHMoz, 1969: 45, 15, for the above and information in general on Angola and Mozambique).

As the census figures indicate, the bulk of Portuguese Africa's population is indigenous African, primarily Bantu ethnolinguistic groups. The two most important of Portugal's five overseas provinces, which altogether total 7 percent of the land area in Africa and whose combined population of some 13 million equals about 5 percent of Africa's population, have been Mozambique, the most populous, and Angola, the largest in size. In these two areas, especially Mozambique, there are distinct differences between Africans and Portuguese and also between the two major African cultural groups as divided north and south of the Zambezi River.

Among the northern Mozambique tribes, for example the Makua, Makonde, and Yao, who are agriculturalists, villages are composed of persons who recognize descent from a common female. There is scarcely any incidence of bride price, although a male performs service in his wife's mother's garden. Puberty rites are quite elaborate, involving a girl's artificial defloration and, among the Yao, excision of the clitoris. However, no value is attached to virginity among any northern groups, a somewhat surprising fact considering their long contact with and assimilation of Arabo-Islamic customs (AHMoz, 1969: 61-3).

The southern tribes, such as the Shona, Nguni, Chopi, and Thonga, are pastoralists; the last two groups supply most of the mine labor recruits for South Africa. Among these tribes cattle are prestige, and descent, social status, and wealth are patrilineal. Unlike their northern cousins, the southern groups have a traditional bride price, value is placed on virginity, and girls go through puberty rites less elaborate than those of northern tribes, in which they are secluded and instructed in their duties as wives (AHMoz, 1969: 64-5).

In both the matrilineal and matrilocal north and patrilineal and patri-local south, the extended family, composed of two or more nuclear families united under one head by kinship ties, functions as a major economic unit and often forms a residential group that comprises a single village. Usually the senior male is head of the family, although inheritance of property and social position is determined by kinship.

In both north and south childbearing is desirable and female fertility is encouraged. However, childbearing is considered a contaminated affair and women must go some distance from the village for that purpose. Since a woman is not supposed to become pregnant for about two years after childbearing and since her husband is forbidden sexual relations with her for a long time, he is apt to take another wife in another village. Tradi-tionally, sexual intercourse was performed as a ritual religious act of purification by a husband and wife before specific important occasions. This may still be the case in certain areas (AHMoz, 1969: 73-4).

In matrilineal groups a marriage is made easily, dissolved easily, and is essentially a contract between two families. Although polygyny has been the preferred form of marriage, it has not been common, especially since Christian monogamous concepts have been introduced and, in African tradition, it has been less likely to occur in matrilocal than in patrilocal areas. Matrilineage and matrilocality have weakened considerably with the increased ability of village men to earn money and, consequently, to be freer from lineage strictures. Divorce is frequent but it is ameliorated greatly by the strength of matrilineal extended families, since at separation children go with their mother while husbands return to their maternal village where they retain prestige. In general, women in these matrilineal village cultures are fairly independent since they own house and fields and can initiate divorce.

Most of these patterns are reversed in patrilineal and patrilocal groups. Polygyny does occur among economic and social elites. In fact, among some tribes if women have sufficient money to pay the *lobalo* (bride price) they buy women whom they lend to their brothers or husbands for pro-creative purposes; then the female "husbands" claim the children for their own (AHMoz 1969: 73-9 passim).

Angola was the largest Portuguese African possession, but in 1960 it had a smaller population (about 5 million) although it had more whites (about 200,000). The predominant black population are Bantu language groups such as the Umbundu, Kimbundu, Kikongo, Chokwe-Lunda, and other mostly Umbundu-speaking peoples. Most populous are the Ovimbundu who comprise about 1.75 million of Angola's population. They formerly had a type of "double descent system" in which each individual belonged to a local patrilineal and a dispersed matrilineal group in which movable property was inherited (Edwards, 1962: 99). There were prohibitions on female contact with men outside of her married family (therefore little social contact between the sexes), and women were always under male guardianship. Now all of this is changed, and there is substantial male-female relationship, reversing all the previous patterns (Edwards, 1962: 99-104).

Traditionally chastity was expected from both male and female Ovimbundu before marriage, which occurred at about age twenty-two for men and eighteen for women, after parental consent but not by parental arrangement (Edwards, 1962: 115-6). Since the nuclear or elementary family has been of prime importance and the individual household has been essentially an independent unit, the wife does not have to contend with mothers-in-law or other women in her husband's family. Of late, and under European influence, close companionship between husband and wife has been developed as an ideal, a change from older days when even married men and women socialized in separate groups (Edwards, 1962: 19-20). Polygyny is preferred for children and for household help and is frequent among the Ovimbundu. Consequently problems arise for converts to Catholicism, which recognizes marriage as monogamous and indissoluble (Edwards, 1962: 123-4). Marriage is "the pivotal institution of the Umbundu kinship system," which brings about "the local concentration of kin which makes . . . a strongly woven community in which both husband and wife can live with relatives near at hand" (Edwards, 1962: 126). The conjugal bond is the closest social relationship between adults, while adultery is frowned upon (Edwards, 1962: 127).

Among Portuguese living in Africa, family remains a major economic and social institution, and in areas where Europeans and Africans have contact, particularly in coastal cities, the Portuguese nuclear family of husband, wife, and children is the basic unit. Polygamy is discouraged; marriage is monogamous, a sacrament, and its dissolution disapproved. Kin groups and extended families are important units, and as among Africans, valued for the communal and mutual cooperation and stability they connote. Portuguese-African marriages are rare, but in many cases Portuguese men follow Portuguese custom and do not involve themselves in activities considered the wives' purview. Her duties are fixed in overseeing child-rearing and household activities, with none of which the male is expected to help. In recent years many Portuguese women in Africa have taken outside jobs with or without husband's permission.

Marriage and family attitudes and values of African and European cultures in Portuguese Africa are changing and adjusting to each other. Portuguese values appear less flexible however; their women do not have the mobility of African women and are not so publicly visible as their African counterparts.

Among the Ovimbundu of Angola the wife can own her fields and her granary, and if the marriage is polygamous, then each wife also possesses her own (Edwards, 1962: 120). Women and men can and do share the work in almost all forms of agriculture, although beer brewing, cooking, maize pounding, and water and firewood gathering basically are woman's work (Edwards, 1962: 121). The Ovimbundu men, unlike in many other Bantu culture groups, not only help their women but also share ownership in fields with them.

Among African groups in northern Mozambique, women cultivate the fields, prepare food, are potters, repair and plaster huts, and care for children and preadolescent girls. Among the African patrilineal groups in southern Mozambique, in addition to household duties and because their men often migrate, females have taken over traditional male tasks. This has created tensions and distrust between women and men (AHMoz, 1969: 72, 75, 78). In 1963 of 3.4 million persons in the labor force between ten and fifty-nine years of age, about half were male and half female. In the country as a whole, "At any given time all but five per cent of the women and about half the men were engaged in subsistence agriculture" (AHMoz, 1969: 260). In urban areas most women were employed in domestic service, but of 610,000 persons who were urban wage earners, only 5 percent were female (AHMoz, 1969: 261).

Education is not one of Portugal's contributions to Africa. A royal decree of 1852 called for a training center in Mozambique for African girls, but in 1873 some 456 boys and only thirty-three girls were in school in Angola while Mozambique schools had similar proportions. By 1909 Mozambique contained only sixty-six primary schools, most of them run by missionaries; only eighteen were for girls (Duffy, 1959: 257-8, 368 n.27; Avila de Azevedo, 1945: 12; Mousinho de Albuquerque, 1934: II, 138-9; Jones, 1922: 224-7; Jones, 1926: 296-315). By 1957 there were only 85,000 students in Angola schools and 284,000 in Mozambique schools. The government paid lip service to equal education between the sexes in some areas. It established training schools for tribal leaders in 1948 wherein the eldest sons and daughters are given instruction together (Duffy, 1959: 315). But, generally speaking, in health, education, and welfare, women and girls receive the least of what is available.

Civil and political rights have been vague for all Portuguese Africans. In Mozambique the Rural Labor Code has provisos for pregnant women and nursing mothers. The Portuguese Women's Youth Organization founded for girls in 1942 is active in socialization processes. Women play a negligible role in politics in a country where only a few thousand Europeans, Europeanized Africans, and Indians are politically active.

In personal family rights, national laws still vary according to custom and practice for African groups. For example, an Ovimbundu widow may remarry six months after her late husband's funeral. Divorce and official separations are common; wives can leave their husbands for any reason, and a formal divorce ceremony exists. Divorce is not approved of for Catholics, but Protestant church courts grant divorces on certain grounds.

Guiné-Bissau, the Cape Verde archipelago, and the equatorial Atlantic islands of São Tomé and Príncipe have been important primarily as bolsters to Portugal's persistence of empire. Guiné-Bissau (Portuguese Guinea), until the late nineteenth century part of the Cape Verde administrative unit, was divided into *concelhos*. Guiné-Bissau's population is twice the average density of Africa in general but, like the continent's population, is basically rural. The twenty or more local tribes, the religious division of a Muslim north and animist south, and the overlay of *crioulo*, dialect of Cape Verdian mestiço immigrants who until the late 1920s had comprised the only non-African residents, has created an ethnic diversity and a geographical unit least affected by Portuguese influence. A disease environment for whites kept them away until the 1930s, and of the 500,000 or so population of today only 8,000 are non-African, mostly Syrian and Lebanese (Texeira da Mota, 1954: 239; AGU, 1967: 48-9). Thus, European values and institutions have had little influence in Guiné-Bissau.

The Cape Verde islands, now divided into twelve concelhos, were uninhabited when discovered in mid-fifteenth century. They soon were populated with peoples from the Guinea coast, Guiné especially, and from Portugal. This simultaneous introduction of two ethnic stocks contributed to a unique Cape Verdian population, a racially mixed society of some 225,000, with cultural patterns reminiscent of rural Portugal (Abshire and Samuels, 1969: 26). On all the islands except Santiago, mestiços are at least 60 percent of the population, but miscegenation and cultural assimilation have been least complete on Santiago, traces of African culture being more prominent there than elsewhere. African heritages, as among the Senegambians of Guiné-Bissau, are of the Sudanic-Negro family rather than the Bantu. Child-raising techniques and female participation in economic and other public activities are part of the Negro tradition. Polygamy is common, especially among lower classes, official marriage rare, and female independence a normal behavior pattern.

A unique African institution that governs the social life of Santiago Island is the *tabanca,* a mutual assistance society, the headquarters of which serves as religious center, social hall, "hospital," and prison; the head usually is a king or chief (Miranda, 1963: 49). A queen controls the activities of all the women and young girls and directs them in welfare activities; this especially is reminiscent of the *candomblé* groups of Brazil, which have their *maes* and *filhas.*

São Tomé (60,000) and Príncipe (5,000) together comprise the smallest Portuguese unit in Africa, each one a concelho. They show not even a shadow of their former importance as major entrepôts of the slave trade. Some 5,000 inhabitants are creole, racially mixed descendants of Portuguese, Spanish, French, Jewish, and West African slaves who live in and around São Tomé city. There are only about 1,000 Europeans and a few thousand *angolares,* descendants of shipwrecked runaway slaves. The remainder of the population consists of African contract laborers from other parts of Portuguese Africa brought in for plantation work (Tenreiro, 1961: 182, 184, 212). As in Cape Verde, there is a Luso-African culture, but home construction, diet, dress, institutions, and values mainly are Portuguese.

These three territories, together about the size of Portugal with a population of 800,000, have contributed little other than reinforcement of Portugal's national ego. Cultural values of African Negro peoples are indistinct, except in isolated pockets and, for the most part, Portuguese values regarding women are emulated by the mixed creole people. But more insignificant than Portugal's African islands are the enclaves of Africa belonging to Spain.

SPAIN IN AFRICA:
THE DREGS OF EMPIRE

Spanish Africa is relatively insignificant, scarcely mentioned in scholarship. The first Spanish institute for African studies was not established until 1945, and not until then did Spain seriously undertake research on African peoples.

Spanish Sahara, otherwise known as Spanish Morocco and Mauritania, was a possession of 11,000 square miles, but one of limited social penetration and more primarily of military strategic importance. The primarily pastoral Arabic and Berber Muslims comprise almost the total population, and little intercourse of any kind has characterized Spanish-Moroccan relations, intermittent in themselves since late fifteenth century. The population, never more than 1 million, is 92-94 percent orthodox Muslim, 6.5 percent Spanish and Moroccan Catholic, and the remainder Moorish Jews. The Rif Berbers comprise about half of the Muslim population and retain their language, customs, and nomadic way of life, while the coastal, sedentary Berbers have assimilated more Arabic and Islamic characteristics and make up the agriculturalists in rural areas and merchant groups in the towns.

Spanish western Sahara, including the enclave of Ifni and main colony of Rio de Oro, comprises 100,000 square miles of Spain's 170,000 square miles of African territory and is mostly desert. Spaniards have been there since the fifteenth century and declared it a protectorate in 1885. The 37,000 residents of Rio de Oro and 35,000 of Ifni are engaged mainly in viticulture, horticulture, grain growing, and fishing. There are about 31,000 Arabs and nomadic Arabized Berbers.

A final possession, the islands of Corisco, Great and Little Elobey, Fernando Po, and Annobón, and the continental settlement of Rio Muni comprise Spanish Guinea in sub-Saharan Africa. A timber, cocoa, copra, foodstuffs agriculture, rubber, and coffee-producing area, Fernando Po's population (40,000) is more important than the larger but less developed Muni River settlement. Of its 200,000 residents, only about 1.5 percent are Spanish or European. Of all the Spanish African possessions only Spanish Guinea has much of a "black" population, consisting of Bantu and Sudanic-Negro families. A considerable mixed group of Negro and Spanish-Portuguese exists on coastal areas, and these people form the bulk of local labor groups (OHI, Morocco, Canary Islands, and Spanish Africa, 1965). There has been little interaction between Spaniards and local populations of Spanish Africa. By and large, females and families fall within the purview of whatever religious and ethnic groups they comprise and their social systems.

The female's role in Iberian African societies has remained relatively traditional, either African or Iberian. The female's position inherently is linked with class, race, and the double standard as applied by and for whites and males. It is still concubinage that is accepted, not intermarriage. In Angola recently only twenty-five mixed marriages were recorded, a few more in Mozambique. Of the twenty-five, one was black and white; four mulatto and black; twenty mulatto and white (Mondlane, 1969: 51). In almost all miscegenation cases the male is Iberian because relations between a white woman and a black man are disapproved.

What is in store for Ibero-African women with independence (Guiné-Bissau, 1973; Mozambique, 1974; Angola, 1975) is not known. For the moment Africa still remains Iberia's black mother.

NOTES

1. For extensive sources on earliest Africa to European contact see bibliographic citations and essays in Pescatello, forthcoming, and Pescatello, 1975.

2. Pescatello, forthcoming, and Pescatello, 1975 and the works of John Fage and Basil Davidson cited therein.

3. Until the discovery and use of quinine in the nineteenth century to counter fevers, only a few Europeans got inland.

4. Radcliffe-Brown and Forde, 1964: 1-85, and sources cited therein are useful for matrilineage and matriarchies. Also consult the African Institute Series of Oxford University Press.

5. Junod, 1913; Earthy, 1935; Barnes, 1931; and Boas, 1923: 41-51, for the following information.

6. The major linguistic families of sub-Saharan Africa are Bantu and Sudanic (Negro). Herskovits and others have determined that while there are hundreds of languages within those two families and such diversity among them that when spoken they are not intelligible to any one not of the specific language, nonetheless all of the languages of a family are structurally and idiomatically consistent. Thus, when people from one part of Africa meet elsewhere they could still develop a communications system within their linguistic family group which, it is being argued, was the case in the Americas. See Greenberg, 1966: 38, and other Greenberg works.

7. Confirming published documentation of this were my OHI in Brazil, December 1969-February 1970, with the *pae do santo* of a major candomblé house, Deoscoredes Santos and his wife, anthropologist Juanita Elbein. It is unusual for a male to hold this position. Didi inherited his from his mother and he and Juanita have extensively researched in Nigeria and Dahomey tracing the "authenticity" of his cult house to Africa. Generally, females are dominant as heads of Afro-Brazilian "cults."

8. Slaves refer here to the pre-European extensive slave trade among Africans. On Akan-speaking peoples see Rattray, 1927; Herskovits, 1938; Meyerowitz, 1952; and Klein, 1969.

9. Crowder, 1966: 49 passim for Sudanic-West Africa states.

10. Herskovits noted that "polygyny . . . not only in West Africa but over the entire African continent, is the rule, an institution" (Herskovits, 1971: 25-6). Plural marriage was represented spatially by several households; each belonged to a separate wife, grouped in a single compound headed by the oldest male. That compound was joined to several others, and all the inhabitants of joint compounds equaled an extended family. Each woman cohabited with her husband for a particular period of time, usually a week as figured in the culture. For example, in Dahomey a week was equivalent to four of our days. "Though a person in most cases belongs to his father's family, the intimate personal relationship is that between a mother and her own children" (Herskovits, 1971: 26). A general rule of descent in most African societies historically has been that descent is counted from either the male or female side and *not,* as in Europe, from both.

11. See Vansina, 1968: 3-45 passim; for a discussion of Kongolese history. Also, see Axelson, 1962-; the Section Archives: Biblioteque-Documentation, Kinshasa; IFAN, Dakar; NA, Ibadan.

12. See Duffy, 1959: 5-23 passim for a fuller discussion.

13. Cited in Cadornega, 1940-1942: II, 529. Some Portuguese women, married to Catholic Dutch or Flemish men, were allowed to remain in Luanda after Salvador da Sa captured it in 1648.

14. See paragraphs item 26 in appendix, Boxer, 1965. These are from the archive of the senate of Luanda, Codex 499, "Registo de Degregados." I was allowed to look through these materials in Luanda but could not reproduce them. Other materials I saw verified Boxer's patterns for other years.

15. See Alvares, 1961; Beccari, 1903-1917; works cited in Rotberg, 1965: 72-3, notes 14-18; and Beshah and Aregay, 1964.

16. On this aspect consult Axelson, 1962-.

17. See Strandes, 1961, and Boxer and Azevedo, 1960, for detailed information on Portuguese-Arab city-states encounters.

18. On the prazo see Vilhena, 1916; *Relatorio . . . dos prazos de Moçambique,* 1889; Texeira Botelho, 1936; Almeida de Eça, 1953-1954; Lobato, 1957; Isaacman, 1969; Isaacman, 1972.

19. Lobato, 1962: 96-116; Johnson, 1972: 203-14, for standard and revisionist examination of the donatary system.

20. See Kuczynski, 1936, and Curtin, 1969, on Muslim and Judaeo-Christian conduct of the trade.

21. Curtin, 1971: 89-90, says two men for every woman were bought and sold in the slave trade.

22. See Torres Texugo, 1839: 38-9, Mousinho de Albuquerque, 1934, passim; Texeira Botelho, 1936; Almeida de Eça, 1953-1954; and Vilhena, 1916 for accounts of Indians in Africa, and the Cruz's.

5 AMERINDIA: THE ANTEBELLUM SOUTH

The Western Hemisphere became the cornerstone of Spanish and Portuguese imperial ambitions. Nowhere else was Iberian culture so deeply transplanted. Because the Iberian story in the Americas has been so complex and consequential, it will be discussed by spatial and time segments. This chapter focuses primarily on the forms and substance of Amerindian family and female life on the eve of discovery and conquest.[1]

Peoples with whom the Iberians established contact in the Western Hemisphere lived in what is today the Caribbean, Central America, Mexico, the continental land mass of South America, and sections in North America peripheral to these areas. Ethnographers and archaeologists have divided these Amerindian cultures into five categories: marginal hunting and gathering tribes; tropical forest and savanna peoples; circum-Caribbean cultures; Andean civilizations; and Mexico-Middle America groups.[2] They were highland, coastal, riverine, and plains cultures, and each enjoyed differences that were integral to their sociocultural milieux and that greatly affected relationships between conquered and conqueror. Differences between Amerindian groups in population, settlement styles, social and political organization, religion, economy, and wealth also determined the status of their females.

The Hispanic conquest (1492-1532) quickly eliminated circum-Caribbean cultures through a combination of ecological and economic disasters, more systematically and juridically countered the Aztéc and Mayan civilizations as well as their subject cultures, and swiftly subjugated the highly centralized and intensely personalized Inca political structure (Gibson, 1948, 1952, 1964, 1966; Sauer, 1969; Vaillant, 1953; Morley, 1946). Many practices and powers of Amerindian women disappeared after conquest. Others were absorbed into the newly bastardized matrix contributing to the varied orientation of new American societies. In this chapter basic social, economic, and political structures of the five Amerindian types will be examined to determine where change as a result of contact seems to have occurred or where basic Amerindian patterns have persisted, and why.

MARGINAL HUNTING AND
GATHERING TRIBES

Tribes of nonfarming Indians customarily have been classified as marginal or peripheral to main centers of culture, remote from inventive and more "complex" cultures.[3] At the time of discovery these nomadic tribes were different from other Amerindians in their display of simpler life styles, lack of technology, existence in an unproductive environment, and a sparse population whose quest for food was central to the organization of their societies.

Space dictates a selective examination among these myriad tribes of female life. The Chono, Alacaluf, Yahgan, and Ona have been chosen. They occupied areas of the Argentine pampas and the Chilean archipelago, one of two major area sources on the myth of matriarchal domination. In Chono, Alacaluf, and western Yahgan societies the elementary family was the basic sociopolitical and economic unit; among the Ona, eastern Yahgan, and aboriginal Pampean and Patagonian groups exogamy was the rule. Recent ethnographic analysis has indicated that these marginal groups had to have maximum flexibility to survive; therefore bilateral social organizations occurred.

The Chono, called canoe people because of the mode of transport they used to traverse their 300-mile strip of "land" in the southern Chilean archipelago, were in precontact association with the Araucanians, who raided the Chono for women and children (Cooper, 1946: 47-54). Shellfish were the principal commodity, and females dove for sea urchin, searched for shellfish and, in general, gathered the food in a competitive environment. There is uncertainty as to whether the Chono were monogamous or polygamous, but it seems that women participated in ritual observance practices of these families (Garcia, 1889:42; Byron, 1768:145-6; Campbell, 1747:61-2).

In the archipelago along the Chilean coast from the Gulf of Penas to islands west of Tierra del Fuego, Alacaluf women also were shellfish gatherers. Polygamy was common but in any sexual relationship the onus of misbehavior was on women, who were liable to beatings by their husbands should they be found unfaithful (Bird, 1946: 55-79). Although they were allowed to attend ceremonies, they were relegated to either end of the ritual house while men and boys occupied the central areas.

In the mountainous islands at the end of the Andean chain near Cape Horn, Yahgan women also carried the major economic responsibility of supplying fish and water (Cooper, 1946a: 81-106). Girls were wed at fifteen or sixteen years, boys at seventeen to nineteen years in primarily monogamous circumstances (Gusinde, 1937: 633). Although in theory the man was the head of his family, his absolute authority was greatly reduced by woman's power through child rearing, food gathering, and canoe managing, major economic levers.

Woman's position in these societies seems one of respected member of family and community, one with a fair measure of mobility and independence, albeit with societal strictures. Female adultery was more disapproved than was male adultery. Yet both sexes enjoyed rights to ownership of food, huts, canoes, and other items belonging to the biological family. The female role as food provider was a crucial one in these societies, and it would appear that the sexual division of labor was far more equal than in other Amerindian societies.

The Chono, Yahgan, and Alacaluf usually were monogamous although forms of polygamy, such as simultaneous marriage to a widow and her daughter, were allowed. Marriage, sexual dichotomy, and age status recognition were sources of ceremonies. Among the Yahgan, and to a lesser extent the Alacaluf, sex distinctions broke down. During initiation ceremonies among the Alacaluf, for example, women were admitted to ceremonies but only after being humiliated by a ritual water dousing.

Ona women also enjoyed a respected status in family and community and a lage measure of independence. The Ona depended entirely upon wild foods, and division of labor was almost entirely on a sexual basis: men hunted, fished, and made weapons while women controlled all other work related to the household (Cooper, 1946b: 107-25).

Wives usually were taken from distant areas and, although monogamy prevailed, polygamy and the levirate were common.[4] Although the Ona, like other gathering tribes, observed girls' puberty with simple rites and a feast, the full-fledged initiation of boys into manhood was the major ceremony. This most important Ona social and religious function, the *klóketen* initiation and men's rite had two basic concepts: first, it was a male device to keep women in subjection by supernatural hocus-pocus (corresponding to a Yahgan rite, the *kina*), and second, it was a boy's initiation rite in which secrets were revealed only to men, male shamans threated women and children, and strong distinctions were made between the sexes (Cooper, 1946b: 120-1). Similar, too, were female activities among the Tehuelche, Puelche, and Poya cultures of the Pampean hunter groups whose territories extended 600 miles north to south from Córdoba and the La Plata river mouth to Rio Colorado and Rio Negro (Cooper, 1946c: 127-68). However, women of certain tribes, such as the Puelche, served as "concubine slaves," being drudges or adopted wives (d'Orbigny, 1835-1847: II, 270).[5]

Generally speaking marginal groups were composed of innumerable localized families that consisted of a husband, and one or more wives, usually obtained through purchase and the levirate. This applied to localized patrilineal bands of the Ona of Tierra del Fuego, the numerous Ge, many migratory families of the Alacaluf and independent family villages of the Tucano. Most rites were limited to men. In some groups, such as the Huarpe, women sometimes were forbidden to see their husbands in bacchanalian festivities. Wives were beaten in some of these cultures (Cooper, 1946c; Métraux and Baldus, 1946 on the Guayaki and later Tehuelche). In some groups young girls married elderly men, and mature women wed younger boys. As widows, some women—for example the Guayaki—often had to maintain a longer mourning period than men (Métraux and Baldus, 1946: 442).

In social, political, and economic considerations there are variances. In these marginal societies in which there was no separate set of governmental institutions, it is difficult to determine what control or power women enjoyed. Women acted in "medical" capacities, particularly as midwives. But they had little control over inheritance procedures. Their secondary importance in significant social and religious events was paralleled by their "typical" occupational household duties, as was the case among the Timbira (Lowie, 1946b: 481).

In many societies in which seafood was a major food resource females had more privileged roles (Steward and Faron, 1959: 413-24). In Chaco societies, whether hunters, gatherers, fishers, or farmers, girls had initiation rites, sexual liberty, and were promiscuous at their own urgings. Abortion and infanticide were common, especially among the unmarried, and divorce was easy and initiated by wives. Thus, there were variations in roles, treatment, position, and attitudes regarding women in these thousands of localized, marginal societies.

It was possible for Europeans to overrun these Amerindians. Most local cultures withdrew into cover of forests, islands, and plains remote from European contact, and there they remain. A few were absorbed into European cultures, the rest annihilated. We know very little about them, but that information seems to confirm that minimal contact of these groups with Iberians resulted in little change for either Amerindians or Iberians.[6] Rather, contact forced continuity, through isolation, of Amerindian lifeways.

THE TROPICAL FOREST
AND SAVANNA

The tropical forest area usually designates the vast Amazon region, the selva, savanna, and forest.[7] Tropical foresters were village groups with a subsistence economy. They cultivated tropical root crops such as bitter manioc, manufactured pottery, and had extensive mobility by utilizing rivercraft on waterways.

Tropical forest people comprise the Arawakan, Cariban, and Tupí-Guarani who are spread over five areas: coastal and Amazonian Tupi; Matto Grosso and eastern Bolivia; Montana and the Bolivian East Andes; western Amazon basin; and the Guianas and left Amazon Basin tributaries. Arawakan ethnolinguistic groups are found mostly north of the Amazon, Cariban also north of the Amazon and in the Guianas, and the Tupí-Guarani speakers were widespread south of the Amazon.

In general, tropical forest cultures are best understood in the context of their adjustment to humid, hot, lowland rain forests. Their culture history can be inferred only from distribution of linguistic groups and their co-relative cultural features. These linguistic groups were primarily horticulturalists whose crop supply was supplemented by hunting and fishing, both culturally prescribed masculine roles. Families were based on kinship and community groups in which environment-induced subsistence techniques for food gathering precluded the accumulation of surpluses to support full-time occupational specialists, multivillage states, or class-structured societies.

Girls were married soon after puberty and in some cases were given to grown men, who then went to live in the girl's parents' homes (Métraux, 1948: 87; Wagley and Galvão, 1948: 143). In many groups it was frowned upon for girls to engage in prepuberty sexual practices, but in other tribes, such as the Tupinambá, it was common except for a girl betrothed to a chief (Métraux, 1948: 116). Female captives often were taken as secondary wives or concubines, and there were longer mourning periods required of females than for males than the reverse.

Exogamy was observed by all these groups. Many were patrilocal; others, such as the Tenetehara and Tapirape, were matrilocal, requiring residence, in the female's home for long periods of time (Wagley and Galvão, 1948; 1948a). Most groups, such as the Tupinambá, also were patrilineal with the exception of Guiana societies, which were matrilineal.

There were many others in which emphasis fell more heavily on the maternal line of the kinship structure. Others, such as the matrilocal

Caraja, where both lines were important, gave slightly more importance
to the female as determinant of village citizenship, adoption, and closest
affectional ties, while moiety membership and chief, priest, and food-
divider offices were determined patrilineally (Lipkind, 1948: 186). In
fact, this was one of the few Amerindian societies in which women probably
functioned as chief.

Tupí groups were predominant in what is today Brazil, parts of the
Guianas, Paraguay, and fringes of the Bolivian Andes. The two major
ethnolinguistic Tupí groups were the Tupinambá and the Guaraní. In
Tupinambá society everything hinged on relative social positions of each
female and male in Tupinambá tribal hierarchies (Fernandes, 1948:
244-6). In social and political organization there is very little evidence
that women had any administrative duties, rights, or prerogatives of
political office, or functioned as shaman. There was a marked separation
of the sexes by division of labor and by segregation of men into a special
house. This latter form, especially, was a feature of tribes of the Upper
Xingú. Political institutions scarcely were developed since the communities
had few functions requiring extensive civil control. Also, the female seems
to have played a secondary role in religious activities although, with the
exception of the Trumai, a linguistically isolated group, women participated
in dancing festivities and frequented village center activities (Lévi-Strauss,
1948: 339, 342-3). Political and religious power, however, was in the hands
of a male gerontocracy (Fernandes, 1948: 271).

On the economic level sex differences entailed occupational specialization. In general, women dominated the economic and household sphere.
They planted, weeded, and harvested; grated and boiled manioc; netted
fish; carried and made hammocks; often were weavers and potters; and
in general controlled production and distribution of the above with the
exception of tobacco cultivation, which was reserved to men (Lévi-
Strauss; 1948: 324; Steinen, 1894; Métraux, 1948b: 388, 1948e: 695).
In some groups husbands were bound to carry their wives and their own
goods while wives poked fun at husbands as they struggled with their
loads (Nimuendajú, 1948b: 292). In general, among Brazilian Amerindians
woman was the principal food provisioner and crafts technician. Upon
her devolved responsibilities for production and utilization of basic
necessities of the communal society; Tupinambá women "work much
more than do their men" (Fernandes, 1948: 113).

Nonetheless, despite such importance in societal activities Brazilian
Amerindians "at the time of discovery were still in the stage of relative
male parasitism, with a consequent overburdening of the female" (Freyre,
1964: 78-160 passim). Amerindian women, with whom Portuguese first
came into contact along Bahian and other coastal shores, were used to
offering themselves to men and thus did so to the Europeans,

rubbing themselves against the legs of males for a comb or a broken
mirror . . . naked . . . unable to say no to anyone, but they themselves
provoke and importune the men, sleeping with them in hammocks; for
they hold it to be an honor to sleep with the Christians. (Padre Anchieta,
in Freyre, 1964: 83ff.)

Indian women reflected a societal attitude that it was most desirable
"to bear sons belonging to the superior race, since according to the ideas
current among them, it was only parentage on the paternal side that
counted" (Capistrano de Abreu, in Freyre, 1964:82). Mothers were "no
more than so many bags . . . in which children are created," and for such
the men used "their sisters' daughters *ad copulam* without any scruple"
(Padre Anchieta, in Freyre, 1964: 92). But Amerindian societies viewed
the exchange of husbands and wives as a natural act; thus there was little
concern about Portuguese exchanging one woman for another since
Indian males often had numerous "wives" whom they freely acquired or
discarded.

As Amerigo Vespucci noted in a letter to Lorenzo de 'Medici:

The Indians take as many wives as they like, and the son has intercourse
with the mother, and the brother with the sister, and the male cousin
with the female cousin, and the one who is out walking with the first
woman whom he meets. (Freyre, 1964: 91-2.)

Guaraní is the name given the Tupí ethnolinguistic groups of the
southern Brazilian coast who migrated to Paraguay and today are the
dominant ethnic group there. Guaraní social organization was based on
the extended family (Schaden, 1960: 72). Guaraní had the same subsistence economy and social structure of nonlocalized patrilineal lines,
and the role of women was essentially that in other similar societies.

Through historical and field documentaion of the Services and
Schaden the Guaraní are among the few Amerindian groups whom scholars
have been able to follow through conquest and postconquest culture
change (Service, 1954: for Guarani of Paraguay; Schaden, 1960: for
Guaraní of Brazil). The Guarani have changed from subsistence to a
sporadic cash crop economy; from polygamous to consensual and matrilineal family; from interfamilial and interpersonal kin patrilineage to
compadrazgo; and from a Guaraní culture to a lower-class Hispanic mode
of life.[8] Thus, for the Guaraní we are able to document a profound revolution in lifeways and extensive acculturation (Schaden, 1960: 179-83).

What is observable for the Guaraní and other Tupian and tropical
forest peoples is absorption, assimilation, or loss of cultural baggage
depending on the degree and style of contacts with outsiders. Those who

did not ally with the Spanish and Portuguese and become somewhat Hispanicized, as with the Guaraní, or Lusoized, as with Tupian peoples in southern Brazil, simply vanished into the tropical forests, some in search of the land of their grandfathers, others to retain their own lifeways in the face of external pressures.

CIRCUM-CARIBBEAN PEOPLES

In addition to marginal and tropical forest peoples with whom Iberians first came in contact were chiefdoms of the circum-Caribbean. Early Spanish chronicles describe these societies as warlike states ruled by priests and military and, unlike marginal and tropical forest people, sharply divided into social classes. Ethnographically speaking, these chiefdoms, at their strongest represented by the Chibcha (Muisca), reflected the interdependence of population density, surplus production, and religious military activities. These chiefdoms included the area of Central America, Colombia, Venezuela, and the Antilles (Hernandez de Alba, 1948; 1948a; Kirchoff, 1948; Métraux and Kirchoff, 1948; Johnson, 1948).

No societies were so "kaleidoscopically varied" as the chiefdoms, for their cultures combined elements of the tropical forest, Andean, and Mesoamerican groups. They differed from marginal and tropical forest people because they were based on surplus production that permitted social differentiation, but they shared features of village and community life. They resembled Andean and Mesoamerican high cultures in military, manufacturing, and religious patterns (Steward and Faron, 1959: 175, 178; Steward, 1948).

Circum-Caribbean chiefdoms were of two general subtypes: the militaristic states, which flourished in the northern Andes of Ecuador and Colombia and among many Central American groups, and the theocratic chiefdoms of the Greater Antilles, eastern Bolivia, and Venezuela. All were based on intensive farming in the highlands and semiarid lowlands. Subsistence on cultivated plants rather than animal foods and a high degree of food production allowed substantial populations that were serviced by well-developed transportation facilities. The chiefdoms supported a four-tiered class structure, although fixed social position was hereditary only in more organized states.

The Chibcha (Muisca) were the major groups of the military chiefdoms and displayed many elements, such as markets, types of human sacrifice, and forms of money, more common to Mesoamerica than to their Andean homeland. Among lower classes the kin group and its functions were organized patrilineally, but among upper classes there was a division: succession to office was matrilineal, inheritance of property was patrilineal.

Among military tribes with Mesoamerican characteristics, especially the Chorotega and Nicarao, commerce centered in markets. Men were forbidden entry to those markets, which were run by women and boys. Women of other areas, such as Cauca valley tribes, dominated weaving enterprises and also totally controlled a labor pool of all children under twelve, who were required to help them (Hernandez de Alba, 1948: 305, 311).

As in other cultures women were supplied to chiefs and other male officials as wives, servants, or in other serviceable capacities. Some tribal chiefs such as the Ancerma had as many "wives" as they could support while others, such as the Catio, were limited to twenty (Hernandez de Alba, 1948:317). Adultery by a woman was punished severely. It would appear that polygyny, polygamy, polyandry, the levirate, and the sororate—the marriage of one man to two sisters or to a woman and her daughter—were widespread. Stealing of women supposedly was a major purpose of warfare, and women captives served as wives, slaves, and concubines. Women in the presence of visitors were to be silent and also could be given to male visitors for an evening. Wives of dead men were passed on to other males as just so much other property.

Theocratic chiefdoms centered in Venezuela, north of the Orinoco, and the Greater Antilles. In Venezuela were the Lache, Chitarera, Arhuaco, and Timotean-speaking chiefdoms, while the Antilles was home to the Arawakans. The Antilles also sheltered two other cultural types: the hunting and gathering Ciboney and the tropical forest horticultural Carib villages. In most theocratic chiefdoms woman was regarded as an inferior and in some groups was treated as an expendable piece of marital property. Among some tribes with a developed class structure, such as those of northern Venezuela, chiefs sometimes had harems of 200 wives (Steward, 1948: 22). Among Caribs, captive wives were kept in slave status. The earliest missionaries and other observers recorded that "Carib" women exhibited unfamiliar language characteristics. This was because so many "Carib" women were, in fact, Arawak captives (Rouse, 1948a: 549). Thus the capture and concubinage of Amerindian women was a well-fixed pre-European pattern.

Some tribes were governed by female chiefs who kept both bondswomen and female servants. Generally, among the Arawak prerogatives were matrilineal, and women inherited high positions.

Columbus noted that women in these societies worked much harder than men (Rouse, 1948: 531). Females were responsible for and controlled the production and distribution of markets and commodities (Kirchoff, 1948: 457).

The Hispanic conquest resulted in a decline of some of these groups, an elimination of many, and the absorption of others at a pace more rapid than in most other culture contact areas. Female experience in family or society did not seem to change noticeably on point of contact.

MESOAMERICA: MIDDLE
AMERICA AND MEXICO

In this large sector of Mesoamerica, an anthropological term for all lands between Texas and the Panama Canal, dwelled two of the three "high civilizations" of pre-Columbian America, the Maya and the Aztec. The former occupied most of southern Mexico, Yucatán, Guatemala, and parts of present-day Honduras and Belize, while the latter were located primarily in central Mexico. While sharing similar culture traits of the region, the two cultures were different in language, history, state organization, and regional subdivisions. Maya-speaking peoples were diffused widely throughout Mesoamerica and had enjoyed 3,000 years of recorded history—oral, mythic, archaeological, and written. They had passed through several historical cycles, having gone from a powerful, unified theocracy to a civilization with pervasive cult symbolism, to theopolitical balkanization into numerous constantly warring city-states. The Aztecs spoke Utaztecan Nahuatl; they were relative newcomers to central Mexico; and they had a centralized confederate empire built on militarism that was politically and economically powerful. At the time of European conquest Mayan and Aztecan civilizations were separated from each other by smaller culture groups of Mixtec, Totonac, and Zapotec (Wauchope, 1970: 3).

The Maya

Maya hieroglyphics and pictorial manuscripts have left us with a more accurate record than any other in aboriginal America, and this has been supplemented by first-century conquest writings, particularly the *Relación de las cosas de Yucatán*, written in 1566 by Diego de Landa, second bishop of Yucatán. Perhaps the most brilliant pre-Columbian civilization, Mayan culture was based on an agricultural system that it spread, with adaptations, to neighboring environs from the Guatemalan highlands, into the lush Usumacinta Valley and, in its final period of decay, into the arid northern part of the Yucatán peninsula.

Yucatecan Maya society had a very important feature, the name group, or lineage, by which every person of either sex had a patronym—the name of a male in the group and, although not always, a matronym, their mother's name. Inheritance and descent were determined through both lines, although among these exogamous societies, inheritance of property and certain political positions was based almost exclusively on patrilineal descent. In Yucatán, caciqueships never could be inherited by women, and although the mother of a family might be highly respected. the father was undisputed household head, so noted in the matrícula of

Tixchel, 1569 (Scholes and Roy, 1968: 474). Three classes of nobles, commoners, and slaves composed a Maya society in which women's roles were culturally ascribed.

Marriageable ages were considered to be eighteen to twenty for boys and fourteen for girls. Juvenile marriage existed among some groups, and although there were instances of child spouses among both sexes, marriages where only the wife was younger seem to have been more frequent; in these cases girls were married at nine, twelve, and thirteen (Garcia v. Bravo, 1570-1571: folios 2117r-2128v). Landa had noted that in "olden times" Mayan girls were married at twenty, but after foreigners came they were married at twelve or fourteen. Monogamy was common among lower classes. Marriages were matrilocal, and female matchmakers arranged them, settled dowries, and engaged priests' services. The Maya had a "marriage in service" in which the man worked in his father-in-law's house for five years after his marriage. The Maya also had a practice comparable to the European feudal lord's *jus primae noctis*, at which the father-in-law or other male relatives had sexual relations with the bride during the first nights of her marriage "to prevent the bridegroom from being menaced by malign influence" (von Hagen, 1960: 49). Mayan wives usually bore from seven to nine children, of whom few survived. An example of European views on Mayan mothers is Bishop Landa's that "they were excellent nurses because the continued grinding of tortillas agitated their breasts, and they do not bind their breasts as we do in Spain and so they have large ones that have a good deal of milk" (von Hagen, 1960:41).

Landa also remarked on the seemingly extreme modesty of Maya women. To enforce this modesty, females were not allowed to eat with their menfolk. Men ate first, served by women, and later female family members ate together in seclusion (Morley, 1946: 33). This modesty was confined to females. Little girls from birth were required to wear *huipiles* (dress) while boys were allowed to play naked. Modesty did not carry into sexual relationships. Promiscuity by married or unmarried females was neither uncommon nor disapproved.

Prostitution, as in most social situations where sexual intercourse is of mixed availability, was not uncommon. It was the role of most older women or widows to introduce boys to sex. Young men brought public women to their quarters and "although the women received pay for it, (a handful of cacao beans), they were beseiged by such a great number of men—one after the other—that they were harassed almost to death" (von Hagen, 1960: 49).

Female slaves frequently were victims of religious sacrifices. Most often females of noble classes were captured, enslaved, and sacrificed, while commoners captured in war were put into slavery. It was said of women and slaves:

The children of slaves were also slaves like their parents until they were redeemed. He who made pregnant any slave women or married her, remained enslaved to the owner of such slave women, and likewise [the same was the case with a] women who married a slave (Roys, 1970;118).

In pre-Columbian Mayan societies religious worship and theocratic affairs were exclusively male preserves. There were only two female members of the Maya Pantheon, represented in the Codices: Ixchel, wife of the head chief Itzamma, goddess of childbirth and weaving, and Ixtab, the goddess of suicide (plate 29 in Morley, 1946: 240-1).

The bulk of the population, commoners, were freemen laborers. Daily economic tasks of females in this population stratum lasted from 3 A.M. until sunset. If the records are correct female activities have changed little in the past 500 years. In addition to household routine women worked to pay labor tribute, a common feature of Mayan societies.

A woman could not hold public office nor was she allowed entrance to any temples. She could divorce her husband, although divorce was frowned upon. Yet, neither ex-mate was prevented from remarrying. However, a widower could remarry a year after his wife's death but a widow was taboo bound not to remarry. Females' property rights were restricted; inheritance was patrilineal with sons dividing the estate, but under their mothers' guardianship.

Maya who did not integrate into mainstream Hispanic culture maintained a fairly consistent continuity in social, economic, political, and other lifeways from precontact to present times. Changes that have occurred have resulted from organic and environmental factors as well as from interethnic contact.

The Aztec

The "post-classic" period of "Aztec" history (900-1519 A.D.) is of particular concern. It marks a period of migration of "Aztec," Chichimeca, Otomi, and Tolteca peoples and a time of expansion and intensification of commerce, military activity, and urbanism (Gibson, 1964: 1-8 passim). Most information on the later post-classic period (an archaeological designation for this period of Mesoamerican history) derives from Aztec pictorial and oral sources committed to writing by Indian informants and Spanish scribes.

The major area of Aztec activity was the seventy-five by forty mile north-south, east-west valley of Mexico, the center of an extensive empire controlled by the island city-capital of Tenochtitlan-Tlatelolco. The valley's population at the time of encounter has been estimated variously as from 1 million to 3 million people, but due to epidemic disasters and prodigious labor enterprises that dense population was greatly depleted.[9]

Aztec civilization is thought to have been in full flower at the time of conquest, having developed intensive agriculture, huge public open-air markets, with restaurants, hotels, and cantinas, numerous neighborhood-type groceries, and also exhibiting a highly stratified class structure and extensive military apparatus. All were indications of a large nonfood-producing urban population and the full-time specializations of fully urbanized centers (Sanders, 1970: 86).

In some respects Aztec society did not differ remarkably from Mayan, particularly as regards women. Boys were eligible for marriage at twenty, girls at sixteen. Marriage was exogamous with consent of parents, bride, and bridegroom. Polygamy was prevalent, since the Aztec military machine consumed much manpower. However, the first wife took precedent in the household hierarchy, and only her children were allowed to inherit property. Concubinage was common, prostitution prevalent. Both utilized girls either sold by their destitute families or captured in war, although many young women sold themselves into slavery to acquire finery (Vaillant, 1953: 118-24).

Aztec legal-marital relations were worked out with care. Desertion was disapproved. A man could throw his wife out if she were sterile, ill tempered, or negligent. A wife could divorce her husband if he were negligent in supporting her or in educating their children or if he mal-treated his family. Since marriages were arranged between families, any neglect of his wife's rights by a husband was a breach of personal con-duct and social contract. Furthermore a divorcee could remarry, but if she were widowed she was bound to marry either her late husband's brother or a kinsman. Married women were expected to be faithful, just as young girls were bound to be virgin; but, a man could have relations with any other female, except a married women (Vaillant, 1953: 118-9). It was customary among Aztec aristocracy for the emperor to bequeath his concubines as wives to his loyal captains and chieftains. It also was a social courtesy among several Mexican tribes for families to present their daughters to guests or allies as a token of friendship; it was considered an honor should their daughters be kidnapped (Diaz, 1908-1916: II, 108; Gomara 1964: 74; Herrera y Todesillas, 1934: II, 340).

In other civic-legal areas females owned property, made legal contracts, utilized the courts, and may have held temple positions, even serving as priests or in other temple offices. In addition to legally recognized prerogatives, personal influence could be great. Women sometimes acted as regents when their sons were not of legal age to assume the chieftainship; also tribal alliances often depended upon the marriage of one chief's daughter or sister to another chief (Vaillant, 1953: 119).

Women were indispensable to the Aztec economy. An early chronicle noted that Indians required women "also as a means of profit, because they set all the women weaving cloth, making mantles and performing other work of this kind" (Motolinía, 1951: 202). Among lower strata of Aztec society women controlled production of market commodities and domestic functions, these roles being passed from mother to daughter.

Theoretically, Aztec society was "democratic," its economy based on communal ownership of productive property. A man attained stature through his contributions to the tribe and thus could win election as clan representative to the tribal council, be elected chief, or become a priest. These positions were not open customarily to women. But females were responsible for any variety of functions that contributed to the social and political rise of husband and family.

As with the Maya numerous Aztec and their subject peoples form what are the mestizo societies of present-day Mexico and Guatemala. Some were able to retain their Indian way of life, encouraged by the Mexican Revolution and particularly by Cardenas who, as president from 1934-1940, encouraged the reestablishment of such Indian institutions as the *ejido* land system. Some found stability and tenaciously have followed "the old ways." The female role in both family and society in these situations has changed little.

THE ANDEAN CIVILIZATIONS

Results of archaeological and other fieldwork indicate that three complex civilizations have existed in Andean areas from pre-Christian times: the Araucanian, the Chibcha (discussed in the circum-Caribbean section), and the Quechua-Aymara.[10] The Quechua, known to us by the title of their ruler, the Inca, were the most technologically advanced of the Andean cultures.

Araucanian territory extended from the Coquimbo valley through the alluvial valleys and mediterranean climate basin of central Chile. At the time of conquest, Araucanians numbered anywhere from a half to 1.5 million; that, in any case, was a fairly dense population. They resided in dispersed patrilineal hamlets located near cultivated fields, supported by agriculture. Although Araucanians shared a common culture and language, Spaniards referred to three distinct groups: Hilliche, Mapuche, and Picunche.

Araucanian and other Andean societies have yielded us little information on sociosexual activities. We do know that females were shaman. Among all Araucanian societies polygamy was prevalent. Commoners owned one or two wives while more prominent men had as many as thirty (Marino de Lovera, 1865: 124; Nuñez de Pineda y Bascuñan, 1863: 453; Brouwer, 1892: 81; Sors, 1921: 38-46, 39:180). Widows in polygamous households often became the property of their late husband's heir.

After conquest there persisted extensive warfare between Araucanians and Spaniards, a situation that ultimately affected almost all spheres of the aboriginal culture. As of 1866 the remainder of decimated Araucanians were put on reservations. During these centuries several changes occurred. Lands and goods, which had been patrilineally inherited, now are subject to less traditional and more controversial disposal. Farming, which heretofore had been the preserve of females, has been taken over by men, who no longer concentrate their energies on warfare. Men now dominate field and cash crops, while women are relegated to small-scale cultivation of vegetable gardens. Patrilineages have become larger, polygamy and wife grading have yielded to monogamy, virginity is no longer so highly prized, and premarital sex is unrestrained (although promiscuity is still frowned upon).

The Inca empire the Spaniards encountered was a young power, which, at its peak, stretched from southern Colombia through Ecuador, Peru, and western Bolivia into northern Chile. It controlled more than 3.5 million people, most of whom were descendants of numerous non-Inca highland and coastal cultures that had preceded the Inca (Quechua) empire. Incan society was thoroughly regimented and characterized by intensive cultivation, masterful construction techniques, and organizing genius in social, religious, and political affairs. The most widespread language in the Incan empire was Quechua, and it is still the major spoken tongue among many Bolivians and Peruvians.

The Inca state was a self-contained, noncommercial, and agricultural unit whose basic irrigation pattern, upon which it was able to build its power, had become relatively definite, at least by 1,000 A.D. The establishment of the Inca at the head of a centralized state was the result of conquests begun by Pachacuti in 1463 against the powerful northern coastal kingdom of Chimu, against states in the Cajamarca region, the Titicaca basin, on the Ecuadorian coast, and down across the Atacama desert to the Maule River in Chile (archaeological and oral history sources for 1438-1532 in Rowe, 1946). Consolidation of the empire throughout Peru, Ecuador, and the southern Andes was complete only by 1525, thus allowing only seven years of cohesion before Pizarro marched to Cajamarca.

Economically speaking, the highland peoples had a common basis. Primary subsistence was intensive agriculture, which was the major task of men, assisted by women (Bennett, 1946: 9). Women had responsibility, as usual, for all household work and as assistants to men in construction work (Larco Hoyle, 1946: 169). Also, Quechua had allocated all pastoral, weaving, and potting activities to women, who still perform those tasks.

Woman's position in Inca social and political organization is reflected by Quechua functional linguistic analysis (Rowe, 1946: 250, 284). For example, male names were *Apo* (lord), *Okapaq* (powerful, wealthy), *Yopanki* (honored), *Sinci* (strong); female names were *Qoylor* (star), *Ronto* (egg), *Oqlyo* (pure). The primary basis of social classification was sex, and while there was a special word for "husband," the only word for wife was "woman."

In the Inca's empire the number of wives a man had was an index of his wealth and prestige, and because women shared agricultural work extra wives made life easier for the family. Ordinary citizens married endogamously and were monogamous; nobles were privileged to take several wives, usually from other localities. The first wife was the principal one, but if she died none of the secondary wives could take her place although her husband could marry another principal wife. This was to prevent intrigue among secondary wives (Rowe, 1946: 256). Additional women were taken from commoners because of their usefulness in labor tasks, but were most often concubines.

Further discrimination existed among Incas in that a widow could not remarry unless she were inherited by her husband's brother. Sons could inherit their father's secondary wives; a man might receive wives from the emperor; or he might capture wives in war, all examples of the concept of woman as property.

The Inca *ayllu* (community) was a patrilineal kin group. When the emperor died his favorite women were expected to accompany him in death and often had to be intoxicated and strangled to ease their journey (Rowe, 1946: 255, 259).

Children were a great economic asset in Inca society, and it was expected that each woman would have many. While pregnant a woman worked at every job but was not expected to work in the field. Actually, women were assumed to have great strength and power. Female fertility was glorified in the Pachamama.

The Inca supported a group of consecrated women, the Mamakona, who were selected from the chosen women—so designated at the age of ten and organized into convents in Inca provincial capitals for services as concubines, wives, or sacrifices. The system of recruitment was based on the visit of an imperial official to each village where he classified all girls at the age of ten. Those of outstanding beauty and physical perfection were educated by the government, organized into convents, and then either given as wives to nobles and warriors, or as concubines of the emperor. A few were sacrificed on special occasions. Girls rejected as chosen women remained in their villages and married commoners (Rowe, 1946: 255ff.).

The other major language group in the highlands, the Aymará, was patrilineal and patrilocal. Each Aymará council was composed solely of men. Yet, as with practically all other Andean peoples, there is little specific information on systems prior to their encounter with either Inca or Iberian. We do know that women were considered as inferiors. This can be seen in economic, social, and political positions. Men were the ayllu and dance group leaders, potters, doctors, and sorcerers, even the "best" weavers and midwives (Tschopik, 1946: 541). The Aymará did not encourage women to participate in the exclusive basis of economy, fishing, and the occupation was confined to men. In agriculture, women planted while men plowed, spread fertilizer, threshed, and winnowed (Tschopik, 1946: 517).

As in other Andean cultures women who committed adultery were punished by death (Cieza de León, 1924: 314; Cooper, 1946d: 721; Nuñez de Pineda y Bascuñan, 1863: 332, especially for Araucanians). Women could not own land and had to be supported by males of their family. This situation no longer exists, for women can own land in the Aymará area of what is today Peru, a factor now blamed for the breakdown of the extended family. Women were required to accompany their male warriors in battle and assisted on communication lines (Bandelier, 1910: 88).

Today the major nation-state of the Andean culture, Peru, is a mestizo country that has derived lifeways from the Amerindian high civilizations and the Spanish. In Bolivia and parts of Ecuador and Chile, some major Indian groups live in situations relatively unchanged from precontact pasts. Indeed, Bolivia still is an Indian nation. While the mestizos or few "pure" Spanish dominate the economic and political life of that country Indians, particularly in the highlands, continue as they have for centuries their lifeways, undisturbed by Iberian intrusions. The female, too, continues her assigned roles in family and society.

AMERINDIAN WORLDS: LOST, RETAINED, OR COMPROMISED?

The pre-Columbian Amerindian societies discussed here comprise most of the ethnic-linguistic groups with whom Iberians came into contact. In these societies we can trace patterns of extinction, withdrawal, acculturation, and assimilation. Some, like the Araucanians, were all but eliminated in South America's versions of our Wild West Indian wars. Tropical and forest groups fled into forest and jungle to maintain their patterns of life and thought. In Mexico and the Yucatán Indian communities were "protected" and encouraged to maintain their traditional patterns. Those who migrated to urban areas in search of work, whether they stayed or returned to their villages, acquired a status as mestizo, whether, in fact, they were. To Indians they had lost some of the Indian ways. Particularly in Andean areas, especially Peru, and in Mexico and Central America there has been much mixing of blood and culture.

For those groups decimated or in retreat we can discern little contribution toward establishment of a generalizeable lifeway for females of contemporary Ibero-America. The other Amerindian groups either changed many customary female activities to those of the dominant Iberian culture, reinforced the similarities in both Amerindian and Iberian worlds, or retained their own styles and structure under impetus of their own needs and not from Iberian pressures.

NOTES

1. Basic ethnographic information is in Steward, 1946-; Wauchope, 1965-1970; and Hopper, 1967.

2. Steward, 1946, Handbook for the National Research Council.

3. Cooper, 1941, on the marginal hunting and gathering tribes of eastern Brazil, the Gran Chaco, and present-day Argentina.

4. Levirate is a custom whereby wives and children become the dependents of the deceased husband's brother.

5. See the various works of Canals Frau, Lothrop, Serrano, Métraux, and Baldus, Nimendajú, and Métraux and Nimendaju, all from 1946, cited in volumes of Steward, 1946.

6. Most information on marginal Amerindians comes from ethnographic, government, and travel accounts, many incomplete.

7. See bibliographies and contents of Métraux, Wagley and Galvão, Lipkind, Nimuendajú, Lévi-Strauss, Holmberg, Steward and Métraux,

8. *Compadrazgo* is a system of contractual spiritual affinity, of interfamily alliances, usually institutionalized through the Catholic ritual of baptism. Although common in varying forms in many cultures, the term applies to Iberian areas.

9. Gibson, 1964: 1-8, utilizes the researches of Sherburne F. Cook on soil erosion, population, food supply, and construction.

10. See the 1946 studies by Hernández de Alba, Kroeber, Park, Murra, Cooper, LaBarre, Tschopik, Rowe, Larco Hoyle, and Bennett, for these materials in Steward's 1946 volume. Most information on Araucanians is from the fieldwork of Louis Faron in Steward and Faron, 1959: 262-83 passim.

6 AMERICA IN THE RECONQUEST: EMPIRE, MISCEGENATION, AND NEW SOCIETIES

It has been stated that the conquest of Amerindia was more than mere racial encounter, economic endeavor, psychological and national exploit, or missionary fervor. It was also a conquest of women (Mörner, 1966). A major point to be kept in mind, however, is that the non-de jure marital-née-concubinage situations involving Iberian males and local females of the contact cultures of Asia, Oceania, Africa, and Amerindia was a customary pattern in the lifeways of local cultures *and* of pre-Council of Trent Europe.

Initial Iberian male and Amerindian female contacts resulted from the peculiarities of migration from Iberia to the New World. Iberian migrant statistics in official state emigration registers (*Pasajeros a Indias*) for the entire Indies indicate movement in the ratio of ten males to one female, although it has been suggested that the higher mortality rate for Iberian males once in the Indies must have closed the gap to a relatively closer proportion between peninsula males and females.[1] In emigration from the Spains the following regulations applied. The *Casa de Contratación* could issue licenses to wives of men already in the Indies; if a merchant left his wife at home, he had to have her written consent to go and also had to promise the authorities that he would take his wife to America or return to Iberia within three years. No peninsula emigrant, even a royal official, could sail without his wife, except with royal dispensation. On the other hand mestizo and creole colonists with wives in the Indies were subject to arbitrary recall to the peninsula. Unmarried women were forbidden to go to America unless they were daughters or servants of migrating families. In October 1544, strict orders were issued for Peru and Mexico that persons without wives be shipped home unless they gave a *security* in money or in kind that their wives would arrive within two years. The confusion of the data—10 to 1 ratio versus regulations—might be explained by noting that males could and obviously did leave their homeland in large numbers without their women for the three years allowed them, then either won extensions on their stays in America or else returned home. All these regulations apparently were periodic, not constant, and probably not well enforced[2] (*Viajes* ii, 257, cédula September 3, 1501; *Col de doc*, ser 1, cédula January 8, 1504; *Ord de la Casa*, 1505: #7; Encinas, 1596: I, 415-22, 424, 426, and IV, 286ff.; *Recop*, lib ix, tit 26, leyes 25, 29; Veitia Linaje, 1672: lib i, cap 29; *Col de doc* ser 1, xxxi, 156). Iberians who came to the Americas were predominantly males and also a socially mixed group. Among Spanish migrants were missionaries, friars, impecunious younger sons of the nobility, legists, peasant and soldier adventurers, artisans, and civil officials. The Portuguese contributed fewer peoples than the Spanish, but generally of the same mix, and also some degregados, who were often guilty only of dissent.

CULTURAL ENCOUNTERS: IBERIAN MALES AND AMERINDIAN FEMALES

The Caribbean and Central America

Initial Hispano-Amerindian contacts took place in the Caribbean between 1492 and 1519.[3] Arawak peoples of the northern Antilles islands spoke one language, had similar economic patterns, possessed the same social organization, and were of the same ethnic stock. There were exceptions to this pattern, primarily among pre-Arawak inhabitants (Ciboney), but basically it was the aristocratic and strongly stratified matrilineal Arawak societies whom Castilians encountered. Early demographic analyses indicate that women on the Antillean Arawak cultures of Hispaniola, Jamaica, Puerto Rico, and Cuba usually bore no more than three to five children, were healthy, enjoyed positions of prestige, and lived to a relatively late age (Las Casas, 1909: chap. 20). Commentaries on influential, sizable, and healthy native groups in the Caribbean would seem to indicate at contact that in Antillean Arawak families, women were not viewed solely as production equipment but played a significant role in ordering community life.

Arawak were often prey for and captives of the other major ethnolinguistic Caribbean group, the Caribs. When the Spanish arrived they drove out the Caribs and were quick to take advantage of social conditions since there were no Iberian women. Arawak women, freed from their Carib captors, initially were utilized as guides to nearby villages and throughout the islands (Sauer, 1969: 71-2). Soon they were being used for other purposes. Spaniards were taking Indian women, "wives and daughters by force without respect or consideration of person, dignity, state, or marital condition" (Las Casas 1875-1876: Book I, chap. 100). Women soon were being collected as slaves frequently and in quantity by Castilians. Las Casas refers to 600 slaves loaded for Castile—actually confused with a February 1495 consignment. Cuneo, another Spanish observer, noted

> . . . our caravels, . . . had collected into the town (Isabela) 1600 men and women of the said Indians, of whom, male and female, we loaded the said caravels with 550 of the best on February 17, 1495. . . . As to the remainder there was given an order that whoever wished might take whatever he liked . . . and when everyone was thus provided there were left over about 400 . . . among whom were many women with babes at the breast. (Sauer, 1969: 87-8.)

Several sources discuss the seizure of women as a primary element in the general enslavement process throughout most of Ibero-America. Bernal Díaz left descriptive accounts of Cortéz's quests for attractive Indian women; in 1547 in the Gran Chaco, Schmidel had noted the enslavement of fifty women and children; in Chile a 1608 law legitimized the enslavement of Araucanian women (Konetzke, 1949; Konetzke, 1946: 19; Jara, 1960: 205-7; Díaz del Castillo, 1955: I, 428, Schmidel, 1938: 113ff.). The collection of female slaves continued until their numbers were reduced by general decline in the Amerindian population. It should be noted that ecological factors as well as maltreatment of Antillean peoples caused a general decline in absolute numbers and, by loss of female population, a reduction in the birthrate.

In fairness to the Iberians, theirs was not solely a matter of taking but also of being given since *caciques* (local Indian chiefs) often presented their daughters and other females to the Spaniards. Presentation of women as gifts or tokens of friendship was considered an important procedural part of Indian foreign relations. Examples of this are cacique Xicotenga offering Cortéz his virgin daughter and giving four other girls to Spanish captains; Guaraní caciques using gifts of women as an excellent means of alliance with Spaniards in the custom of *Tobayá* (brother-in-law); or Peruvian Indians establishing alliances with the Spanish through the birth of "Spanish" children to Indian women (Konetzke, 1946: 24-5; Varallanos, 1962: 45). The gift of women created lasting kin relationships and also aided the Spanish in their conquests since Indian kinfolk paid homage to the Spanish male as an idol and also served him as a relative.

Since Indians paid their tribute in slaves they often sold female slaves to Spaniards for "domestic servants," a practice later prohibited in the New Laws (*Recop,* 1681: VI, 1-6). Sometimes these women served as slaves or as a kind of serf (*naboría* in the Caribbean, *yanacona* in Peru), while at other times they acted as free servants. In whatever capacity a female served, the civil administration's only requirement was that she become a Christian before having intercourse with a Spaniard, a requirement judiciously noted in reports (Gutiérrez de Pineda, 1963: I, 183). At upper levels of Antillean Arawak society queens and princesses whom Spaniards encountered were the Iberians' first exposure to a ruling matrilineal society, and the mores of a society in which males did not make the rules were incompatible with the conquistadors' backgrounds. As a result women who enjoyed high rank were treated inconsistently by Spaniards. Contrast the preferential treatment accorded Anacaona who, as widow of the West Indian Chief Caonabo, in 1496 was allowed by the Spanish to practice the power prerogatives of her society by sharing responsibilities with her brother, the new king, for the elaborate court ceremonial honoring the adelantado (Las Casas, 1875-1876: Book I, chap. 116). Yet, in 1503 when that same adelantado Ovando marched to visit his new realms, Anacaona, now ruler of western Hispaniola, "the first señora of the island, whom all obeyed and served," was hanged, probably not because of her sex but rather because of shifts in Spanish policy (Sauer, 1969: 149). In either case, the chivalric code had its flaws.

Iberian groups in initial contact with Central America, particularly Honduras, in 1502 noted prominent commercial and military roles of Indian females. One group referred to a canoe with men and women merchants, Mayans returning from distant fairs. A 1510 commentary noted that in Cartagena (north Colombia) at the most important harbor on Tierra Firme, women were valued as warriors but were somewhat immodestly dressed "their hair long and . . . dressed in cotton from the waist down (Sauer, 1969: 171; Herrera, 1601-1615: Decade I, chaps. 14ff.; Simón, 1882-1892: Part III).

Evidence of intermarriage in the Caribbean is available, although in the early decades weddings were recorded with care only for *vecinos,* residents of a particular neighborhood or, as in this case, too, colonizers. Religious sources indicate that although wives from Castile were present in all towns except Salvatierra in 1514, about one Spanish husband in three had a native wife, thus encouraging *mestizaje* (the process of miscegenation) and signaling the persistent role of native females in mestizo colonization (Sauer, 1969: 200).

In addition to Amerindian women African women also were available. Although they did not appear in the earliest black slave arrivals, which supposedly occurred in 1502, African males and females between fifteen and twenty years of age were ordered brought to America in 1517 under license, married to each other, and placed in villages to live and work together (Sauer, 1969: 207).

In Darien and other areas of Central America, it seems also that Spaniards adjusted to the lack of Iberian women by taking wives and daughters of native men (Peter Martyr in Sauer, 1969: 235). In regions with no female rulers it appears also that there was intermixing between Amerindian females and African males, and vice versa (Oviedo, 1950: chap. 10; Sauer, 1969: 284).

In initial decades (1492-1519) of Castilian-Amerindian contact, "the Spaniards, unbeknownst to them were preceded by their terrible allies, the European epidemics, smallpox, pneumonic plague, and typhus." (MacLeod, 1973:38). The result of this demographic and concomitant ecological disaster was to leave the Antilles depleted, desolated, and depopulated, lending a ghostly air to the lands. By the end of the first half-century of contact, the native female population had suffered a severe loss in numbers and the islands of Hispaniola, Puerto Rico, Cuba, and Jamaica contained not millions but only tens of thousands of inhabitants. Not more than 1,500 were Spaniards and about 20,000 Africans; the most populous island, Hispaniola, supposedly had 12,000 to 13,000 people (Velasco, 1894: passim). Despite demographic devastations new colonial communities were cemented by Castilians in the Caribbean islands, thus continuing small but steady permanent development.

Mexico, the Main, and the Mainland

Permanent Castilian colonization was confined during the early decades to the Caribbean and scattered northern coastal sections of the South American mainland. Only after the Hernández de Córdoba and Grijalva expeditions of 1517-1518 did Castilians learn of the continental civilizations. Spanish relations with Mexico (New Spain) and the mainland commenced with the arrival in 1519 of Hernán Cortéz and his army, from Cuba, on the Main.

There has been considerable controversy regarding the impact of conquest. Demographic, ecological, and medical data indicate that Mexico's Indian populations were decimated by mistreatment, excessive labor demands, flood, drought, and, especially, disease epidemics, the most severe in 1545-1548, 1576-1581, and 1736-1739. Demographic analysts now project that the population of the Americas was larger than the population of Europe in 1492, although population statistics vary for Amerindians on the eve of encounter. Sapper (1924) and Spinden (1928) estimated about 40 million to 50 million Amerindians, but Kroeber (1939) noted about 8.4 million for all the Americas, while Rosenblatt (1945; 1954), whose figures have been accepted by many historians, suggested 13.385 million in 1492. Rosenblatt determined

4 million to 5 million for Mexico and 2 million for Peru. But the Berkeley group of Simpson, Borah, and Cook indicate a population of at least 25 million for central Mexico, while Borah conjectures a New World population of about 100 million (Cook and Simpson, 1948; Borah and Cook, 1962, 1963). Statistics on the Incàn empire range from 3 million (Kubler, HSAI, II, 339) to 32 million (Means, 1931). Jaramillo Uribe (1964) believes that fewer than 1 million Indians were in Colombia. Dobyns (1966: 395-416) has arrived at more than 100 million for the entire hemisphere, although he suggests that only 10 million survived the first century of contact.

Given the ecological situation, agricultural development, and temporal-spatial factors it seems the lower figures would be more reasonable population estimates. Although it is presumed that women comprised 50 percent of any native population, in fact all demographic data for the entire colonial period record more women than men in all age categories. For example, late eighteenth-century Mexico City showed a ratio of 100 Indian men to 128 Indian women (Garcia Pimental, 1897; Humboldt, 1882: I, 254).

Casual intercourse and concubinage were the most common types of postconquest sexual relationships, although polygyny was considerable and monogamous marriage was occasional. By a 1501 ruling the Crown explicitly permitted intermarriage, and succeeding instructions—to Governor Ovando of Santo Domingo in 1503, in the royal decree of 1514, and in many later proclamations—noted the necessity of intermarriage as a means of Christianizing Amerindians through female converts. Spanish men and Indian women, living together, were persuaded to marry, although most European males married to Indian women usually were of the lowest social stratum.

As with almost all statistics, miscegenation data for Mexico are unreliable but sources available indicate that racial mixing was more common in Mexico City, the larger towns, and haciendas than it was in rural areas, villages, and smaller towns (AGN; BNM, Padrones, III-XXIX, and *Civil* volumes). Formal marriage remained rare because of civil and ecclesiastical restrictions. Mestizos, mulattoes, zambos (African-Indian mix), and other *castas* (specifically lineage groups, part of the elaborate Hispanic hierarchical social order) were bastard children of Spaniards, Amerindians, and Africans (Mörner, 1967: 35-41 passim). Gibson's (1964: 144) references to 7,094 mulattoes and to 19,357 other castas for 1790s population of 112,926 in Mexico City not only indicate a fairly substantial exploitation of the female sex but also probably do not show the entire bastard number since Spaniards often categorized mestizos and other half-castes as Indians to avoid parental responsibilities (Gibson, 1964: 144). It is curious to note that only a few marriages between Indian men and Spanish women were recorded. Did more occur?

It would appear that the vacillating and uncertain Spanish Crown policy ultimately was successful in preventing Spanish girls from emigrating. Humboldt noted in 1803 that European-born Spanish men in Mexico out-numbered European-born Spanish women ten to one. To the contrary, colony-born (creole) women of Spanish blood outnumbered males 135 to 100, and mestizas and mulatto women were numerous (Marshall, 1939: 170ff.). As a matter of comparison with the Caribbean, Haiti by 1789 had only 10,900 women for nearly 247,000 white men; many women died in childbirth or from disease and climate (Garran-Coulou, 1798: X, 16). In 1774 of a total of 7,000 free women of color, 5,000 were living in concubinage with whites and consisted of almost the entire courtesan court population (de la Croix, 1819: I, 278).

Even given that Africans were discouraged by officials in colonial Mexico from marrying outside their racial group, there was considerable intermixing, usually by extralegal unions. Miscegenation resulted from the importation of three times as many African males and females and prohibitions on Africans and Afro-Mexicans living in Indian neighbor-hoods, although Africans were not specifically prohibited from marrying outside their racial group (Love, 1971: 84). Extralegal unions resulted from difficulties of acquiring money for marriage, and other mainly financial reasons (Love, 1971: 83, 91). And a conclusion to be drawn from recent research is that marriage was neither the sole nor major basis for mestizaje or *mulataje*.

It appears as if there were as strong native matrilineal elements making for female involvement in Mexico in the early 1530s and 1540s as there had been in Central America and the Caribbean (Carrasco, 1964: 199). Furthermore, native women were in as great demand as when Columbus first had noted that a woman was worth 100 *castellanos*, a unit of exchange of some worth, or as much as a farm; when nine- and ten-year-old girls were priced for sale, merchants did a lucrative business in this traffic since there was a market for women of every age—so Columbus reported to Prince Juan's nurse (Navarrete, 1825: I, 271-6).

One means of obtaining women was through the institution of encomienda, a grant of a specified number of Indians to a Spaniard for purposes of providing tribute. *Encomenderos* (encomienda grantees) often asked for females as domestic servants although they utilized them more as concubines. In such diverse areas as Mexico and Ecuador Indian males helped these processes by sending their wives and daughters to carry Spaniards' luggage and also paid their tribute in females, or occasionally sold females as slaves, a custom lamented by Bishop Juan de Zumárraga of Mexico to Charles V in 1529 (Mörner, 1967: 24; Marshall, 1939:173; Cieza de León, 1945:145).

Women also were obtained through inheritance of an encomienda. Despite some varied Iberian laws prohibiting property inheritance by females, it seems that females' rights to inherit property and then male acquisition of both the rights and women were an in-flux policy, depending on the time and place. This also was related to population decline, which caused loosening of restrictions. Official encouragement of marriage to increase Spanish populations in Mexico and elsewhere made "marriage of Spaniards with Indian women a very general fact" (Las Casas, 1909: chap. xxiv). Las Casas also observed villages where this pattern was true, and in one town of sixty inhabitants, mostly hidalgos, he noted that all were "married to native women" although another writer said that "many of those married to *cacicas* [female chieftain women] . . . are persons of little esteem and consequence" (Serrano y Sanz, 1918: 384, 569). In a census taken in Santo Domingo in 1514, of 689 Spaniards living there, 171 were married, 107 had Spanish wives (five at home in Spain), and only 64 had native wives; those Spaniards married to Amerindians were from the lowest social strata (Konetzke, 1946: 215-8).

Women were necessary in parceling out encomiendas, but Rodrigo de Albuquerque's sixteenth-century report is an indication of the dichotomous status of women. In his distribution figures on 692 encomiendas, he showed the following pattern: 63 were granted to Spaniards with native wives; 19 were given outright to women; and 475 were awarded to single men, which shows that only 82 of 694 or 11.8 percent involved women in the grants and only 19 of 692 or 2.7 percent were given outright to females (Serrano y Sanz, 1918). In systematic examination these data for all sections of colonial America can be interpreted as examples of discrimination on the basis of sex. They also indicate approximately how many European women there may have been in the initial century of conquest and afford quantitative evidence for investigation into general female involvement in early colonial affairs.

Initial sixteenth-century Spanish policy, as in the July 28, 1513, Clarification of the Laws of Burgos, had been protective of native women and prohibitive of illicit unions. Then the Crown revoked early policies against mixed marriages and actively encouraged free intercourse and intermarriage between European and Amerindian. The Crown gave inducements of general and permanent distribution of land and labor in Mexico to those who would marry either Spanish or Indian women and also ceased early efforts to abolish the encomienda by declaring in 1536 that those estates could be inherited by female as well as male heirs for two or three generations. The royal decree of 1539 provided that encomiendas be given only to married people and indicated that for positions in local government or posts of corregidor (officer in charge of a district) a wife would be an essential qualification. Note that in 1534 the Spanish town in America of La Puebla de los Angeles had a male population of 80, of whom 38 had Castilian wives, 20 had Indian wives, 4 had wives in Castile, and only 18 were single, while in Antequera City near the end of the sixteenth century, of 300 vecinos, 200 had Spanish wives and practically all the rest were married to mulattas and mestizas (Marshall, 1939: 164 ff.).

Any woman, regardless of race, who possessed any property had little difficulty in marrying since, as Juan de Carvajal, a conquistador in Venezuela noted, "no one in these parts who has a homestead can live without women, Spanish or Indian" (Friede, 1961: 405). Furthermore, Viceroy Mendoza had established a home for orphaned mestizas and also provided them with a good education and dowries in the form of money from the royal treasury, *corregimientos* (an administrative unit, often a magistracy or sheriff's office), or other posts, and later local governments supplied dowries for poorer Castilian girls who were unable to compete for spouses (Marshall, 1939: 166-70).

Peru and Andean America

Spaniards first arrived in Peru in the 1520s, primarily as explorers, but the beginning of permanent contact began in 1532 after Francisco Pizarro's capture of Atahualpa, foremost claimant to the Incaship. Almost immediately contact was made between male and female, and the majority of Indian women became either personal servants or concubines. It appears that more Indian women than men were enslaved (Lockhart, 1968: 202). Some females became senior servants who supervised households. Others of higher station were treated quite well and assigned roles with enough status to enable them to marry Spaniards. Daughters of lesser caciques married artisans and merchants. Some Indian noblewomen received en- comenderos, although it should be noted that females of Incan aristocracy never wed into the highest stratum of Spanish society but into lower upper class and lesser levels (Lockhart, 1968: 210).

Substantial evidence suggests the existence of harems, and practically all Spanish bachelors kept Indian women. If Europeans were married they maintained liaisons with Peruvian females until their wives arrived. Some Spaniards kept numerous mistresses: "The Indian mistress and servant was important in the evolution of other varieties of town Indians" (Lockhart, 1968: 216). Lockhart also noted an encomendero who claimed six children and six women and a seventh pregnant by him, all living in his house (Lockhart, 1968: 216).

Interracial concubinage continued as did the stabilized relationship of *barrangania,* a consensual union common to medieval Spain and tolerated in the Siete Partidas. Even until the mid-eighteenth century, concubinage in the viceroyalty of Peru was still so prevalent as to be considered a com- pletely normal social procedure, so much so that even clergy generally kept women (Juan and Ulloa, 1953: 374ff.). Throughout the colonial era it seems that females within the concubinage system comprised the core element of interethnic relations. The singular Indian woman servant often was an abandoned mistress; some ex-concubines operated houses of prostitution, but in whatever role, women were the economic and social servants of their Spanish masters.

Afro-Indian concubinage, usually African males and Indian females, was resisted ferociously by local authorities, yet social conditions made it inevitable. The first Africans had arrived in Peru in 1533 and shortly thereafter black women were in the colony as household servants, as cooks for carting companies or mining gangs, and as sellers of food and merchandise (Gutiérrez, 1963-1965: 55-6 n494; Salinas, 1957: 42-3 n723). Free Negro women arrived from Portugal or Spain, and if they did not marry, usually to free Negroes, either became mistresses to Spaniards and other foreigners or became associated with certain commercial enterprises in the city, such as bakeries and produce markets. Some of them, such as one Catalina de Zorita, owner of a bakery and confectionary, maintained more than ten black slaves and arranged a 3,000 peso dowry for her daughter, an example of how important black women were in early Peru (Lockhart, 1968: 193).

Another group of females were *moriscas,* although there were scarcely more than a few hundred for the first three quarters of the sixteenth century. Among Moorish people women outnumbered men four or five to one, so that morisco slavery really meant female slavery. The morisca, a Caucasian, Spanish-born Christian convert, was primarily a concubine. She supplied the dual need for housekeeper and sexual partner before free Spanish women were available in quantity. Once Spanish women arrived, moriscas usually were freed but then were viewed as members of a despised class and, as such, remained as servants or in other marginal capacities (Fernández, 1963-1965: I, 357). Paradoxically, since they were primarily "Spanish" women and had been in Peru for a while, they enjoyed a certain measure of prestige and could and did marry into the highest echelons of Peruvian society. Some married encomenderos, and one even wed the royal comptroller (Lockhart, 1968: 197-8).

Writings on non-Iberian women for the colonial years are limited to mention of their importance either as servants, slaves, or concubines, these being Indians, Africans, mestizas, or mulattas. The white woman has received only slightly better attention in the substantial historical and social science analyses of Iberian contacts. People are prone to view Latin American history as the result of the activities of men, but females who accompanied these men must be considered. Nobles, artisans, farmers, merchants, lawyers, and other officials began bringing their wives, their daughters, and other chaperoned marriageable girls in seach of husbands. Within a decade of the establishment of Hispaniola colony, Iberian women had begun their roles in the European conquest and colonization of the Americas.

IBERIAN NEWCOMERS TO AMERICA

Iberian law codes identified women as an *imbecilitas sexus,* an imbecile by her very nature, and in all laws of Castile women were classed with children, invalids, and delinquents. Any widow who remarried was deprived of custody of her minor children and the right to administer their property (Careaga, 1967: 179). The aura of inequality between the sexes was paradoxical since, on the one hand, women were recognized as necessary for certain social and economic functions and used as pawns in Crown policy, while on the other hand their permanent position always was legalized as one of servant-slave to a male master. Women were encouraged to emigrate from the Spains to America and thus were involved intimately in Crown colonization schemes to create the stable population the royal authorities desired. Despite their legal inferiority Iberian women were a biological, social, and economic necessity.

The first females from Spain to come to America comprised thirty of the 330 passengers on Columbus's third voyage. When Ovando arrived in Hispaniola in 1502, he brought seventy-three families among 2,500 settlers; a few years later women arrived in Cuba. Cortéz married in Cuba and brought his wife, her sister, and many other women to Mexico. But this was not the rule. Konetzke (1945: 124ff., 145ff.) noted that generally the number of single women emigrants was larger than the number of married women, one possible reason being an excess spinster population in Iberia. Few mothers accompanied their children on their travels; men often came without their wives but with their daughters in order to provide greater opportunities to find husbands for their girls and to accumulate dowries for them more quickly than could be done in the peninsula (Diaz, 1908-1916: IV, 228, 236-7).

Diaz (1908-1916: V, 125, 184, 222-49) cited numerous Iberian women in Mexico. In his account of a battle in Tuxtepec he noted that sixty Spanish men and women from Castile were killed. From his and other reports we know that other Spanish women were with the earliest conquerors and that on one of his Pacific expeditions, Cortéz took thirty or forty married men, making a total of at least 300, including the married women. (When Narvaéz embarked on the conquest of Florida in 1528, a large number of women accompanied their husbands, and Pedro de Alvarado took twelve Spanish noblewomen with him to Guatemala in 1539 (Pereyra, 1920-1926: V, 143 n. 1). In 1535 Dona Isabel de Guevara accompanied Pedro de Mendoza to Argentina and she, along with twenty other women, arrived at Rio de la Plata in January 1536. These white women assumed expeditionary responsibilities because of illnesses of the men and were, apparently, very prominent on river expeditions and in the founding of Asunción (Pereyra, 1920-1926: IV, 75-6).

In general there were too few women for too many men. On the Argentine trip there were only twenty-one women. The expedition of Juan de Salazar de Espinosa left San Lúcar on April 10, 1550, with only fifty married and single women (Sosa de Newton, 1967: 15). The male leader died unexpectedly, command was assumed by his wife Mencia Corvalán, and they arrived eleven months later on the shore of Brazil, then went on to Paraguay (Pichel, 1968: 13-4).

Iberian policy was as contradictory for white women as for Indians. On the one hand it encouraged protection of native women. As early as 1505 authorities were instructed that in sexual offenses, Indian women be treated with leniency but Spanish males be punished severely (Gutiérrez de Pineda, 1963: 267). On February 23, 1512, King Ferdinand ordered the Casa de Contratación to send white Christian slave women to the Indies (AGI, Indiferente General 418, Lib. 3, 236; Torres Revello, 1927: 263-71). Documents testify to the presence of white "slave" women in the Platine— Argentina, Uruguay, and Paraguay—and in Mexico, in part to discourage Iberian men from taking advantage of local women (Torre Revello, 1927; Villafane Casal, 1958: 90). Royal licenses as widespread in time as those of 1528, 1533, 1633, and 1730 demonstrated that white women also were introduced specifically for domestic duties and especially for marriage to Spanish authorities (Torres Revello, 1927, as a 1728 fragment in Villa-fane Casal, 1958: 90).

In the archives of the Indies are many records that indicate women were branded as slaves. For instance, there is a document by which the adelantado Alvar Núñez Cabeza de Vaca ordered a slave branding iron for Indian women taken in wars; such brands were applied to white women, too (AGI, est 52, cajo 5, leg 2/10 pieza 2.a, 6 de marzo de 1544. This decree was abolished by royal cédula on February 4, 1785). An example in branding was Doña Isabel transshipped to be the spouse of the adelantado don Hernando de Soto and who "was a white slave who had been branded on the face" (Villafane Casal, 1958:90).

White and Amerindian women alike were forced into the conquistadors' polygymous *mancebías* (harem-households). The attitude carried through the centuries and even developed "religious" overtones, for when a cacique was questioned as to why he preferred "Christian women," he responded, "They are whiter, taller, and very fair . . . ; that Christian girl is prettier" (Mansilla, 1907: V, 197, 198).

Yet another document is one of 1586 by Juan Ramirez de Velazco who informed the king on how Tucumán was being governed. In Santiago del Estero in Argentina, a city he considered exemplary of many others in the less settled areas of the empire, he found more than 200 poor virgins, daughters of conquistadores who had no one to care for them, with the exception of a few "kind" men such as himself. Many of the girls possessed two or three *repartimiento* grants (part of a system of rewards that provided a certain number of persons to give their labor to whomever held the grant; it was similar to the Aztec labor tribute system). The result was that soldiers and vecinos would marry them in order to obtain those rights. This pattern of frontier life apparently was common, and these daughters of adventurers appeared in almost every town in the more remote regions of the empire (RBPBA, 1881: XX, 35). It was so especially for backwater areas such as the Platine, regions of Bolivia, Argentina, or Chile near the Andean borders, or in the relatively uninhabited Amazonian backlands.

Thus we see that Iberian-descendant females as holders of repartimientos in frontier areas held control or access to control of both labor and an Ibero-American device to recruit labor. Iberian women were involved in numerous other acculturating activities in early colonial centuries. Women as *curanderos* (medicine women) and in other medical activities are cited frequently in materials from expeditions and scholarly researches in the Platine. Such was mentioned by Gorman, the first doctor in Pedro de Cevallos' expedition in 1790 and in the deposition written against curanderismo by Vértiz in 1779 (Gorman, 1790; Villafane Casal, 1958: 93; Mantegazza, 1949; Botarro, 1921; Granada, 1896).

The scarcity of Iberian women, however, led not only to exploitation of Amerindian women but also to problems for Iberian women, either at home or in America. Despite extensive codification that included sections protecting females, both in legislation and in practice women within the family were inferior socially because usually they were completely dependent (Garcia, n.d.). Sosa de Newton (1967: 19) shows this especially in the extensive notes of the Leyes Indias. Women were under a double yoke of inferiority in social organization and in family, regardless of whether they were Indian or Iberian. Furthermore, women were impugned for behavior considered unacceptable to the Iberian family and thus were the object of many *autos de fe* (a Christian faith trial). One example is the case in Lima of Angela Carranza who, in a typically moralizing trial, was condemned and accused of blasphemy and heresy (Sosa de Newton, 1967: 23-4).

PORTUGUESE AMERICA: BRAZIL
AND THE MARANHÃO

Portuguese women who first came to America were few.[4] Some of them appear in accounts on Peru and other Castilian colonies before they are noted in Brazil. The first white woman of whom we have notice, Dona Brites de Albuquerque, the wife of Duarte Coelho Pereira, first lord-proprietor of Pernambuco, arrived in 1535 with her husband. Although very few women acquired administrative power, Dona Brites has the honor of having been the first woman governor of Brazil (and in the Americas) during her husband's absences. At times she shared these responsibilities with her brother Jerónimo. Duarte Coelho Pereira's example apparently was not followed by most colonists since Padre Nóbrega complained only fifteen years later of the excess of orphans, the lack of white women, and an absence of a sense of decency among the colonists, in a letter of

1552 to the Portuguese king (Thomé, 1967: 44; Dutra, 1973: PC). Other women may have arrived earlier but they are not noted in available sources. In succeeding colonial centuries some females followed their men on land and water expeditions (*bandeiras* and *monções*) as bearers of food, guns, and children, or they took on traditional roles as midwives or ministerants to the sick. But for the most part, in plantation areas, patterns of living for most Portuguese women had been predetermined by social organizations transplanted to the Americas.

One major social organization the Portuguese transplanted to America was the patriarchal, extended family, which, when developed in Brazil and the Maranhão (Cabo São Roque to the Amazon), flourished best in areas dominated by plantations. Brazilian *fazendas* (equivalent of Spanish haciendas, a type of large estate) grew in a frontier environment in which each estate was isolated and thus, by necessity, was self-sufficient. A large extended family of blood and affinal relatives, friends, workers—slave and free—lived and functioned within this unit that was controlled absolutely by the patriarch. The "family" dwelled in the *casa grande* (literally "big house," or patriarchal mansion), which, with all its members, constituted a single household. All were fed from the casa's kitchens, and on some plantations this meant several hundred persons daily. The family performed all the economic, social, political, and cultural functions in true conformity to Ariès' concept of the "premodern" family. Stability, solidarity, continuity, and unity were prime elements. Kinship ties were "reinforced by interdependence, common industry, and the sharing of a common culture" (AHB, 1971: 124).

In this patriarchal family marriage was a bond between families of a similar class, and often of kin. Courtship was controlled, chaperonage was de rigeur. Within the marital bond the senior male was considered as a "medieval lord. . . . The pattern of male dominance evolved from the Portuguese model, but the circumstances of colonial life strengthened it" (AHB, 1971: 124). In Portugal the wife was guaranteed certain rights and prerogatives by her family. However, life in a wilderness society changed certain rules. It is one theory that the rules were changed when the earliest Portuguese male settlers mated with Indian or African women whom they considered economic and social inferiors. This pattern hardened into tradition so that once Portuguese women became involved in settlement processes they entered into relationships in which their status and prerogatives had changed from their homeland experience (AHB, 1971: 124).

In colonial Brazilian plantation society, women were required to be mothers, housekeepers, managers of households and family community activities, and supervisors of all social festivities, most of which revolved around the Church. Girls growing up in such an environment were kept un under surveillance after reaching the age of six, the age of "theological

reason," after which time distinctions between the sexes were made. In or
after puberty girls either were married or ensconced in convents. A major
requirement of male members of any family was to protect their women's
honor and to avenge any dishonor, which would reflect upon them.

It should be remembered that while this patriarchal extended family
was a prevalent ideal type and its values and codes persisted, variations
in geographic and demographic processes of colonization and settlement
presumed the development of other kinds of social familial relationships.
There were, in regions of the vast Brazilian subcontinent, maintenance of
Amerindian customs among Indian and Indian-influenced settlements;
of African traditions among African and Afro-Brazilianized groups in
their familial patterns; and also continuation of values and social patterns
common among Portuguese rural communities, pastoral and agricultural,
who settled in Brazil. All these ethnic-cultural groups reflected and perpetuated experiences that were divorced from the casa grande weltanschaaung

The more aristocratic elements, by virtue of money or position, were
able to engage in enterprises and colonization. Some of the early settlers
brought families and, in 1549, the first captain general, Tomé de Souza,
brought some orphan girls with him. Throughout colonial Brazil and to
the late eighteenth century, most single women (other than orphans) were
prostitutes. The small number of immigrant women combined with the
Portuguese penchant for placing girls in Iberian and Brazilian convents persisted until Pombal, in mid-eighteenth century, forbade parents to take their
daughters out of marital circulation without permission of the king. Simultaneously, Pombal ordered entire families, totaling some 20,000 people,
to America, the first large addition of white women to Brazil since the
sixteenth century (Southey, 1810-1819: III, 586-92). This mid-eighteenth-
century influx perhaps accounts for the fact that from this time more
women are mentioned in regional records of Brazil. More than forty European women were counted in the household of a senhor de engenho (owner
of a sugar mill estate) between 1761 and 1763 in the Amazon, and that
example is typical of the sudden proliferation of entries on females in the
registers (Queiroz, 1961: 40ff.).

Among upper classes marriage always has been a major method of
socio-economic-political linkage. Young, ambitious Portuguese and
Brazilian administrators and lawyers, usually from undistinguished social
and economic stock and the like, sought marriage to daughters of socially
and economically prestigious Brazilian families. Prior to 1759 "at least
17 percent of the 168 desembargadores [high court magistrates]" were
married to Brazilian women (Schwartz, 1973a: 177). Marriage, more
specifically the pawning of a woman, created a web of familial and social
ties and obligations (Schwartz, 1973a: 177ff.).

Restrictions on and scarcity of European women available to Portuguese
colonizers resulted in a natural reduction in the number of legal weddings

while, coevally, bachelor colonists were clandestinely involved in "immoral" sexual behavior with girls of the most prominent families (Azevedo, 1962: 4). There was intense competition among Lusitanian bachelors to obtain as their wife one of the white servant girls sent from Portugal by wealthy families. The alternative was to take Amerindians, mulattas, mestiças, or African women as concubines since marriage between races was not always disapproved and de facto unions gradually were regularized by the Church (Azevedo, 1962: 4; Mörner, 1967: 35-41 passim). An indication of religio-legal efforts to correct Brazilian population deficiencies was the seventeenth-century Portuguese law recognizing *casamento Conhuçudo* (common-law marriage) as legally binding. Socially, Portugal developed a great tolerance for all varieties of union, and even the Church recognized *de juras* marriage (any relationship consummated by intercourse; a simple marriage ceremony in which mutual consent of both parties was affirmed by an oath before a church representative but without sacraments) (Herculano, 1907: 30ff.). In addition to interracial and intercaste "exploitation" of subject females, "women in sin" continued to be shipped to the colonies for marital and other purposes. Even the Portuguese queen donated some orphan girls from among those she maintained in Lisbon to be white wives of early colonists.

The traditional double standard of morality, which still, theoretically, regulates Iberian and Ibero-American lifeways and that allows ample sexual freedom for men but enforces strict rules to protect virginity of girls and fidelity of wives, found room for amplification and accretion during early colonial days. It should be borne in mind that the strict double standard and seclusion of women was an ideal behavioral norm that often differed considerably from real or expected patterns, especially among lower economic sectors (Willems, 1953, 1955, 1962). Nonetheless supposedly it gained enforcement by establishment of systems of Amerindian and African slavery in Brazil, with demographic, geographic, and ecological problems during Brazil's early centuries, from the economic system and social values derived from Iberian Catholicism, and from Portuguese and Spanish racial attitudes resultant from their contact with populations in Asia and Africa. Brazilian and Hispanic wives traditionally were property of their husbands, a situation that afforded protection to the female but, at the same time, practically isolated her from any social and cultural contacts. It was not only upper-class women who were segregated but often also those of working classes, such as is demonstrated in the careful segregation of Indian male and female workers in the cotton mills of the Amazon region (BAPP, codice 703, documents 80 and 81 for a mill for the years 1756-1797).

Since the Portuguese administration made serious efforts to colonize Brazil after the mid-sixteenth century, it was not unusual for wealthy persons and certain institutions, such as the *Misericordias* (welfare houses)

to advance a policy of underwriting marriages with Portuguese girls. The
Crown acceded to requests in Brazil, as it had in other parts of its empire,
to send white orphan girls of marriageable age, "orphans of the King,"
although few of them seem to have survived the rigors of marriage or
the tropical climate. A contradictory practice was to send daughters
from these marriages to Portugal to wither in convents. This was a policy
prejudicial both to young men and women as well as to the Brazilian
economy and society.[5] Other girls, thirteen to fifteen years of age, were
married from the casa grande to husbands twice their age—either older
Portuguese merchants, officials, physicians, or other plantation owners—
and were used as pawns in the patriarchal society to suit the social and
economic desires of their parents. The necessity for marrying a virgin
became almost a prejudice, and it appears that a major reason for marrying girls at twelve or thirteen years of age was to ensure that she would
be a virgin. Within the confines of the casa grande, as daughter or wife,
the Portuguese woman lived a life of lassitude and illiteracy.

To compensate for what proved for centuries to be an inadequate supply
of women, Brazilian men relied on female slaves, Amerindian but most
often African, to supply them with sexual comforts. Slave women were
raised to be "generative bellies," but it should be noted that Brazilian
male planters displayed similar attitudes in their relationships to any
woman, be she wife or slave. A description of life at the end of the eighteenth
century noted that

> Negro and mulatto girls, for whom honor is only a chimerical word
> that signifies nothing, when they arrive at adolescence are ordinarily
> the first to corrupt their adolescent masters, giving them their first
> lessons in that sexuality which has enveloped the girls since infancy.
> (Santos Vilhena, 1922: I, 138.)

Even as little girls blacks were used by their masters. Female slaves served
as mistresses, concubines, and in other domestic capacities, whereas white
women in the society were secluded. Colonial authorities in puritanical
moments legislated often but unsuccessfully against the money and finery
lavished on mulattas by Brazilian males often to the impoverishment of
their white wives and for exemplification of male psychological gratifi-
cation (Barbinais, 1728: III, 204; Calmon, 1941: 164-9).

Personal favoritism to mulattas was counterbalanced by social and
legal discrimination against them, and colonial legislation generally was
applied more rigidly to female or males of Euro-Amerindian mix, although
females in all mixed-blood categories suffered discriminations (See
Purificação, 1640). Examples are frequent. Offspring of Euro-Amerindian
unions, *mamelucos,* if recognized by their father were given Portuguese

names and accepted as subjects of the Crown. However, if they were raised by their mothers, they were raised in Indian villages and regarded as part of the subject Indian population. Similarly, if mulattoes were recognized by their fathers they obtained, usually, manumission from slavery, but if not recognized they, and *cafusos* (Indian and African mix), kept their mother's status as servant or slave (Poppino, 1968: 58). In January 1726, the Crown on the advice of the overseas councillors, promulgated a decree that indicated that only white women were acceptable as marriage partners. Five years later the captain general of Minas Gerais, Lourenço de Almeida, noted a severe lack of women for the male populace to marry. And more than a century earlier, Diego de Vasconcellos, in 1612, had sent a letter to the Portuguese king forewarning him of the disasters for the colony should he not send out more women.

In economic matters it appears that some upper-class Portuguese white women in Brazil enjoyed a measure of financial power or privileges of property. One was the daughter of Governor Mem de Sá who, in the 1560s, inherited the largest and most famous sugar plantation in colonial Brazil, the *Sergipe do Conde,* which she administered until her death in 1612 (Schwartz, 1973: 149). Often widows assumed the property and responsibility of their husbands in some sections of Brazil, most notably Bahia, and sometimes women were the most prosperous plantation owners, such as one Beatris Delgada whose estates produced large quantities of sugar at Sergipe do Conde in the 1620s (Schwartz, 1973: 178). Also, three women who were *lavradores de cana* (female sugar cane growers) at the *Engenho d'Alimbero* were some of the largest and most important sugar producers in Pernambuco (Dutra, 1973: PC; Schwartz, 1973: 178; van der Dussen, 1639). Many of the women who were widowed, because of their wealth and their ethnic (Portuguese) credentials, were in demand to remarry and a seemingly large number of women were active planters or became *senhoras de engenho* (female sugar mill owners), a contradiction to the supposed seclusion and protection of Portuguese women (Schwartz, 1973: 179). Among less affluent groups the 1639 descriptions of Pernambuco and Alagoas note that 24 or 17 percent of the 144 lavradores de cana were women and in some areas all lavradores de cana were women as, for example, at the *Engenho d'Alimbero* (Schwartz, 1973: 178; table IV for women lavradores de cana, 1611-1712). In 1754-1755 some 16 of 172 or 9 percent of the engenhos in Bahia were listed as owned by women (Caldas, 1951: 429-38).

Not all widows remarried. Many took the veil. Others actively involved themselves in the affairs of their late husbands. The widow of Matias de Albuquerque, governor of Pernambuco and governor-general of Brazil in the 1620s, publicly was proclaiming her late husband instrumental in the discovery of the Pará and Amazon rivers (Dutra, 1973: PC; and in 1973, Dutra's citations for information on Señora Albuquerque: AGS, Sect Prov. lib. 1465, fls 175-181v; lib, 1467, fls 688-691v).

Attitudes fluctuated with the times and circumstances and persons involved. The prosperous land grant of Pernambuco was unguided after 1572 for nearly a half century until a male member of the donatory's (lord-proprietor) immediate family came to run the captaincy (Dutra, 1973: 24). Another instance of Portuguese American women's involvement in public affairs is in royal dispatches of late seventeenth- and early eighteenth-century Bahia, which condemned as shameful the practice of women slave owners living on the immoral earnings of their female slaves who were forced into a life of prostitution. Female slaves also could hire out as cooks, seamstresses, and street hawkers and then pay a fixed sum from these earnings to their owners, a practice that continued until the abolition of slavery in 1888 (CR, 1 March 1700, in Accioli-Amaral, 1919-1940: II, 149; Marques Pereira, 1939: chap. xiii; Barbinais, 1728: III, 202-4).

THE COLONIAL MILIEU: SOME
CONTRIBUTIONS IN TIME

Pre-nineteenth-century colonial documentation offers few specific examples of social, cultural, and intellectual activity and relatively little personal insights since most women could not write and therefore were unable to record their thoughts or viewpoints on societal situations. What comes clear in the few writings by women is that many felt themselves in a position of inferiority in their relationship to men, a prejudice supported by legislation and noted by travelers.

We also have little way of knowing what influential works regarding female life and work, written by and about women in Europe—such as Madame de Lafayette's *La princesa de Cleves* (1678), Madame de Sousa's novelas of 1793 to 1808, Madame de Staël's *Delfina* (1802) and *Corina* (1807), Madame Guizot's *Contradiciones,* or the life of Madame Roland and other eighteenth- and nineteenth-century European women—ever reached Iberia or Iberian America. This is related to the more general problem of determining the effects or extent of the Enlightenment on Iberian societies.

So difficult was the social position of most women that in the Platine, for example, there was a hospital de *mujeres* (women) and a house of correction for women in order, as the records say, to rid the society of evils of these bad women and to correct the affrontery to God, to return the society to correct living (Vértiz, notice from the 1801 *Telegrafo Mercantil,* in Zinny, 1941). Testaments of *hacendados* (owners of haciendas, in Portuguese *fazendeiros*) and even a few of their daughters indicated that their women did not know how to read or write, although their documents afford an idea of how some women knew how to take care of records. For example, a hidden will recorded an act of the Buenos Aires *cabildo* (city council) of August 28, 1702, that gave a license to a woman to "sell 9000 head of cattle; mentioned that she had previously supplied the market with same; and recognized her legitimate rights to pursue wild cattle" (Garrido de la Pena, 1942, cited in Sosa de Newton, 1967: 29). Nationalists and patriots can point with pride to Sor Juana Inés de la Cruz, famous poetess and writer-nun of the late seventeenth-century Baroque period in Mexico. She composed verse and morality plays and attempted innovations in meter, medley, and form. While she was outstanding in intellectual achievement, apparently her personal life was one of repression and disillusionment (Arroyo, 1952). Sor Juana was an exception to the seventeenth-century rule in America and Europe when women seldom had independent lives and were chattels of their fathers, brothers, and husbands and when it was axiomatic that they be of inferior intelligence.

One colonial area for which we have some substantive published information regarding the multifarious roles of women is sixteenth-century Peru in Lockhart's (1968) rare account of female activities in an Iberian colonial society. He does not neglect the very important fact that in many areas of Spanish America there were enough European women to retain intact their peninsula traditions, whereas their Portuguese counterparts possessed numerous settlements without European women so that Portuguese customs, language, and religion were either lost or modified. For example, Tupí was the lingua franca in the Brazilian south until mid-eighteenth century. This factor alone not only indicates the significance of the female per se but also demonstrates that transferability or retention of customs, traditions, and lifeways are reliant on females because of their role in the household and family.

Technically, females were restricted from ownership of encomiendas and property, from holding public office, and from any legal involvement in colonial administration. Yet, colonial life had some special problems that tended to pose contradictions between theoretical concerns and practical activities. For example, in sixteenth-century Peru, although there were fewer women than men, not only were females substantial in number but also because of necessities of colonial life they contravened convention and contributed culturally and biologically to the growth of a Spanish society in Peru. From 1532 to 1560 about 550 were listed in notarial records, but since there was little reason for all Spanish women to be cited it is reasonable to assume that the 550 accounted for only a portion of the total Iberian female population. Lockhart, noting that a minority of moriscas, mulattas, and mestizas were included under the rubric of Spanish women, estimates that from the early 1540s on, Peru probably had one Spanish woman for every seven or eight men, or about 300 to 400 women in 1543 and 1,000 by 1555. Spanish women who appeared in the Caribbean contributed to population in Peru and other Spanish American areas; for example, Santo Domingo remigrated a significant number of Peru's Spanish female population (Lockhart, 1968: 151-2).

Throughout the colonial era, and following the early Peruvian example, women from every strata of Spanish society appeared in South America, and about 90 percent of all adult peninsula women in Spanish America were married (in general see Otero Muñoz, 1936: passim; Ots Capdequi, 1920, 1934: passim). In Peru, by 1542 about a third of the encomenderos were wed and by 1563, 468 of nearly 500 encomenderos throughout all Peru were married, almost all to Spanish women (Lockhart, 1968: 155).

For the female, family and regional ties remained most important. Most women continued to arrive as part of a family or were sent by male relatives already living in America since practically all marital alliances were arranged to enhance the economic well-being or social standing of the family and the male. While males could enhance their position through ways other than marriage, the female could do little independently to alter her status, so it was to her advantage that most encomenderos chose their wives from the female relatives of people prominent in politics, church, or land. Immigrant women had little to say in any match, and marriage almost always was arranged while the brides were still in Spain.

Encomendero wives were the most important and influential in Peru, partially from their household position and partially as a result of marital alliances. On their husbands' deaths, encomendero wives often became influential and powerful heads of households consisting of relatives, servants, and slaves, and often women acted as trustees of their husband's affairs. As managers of encomiendas many were considered to be ruthless.

Female cruelties did not go unchecked nor did their involvement in illegalities, either as mistresses of plantations, holders of encomiendas, or as single women involved in commercial affairs. A letter from Philip II, January 13, 1596, proclaimed that unmarried women were not to be exempted from punishment for selling without licenses, and encomendero wives had been reprimanded frequently for "irregularities of conduct" (*Col de Doc,* ser 1, xix, 47; *Recop,* lib. ix, tit 27, leyes 12-17).

Areas in America, especially Peru, retained much social status consciousness of Spain, but a severe decline in the male population because of wars, revolts, and the like placed females in the forefront of daily life. It is clear that the Spanish Peruvian woman played a crucial role in adjusting class status to colonial reality, in the transmission of social customs, and in the direction of economic activities. In Lima and other towns, women owned and directed much real estate but because of societal conventions did not appear openly as the owners of property or livestock. However, their ownership of a large proportion of black house slaves involved them in extensive market transactions, and their accumulation of money allowed them to function as silent partners in investments.

Aside from their roles as wives of encomenderos or wealthy community leaders and the social prerequisites and restrictions which that class position designated, women were prominent in other socially ascribed roles. Those in the rank next to the upper stratum of society were women of artisan and merchant classes. In their "bourgeois" positions they enjoyed many material accoutrements of their new wealth, although not always the social seniority. From Lima to La Paz unmarried women, especially those of the lower classes, usually were involved in specifically approved occupations such as bakeries, midwifery, running inns or boardinghouses and similar jobs, and owning real estate (Lockhart, 1968: 160). The frequency of reports on women property owners points up a curious contradiction in Iberian attitudes of achievement of status through property. The allowance of females to engage in this activity points out, possibly, that since women were considered of inferior status, they were likely candidates for these money activities. Much the same role was reserved for Jews by Christians.

In mining areas of Mexico, Peru, and elsewhere, females were used as laborers. But sporadic reforms, as early as the Laws of Burgos (1512-1513), prohibited compulsory female labor in mines or elsewhere without their own or their husband's consent.

The rather casual attitudes toward women as perceived in Spanish American colonial society are amply demonstrated by the persistence of types and social categories to which they were "assigned" in the Iberian male value scheme. Unless a Spanish man already was wed to a woman living in America with him, it was likely that he would form an alliance with prostitutes or another woman who would become his mistress. He desired female companionship but did not want to marry until he had the means to acquire a wealthy upper-class woman. Once this was done, the male usually discarded his mistress, sometimes endowing her with adequate means to live. Of course, this does not mean that the married man might not continue to have illicit relations once he had wed a wealthy woman and become lord and master of her and all her properties.

Prostitution was widespread. The first notice we have of the establishment of *"una casa de mjueres publicas"* is in Puerto Rico in 1526. In other regions of the Americas many prostitutes also were singers and entertainers in colonial cities following the tradition of soldadeiras. Prostitution was one of the occupations most likely to be followed by lower-class women since general employment opportunities were rare or else many unskilled jobs carried with them a built-in impulse for socially unacceptable behavior. The "loose" female was subject to some Spanish colonial administrators' fears. For example, orders by Viceroy Francisco Toledo in Panama denoted that because of the great number of mistresses in that city, all unmarried women were to be apprehended and banished from the area (Ots Capdequi, 1920: 254; Lockhart, 1968: 151; Bagú, 1952: 116-8; Haring, 1964: 151). In general, single or widowed women who neither inherited wealth nor came by it by various means in their own lifetime apparently led lives of uncertainty and misery often channeled to prostitution. This was common throughout all colonial Spanish America. It was not until 1772 and 1776 that the state even provided pensions for widows of its functionaries.

Most scholarship to which we have access has, heretofore, reflected primarily on the "visible" or upper-class females; very few have probed the lives and values of the socially predominant lower strata. Some travel accounts, most notably eighteenth-century ones, offer insights into the development of Iberian colonial society and, occasionally, provide information on daily life of lower, particularly nonwhite, groups in Latin America. These accounts supplement the rich archival data awaiting an army of researchers but, unfortunately, reflect the class of the observer and the intellectual style of the era and too often evince concern for costume rather than content in their accounts. Juan and Ulloa (1964 ed.: 28) in their famous eighteenth-century journeys observed activities of peasant and working women in Andean and neighboring areas and noted, "If any Whites, especially women, are met with, it is only accidental." Indeed, most descriptions of eighteenth-century Spanish American ladies is contradictory to their Iberian peninsula counterparts who seemed to enjoy the frivolity and freedom of Bourbon Spain.

We assume fewer socio-moral restrictions for lower-class women, especially those of color. We are told that female slaves in eighteenth-century Cartagena either lived on *estancias* (ranches), where their husbands also worked, performed usual domestic and field chores, or resided in the city. In that case usually they "sell in the markets all kinds of eatables, and dry fruits, sweetmeats, cakes made of the maize and cassava." (Juan and Ulloa, 1964 ed.: 29). In Lima, black women and mulattas usually performed domestic services or followed occupations they had been noted for two centuries earlier, while their Indian and mestiza counterparts were active in farming, plotting, and provisioning the markets (Juan and Ulloa, 1964 ed.: 195).

In Brazil, too, class patterns followed previously established ones through the colonial centuries but, again, here we are better able to document lives and attitudes of upper and urban classes. Salvador (Bahia) was a complex, urban society similar to Spanish American cities in organization, functions, and milieux (Russell-Wood, 1968: passim). Through several decades Salvador's influential citizenry increased its concern for prestige and "proper credentials" and, as Mörner (1967) has noted for all Spanish America in the eighteenth century, socioracial prejudice was growing.

Preservers of class and family were females, and the basic pattern of life in eighteenth-century Salvador for an upper-class girl seemed to be the following: raised in relative isolation, either married to a man of rank and stature or required to enter convents to ensure no mesalliances with males of unacceptable socio(racial)-economic station, and thereafter to live in relative seclusion. These women could and on occasion would rise to positions of social and economic power but seldom, if ever, were they allowed access to juridical, political, or administrative control (Russell-Wood, 1968: 177-81).

For lower classes in Brazil, circumstances varied. The more "fortunate" black and mulatta slaves who could gain the affection and concern of their white masters were treated well and were bequeathed substantial inheritances on the deaths of their masters (Russell-Wood, 1968: 177-81, on wills and dowries; ASCMB XLI, ff 134v-140v, 42v-44v, and XL, ff 28v-33v). On the other hand most of Salvador's population lived at subsistence level. Wages were low, especially for people of color, and created a tenuous existence for poor women, especially blacks and mulattas, in a society where both African and Portuguese custom condones informal relationships, thus creating no family for security or sharing. Many Afro-Brazilian or poor white Portuguese-Brazilian females assumed temporary residence with immigrants to mining areas and cattle ranches in the interior, with soldiers on frontier garrisons, or with merchants and other urban functionaries who would never marry them. Because of the temporary nature of their social relationships, most of these females comprised a substantial segment of Salvador's working class as street vendors of foods and clothing, as laundresses, as cooks, as bakers, and in domestic service. There was little Indian or mestizo element, as there was in Spanish America, with whom they had to compete, and many lower-class whites, male and female, shunned menial labor, leaving it to blacks and mulattas (archival sources and travel accounts, impressions).

Two areas in which women can be compared in Spanish and Portuguese America were education and religion. As early as 1530 female teachers and nuns as well as pious women had been brought to Mexico to establish girls' schools with missionary indoctrination. Nonetheless illiteracy was widespread and customary throughout the colonial era, and females generally benefited least from the scant formal education system. The English explorer Vancouver visited Chile in 1795 and found that few upper-class women could write their names. An Argentine historian noted that "at the beginning of our century [nineteenth] there were still very few married women who could even read a single page." In Buenos Aires there were only four schools with 700 students for a population of 40,000; Santiago (Chile) had only 500 children in primary and higher schools of some 30,000 residents; and the situation in Peru, New Granada, and other areas was similar (Altamira, 1928-1930: IV, 340; Barros Aranha, n.d.: VII, chap. 27, n. 2; Prado, 1941:1, 144-5; *Relacion de mando del Virrey . . . Gongora,* 1789: VII, 236-55; *Relación del Virrey . . . Espleta,* 1796: VIII, 322-39; López, 1957: I, 243). It seems that the purpose of most Spanish American schools with women lay teachers was to keep Indian and mestiza girls and to teach them the vocational arts, not the three R's. The remaining few girls were being prepared for their only purpose in life, marriage. Yet, after a generation or so most of these schools were unsuccessful and unsupported by the administration (Ricard, 1933: 262-76). Curiously, the Indians opposed female education and always had reared their girls in almost rigid absolute confinement.

The few educated Spanish women or the small number who were teachers were far outnumbered by those involved in general religious activities, for within a few decades the colonies usually had developed convents for either regular nuns or beatas. Not until later did missionary nuns appear. Dominicans and Augustinians sponsored many religious institutions that in several areas were run much as country clubs. Nuns maintained slaves, and often ceremonies for a girl's entrance into a convent were tantamount to a contemporary debutante party.

The situation in both Spanish and Portuguese America exhibited certain similarities as well as specific differences owing both to variations in ideas and values of the mother countries and to geographic settlements in America (Calmón, 1939-1943: I, 93). In Mexico, as elsewhere in colonial Latin America, convents were important in the economic life of the viceroyalty. As Lavrin has explained, "The growth in economic importance of nunneries corresponded to the establishment of a certain type of landed economy in the hands of a creole nobility and a class of hacendados, miners, and merchants," all interacting with religious organizations (1966: 372). Preoccupation with social prestige and family honor, which had become a characteristic of upper classes, and the concomitant concern for "virgin" daughters or other female members, undoubtedly motivated creoles and peninsulares in Mexico, Guatemala, Brazil, Peru, Chile, and elsewhere in Ibero-America to establish and support nunneries. Nuns themselves donated monies and bequeathed properties to their convents. In some instances when they considered administrators and majordomos to be mismanaging convent affairs, nuns took over administrative and financial operations and reorganization of their convents (Lavrin, 1966: 373-4, 387).

In eighteenth-century Lima there existed fourteen nunneries for women of the regular and recollect orders, and four other conventual houses, of which one specifically was for poor women, one for Indian women, and one "a retreat for women who desire to be divorced from their husbands" (Juan and Ulloa, 1964 ed.: 179-80). That affluent city also supported an orphanage for girls and schools, with more of a technical

and domestic curriculum than an intellectual one, oriented toward
training upper-class girls to be good wives and mothers and servant girls
to be well trained in domestic arts.

The Portuguese seemed overzealous in safeguarding their women, especially those who resided in the northeast, particularly Bahia. Travelers
and prelates alike noted that the Portuguese propensity to protect and
seclude their women already had caused several convents to be established,
not including a separate institution for little girls, and that in Bahia alone
by 1755 there were seven convents for women (Calmón, 1939-1943: I,
86-90). At eight or nine years of age, girls entered convents that resembled
dormitories with lenient matrons. Many nuns from monied classes were
not sincerely religious and often carried on affairs with young men outside
the convents. The profusion of letters of bishops and governors concerning
these "scandals" indicates that they were widespread. (Russell-Wood, 1968:
174-84 passim, 310-2, 320-2; Soeiro, 1973).

The number of nuns resident in a convent in Portuguese America was
limited to fifty, but by practice this restriction was relaxed so that some
nunneries could accommodate both the ladies and their female slaves.
At one point a suggestion was made that these people be identified as two
different social groups, one higher and one lower. But in 1719 the overseas council rejected that proposal, saying that that kind of class distinction would be incompatible and even resented since even the humblest
person in Brazil had "the airs of a great fidalgo" (Boxer, 1965: 92-3). By
the eighteenth century residents of convents, such as those controlled
by the Poor Clares in Salvador, by virtue of their dowries, legacies, and
alms, began to enjoy a sumptuous life style. The French traveler La
Barbinais viewed a theatrical presentation in 1717 in Bahia's *Desterro*
(Exile) convent, a convent founded specifically for Brazilian-born girls,
and noted that the girls "posed in ways inappropriate to the place and to
themselves" and that the convent was decorated with "worldly" scenes
(*Documentos Históricos,* 1928-ff: xcvii, 189-94, 271ff.). In 1764, the
the Bahian prelate Manuel de Santa Inez noted that "nonobservance of
the laws appropriate to the state and profession" were the rule. This
also was the case in Mexico where marriage or religious seclusion were
the only careers open to respectable females, although nuns were allowed
the amenities of secular life, including personal slaves (Muriel, 1946:
passim).

The numerous brotherhoods founded in Brazil and in full flower by
early eighteenth century, while restricted in membership to males, allowed
women to watch their processions, which was one of the few diversions
permitted females in colonial days. The Portuguese proverb was that a
virtuous, (i.e., upper-class) woman left her house only three times during
her lifetime: for her christening, her marriage, and her funeral. Such
seclusion was noted by practically every traveler to Portuguese possessions

from Linschoten in sixteenth-century Goa to Graham in nineteenth-century Bahia. Some parents rarely let their daughters out to hear Mass, never mind for any other reason, and this applied both to white and colored women (Boxer, 1962: 126-61 passim).

The educational system, whether run by city councils (*camaras*) or by the Jesuits and other orders, did little to enhance Brazilian intellectual life since only a few secondary schools existed and those primarily for boys. Furthermore, it was the conscious policy of Portuguese colonial society to confine instruction and education to a few and those of the class able to pay, hence guaranteeing that only a minimal number other than the privileged class could enjoy education. An example of this rare practice of educating women was in the eighteenth century a fairly well-known Brazilian writer, one Dona Teresa Margarida da Silva e Orta (1711 or 1712-1793) (Ennes, 1947: 11-92, 211-66).

Traditional scholarship has neatly divided Latin American history into the colonial—arbitrarily 1492-1825—and the national, thereafter. Only since the 1960s has the periodization been shifted to encompass more exactly the events and processes of history, thereby better enabling us to perceive nearly 500 years of historical change and continuity in twenty distinct Iberian-influenced societies. Yet, within this reordering, it is impossible to write social, economic, or political histories of Latin America in which women are pivotal. It is, however, possible to adumbrate some types of female involvement at varying times and in varying places.

Some conclusions, perhaps more hypothetical in nature, can be drawn from discussion of the colonial mileux. In basic social relationships, external to any formal structure of alliances, race or national origin seems of lesser importance than economic condition, more specifically "class" ranking, and sexual necessity, for no man could "live without women, Spanish or Indian" (Friede, 1961: 405). Furthermore, values placed on "purity" by inheritance through mother's line remained characteristic of several Latin American ethnic groups. The condition of the mother determined whether her children would be slaves but recognition by the father often mean freedom, with the mother disposed of "as he sees fit" (Aguirre Beltrán, 1946: 263-8). Utilization of women under conditions akin to "chattel sex slavery" was not confined to Europeans, for I have noted its existence among Amerindian groups, African groups, and Africans in America who kept "great numbers of Indian women, some of them voluntarily, others against their wishes" (CDFS: I, 81-2, 99-100, 185, 210; Aguirre Beltrán, 1946: 256-7).

There also is tantalizing evidence to indicate that some colonial mileux might have offered more freedom of social choices and economic opportunities for women, a situation that some scholars would attribute to the "frontier" character of Latin American colonization. However, the evidence indicates that for Iberian, African, and Amerindian, forms of "exploitation" coexisted with very real social, economic, and political influence by women within both family and society. Real power and influence seem as much a result of behavior and values inherent to any of the contributing societies as they do to events peculiar to the colonizing experiences and processes. When more specific monographic analyses of the structural implications of sex, race, and class phenomena are available, then perhaps we shall better be able to get behind observed reality biased by a consistent male view and understand the coexistence of seemingly polar values of female power and male authority.

NOTES

1. Konetzke, 1945: 123-4, 146; Friede, 1951; Boyd-Bowman, 1956; Céspedes, 1957; *Pasajeros a Indias,* 1940-1946, for statistics on origins, numbers, and proportions of immigrants to Latin America and the first generations-societies. Spain could ill afford large numbers of emigrants and those emigrants, especially from Castile, must have had great natural increases, because from the beginning to the end of the seventeenth century the white minority population in Spanish America had gone from 300,000 to 600,000. Registers of Seville's *Casa de Contratación,* where all passengers to the Indies were required to register, are not complete and show only 150,000 for the first three centuries, but it is likely that clandestine emigration tripled these figures. Further, Spanish policy in the Caribbean was the reverse of its general policy of restrictive emigration because Spain wanted to thwart European interference there (see Peréz Bustamente, 1941; Domínguez Ortiz, 1971: 295-7, 330 n.2).

2. John Leddy Phelan (1960) and Margali Sarfatti (1966) analyze the vast discrepancies between policy and practice common to any bureaucratic structure.

3. For an excellent discussion of geographic and placement terminology in historical context, see Sauer, 1966: 1-6.

4. For nearly a century and a half Brazil was divided into two administrative units: Brazil and the Maranhão.

5. *Misericordia* records, state and local archives, and Inquisition records (see Rego Quirino, 1966) and the AN Códice 952, vol. 26, fls. 395-405 as examples, are rich in sources on all aspects of women in Portuguese America and the empire.

7 THE NINETEENTH CENTURY: ENLIGHTENMENT, INDEPENDENCE, AND TRANSITION

The nineteenth century is a neglected one for Latin American history. Latin America's nineteenth century has been defined as one characterized by two trends that had begun before the eighteenth century and continued into the twentieth century: Europeanization and modernization (Graham, 1972). The first trend implied closer contact with mainstream European development, while the latter included a complex of changes in man's view of himself and his world, in no longer perceiving society as divinely ordained and permanently ordered, in realizing that the individual's place within society was no longer immutably fixed and that the economy was more open to free enterprise and individual involvement. Graham suggests that this was not merely an Anglo-Saxonization, for much of the impulse for change came from Bourbon Spain. Furthermore, establishment of political independence by numerous Spanish American regions between 1808 and 1825 was a major move toward integration with Europe as a whole (Graham, 1972: introduction, passim).

For Latin American colonies the nineteenth century represented both an experimental entrance into a world in socioeconomic metamorphosis as well as the age of loosening political bonds from European parents. The century began with the fragmentation of Spanish America into unstable political units separate from Spain and the consolidation of Portuguese

America into one nation with the legacy of imperial domain. The early nineteenth century also reflected some understanding of the Enlightenment, as translated in the Americas, and crystallization of its body of ideas concerning the role and influence of women in male-dominated societies and in American colonial milieux.

Enlightenment ideas had created a new basis for interpretation of the status of women. Prior to the eighteenth century it had been questioned whether women were equal in human nature, but Enlightenment philosophies shifted the question to one of whether women were capable not only of service to mankind but also of being enlightened. Initial impetus for changing ideas concerning females came neither from Iberia nor from the eighteenth century but from earlier European reformers and traditionalists, particularly Frenchmen such as Archbishop Fenelon (1651-1715), a reformer of female education whose *Traité* reflected his ideas that women were intellectually less capable than men and consequently needed more education, and whose *Telemaque* was an allegorical study that encouraged devotion to domestic duties. Other Frenchmen such as Voltaire and Rousseau reflected the more traditional view of the place of women, observing that they should be content to please men with little reward to themselves. On the other hand Condorcet and d'Holbach urged equal education and citizenship for women, demanding that females have the same political rights as men, and advocating the election of women to public office (Fenelon, 1699; Voltaire (n.d.) Rousseau, 1775, 1762; d'Holbach, 1772; Condorcet, 1795). And the Englishman John Locke had *Some Thoughts Concerning Education* of women and advocated the private schooling of young ladies (1693).

Iberians were quick to enter discussion regarding the role of females. In Spain Padre Benito Feijoo y Montenegro produced a work in which he questioned the absoluteness of categorizing men as the superior sex. Despite his attempt to redefine the social role of females and his search for areas in which women could excel, Feijoo revealed the prejudices of his age by his anatomical discussion in which he suggested that the female's brain was too soft for her to comprehend as much as a male. He did, however, give credit to outstanding Iberian women such as Castile's Isabella and the colonies' Sor Juana de la Cruz, both of whom he accorded the highest honor by equating their achievements with comparable ones produced by men (Feijoo y Montenegro, 1778; Glauert, mss. and documents.

A variation in viewpoints in the colonies is seen in opinions of Feijoo's Mexican counterpart, Fernández de Lizardi. He tended to accept Rousseau's dictum about women's existence being of value only so long as it benefited men (1967).

An important element of Enlightenment thought was the idea of equality, an idea that was woven into arguments for the education of women and redefinition of feminine roles as well as being intricately involved in reassessments of the entire society. Salient theories on equality of Voltaire, Rousseau, Condorcet, d'Holbach, Fenelon, and Feijoo influenced development of nineteenth-century Ibero-American thought.[1]

From this philosophical flowering also came a desire for political independence. Early dissident movements reflected a tradition in which Spain's dominions manifested disdain for metropolitan economic, political, and social discrimination at elite levels and chose rebellions reactions. In these articulated and armed conflicts women often played an important, though nonpolitical part. Some upper-stratum females, such as the lover of Simón Bolívar, wielded power. Manuela Saenz was a Quiteno by birth, wed to an English merchant living in Lima, who became a member of the patriot underground in Lima. She met Bolívar in Quito and became his lover, left her husband, and aided Bolívar in the Spanish-American wars for independence (von Hagen, 1952: passim). But most such women did not make the same consistent contribution to independence causes as did lower-class women.

During the Spanish-American wars for independence and other upheavals or military actions, women, mostly *criolla* (female American-born Spanish women) and mestiza, played important auxiliary roles aside from their traditionally ascribed domestic duties, acted with bravery, and were cited for their patriotic actions (Sosa de Newton, 1967: 38-75 passim; Bernard, 1941; Sarmiento, 1911; Carranza, 1910; Paz, 1935; Frias, 1907; Aráoz de Lamadrid, 1947: I; López, 1939; Pérez Godoy, n.d.; González Arrili, 1950; Levene, 1942; Dellepiane, 1923; Mabragana, 1910). Occasionally some were noted as leaders in rebel forays, and there are innumerable references to them in various battles against the Spanish in which they served as military messengers, fulfilled nursing and cooking duties, and performed a wide range of needed functions, although never in positions of command. Thus, the early years of independence saw women in the forefront of activities to attempt to reassert the influence begun during the wars:

> Without the women America never would have obtained her liberty. Many of the circulos, clubs, and conspiracies which formed in South America were born of the impulses of heroic and passionate women. . . . They were the first to carry the revolt to the street, in displaying the revolutionary flag, in singing patriotic songs. . . . They followed their husbands or their lovers to the field of battle. . . . (Ludwig, 1942: 83).

Recognition of services rendered took different forms in the individual independence movements. In Argentina, as thanks for their valiancy, the *Sociedad de Beneficencia* (Beneficient Society) with thirteen women as charter members was created by the decree of 2 January 1823. "For the first time in the Rio de la Plata region was officially recognized the woman's right in society to an equal place with that of the men" (Galván Moreno, 1940, in Sosa de Newton, 1967: 61). Besides legislating a measure of dignity and self-respect for women, this decree also put education at the disposal of females and provided protection to young women.

Generally speaking, however, women were barred from literary academies, "universities," offices, and other organizations, a situation prevalent in all of Spanish and Portuguese America. The irony of the independence movements and the fostering of "democratic" governments by liberals, most notably in the Hispanic ex-colonies, was that these revolutionary regimes were superimposed on patriarchal societies in which ex-slaves, women, and other class and racial groups had little effective voice in government. In the nineteenth century females remained almost totally ineffective politically while upper-class women attempted to gain a modicum of leverage through associations.

THE HISPANIC AMERICAS: AFTER INDEPENDENCE

Transitions in socio-economic-political systems of nineteenth-century Latin American nations provide a framework for theorizing about changes for females in all those societies. While I have examined materials for all Latin American countries I shall discuss only those for which the most materials are available.

Nineteenth-century Argentine females who lived outside city limits were of several types: shopkeepers, farmers, wives of soldiers, or "women" of the troops—the cuartelera and militia. Sarmiento noted that women on the Pampas played "extremely important roles" with the military, that cooking and washing were their primary functions in camp. He spoke of women who accompanied Ramirez and of the courage of some 1,800 women in Urquiza's excursion into Entre Rios (Villafane Casal, 1958: 15-6). He said of another camp situation:

> . . . the women, far from being an impediment in the campaigns were, on the contrary, the most powerful help to the sustenance, discipline, and service of the montonera [group of revolutionary horsemen]. Their intelligence, their suffrance, and their following served to maintain the soldier's faith. (Villafane Casal, 1958: 19-20.)

All types of camp follower are cited with the armies of Roças, and it is these females whom Avallaneda and Zeballos commended for their contributions to Argentine development (Ramayón, 1921; Cadete X, 1878; Villafane Casal, 1958: 12-13). Women in the military—as auxiliaries, as family members, even as camp followers—were needed and deserve more credit for their duties than simply being cited as good washerwomen and good cooks (Villafane Casal, 1958: 27-39 passim).

During the War of the Triple Alliance (1865-1870) Paraguayan women distinguished themselves in a number of campaigns and gained the respect

of soldiers as primary ordnance, material, and food suppliers to the army
(Vittone, 1968:8-9). The combined Argentine, Brazilian, and Uruguayan
forces decimated the ranks of Paraguay's population, so that by 1870
of some 120,000 Paraguayans still alive, women outnumbered men approximately six to one (AHPg, 1972:3). Less than a century later women
gave a repeat performance in the Chaco War (1932-1935), that conflict
engaging two of Latin America's most downtrodden and exploited
peoples, the Paraguayans and Bolivians, and again leaving a surplus of
females in Paraguay.

The condition of white and Amerindian women captured during conflicts on the Pampas caused General Mansilla to comment, "Who is not
moved by the sad look and tears of a woman?" (Villafane Casal, 1958:
43). In Argentina there were attempts to rectify the servile situation of women captured during Indian wars on the Argentine plains.
In 1826 a document signed by fifty caciques and caciquillos provided
for the exchange of female captives in war (Villafane Casal, 1958:43).
In 1857 when congress reconvened in Paraná, provisional capital of
the Argentine confederation, it sanctioned a law authorizing the executive power "to spend up to the amount of 25,000 pesos for the re-
acquisition of Argentinas captured by the savage Indians of the Province
of Buenos Aires" (Villafane Casal, 1958:43). Women captives in Argentina were romanticized and brought to public awareness by Esteban
Echeverria's *La Cautiva* (1837), a story of Rosas' campaign.

Among upper classes in nineteenth-century rural Spanish America,
the role of the married female often was one of being subordinate to her
husband. The male, whether father, husband, governor, priest, military
chieftain, or judge, held the highest rank in the social hierarchy, while
the female was expected to cater to male society's needs. Yet the sub-
missiveness was contradictory, for at the same time she was (and is) held
responsible for attitudes and values developed in her society. For example,
the influence of an uneducated mother over her children perpetuated a
system that deprived society of participation from all its members and placed
a psychological burden on the overall society.

There were some exceptions in public activities that can be pointed
to as examples of the "tolerance" of a social group or flexibility of a
system. Female control in some economic areas is evidenced in letters
from *estancieras* (female ranch owners) who requested licenses for sale
of haciendas, such as the letter from Josepha Prado to the Alcalde de
Primer Voto, 2 February 1789 (cited in Grenan, n.d.). Specific examples
of women as administrators, owners, and *majordomos* (foremen) of
estates are seen from notices such as: one Doña Magdalena de Arguëllo,
majordoma of an estancia of Don Luis Dias; Doña Marsela de Salas y
Valdes, aide to Alcalde y Sargent Mar Don Carlos Villagran y Mendoza;
or one Doña Carlota Guzman who, in 1826, arrived at Chivolcoy bringing

a flock of sheep and who, according to the chroniclers, was the first woman and third person in that part of Buenos Aires province (Grenan, n.d.; Villafane Casal, 1958: 53-4). Upper-class rural and estancia women also were captured in romance by W. H. Hudson whose *Alla lejos y hace tiempo* is a series of biographical sketches about women he saw on estancias.

In addition to their military services and occasional estate management, a primary area of lower-class female involvement was in domestic work. In that sector, young women, fifteen to twenty years of age, and old women, especially those of the interior, served in varying capacities, and some apparently were treated harshly by their señoras (married woman, presumably the household head). Other rural women were field laborers and tenant farmers, while women living in the environs of *pueblos* (towns) formed unique defense units. In these areas woman's work was constant, lasting all day long, both in the home and in the field. Night work was the most onerous of all tasks, and this was often given over to women, on the frontiers especially (La Tribuna, 1854: I, 30, 31; Alsina and Osuna, 1880: I). Poor whites, mulattas, mestizas, and occasionally Indians comprised the peon women of the estancia, the praises of whom were sung by romanticizers of the plains (Silva Valdes, 1952).

Documentation regarding stores enumerate many saleswomen despite some official suggestions that few women seemed inclined to work in *pulperias* and *cantineras* (types of rural stores and taverns). Several pulperias owned by women have been noted in writings of military men and foreign travelers. These frequent references to female ownership and management of retail trading establishments on "highways," in the pampas, and elsewhere provide useful material for investigation into the role of women. For example, in 1843, on the road from Lima Verde to Buenos Aires was the pulperia of one Doña Serafina; the descriptions of it detail its service and food (Pellington, 1939).

Women also were involved in the "medical profession." The curandera was of great importance in the rural ambient, where certified doctors were not found. The result was that "la medica" was the only recourse to those who suffered. "It is known that in this profession the two sexes are equal," and so scarce were doctors in certain instances that the cabildos refused to accept the demands by some licensed professionals to transfer to another locality, with resultant abandonment of the public weal (Beltrán, 1937).

In addition to their medical activities females functioned as *carteras* (letter carriers) and *maestras de posta* (postmistresses). There are many references to them in documents, and travelers to the Platine also mentioned both (Bernard, 1941; Beaumont, 1826-1827; Grenan, n.d.; "Patricias cordobesas, Seccion patriotica," 4). In this area, women were also *maestras* (schoolteachers). There is abundant legislation, reports, and letters concerning education of women and the appointment of schoolteachers (Villafane Casal, 1958: 69-85).

Education for females was a theme in many early nineteenth-century journals, particularly those of Mexico, Peru, and the Platine, and it coincided with male musings on the role and place of women in society, household needs and management, and beauty tips. Some journals were sympathetic to the civil position of females. The editors of *El Diario de Mexico* noted that "women are the most abandoned of creatures in the area of learning" and suggested that their talents be used for more than household occupations (13 December 1805: LXXIV, 325). This attitude is reflected in a number of other journals also. Perhaps the Enlightenment encouraged discussion on the education of women, making men aware that the care and education of their sons was in the hands of illiterate and ignorant mothers. Perhaps motives for supporting feminine education, for removing it from the superstitious recesses of convent and church, were not altruistic but merely a concern for implementation of their male progeny's enlightenment.

Two Platine countries seem to have been forerunners of enlightened legislation for social, economic, and political freedoms and responsibilities for women. Uruguay was a leader in education and female education in mid-century under José Varela, a disciple of the Manns and Sarmiento. Under Varela's influence in 1877 a law was enacted establishing free, compulsory, coeducational primary schooling and free, secular, coeducational secondary and teacher-training education. The Argentines, also followers of the Manns and highly emulative of United States procedures, adapted educational opportunities for its women, earlier than most of the rest of Latin America although it was a long struggle.

Until 1810 in Buenos Aires there were only two educational establishments for girls, and the offerings prepared females for such "nonmasculine" activities as singing, painting, and dancing, as well as languages, reading, writing, and virtue (Gregorio Lavie, 1947: 6-7). Rivadavia in 1823 founded the Beneficent Society for the education of girls under state auspices, a social reform of great significance. In 1854 Juana Manso began her campaign for education of women with the idea that "the curriculum of the female is indispensable for the education of the people" (Gregorio Lavie, 1947: 8). She was supported by Juana Manuela Gorriti (1820-1894), another feminist precursor who exposed the "terrible situation" of women, and it was the result of efforts by these and other feminists that the first normal schools for women opened, with new opportunities for education without traditional barriers of male prejudice.

Argentina's educational system had been encouraged by Americans, the Horace Manns, and their enthusiasm had prompted Sarmiento to establish a free public educational system, devoid of Roman Catholic Church control and staffed by only lay teachers. It also was Sarmiento's intention during his presidency (1868-1874) to develop professional schools. One normal school graduate whom he encouraged personally was Cecilia Grierson. She entered the School of Medicine of the University of Buenos Aires and after enduring the "persecution" of male staff and students became the first female graduate (1889) in medicine. She later founded the first school of nursing and public-health facilities in Buenos Aires city although she was refused teaching positions at the university and was forced to relegate her pedagogical activities to secondary schools.

If we are to judge by journals it appears that *porteños* (residents of the major port of Buenos Aires city) were the most enlightened in their attitudes toward women. That thought is best represented by *Telégrafo Mercantil,* whose editorial policies and articles appeared to be favorable to the feminine cause and many of whose letters to the editor were written by women, a rare source of prose material by literate Spanish American women. A series of these letters, initiated by one entitled "Portrait of a Respectable Woman," sarcastically intones the virtues and queenly qualities of a porteña in her realm of religion and romance and questions why women cannot become involved in useful work. Why must women be ascribed the role of complacency and acceptance of fate in their relationships with men? Why do they know little of their own interests? The conclusions that she draws are that women have more than physical virtures to offer men; that education at an early age may prevent boredom of daily adult life, and that women are human beings with the ability to learn (TM, 27 December 1805).

Material life in the decades between independence and the end of the nineteenth century was not a burden for all Latin American women. The persistent preoccupation by male society with the softer, feminine qualities of women was reflected in attention, particularly at the middle and upper levels of society, to "respectable" conduct and "proper marriage." We have much information on the comfortable aspects of female life. This appears in written criticisms of woman's squandering of household monies on luxuries that ultimately led her husband to financial ruin (SE, 19 April 1810: II, 16). These criticisms are merely additives to an extensive list of defects in the female personality, such as woman's inability to enhance her position economically or socially other than through marriage; her weakness of character, which caused bad behavior in her children; or her squandering of her husband's finances in extravagant and ostentatious habits. Leisure was both an important concept and an important activity for women of the upper classes. The list of establishments catering to these activities, in Peru for example, included an Italian school of dancing and a school of design, both of which appeared representative of the culture and comfort of Lima.

Despite the "freedom" of ladies of leisure, anxieties persisted. Concerns of Latin America males were given some measure of attention with long discussion in the *Mercurio Peruano* and the *Diario de Mexico* on maternal duties, protection of pregnant women, and problems of prenatal care. These discussions stressed that women had the most serious tasks in human existence—preservation of the species—and warned against utilization

of folk medicine curanderas who preyed on the superstitions of the uneducated (MP, 26 May-27 November 1791: passim; D de Mx, 28 January-5
July 1806: passim). The journals also inveighed against dangers of venereal
disease to mothers' health and possible resultant sick children, as well as the
questionable role of wet nurses in the rearing of healthy children.

Whereas the journalistic medium demonstrated a reasonable amount
of concern about middle- and upper-class women, especially those in
Argentina, Mexico, and Peru, very little care was shown for conditions of
working-class women. Generally, life for these women in the nineteenth
century was not the best of all possible worlds. They were unwitting
victims of the revolutions, civil wars, international conflicts, gaucho strug-
gles, and other bloody actions to settle Latin American "frontiers"
(Blomberg, 1933; Mansilla, 1933; Arciniegas, 1961; Vega Díaz, 1955).
Although Argentina was to gain a reputation as a leader in instilling
dignity into woman's existence, it was not until May 1890 that a petition
was presented to Argentina's national congress with some important measures regarding the labor of women and minors: prohibition of work for
girls under fourteen and reduction of the workday to six hours for boys
and girls from ages fourteen to eighteen; prohibition of work in industries
that affect female organs; abolition of night work for women and for minors
under eighteen years of age; prohibition of piecework and subleasing work
(Pichel, 1968: 58-9).

In general, however, Argentines evinced contradictory concern with
growing social problems. As long as prostitution did not utilize their own
women, xenophobic Argentines could wax condemnatory of foreigners who
brought their white slaves to Buenos Aires. By the end of the nineteenth
century when numerous immigrant girls were engaged in prostitution, the
only sentiment exhibited by Argentines was that they were foreign harlots,
not that they were exploited women. (Solberg, 1970: 100-1).

Some upper-class Argentines viewed all women as deceitful creatures
and thought the war between the sexes essentially was one of sham in which
women's modesty and morality chiefly were pretenses designed to interest
men in their bodies, and their affection was little more than a lure to matrimony (Crawford, 1966: 121). Some Argentine and Spanish writers popular
in Latin America, such as the traditionalist Perez Escrich, wrote novels
that counteracted the rising romanticizing tendency that glorified the
relationships that could exist in equal honesty between men and women
rather than dwell on the subservient role of women that society demanded.

Señora Calderón de la Barca has left us some superficial glimpses of
female life in nineteenth-century Cuba and Mexico that delineate the
different social roles of females of varying ethnic groups. In Cuba she
noted numerous aristocratic and wealthy women who apparently were
seen frequently at the opera and in theaters and who had large enough
fortunes to entertain sumptuously (Calderón de la Barca, n.d.: 23-9 passim).
Curiously, in Mexico City and Lima, the appearance of women at the

theater was frowned upon. Calderón de la Barca noted also that shop-keepers had to take their fashions and other items to private homes because in Havana it was not an acceptable custom for women to go into shops. A striking contrast within the society were "liberated Havana ladies, with their white faces, and black eyes" attended by many Negresses.

In Mexico, similar situations were noted, although Mexican society seems not so splendiferous, not so openly "scandalous" as nineteenth-century Cuba. Upper-class Mexican women were, for the most part, restricted to church, some cultural affairs, and care of the household. On the other hand, the "Yankee" Señora Calderón seemed somewhat squeamish about the immorality and unkempt nature of lower-class Ibero-American women, especially *galopinas* (kitchen maids), who, it seems, earned little and therefore stole much (Calderón de la Barca, n.d.: 197).

Señora Calderón described women in nineteenth-century Mexican urban society:

> others, now that their church-going duty was over, equipped in velvet or satin, with their hair dressed . . . leading their children by the hand, dressed [in] Long velvet gowns . . . diamond earrings . . . high French caps. . . . As a contrast to the Señoras . . . were the poor Indian women, trotting across the square, their black hair plaited with dirty red ribbon . . . and a little mahogany baby hanging behind. . . . All the groups . . . were here collected by the hundreds; the women of the shopkeeper class, or it may be lower, in their smart white embroidered gowns, with their white satin shoes, . . . and rebosos . . . thrown over their heads; the peasants and countrywomen, with their short petticoats of two colours, generally scarlet and yellow . . . or bronze-colored damsels. . . . And above all, here and there, a flashing Poblana with a dress of real value and much taste. . . . (Calderón de la Barca, n.d.: 145-6.)

Señora Calderón also noted that while men could sit in high-backed chairs or on benches in church, women had to kneel or sit on the ground, and their position at other public events usually was of the same subservient character (Calderón de la Barca, n.d.: 147).

On feast days women were predominant in the churches. On Good Friday, "ladies all issue forth in mourning." On Sundays they would pour into the main square from Church, some wearing black gowns and mantillas" (Calderón de la Barca, n.d.: 147).

Calderón found that convents were rich, that each girl who entered had paid a sizable sum, and that a sample convent contained about three dozen to four dozen nuns and novices, She also suggested that once a girl entered or was put in the convent, there was little opportunity for her to return to secular life.

Education occurred only among the upper classes and then, primarily, through tutors. Women were taught reading, writing, and what we today call home economics or domestic science. Furthermore, in addition to there being no schools there were neither public nor private amusements. In the rare cases of young girls and boys attending school together, it was under the tutelage of an old woman. At the age of twelve, the sexes were separated. Calderón de la Barca indicated that she knew of not more than a half-dozen married women or girls older than fourteen years of age who read anything other than a Mass book.

Generally speaking, nineteenth-century Spanish America was a society in which woman's place was dependent in part on economic conditions that determined her social stratum and her role in society. There were definite divisions between upper- and lower-class, between rural and urban women, between females of various racial and ethnic groups. The "occupation" and the behavior of women in their societies was determined and influenced by all these factors. This generalization remains true for almost every area of nineteenth-century Hispanic America with a peculiar twist in Paraguay where a persistent shortage of males had modified family organization and marital standards and allowed or forced women to control and participate in many areas of public affairs. This exercise of female power was enforced by an almost total elimination of the upper classes during the last three decades of the nineteenth century and the loss of much of the male population; thus, there was a need for informal marriage arrangements to perpetuate Paraguay's population.

Upper-class peninsular and creole families transferred basic characteristics of Hispanic traditions to their upper- and middle-class counterparts in the numerous nineteenth-century Spanish American republics. Basic outlines of this tradition included extended families and a thriving institution of compadrazgo relationships; a patriarchal society dominated by an authoritarian male figure; familial and social patterns of behavior in which the wife's purview extended to domestic management and the socialization, education, and religious training of her children, albeit in all other areas she was subject to her husband's authority.

Among the lower classes, variations existed. Nomadic *gaucho* (cowboys of the Pampas, the vast plains areas of the Plata River region) groups in Argentina, Uruguay, and other pastoral areas maintained rather loose connubial ties with whatever females were convenient. Agricultural families in villages or distant countrysides usually were less casual but still found loose alliances more convenient, as did many urban proletariat. Both rural and urban workers functioned within a smaller, more circumscribed family group than did their wealthier kin.

Despite many similarities Brazil shares with other Spanish American countries, contrasts between the Ibero-American states and their approaches to and achievement of political independence and economic development bear some suggestions for differences of roles and attitudes regarding

females. The relatively quiescent attainment of Brazil's political freedom
from Portugal contrasted sharply with the violent upheavals of Hispanic
nations against their mother country. As Graham (1972) noted, the traditional, corporate society survived in Brazil with all that that implied for
each stratum and its individual members.

THE NINETEENTH CENTURY IN
BRAZIL: THE IMPERIAL YEARS,
1822-1889

Socially, the life of a nineteenth-century Brazilian woman depended on
her class and color to determine whether hers would be a secluded life.
It could be said that for a female in nineteenth-century Brazilian society,
it was not necessarily the best of all worlds to have been born white.
Sobrados (one- or two-story dwellings) had sprung up in the cities and
secluded in them were upper-class white women. Their rooms were removed from the street and often deprived of light and air, this sequestering
being, supposedly, a Moorish survival into the nineteenth century (Morse,
1958: 35). Morse also pointed out that these "Moslem" vestiges officially
had been banned from Rio de Janeiro and other cities, except São Paulo,
by early nineteenth century. At family gatherings women were expected
to occupy the cane-bottomed sofa at one end of the parlor and often they
did not appear, even at the dinner table, before male guests (Morse, 1958:
36). Further, Morse, in quoting Sarmiento's *Recuerdos* (1916: 191), notes
that rural Argentina maintained this divan, "inherited from the Arabs"
and originally used as a protective place for woman. One traveler in
Pernambuco, Tollenare, observed that "there are many parents who do
not wish their daughters to learn to read and write," and so uncultured
were these women that when some became baronesses and viscountesses
under the empire, they were illiterate and smoked like backwoodsmen
(Freyre, 1964: 314).

Brazilian girls of good family married as young as thirteen and fourteen,
and the famous traveler, Richard Burton, noted that it was still common
in the mid-nineteenth century for fifteen-year-old girls to marry seventy-
year-old men. Regardless the age, once married females were occupied
forever after in the humdrum tasks of lacework, sweetsmaking, and so on,
swathed in cloaks, high collars, and mantillas to protect them from unfamiliar males. The English observer Alexander Caldcleugh noted that
"marriages are formed when the parties are very young and it is by no
means uncommon to meet with mothers not thirteen years old," while
Walter Colton wrote that in Rio de Janeiro he met a twelve-year-old who
was a "respectable married lady. A mother as well" (Freyre, 1964: 320).

Women usually were devotees at religious affairs, always expected to be
present at family prayer sessions, and usually combined their religious
responsibilities with the chance to show off their scant finery (Morse, 1958:

passim; Freyre, 1963, 1964: passim). Freyre has discussed "the creative maternalism which from the first century of colonization stood out as typical in the colonization of Brazil" and has blithely asserted that "the presence of European women in greater numbers is perhaps the element most actively responsible for the development of the great cities and the architecture of elegant colonial residences" a queer contradiction that does nothing to dispel the widely noted repressive patriarchalism of Brazilian families (Freyre, 1963: 30-1). For, as he also noted, development of cities and the movement from plantations to townhouses meant that by the nineteenth century, city mansions had become the prisons of Brazilian virgins who were shut up in their rooms among their servants. Women hardly had anything to do but the domestic routines of cooking, sewing, and of scurrying to hide when male visitors came to call. Travelers in the first half of the nineteenth century noted houses with high walls of difficult access to strangers because "inside jealous, brutal husbands held sway." Unmarried girls were not present at wedding festivities, were not in promenades on the streets, and were just beginning to appear with thei faces uncovered at theaters. An American scientist noted that "as a rule, the old Portuguese custom of seclusion is still dominant in all the Amazonian country towns" (Smith, 1879: 122-3). Another American visitor noted that "the life of the Indian woman . . . seems enviable, in comparison with that of the Brazilian lady in the Amazonian towns" (Aggasiz and Aggasiz, 1868: 269). The only women who appeared frequently on the streets in Rio, São Paulo, Minàs, Recife, or other places were Negresses and mulattas (Stewart, 1856: 148; Graham, 1824; Saint-Hilaire, 1830: I, 210; Mello Leitão, 1934: 84).

The cult of the woman became an obsession in urbanizing societies in the nineteenth century, and in Latin America as well as Europe women were expected to conform to ideals of what males considered pleasurable. For example, the feet of upper-class Brazilian women often were deformed because of efforts to keep them small, women's waists were laced to the point of excruciation, and hair was grown long and fixed in elaborate coiffures or adorned by combs. On the contrary Afro-Brazilian women, at least during the first half of the nineteenth century in Bahia, had to wear their hair short and cleanly covered in a turban as a contrast to women of higher standing.

Despite these glorious ideals of woman as an artificial creation of the male ego for his sexual pleasure, other images of Brazilian women remained. To the outsider persistent images were the fourteen- or fifteen-year-old girl, with narrow chest and sunken, romantic eyes; the mother of eighteen or twenty years, with a soft, puffy, unhealthy obesity; the woman who died old at the age of twenty-five, at the birth of the eighth or ninth child, whose only intimacy with her husband had been that of the marriage bed (Freyre, 1963: 91).

In 1882 a prominent physician reported that in the richest homes of Rio pulmonary tuberculosis among young girls was frequent, while another doctor noted that the Brazilian woman was

> a slave who has not yet received, nor will in the near future, the benefits of emancipation. . . . She was not even a human being . . . this pathetic creature whom they indoctrinate from a tender age with the idea that woman should be a slave of dress and outward show so she may more easily become the slave of man. (Torres Homem, 1870; Correa de Azevedo, 1872: 416-40.)

There is little doubt that the upper-class Brazilian female's health as well as her short life span was due to several things: constant care by and association with servants who themselves suffered chronic skin irritation; being dressed in clothing so tight as to prevent the proper development of internal organs, especially the uterus; and confinement to indoor quarters.

Despite their segregated existence and the likelihood of the wife becoming a sickly, deformed person because of her seclusive role, some able women in both plantations and mansions came to run all family activities. These were such women as Dona Brites de Albuquerque in colonial days (see Chapter 6 above), Dona Joaquina do Pompeu, Dona Francisca de Rio Formoso, and others (Freyre, 1963: 75). In the latter half of the nineteenth century, as cities began to grow in size and sophistication, some semblance of freedom developed for the white female. It was said that "[at] Pará, one no longer sees ladies shut up from all intercourse with visitors, and banished from the table" (Smith, 1879: 50). Theaters increasingly were patronized by women, and a woman's emancipation society appeared in April 1870 with the dual goal of freeing "the wombs of . . . female slaves" as well as "themselves from the narrow, subdued life such as had been imposed on them by the mold of colonial times" (Morse, 1958: 144, 147, quoted from the *Correio Paulistano*, 10 April 1870). There even was evidence of girls eloping with their sweethearts, a pattern that alarmed some writers and parents who saw bad influences in theater and literature such as in the novels of José de Alencar whose "portrait of proud, capricious women . . . may lead an innocent young girl astray" (Goes Bettencourt, 1885; her novels include *Jephthah's Daughter* and *Forgiving Angel*).

Advances in education during the empire included the development of public elementary schools. Although there were many more schools for boys than for girls and with separate curricula, some females were able to acquire an education. Also, a number of private elementary and secondary schools were established for girls, particularly in the south. Some teacher-training schools were organized but girls who entered them were considered

immoral, and women were excluded from the prestigious Colegio Dom
Pedro Segundo. By 1883 the majority of students in coeducational teacher-
training schools were women. In 1881 the first female medical student
appeared, joined in 1882 by three other women (see Havighurst and Moreira,
1965, for an elaborate discussion on education).

In the decade immediately preceding the establishment of the Brazilian
republic, there was a general increase of women in the liberal professions,
unescorted ladies in the streets, and more participation in public functions.
Nonetheless, it was not until 1886 that a woman was appointed to serve
in a São Paulo post office and not until 1898 that the first female graduated from the law school, although thousands of women already were
working at stenographic and industrial jobs (Morse, 1958: 215). Brazil's
assembly of 1823 had included a project of instruction for women, and on
15 October 1827 a law was passed to provide schools in "cities, towns
and the most populous places" for young girls (Thomé, 1967: 45). But
by 1854 the project barely was off the ground, and in 1857 a professor
of São Vicente had to present an oficio to the inspector general of public
instruction for reading and writing (Thomé, 1967: 45).

It has been indicated that among rank-and-file laborers, women as well
as men were sought from abroad by Brazilian mill owners to run machinery
and to train Brazilian operatives of both sexes (Stein, 1957: 51). Also, in
the latter half of the nineteenth century both young men and young women
of poor families were being trained as mill operatives and were employed
in other positions in factories. In Bahia's Todos los Santos mill, seventy
of the 150 employees were women. However in the 1890s a white man
might earn the equivalent of two shillings a day—a pittance—but the
female earned even less: two pounds, two shillings a month for piecework
(Stein, 1957: 51-3).

Stein also has given us an informative picture of nineteenth-century
plantation life for females in his study of the patriarchal, compadre-
dominated society of Vassouras município in the present-day state of
Rio de Janeiro. The roles of slave and free women on nineteenth-century
plantations were quite different. Free women, passive creatures of planters,
merchants, and professional men, contrast with economically and socially
more mobile slave women who, Stein infers, were more independent after
manumission than were upper-class women. Among slaves themselves,
travelers noted that because of the separation of married slaves, "most of
the slave children have only one parent, the mother" and that was the
result of the disproportion between male and female slaves (Couty, 1881:
25). A report in the Rio de Janeiro province noted a third fewer women than
men among slaves in 1841 (Stein, 1957a: 155). After abolition female slaves
abandoned their chores as cooks, washerwomen, dishwashers, housecleaners,
and nursemaids but later returned to work as piecework coffee pickers.

A Vassouras schoolteacher in 1873 noted of free plantation women that "a woman in Brazil is still the image of what she used to be; she still bears on her wrists the marks of chains; she has not yet taken the place which is rightfully hers" (Stein, 1957a:152). Wives of plantation owners "deferred as submissively as did their children"; Stein noted one planter who for fourteen years forbade his wife to visit her mother; a woman who fled her husband; and another who, after twenty-three years and eight children, could no longer tolerate her husband (1957a: 147, 158). There were only a few ways by which upper-class plantation women might achieve economic and intellectual emancipation, such as by administering property after a husband's death or managing an estate.

Only in the second half of the nineteenth century did it become more common for wealthier planters to permit their daughters to attend school, parties, church, and the theater, although that in no way changed the practice of marrying daughters barely in their teens to enhance family position or fortune. In the interlocking alliances of traditional societies, marriages were major social events, and daughters of upper-class families were pawns in these arrangements, as were daughters of poor freemen whom the wealthy protected (Stein, 1957a: 154). These nineteenth-century Brazilian females were reared to accept traditional submission to family males and in their role as wife to tolerate the man chosen for them and also his extramarital relations with female slaves.

African and Afro-Brazilian women were a substantial part of nineteenth-century Brazil's population. Many were freedwomen who dominated produce and retail market activities. Prior to abolition (1888) African-born slave women in Rio de Janeiro were apt to acquire their freedom more quickly than men. It was easier for women to obtain freedom because they usually had more opportunities for closer relationships with white men and also more opportunities, particularly on an *ao ganho* (self-earn) basis, to earn money to purchase their freedom (Karasch, 1972: 421-2). Also, women cost less; the prices for purchase of liberty were lower than for males and, further, women were valued less for the labor than for services a master could obtain whether a woman was slave or free (Karasch, 1972: 424).

In the north and northeast as in Rio de Janeiro and other areas of southern Brazil, it appears that urban slaves, partly free, and freedwomen were active in marketplace and domestic activities. It seems that regardless of the area or whether the scene was rural or urban, the African and Afro-Brazilian female had more opportunities than her male counterpart for obtaining freedom. Also, the black and mulata established power patterns in economic activities and social relationships that developed during colonial days and carried through the nineteenth century, thus delineating patterns of behavior for the twentieth century.

8 TWENTIETH-CENTURY WOMAN: THE HERITAGE OF HISPANIA

Latin American females reached the twentieth century still bound by attitudes nurtured in the precepts of *Las Siete Partidas* (thirteenth-century law codes) and the Laws of Toro (a recompilation of principal civil codes in the sixteenth century). Toro Law 54 stated that no married woman could accept or repudiate inheritance except by permission of her husband or, as the famous Hispanic American jurist José Maria Ots Capdequi observed of woman in the Spanish Indies:

> In Spanish law . . . only in exceptional situations, does the woman enjoy full civil rights. . . . The single woman is always submissive to paternal authority . . . the married . . . inside the orbit of a new power as *acusado* as the first. Only the state of widowhood permits the woman to earn her full civil rights. (Pichel, 1968: 42.)

The twentieth century, however, has brought increasing pressures on the customary pattern of male-female relationships, on family traditions, and on the general social fabric, especially in light of subtle shifts in the status of females within family and society. These changes have occurred as a result of pressures from within and without. Some evolved from gradual reforms in the Spanish American republics while others, more revolutionary in

176

nature, resulted from contacts outside of Latin America. Not only did more Latins travel to North America and western Europe, but more "western" ideas and women traveled to or remained in Latin countries, and this dual intercourse influenced external relationships and internal habits.

Another factor of change has been the growth of cities, making available transportation and communications that bring new ideas and threaten traditional family structure. With twentieth-century urbanization has come an increase in the tempo of life, from unhurried to rushed, and a change in living style: people have moved out of patriarchal mansions and into small homes or apartments. These changes have whittled down such notions of privacy and family relaxation, as represented by enclosed backyard patios, and have replaced them with innovations such as the openness of American front yards which, ironically, few families use.

In addition to new ideas of family relations, communications, housing, and urbanization, the impact of industry has induced changes in the economy and thus in occupational opportunities for women. Females first entered the teaching and clerical professions, then went into business, government, sales, and nursing, and now those from the provinces who otherwise would have become domestic servants in urban households come from the villages to labor in urban factories. With new freedoms and responsibilities of wage earning, gradually females are changing their ideas about matrimony and maternity; nations have made constitutional changes regarding divorce; and civil-rights guarantees for women are becoming more commonplace. Latin American women slowly but surely are moving toward both the benefits and the hazards of behavior norms accepted by twentieth-century Western society.

THE SPANISH AMERICAN MAINLAND

Education

In Latin American countries there have been relatively few formal restrictions on women's access to education in this century, but this is countered by traditional attitudes regarding capacities and aptitudes of women. Education is recognized by some Latin intellectuals as fundamental for their nation's social independence, and thus some countries have sought to upgrade education and professional training of women, which, nonetheless, remains inferior to that of men. But in addition to extreme differences in attitudes toward female education among Latin American nations, there is a variance in general female educational opportunities between urban and rural areas. For example, functional literacy and general intellectual achievement is much higher in Buenos Aires, Santiago, Mexico City, or Lima than it is in remoter rural regions where below-subsistence standards of living are handmaidens to illiteracy rates of 90 percent or more.

It would appear that the student selection process is linked to the degree to which families are economically privileged or underprivileged. In 1950, 49 percent of Latin America's population over fifteen years had none or less than one year of schooling; of 44 percent who had more than one year of primary education, only 8 percent had finished; of 6 percent who had secondary schooling, only 2 percent had graduated; and only 1 percent of the fifteen years and over group had attended an institution of higher learning (Silvert, 1967: 207-9). Only in Argentina, Chile, Cuba, and Panama have people completed four to six years of primary education, thus providing a broad enough base for social heterogeneity in secondary schooling (Silvert, 1967: 207-9). In all of Latin America in the mid-1950s only 350,000 students were registered in state and private institutions of higher learning. Of these 40 percent were in Argentina and nearly half that total at the National University of Buenos Aires (Silvert, 1967: 207-9). Despite the vagaries of statistics gathering, even the highest enrollment in 1960 does not exceed 550,000 for Latin America.

Argentines seem to have thought and written more about "the woman problem" than most other Ibero-Americans. Also, it appears that Argentine women rank in the highest figures for Latin America for education and other categories. Most studies on the Latin American female stress the few successes she has been able to make despite her position in the overall society. In Argentina woman has been in the forefront of Latin American feminist movements, the fight for education, as writer and journalist, as painter and scientist, and, in the process, has attained a decent but low visibility position in national stature. (For a general discussion see Sosa de Newton, 1967: 141-60 on feminism, 161-80 on education, 181-96 on writers, 197-208 on arts and sciences; Dellepiane, 1921; Schultze de Mantovani, 1960; Pagés Larraya, 1965; Ocampo, 1966; Caillet-Bois, 1952; Machado de Arnão, 1965.)

All areas were a difficult struggle for Argentine women. Although Cecilia Grierson had graduated from the medical school in 1889, not another woman graduated in medicine until 1902. It remained an uphill battle for female medical education.

The first Argentine woman be become a lawyer, Cecilia Tapias, matriculated in 1911. In 1918 the first female engineer and in 1919 the first woman architect were graduated. These were initial achievements of improved female education, for at the start of Sarmiento's drive for literacy in 1869, with the exception of Buenos Aires and other areas, the majority of women could neither read nor write in a population itself two-thirds illiterate. By 1914 only one-third of the population was illiterate although Buenos Aires enjoyed a much higher literacy rate—some 80 percent— than outlying towns and countryside (Scobie, 1964: 154-5, 170). By 1940-1941, Argentina was educating annually 1,014,531 boys and 931,694 girls in primary schools. Only 9 percent of those who left primary school were accepted into secondary school and in secondary schools young women were 49 percent of the total. They comprised 74 percent in normal (teacher-training) schools; universities enrolled some 18,146 men and 3,112 women; enrollment in commercial schools was 61 percent male and 39 percent female, in industrial schools 98 percent male and 2 percent female, and in professional schools, 4 percent male and 96 percent female *(Memoria . . . Educación,* 1941; Recopilacón estadistica, 1941). At the same time the 13,727 schools in Argentina had 11,727 male and 62,609 female instructors.

Under Perón education in general and for women in particular continued to grow, and by 1960 Argentina had the highest percentage among Latin American nations in its primary schools. Its secondary school enrollment was 31 percent of the school-age population (Solari, 1967: 458-9). The latest available data on University of Buenos Aires students show that of 65,328 registered, 32 percent were women and were distributed among schools or colleges in the following percentages: philosophy and letters, 75.1; pharmacy and biochemistry, 55.3; odontology, 49.2; natural sciences, 42.6; law and social sciences, 33.9; medical science, 32.3; architecture, 29.5; economics, 23.8; agronomy and veterinary science, 11.7; and engineering, 3.0 (Sosa de Newton, 1967: 178-9). Of 150,000 diplomas granted by the University of Buenos Aires between 1900 and 1960, 25,000 were to women, according to the following breakdown: the number of females graduates was 36 in the decade 1900-1910; 541 in 1911-1920; 1,599 in 1921-1930; 2,695 in 1931-1940; 6,457 in 1941-1950; and 16,376 in 1951-1960 (Sosa de Newton, 1967: 179). As of 1964 outside of the University of Buenos Aires, the rest of the eight state universities boasted 10,053 women of a total enrollment of 52,715 students (Sosa de Newton, 1967: 179).

As of 1965 numbers and percentages of female professional graduates from the University of Buenos Aires were as follows: in medicine, 1,323 or 20.26 percent; law, 568 or 22.04 percent; pharmacy 545 or 55.44 percent; biochemistry 149 or 51.55 percent; dentistry 938 or 48.80 percent; architecture 274 or 27.8 percent; agronomy 27 or 9.18 percent; civil engineering 17 or 2.34 percent. This is better than for most of Latin America.

Like Argentina, Chile has been an exception to the rule of widespread functional illiteracy. Chile's illiteracy rate of 19.4 percent for men and 11.9 percent for women in 1968 and its female university population at the University of Chile of some 46.1 percent gave the country one of the highest averages in Latin America and in the world (LaBarca Hubertson, 1952; 16ff.).

Chilean women, especially those of the strongly aspirational middle class, have done well at professional educational opportunities. By the mid-1960s women comprised 8.5 percent of Chile's 4,729 doctors and

32 percent of its dentists, and they were prominent in pharmacy, architecture, law, and as paramedics. (Blitz, 1965:104). Furthermore, many middle-class Chilean women have seized the advantage in jobs and education training for jobs, derivative from the technological age, which have not yet had the opportunity to become sex stereotyped, such as computer programming, economics and other fields of social science, and statistical work. As in Argentina, Chilean women seem to be moving into areas of traditional "masculine" professions with some impunity and considerable success.

In Mexico, a by-product of the revolution was an upsurge in education for women as a result of both an ideal and of society's manpower loss. By 1925, education for Mexican women had moved from narrow curricula of music and fine arts to more practical programs to prepare them for professions and public service. Estimated distribution of 2,602 women in the University of Mexico in 1925 in the following schools and colleges was: 906 in philosophy and letters; 569 in medicine, including midwifery and nursing; 176 in public administration; 59 in chemistry and pharmacy; 21 in dentistry; 4 in law; 1 in engineering; 625 in music; and 241 in fine arts (PAU Bulletin, 1925: 842-3). By 1924 Mexico City had five trade schools for women, and one of the four commercial schools was exclusively for women. Usually middle-class women continued on to teaching or commercial colleges, but upper-class families still frowned on educating a female past the age of fourteen and lower-class families often could not spare their daughters from needed income-producing jobs (Inman, 1922: 353-4).

Yet it should not be assumed that Mexico has made great strides in its educational programs, for by 1960, as compared with Argentina, only 12 percent of Mexico's school-age population was in secondary schools and only one in every 1,000 who began primary school finished a university education. Broken down on a sex ratio basis, by 1969 the education pattern of male and female percentage of the population per years of study was as follows: 8.3 percent male and 10.3 female had no years of study; 19.7 male and 22.7 female had four to six years; 28.7 male and 27.0 female had seven to nine years; 9.2 male and 14.0 female had ten to twelve years; 6.5 male and 4.9 female had thirteen to fifteen years; 14.3 male and 1.4 female had sixteen or more years; and 0.1 percent each male and female had an unknown number of years (Solari, 1967: 459; Silvert, 1967: 208; Elu de Lenero, 1969: 54). Notice the fairly even distribution until the college years; the sharp decline in the percentage of women is due partly to family resistance, to marriage, or to unavailability of resources for females to continue their education.

In some Spanish American areas, the level attained in female education is not so inspiring. In Lima, at the turn of the century, a Centro Social de Senoras was founded to establish a lycée for young women, a preparatory section of Primera Enseñanza (primary school), a commercial section, a domestic school, and other annexes (Aurora Cáceres, 1909: 204). This project provided some kind of secondary education for females, the lack of which was lamentable for Peru, a country that still maintains a very poor school system. In Bolivia, things are not much better. Women make up 38 percent of the student body in primary schools, 40 percent in the secondary schools, and only 11 percent in the universities (*Orientación Revolucionaria,* 1966: 55). There is irony in this, for Peru boasted one of the first higher education policies in the Western Hemisphere; and the University of San Marcos, with Mexico's one of the two oldest in America, in colonial days was a major training area for elites of Peru and Bolivia.

Other countries, especially Colombia and El Salvador, have engaged in an energetic campaign against illiteracy—Colombia with its elementary education plan and El Salvador with its rural literacy program. It seems to have worked, especially in Colombia where, by 1968, of 3,419,392 students in all educational institutions, females comprised slightly more than half, or 1,712,522 pupils (*El Censo Educativo Nacional,* 1968). In Colombia in 1938 some 47 percent of the female population were illiterate as compared to 1964 when that figure had been reduced to 28.8 percent (BME, April 1972: #249). As of 1970 some 39.5 percent or 4,501 of the public university students were women (BME, April 1972: #249). The percentage of women among all university students in Colombia, private or public schools, was 25 percent in 1971 (Cohen, 1971).

In neighboring Venezuela, far richer than Colombia, education is free and compulsory up to the age of fourteen, with a fairly equal distribution of boys and girls. In higher education, however, Venezuelan women comprised only about 34 percent of the student enrollment (AHV, 1971: 131-6).

Two smaller countries, Paraguay and Uruguay, almost diametrically opposite in social welfare programs, have similar educational accomplishments. In Paraguay, primary school enrollments indicated 220,308 boys to 195,483 girls, while secondary figures noted 25,880 boys to 25,528 girls with no explanations suggested for the closeness in secondary enrollments. In most areas of Paraguayan education, female participation is fairly close to male enrollments, the total figures in all schools in 1969 being 250,818 males and 224,031 females (AEP, 1969: 54-5, 59-63).

Uruguay not only has a proud educational tradition, but women are a vital part of its educational system as a result of José Varela's nineteenth-century reforms. Uruguay enjoys a 92 percent literacy rate. Boys and girls are on a par percentagewise in preuniversity institutions, and women total 40 percent of university rolls and 90 percent of all primary school teachers (AHU, 1970:121, 217).

In general women, including those in the labor force, possess a much lower educational attainment level than do men. A common case would be Peru where the 1961 census showed 44.2 percent of the population without

schooling of whom—including those of working age—25.6 percent were men
and 51.8 percent women (Chaney, 1973:47 n. 13). Female education in
urban and industrial areas is being intensified, but the types of education for
women are not necessarily the intellectual's curriculum. More often it is
a practical course that supplies women with the skills to earn a living at
trades, commerce, and clerical work.

However, the degrees and kinds of change vary in different countries,
and female education still suffers from basic problems of Latin American
education, problems that result from the perpetuation of such deficient
methods as rote learning or memorization of facts and insistence on esoteric
subjects far removed from basic national experiences. These deficiencies
infect Latin American universities, especially in the humanities, and stem
from the proposition that mere repetition of humanizing materials will
result in a better society. This is not to say that the basic process of education
is not to humanize. It is just that at this point in their historical time, Latin
American nations require other transfusions into their curricula and need
more diverse kinds of education. A few countries are doing something about
it. For example, Uruguay has established a vocational university for the
practical training of women, Ecuador has established a technical baccalaureate
and a coeducational technical university, Venezuela has begun the Center
of Studies for Development, and Guatemala has its Technical Vocational
Institute and gives courses in industrial and vocational training at primary
schools (Marti, 1967: 198; Rogers, 1970, 1971, passim, for current materials
on education).

Civil Rights

In the area of civil rights the wheels of change have ground a slow but
steady pattern. Spanish American colonial life traditionally had been based
on patriarchal customs of the Iberian family and Castilian laws in which
rights within a family were dictated by the Roman system of supremacy
of the husband-patrón. Transformation of this began only with Vélez
Sarsfield's monumental Código Civil (Vélez Sarsfield, 1870).

Laws reflected the "capitis diminutio" role of woman in the family,
in marriage, in the home, and in ordinary life. However, customs that
existed in Spanish American society a hundred years ago were more restrictive of fundamental female liberty than any laws previously enunciated.
The man was granted property and rights of administration and also the
right to administer and judge the family's welfare, notwithstanding the
rich husband and wife who often "abused custom." In illicit relationships
in which there were illegitimate children, the man assumed no responsibility while the woman endured all of it, since "there is no judicious way of
defending the well-being of women" (Gregorio Lavié, 1947: 10).

Not until the twentieth century were reform projects begun for women's
rights. In Argentina they were written into the Código Civil. Drago, in his

"Emancipación civil de la mujer," attempted to give financial security to wives and drew the wrath of conservative males on his suggestion of divorce. In 1907 Alfredo Palacios and in 1919 Del Valle Iberlucea presented reforms or plans to study ways to reform the civil code on marriage (Moreau de Justo, 1945: 205-7). But it took twenty-one years, from 1905 to 1926, for the Argentine legislature to promulgate the woman's civil rights law, which provided for an improved legal position for women regarding administration of property after divorce and the like. Since that time, all women in Argentina have been qualified for all civil actions, and in marriage they are considered equal to their husbands.

Unfortunately, practice departs from theory, and there are few Ibero-American countries where these ideals have been translated into practical working resolutions. Other countries have had their defenders of female rights, the activities of which were pressed by leagues such as Colombia's Academia Femenina, the Unión Femenina de Colombia, and the Colegio Internacional de Mujeres Escritoras y Periodistas. One of the most active participants was Señora Melo Lancheros, whose book (1966) is a useful compilation of important Colombian women, all of whom are white. Panama's Mesa Redonda Panamericana, Club Interamericano de Mujeres, Asociación Soroptimista de Panamá, Unión de Cuidadanas were societies with programs for the civic and cultural advancement of women (Tejeira, 1963: 161). Chile has followed its neighbors' programs, and the Chilean Civil Code, very close to the Argentinian, was modified by a law that eliminated civil restrictions on women.

In Uruguay, women achieved their political rights in 1917 before attaining civic equality, the measures for which were initiated in legislative reforms of 1926. However, in Uruguay women have certain civil rights that only recently have begun to make inroads in other areas of Hispanic America. Civil marriage, which since 1885 has been the only legally recognized form, has enjoyed several amendments aimed at sexual equality. For example, although the married couple holds property in common, each has the right to individual ownership. Further, since a 1927 amendment the woman no longer has to promise obedience to her husband although both vow to respect each other. In divorce actions—since divorce was legalized in 1907—women can sue on grounds of cruelty, adultery, attempted murder, or desertion for a period of longer than three years; in such instances, she is granted alimony but custody of the children is agreed upon mutually (AHU, 1970: 85-6). In other civil matters Uruguayan women and men enjoy the same equal rights.

Ecuador places great civil restrictions on women representing one of the most traditional national patterns of male control over almost all female activity. A wife is considered legally incapable of entering into any property or commercial dealings, although some softening has occurred in limiting husbands' powers. Women now can file for civil divorce but, in general, divorce is frowned upon for all Ecuadorians primarily because of the influence of a conservative and orthodox Roman Catholic clergy. Premarital property settlements are permitted by law and usually are adhered to (AHEc, 1971).

In Venezuela civil action is directed more toward activities other than marital rights. A growing middle class in that oil-rich nation has produced a vociferous segment of feminists who have acquired full civic and political rights. In general, however, civil codes of most of Spanish America still place the male at the family's head and allow the husband to decide on the place of domicile except in special circumstances. This is the law in Argentina, Uruguay, Chile, Venezuela, and Peru as it is the rule that paternal rights over children far outweigh maternal rights and as it also is the rule that husbands control and adminster family property (AHV, 1971).

Peru had had an active woman's rights program since the Consejo Nacional de Mujeres was founded in 1923. It is a nonprofit, voluntary organization comprised mainly of upper- and middle-class women. It counts as its greatest success Law 17838, which requires a husband to obtain his wife's signature on their communal property (although he remains the sole administrator). Their other activities have included health, welfare, and literacy campaigns. Generally speaking, however, as a basically elitist organization in one of the most conservative and elite-conscious Latin American nations, it is limited in its effectiveness for all Peruvian women (Schipske, 1975: passim).

Economics

In Latin American countries the hearth traditionally was considered the place of work for women, as were all domestic-service areas. In modern times, the problem of women as workers generally depends on the rate of social and economic advances of their country as well as the conditions under which they must work. Little has been done to train women for industry except in Argentina and Brazil, and despite the relatively large numbers of girls who wish to have vocational training, traditional attitudes prevent young women from entering vocational school and otherwise restrict their choice of occupation (ILR, 1952: #1). There has been reinforcement here of a theme common to repressed groups: certain tasks are regarded as suitable only for women and women are suitable only for specific tasks. Coupled with this is the relatively recent involvement by females in industry; hence their inexperience has tended to reinforce the idea that women are not capable workers, and this reinforces the practice of unequal pay for equal work. Only in public service and teaching does equal pay seem to prevail in most of Latin America (ILR, 1956: 189, for a detailed discussion of wages and regulations for women).

Women in Latin America are the least active economically of women and/or men in any major region of the world. In contrast to 41.4 percent of Soviet Union women, 14.5 percent of African, 27.6 percent of European, 21.3 percent of North American, and 28.1 percent of Asian women, Latin

American females as a whole comprise a small portion of the labor force, for only 13 percent are active in Latin America's labor force (UN, Report I, 1962). Of this rate in Mexico, Central America, and the Caribbean, women are 14.2 percent, while the rest of Latin America has 13.1 percent of its women in the labor force. In the entire world, some 272. percent of the world's workers are women (UN, Report I, 1962). Two out of every five actively employed Latin American women work as domestic servants, while the rest are employed as dressmakers, retail sales clerks, office workers, and primary school teachers (Gendell and Rossell, 1967: 8ff.). The largest percentage of actively employed women is in agricultural activities, although the number differs significantly from country to country. Some 32 percent of Peru's active women workers are employed in agriculture, while only 4.7 percent of Chile's are; in Chile, some 76 percent of its working women are in service sectors (*OAS América en cifras*, 1969: 102-7). In toto, according to the above studies, at least 60 percent to 70 percent of all women workers in Latin America are involved in the above activities. Very few Latin countries have a strong industrial sector and, consequently, very few women are employed in jobs derivative of such a structure. Also, few married women are in laboring activities—perhaps only 10 percent for all Latin America.

In all Latin America Argentina provides more available statistical data and can serve as a model for comparisons of economic problems relative to the female sector. We should be mindful that all Latin American nations reflect differences in style and tempo of change, as well as conflict between modernizing and traditional influences in occupational opportunities for women.

In Argentina women began working in large numbers as milkmaids and cigar makers, the latter occupation almost exclusively in the hands of women (Wilde, 1961). Later, females entered mills and workshops; employers did not have to pay them as much as they were required to pay men. Women and children were docile instruments whereby Argentine businessmen could make fortunes, a situation that was not questioned until the 1924 law "Of the work of women and minors." An example of discrepancy of opportunity is seen in the 1914 general census for Argentina. Of an economically active population of 3.4 million, some 714,893 women worked in industry, the liberal professions, and commerce, representing only 22 percent of the total number of laborers more than fourteen years of age. The highest percentage and ratio of women employed was in personal service as is seen in the following figures for 1914: 252,999 female of a total 841,337 workers were in industrial and manual arts; 182,711 women of 218,619 workers were in personal services; 41,578 of 529,866 were in agriculture and animal husbandry; 21,217 or 293,646 were in commerce; 43,640 of 83,184 were in instruction and education; 4,368 of 14,763 were in sanitation; 6,279 of 108,852 were in public administration; 1,799 of 14,192 were in fine arts; and 915 of 8,809 were in arts and sciences (*Tercer censo nacional,* 1914: I, 252). In geographic areas there were 194,517 female workers in the federal capital of Buenos Aires city and some 101,243 in the province of Buenos Aires, while the rest were distributed rather evenly throughout the country: Santa Fe, 46,035; Córdoba, 69,755; Corrientes, 41,779; Santiago del Estero 49,530; Tucumán, 41,603; Entre Ríos, 36,413; Mendoz, 19,008; San Luis, 16,487; San Juan, 8,866; Catamarca, 16,322; La Rioja, 14,590; Salta, 22,950; Jujuy, 15,642; Territorios nacionales, 20,104. (*Tercer censo nacional,* 1914: I, 252).

Recent statistics of women in professional activities are revealing regarding female involvement in traditionally male activities. For example, for graduates of the University of Buenos Aires in predominantly traditionally feminine fields in 1965, of 119 graduates in teaching some 101 or 84.87 percent were women; both library graduates were women; 64 of the 67 or 95.52 percent of the social worker graduates were women, as were 48 of 73 or 65.75 percent of the physical therapists; and all 117 of the midwives were women. For graduates of the University of Buenos Aires in predominantly masculine (so-called pioneer) fields in 1965, of 485 graduates in law some 106 or 21.85 percent were women; in medicine of 1,467, some 311 or 21.19 percent were women; in pharmacy 85 of 148 or 59.44 percent; in biochemistry 20 of 41 or 48.78 percent; in dentistry 240 of 480 or 50 percent; in architecture 65 of 216 or 29.68 percent; in agronomy 7 of 62 or 11.29 percent; in all engineering sciences 8 of 376 or 2.17 percent; in all exact and natural sciences 56 of 162 or 34.56 percent; and in veterinary science 9 of 46 or 19.56 percent were women. The percentage of female instructors in various educational establishments in Argentina in 1965 was: in preprimary schools 4,381 women of 4,402 instructors or 99.5 percent of the total; in primary schools women were 116,254 of 130,743 or 88.9 percent of the total; in junior high they were 50,383 of 85,083 or 59.2 percent; in high school they were 920 of 2,230 or 41.2 percent; and in universities they were 517 of 6,049 or only 8.5 percent (*Departamento de la Mujer, Ministro de Trabajo y Seguridad Social,* 1965: passim).

Comparatively speaking the relatively high participation of women in professions holds true for most Hispanic countries. For example, in heavily rural and relatively poor Paraguay in 1969 more than two-thirds of the dental, nearly one-fourth of the medical, and two-thirds of the chemistry-pharmacy students were women who also fed into the active professional labor force in about that proportion. Similarly, in areas of veterinary medicine, fine arts, and philosophy women outnumbered men (AHPg, 1972: 83-4, 105). A major, if not the major, reason for the prominence of women in public activities in Paraguay was that the Chaco War of the 1930s almost wiped out the entire male population. This followed not too many generations after the equally disastrous Triple Alliance War.

In 1933, suffering the whiplash of depression, women workers did not fare so well although they did better than one might expect given the economic circumstances of the times. In that year in Argentina, of a total of 526,495 industrial workers, some 88,535 were women; by 1947 of a total of 5,490,174 workers, some 1,234,102 women were employed in industrial and commercial establishments. In 1957 of 3,138,095 workers in commerce, textiles, food preparation, metallurgy, confections, meats, chemicals, and domestic service there were some 1,685,279 women (Sosa de Newton, 1967: 218). The Dirección Nacional de la Mujer data noted that in national and provincial public works, women numbered 127,257 of 564,227 employees.

According to the following data we see other discrepancies in employment. The economically active Argentine population by age groups shows these percentages of women workers: of each 100 workers fourteen years of age and over, 6.9 percent were female in 1895 and 6 percent in 1914; by 1947 they were 19.7 percent (Mafud, 1966: 29-30). There were variations in female workers in various sections of the country. In the federal capital women were 31.2 percent of the economically active population broken down as follows: the fourteen to eighteen year age group was 33.9 percent, the eighteen to twenty-nine group was 46.5 percent, the thirty to forty-nine group was 29.9 percent, and the fifty and over group was 14.8 percent. All these percentages respond to factors of mobility, necessity, and availability (Germani, 1955: passim).

By the late 1950s Argentine women composed the following percentages of the total work force in these occupations: clothing, 95 percent; ceramics, 90 percent; tobacco and sanitation, 80 percent each; textiles, viticulture, and perfumes, 70 percent each; tinters and dyers, 70 percent; food, 60 percent; elastics and chemicals, 50 percent each; commerce, 45 percent; plastics, 40 percent; meat packing and pastas, 30 percent each; metallurgy, 25 percent (Stabile, 1961: 62ff. for a breakdown of all sectors and regions of Argentina, by percentage, number, and type of work). In general, it should be noted that the twenty to twenty-four year age group is the highest activity group for all Latin America.

Estimates of Argentina's working population of 8 million out of 20 million in 1962 show that 23 percent of the active labor force were women, a rise from the 1947 count when women were 19.7 percent of the active labor force of 6,267,313 (Stabile, 1962: 122, passim). Yet there were 10 million women in Argentina. Twenty-six occupations had a high percentage of female labor, but dispersion of occupational statistics indicate persisting attitudes regarding types of work suitable for women. Furthermore, differentials in pay for the same tasks gave men 7 percent to 15 percent higher wages than women and, more important, Argentina still lacks adequate legislation to correct these inequities (Stabile, 1962: 122ff.; Mafud, 1966: 30).

There had been lacking three major elements in campaigns to correct women's working conditions: no inspection of conditions; little education of workers in certain areas of specialization; and no organ especially devoted to problems of women workers. In 1934 in Argentina, steps were taken for rights of workers who were pregnant or who did dangerous tasks; licenses became required for work, and the Seguro de Maternidad was established and administered by the Caja de Maternidad for all female workers, whatever their civil state, from fifteen to forty-five years of age, working in industrial or commercial establishments. The commission is organized so that women workers pay a specified amount of their monthly salaries to the Caja, an equal sum of which is matched by the employer. Coverage salary is paid during maternity leave, and no woman can be fired because of pregnancy (Gregorio Lavié, 1947: 13-4). Under Perón female and male workers acquired a previously unattained power through labor legislation. His legislation was a boon to female workers because it aimed at the workers, and his *Derechos* (Workers' Rights) signaled a transcendency of worker and female in Argentina. The Peronist *Derechos del Trabajador* were incorporated in the International Charter of Sindicalist Rights of the United Nations. This began the wave of "equal salary, for equal work." In 1944 Eva Perón added provision to laws for working women, foremost among them the guarantee of free medical care, free hospitalization, a delivery grant in cash, and a layette.

In almost all Spanish American nations it seems that the number of females in low-paying or low-esteem positions coincides with their racial or ethnic groupings. Except for some positions that traditionally are viewed as "mammy roles," when there is economic competition jobs to white women. But first and foremost women are employed because they can be paid less and because they will do jobs a man will not.

In Paraguay of a total labor force of 800,000 or 32 percent of the population in 1971 (of which 52 percent are in farming), about a third are women and nearly half of them are self-employed. This indicates substantial concentration in domestic services and home industries such as spinning and sewing, laundry work, and the like. Only a fourth of Paraguay's female labor force are white-collar workers (*YBK Labor Stats,* 1970: 199).

In Uruguay a similar three to one ratio exists. As of the 1963 census, the first in Uruguay since 1908, of a labor force of 1,015,500, some 254,900 were women, many of them in education, clerical, and professional activities (*YBK Labor Stats,* 1970: 23, 192-3).

In 1962, of Ecuador's 4,581,476 people—a third to a half Indian, 10 percent white, 10 percent black or mulatto, and the remainder mixed— about 1.5 million were in the active labor force; more than 50 percent were in agriculture, and only 17.8 percent in the total labor force were women *(Ecuador, Censo de Población,* 1963). Ecuador's labor statistics included both sierra and coast, rural and urban. Urban women of the sierra and the coast participated mostly in services and manufacturing, while in rural areas they were most active in agriculture, fishing, and domestic services (Banco Central del Ecuador, 1963: 68).

In Colombia, 20.8 percent of the population is unemployed or under-employed, and of the total unemployed in the economically active labor force, 11.8 percent are women (BME, May 1971: #238). In 1951 women comprised only 18.7 percent of the total work force and by 1961 had declined slightly to 18.3 percent of the work force (CEDE, 1968).

Venezuela is an interesting case of female participation in a labor force dominated by an oil economy. Anyone over nine years old is classified as economically active, and in 1970 only 20.5 percent of females so classified were in the active work force as compared to 71.5 percent of males (Bamberger, 1973a: 6). But this is a slight rise from 17.5 percent in 1950. Female participation rates also have risen from 17.8 percent in 1950 to 21.6 percent in 1970 (Bamberger, 1973a: 7). These changes have been due partly to an increased demand for labor and an insufficient male labor supply.

An aftermath of the Mexican Revolution was the constitution of 1917, which was quite liberal regarding the protection or working women. Article 123 prohibited specific unhealthy and dangerous occupations and pro-vided overtime for women and children under sixteen and equal pay for equal work, regardless of sex. However the laws were not enforced until the working women organized into an industrial cooperative, the Society for the Protection of Mexican Women, which was founded in 1931. Partly as a result of woman's organizations, the Federal Labor Law of 1931 was adopted, providing for guarantees of jobs, wages, protection, medical and pregnancy care, day-care centers, and a six-day, eight-hour work week. In addition there were provisoes for women in agriculture, such as the Homestead Decree of 4 August 1923, which gave widowed Mexican heads of families equal rights with men to own and cultivate national lands and other properties not reserved by the federal government (PAB, December 1923: 57, 624).

Mexican offices and shops today are filled with women workers, largely from "better" classes, while hospitals, schools, beauty parlors, and factories are staffed by Indian and mestiza girls. In 1949, some 12 percent of the urban female population were employed in these occupations, and at least a half-million of all Mexican women were engaged in business and professional activities (Royer, 1949: 168). However, contrary to idealized ideas of the Mexican Revolution as the positive result of female participation in these activities, it was because of the negative aspects of death and exile of males by the revolution that women were able to come into a position of responsibility in labor, business, and the professions. Further, while more women do work and have independence, there still are a majority of Mexican working girls who, when day's work is done, are guided home by another family member. Thus, while she is allowed to earn, she may do nothing more than yearn to change other circumstances of her life.

Basically Latin countries have proceeded at an acceptable rate by North American standards for their traditional societies vis à vis the employment of women. On the eve of the Cuban revolution only two Latin American countries, curiously Cuba and Mexico, showed less than 10 percent of their total female populations as gainfully employéd (ILR, 1956: 178; *YBK Labor Stats,* 1970: 192, 193, 199). However, it is of lesser importance that women are gainfully employed than to know in what types of jobs they are employed. Agriculture remains the major economic activity in Latin America, but in such countries as Argentina, Mexico, and Venezuela, few females are employed in agriculture, while in Bolivia, Colombia, Ecuador, Paraguay, and others, more women are employed in agriculture than in any other single activity, these women being seasonal workers on large estates that produce coffee, cotton, rice, sugar cane, and the like (ILR, 1956: 178). In such circumstances, when women are not preoccupied with harvest labor they work in cottage industries as unpaid family members, producing traditional handicrafts such as carpets, shawls, hats, pottery, and lace (ILR, 1956: 178). Another major occupation remains domestic service, and in Argentina, Chile, and Mexico females are employed in all lines of service from private homes to hotels (ILR, 1956: 179).

Other than agriculture, home industries, and domestic service, females work mostly in manufacturing industries, primarily light work, in positions requiring manual skill, patience, and accuracy. These are textiles and clothing; for example, women comprise more than 50 percent of Chile's textile workers and more than 75 percent of its clothing industry workers. In Peru, women were about 80 percent of the workers in these jobs, and in Brazil close to 60 percent. Women also are employed in glass, paper, leather, foodstuffs, and related industries, comprising from 23 percent of the labor force in these activities in Costa Rica to 70 percent of the leather workers in Guatemala (ILR, 1956: 179). Women in cities and suburbs are increasing their involvement in home work; instead of hiring out for laundry, weaving, sewing, potting, and the like, women do this in their homes on a hired basis. For example, Uruguay's registered home workers covered by the Minimum Wage Act numbered 50,000 in the year 1 July 1952 to 30 June 1953; in Argentina in 1954, some 150,000 women in Buenos Aires alone were registered home workers (ILR, 1956: 179).

Nonetheless, a few activities in which women are gainfully employed require vocational training, and the lack of vocational qualification makes women workers more vulnerable than men regarding wages, security, employment, and the like. Women employed in building sites, transporting salt, or other hard activities are paid lower wages than are men who do the same kind of work. Generally speaking, women workers still are limited by cultural customs and male prejudice to traditionally female occupations, although there are considerable differences, not only among countries but among regions in different nations.

Politics

Latin American women increasingly have become active, particularly through associations, in the democratic development of their country and what they perceive as woman's role in this activity. Argentina, again, has been a leader in actively encouraging political participation of its female population. In 1900, an Argentine action organization, the Centro Feminista of the First Congress of Free Thought was initiated for female franchise. The association worked in the International Feminine Congress of 1910 and since has persisted in presenting projects and demands to better the condition of children and women. In 1910 the spectre of war in Europe transformed some attitudes about women's capacities, and other political groups developed, such as the Association for Rights of Women, which badgered Argentine legislators into action on women's rights.

In 1916 Progressive Democrat deputy Dr. Francisco Correa promised the municipal vote to single and widowed women. On 25 July 1919, a Radical deputy, Dr. Rogelio Araya, presented a project to modify Article 7 of Citizen Law 346 for all "Argentine women who are 22 years to enjoy the political rights conforming to the Constitution and laws of the Republic" and modified Article 1 of the electoral law to give similar rights to "the natural born and naturalized citizens from 22 years of age. . . ." De facto political rights of Argentine women date from their receiving rights to cast ballots in the 1921 municipal elections in Santa Fé province, although only women of majority age who were free to administer their own estates or who had university degrees that allowed them to work in professions had the vote. Full civil rights were obtained in 1926, although they lacked full participatory political punch.

As early as 1910 Argentina had been influenced by English suffragettes and had their own counterpart of Dr. Pankhurst in Dr^a. Lanteri. The Partido Feminista Nacional was founded in 1919 and drew much reaction from other suffragette groups who thought the PFN too radical. In 1932 other political groups, the Argentine Association for Female Suffrage and the Patriotic Women, were begun. They assembled 100,000 adherents, aided in obtaining the halfway law of 1932, and in this effort were aided by petitions of the Woman's Council of the Argentine Republic. In that year Argentine women "native or naturalized from 18 years of age have all the political rights of the men conferred by the nation. They also have an obligation of asserting these laws or in the exercise of political rights with the exception of military service."

In 1945, another intense feminista campaign was begun with stragglers of the older associations. The appearance of the Statute of Political Parties, which barred women from political parties, made the neosuffragettes decide on immediate action to gain the vote. Women from all social sectors and organizations joined the Association for Woman's Suffrage. Thus organized, they presented themselves to the Division of Work and Assistance to Women, the official government agency for female issues, to solicit support for presenting the petition for the franchise to the country (Gregorio Lavié, 1947: 17). They were opposed by a female group, Democrático, which initiated an inflammatory campaign of opposition.

The Pan American Act of Chapultepec contained recommendations for political rights for women in all Latin America. It was ratified by the Argentine Superior Gobierno de la Nación. On 26 July 1945 thousands of women expressed their civic and political approval, and on 19 July 1946 the Argentine Senate unanimously approved full political rights for all Latin American women. A major source of help was Eva Perón who, by encouraging a united female-worker political front, did much to correct situati that permitted exploitation of female workers, including lower salaries. Workers' syndicates acquired importance, and women, accordingly, were able to attract politicians and associations to other problems.

On 24 August 1949, in keeping with the Peronist administration's appeal to working classes, Eva Perón addressed an assembly of the Inter-American Commission of women under the auspices of the Secretaria de Trabajo y Previsión. She suggested that Argentina, by involving women in constructive action, would be in the forefront of obtaining social justice, political sovereignty, and economic liberty (Perón, 1952). In addition to giving credit for female labor advances to President Perón and noting that the Argentine women's movement was a perfect feature of the "just politics" of the general, she suggested that such a movement would be a stimulus for the rest of the women of the Americas (Perón, 1952: 12).

Eva Perón has been the most prominent and best known Latin American woman, and because she exerted such overriding influence in the affairs of her country something should be said here of her life and career. Born Eva Duarte, she was an illegitimate, poorly educated, rural girl whose career as a radio actress and party girl led to her involvement with Juan Perón, a high-ranking military officer. After becoming his wife, Eva assumed immense popularity among Argentina's masses by using her radio broadcasts to attack Argentina's oligarchs, to defend the *descamisados* (shirtless ones), and to better the educational and economic situation of the people. After all, Eva was, in fact, one of them; Argentinians saw in her a true "Cinderella story," and she rewarded them by distributing her monies, energies, and time to lower-class women and men alike.

Naturally upper- and middle-class women and men did not share in the enthusiastic reception of Evita, as she was called. People of those classes who protested often found themselves in jail, lodged in the same cells with prostitutes and drug addicts. For middle- and upper-class Argentine women this was a humiliation never to be forgotten. Since the modern "feminist party" of Argentina is associated with the Peronists it has, for these and other reasons, not won heady support throughout the upper-class Argentine electorate.

Nonetheless, Eva was largely responsible for the strong consciousness of pride and place among Argentine women. Political activities under her purview were carried out by her husband after her death in 1952. Immediately after Perón's fall in 1957 the number of women deputies and senators noticeably decreased, but Frondizi, after 1958, did attempt to attract women to the federal government. Frondizi's support, it should be noted, was middle sector while Perón's was lower.

In 1951, women constituted 48 percent of Argentina's citizenry, thus 4,225,467 voters; this encouraged the election of numerous women to local and national offices and the election of the Partido Peronista (for figures, percentages, and breakdown of voting patterns and votes, see Pichel, 1968: 90-103). As of 31 December 1965, the national registry of voters counted 6,105,510 women of 12,296,585 registered voters (Sosa de Newton, 1967: 159).

After a period of military rule, Perón was allowed to return to Argentina with his third wife, Isabel. He was elected president, she vice-president. After Perón's death in 1974 Isabel Peron became the first female president in the Americas. She seems, however to have neither the charisma nor qualities of leadership Eva displayed, and time will tell how far she will go. She is in the lion's den!

In Bolivia, the late-blooming feminist movements have begun an organized push to apprise women of all classes of their social, economic, cultural, civic, and political rights (*Orientación Revolutionaria*, 1966). Through such organizations as the Alianza de Liberación de la Mujer Americana (ALMA), the Consejo Nacional de la Mujer, the Oficina de la Mujer, and others they have struck especially at the exploitation of campesinas, who comprise 74 percent of Bolivia's females.

In Colombia Law 28 (1932) was of major importance for females since it proclaimed economic emancipation for married women and allowed them to manage matters of their own welfare. Yet, some of the benefits therein were modified by Law 48 of 1946, with serious consequences for women, (Uribe de Acosta, 1963: for it again restricted their political and economic participation in national life. (Uribe de Acosta, 1963: 331-47, for texts and commentary on these laws.) Political education for women has remained essentially as it was in 1800—negligible, although there is a nonparty politically active Women Citizens' Union that is engaged in a nationwide program of political and citizenship education, primarily for women, but also for the citizenry as a whole.

In Ecuador all voters must be eighteen years of age and literatè, a factor that effectively excludes much of the population. Further, while voting is compulsory for eligible men, it is merely optional for women (AHEc, 1971: 246).

In Mexico political privileges for women, as well as solutions to economic, labor, social problems, and civil rights, came as a result of feminist movements in existence since 1916, although Mexico has not developed

as militant a movement as might be expected to have arisen from the
revolution. It was during the presidency of Lazaro Cárdenas (1934-1940)
that women were first able to enjoy significant involvement in political
matters. In 1934 Cárdenas permitted the woman's wing of his National
Revolutionary party to begin a nationwide fight for the vote with his aid
and consent. A strong strain of feminism developed in Mexico with an
active United Front for Women's Rights in the vanguard, endorsed by the
National Council of Woman Suffrage. The National Revolutionary party,
which had recognized full rights of women in the political and economic
order later, as the recognized Party of the Mexican Revolution (PRM),
maintained a very active feminine action group, joined by many communist women members.

The PRI, or Institutional Revolutionary party, continued the move for
female rights, and Miguel Alemán, in search of a presidential victory in
1946, sought to secure full female support and activity in the party. By
31 December 1953 the Mexican female finally had won the franchise when
Congress passed an equal voting rights law. Suffrage was attained in the
American nations in the following years: Argentina, 1947; Bolivia, 1952;
Brazil, 1932-1934; Canada, 1919; Chile, 1940 (finally ratified in 1949);
Colombia, 1957; Honduras, 1955; Mexico, 1953 (finally ratified);
Nicaragua, 1955; Panamá, 1941; Paraguay, 1961; Peru, 1933; United States,
1920; Uruguay, 1932; Venezuela, 1945 (Moreau de Justo, 1945: 77-9, for
some of the above).

Even considering the Argentine example, what do political concepts and
ideologies mean? If we consider a fundamental measure of democracy to be
the acquisition and dispensing of power, where does the female fit on this
scale of acquisition and dispersion of political power in Latin America?
Some writers have claimed that the female failure at and lack of participation in political power in Latin America has been due to the passivity
and indifference of women, and they have related this to the persistent
influence of religious ideas on women (Moreau de Justo, 1945: 28-9). The
theoretical framing of political rights was a painfully gradual process, and the
application of those legislated rights evince a similar gradual retreat from
traditional practices.

The attainment and exercise of political rights show as similar differences
between theory and practice as in any other human activity. In order to
examine trends in the acquisition and dispensation of political prerogatives
I shall discuss women in politics in two Hispanic American nations that
represent extremes of so-called progress and tradition: Chile and Peru
(Chaney, 1973: passim).

In the past two decades Latin American women in general and those
of Chile and Peru in particular have made halfhearted entries into the
arena of political activity. Commensurate with their limited involvement
women hold very few posts in the upper echelons and only rarely are
involved in decision making. Elsa Chaney, in her provocative study on the

female in Latin American politics, determined that of the Peruvian and Chilean women in public life, only a small percentage of them had any aspirations to rise in government or party hierarchies and to acquire positions from which they could make decisions. Furthermore, Chaney discovered that not only were Peruvian and Chilean women quite similar among themselves and between their two culture, but also that the majority of women in government positions throughout the Americas occupy positions that they and others tend to look upon as extensions of their traditional family role to the public arena. Chaney postulates that since Latin, and in this case Chilean and Peruvian, societies assign females only one honorable vocational option, any deviance from the norm must be justified vis à vis the universal model, hence a woman official often views herself as a supermadre in the larger casa of the municipality and the nation (Chaney, 1973).

Chilean women acquired the right to vote in municipal elections in 1934, but only when they acquired the right to vote nationally (1949) did they begin to exercise their franchise even in local elections (Chaney, 1973: 1, 12-3). Peru was even later in granting universal suffrage, and the act of enfranchisement there in 1955 finally was followed by two hold-outs, Colombia (1957) and Paraguay (1961). Despite only a six-year difference in time of granting the franchise, by the mid-1960s only 33 percent of Peru's women were registered to vote as compared with Chile's 61 percent, while the 1968 pre-coup figures for Peru showed women to be only 37 percent, and Chile's 1971 figures are not much higher, with women only 44.4 percent of the registered electorate (Chaney, 1973: 12-3).

Voting studies show that in Chile participation in politics, especially elections, tends to increase among women as socioeconomic status increases, unlike men for whom no explicit pattern in that category is discernible. In Peru, exercise of the franchise has not yet become a legitimate political activity among any class of woman, and most observers tend to view the situation as one in which hardened Hispanic traditions consider political involvement as a male purview and their legitimate option. Another reason, not only for Peruvian but for Chilean women, is that women in neither country tend to study in faculties that are highly politicized and therefore would be likely to encourage political participation.

Involvement in parties is low among women, but that is not unusual for the populace as a whole. Since general membership in political parties is a fairly recent phenomenon in Latin America, a very low percentage of either sex is registered as voters of any party. Recruitment of both men and women to parties in Peru and Chile has increased in recent years. In Peru, the Apristas were the first to enroll women and the Christian Democrats the second. In 1967 women made up about 30 percent of Peru's Christian Democratic party and Belaunde's Acción Popular had a similar percentage. In Chile the Radical party was the first to enroll women (1888), and Chilenas marched with the communist party in 1911, the only party never segregated.

Segregation of women into separate cadres within political parties is resented greatly by many female leaders, and it is a fact that it lessens the potential influence that women might have on party policy. Even though most parties have at least one woman member on executive committees, females rarely have much influence in determining policy.

Usually Latin American women received the right to hold public office when they received the franchise, and laws usually are quite explicit, as in both Chile and Peru, that women "can elect and be elected." Nonetheless, very few women are found in the uppermost elective or appointive positions of the executive, legislative, or judicial branches of government, although the judiciary is, in some countries including Chile, a special case. In early 1970 only four women occupied cabinet-level positions in all Latin America: the minister of development in Venezuela (who lost her post in a shuffle in August 1971); labor ministers of the Dominican Republic and Puerto Rico; and the secretary of social welfare in Guatemala (Chaney, 1973: 29-30). Peru never has had a woman in a cabinet-level post, and Chile does not at present possess a woman cabinet officer (although there has been one in the past).

Women serve in legislatures throughout the Americas, but they are relatively few. Prior to the 1968 coup Peru had two women in its parliament. Nine women had won election to the chamber and one to the senate in Chile's 1969 elections.

In the judiciary Chile always has had significant female representation. About 28 percent of Chile's justices are female, and Chilean women, because so many of them study law, are continuing to enter the judiciary. They do so in part because of their inability from external pressures to establish a going law firm or to acquire partnership in existing concerns. Another factor is that the judiciary in Chile traditionally is low paying, albeit prestigious, and men might be less inclined to enter that branch for economic reasons. Peru, on the other hand, has only 1.1 percent female judges, just as the percentage of women represented in the law profession is miniscule.

Chaney drew a profile of a "typical" Peruvian and "typical" Chilean woman official to demonstrate comparison and contrast among latinas in public affairs (1973: 34-7). The Chilean would be just over forty-six years of age, married, or had been at one time, would have three or fewer children, and would confine her activities to municipal affairs. She likely would be from the middle class, have spent her childhood in Santiago or another large city, and probably would be five years older than her Peruvian counterpart. She quite likely would have been a recent descendant of immigrants, at least on her father's side, and would have been educated at the secondary level in a public *liceo*. The Peruvian woman likely would be just over forty, raised in Lima or Callão, could belong to either middle or uppr class, and would have attended a private, probably parochial, secondary school. Like her Chilean counterpart she would be or would likely have been married, have at least four children, and defnitely would restrict her activities to the local level. She would be twice as likely as would a Chilean to be an aspirant for higher political office.

In offering some tentative conclusions for relative similarities in political voting and involvement among the "conservative" Peruvian and the "progressive" Chilean, Chaney posits that the "political club" is the last male stronghold women have attempted to breach but with a residue of doubt accumulated from tradition as to whether they are doing the "right" thing. Tradition, sex-role differentiation in action and attitudes, and a pervasive tentativeness contribute some measure to the shadowy involvement of women in politics.

Social

All aspects of twentieth-century female life—education, civic and political rights, economic positions—influence and are influenced by the social status of women in Latin America. Differences in rate of change for female behavior in areas of public life are part of circumstances peculiar to each nation's past and present conditions. Prior to nineteenth-century independence movements and their accompanying bastardized Enlightenment ideologies, the social position of females derived from the customized organic fabric of Iberian colonial culture. After the first quarter of the last century, national independence meant national judiciaries and national ideologies which creole elites extracted willy-nilly from European and North American models and applied to preexisting traditional social orders. These varied and often irreconcilable mixes of social customs and codes of "progress" guided Latin America into the twentieth century, thus, depending on the degree of "enlightenment" in the society as a whole, determining the social status of females.

At the turn of the twentieth century, few women participated in public activities. Elites attended their closely restricted festivities but the relatively open life of lower-class women was frowned upon as something "indecent" and "perverted." In marital relations an entrenched patriarchal pattern determined the legal and social insubordination of wife to husband, although often this was done under the guise of protection for precious females. Husbands owned family estates, including all that their wives brought in dowries and all that they later received as gifts, earning, or inheritance. A wife could not inherit property from her husband, and only if she were left penurious by his death could a widow receive a quarter of his estate (Marti, 1967: 192-3). In no case could she receive more than 100 pounds in gold, no matter how large an estate her husband left. In her role as a mother the woman had limited legal rights in relation to her children and essentially this was to give permission to any offspring over twenty-five years who wished to marry, but only in the absence of the father (Marti, 1967: 193). A father had the legal right to pawn and even to sell his children in cases of necessity.

But the female continued to be the core of Hispanic-American society by virtue of her idealized role in the family and was entrusted with supervision of all housekeeping and household crafts. In upper-class families usually she guided the work force of slaves and servants, but in lower-class families usually she had much more autonomy and prerogatives since her husband spent little time in the home or was absent for long periods of time. It seems that relative lack of material wealth and accoutrements probably have guaranteed more social fluidity for lower-class women since enforced responsibilities tend to be the foundry for personal freedoms.

In addition to differences in class strata, the position of women in rural and urban sectors of Spanish America has helped create a dichotomy in social attitudes vis à vis the female. Since the basis of rural economy is agriculture, supplemented by household industries and since women are actively engaged in these pursuits, the structure of family and society in the countryside is different from urban social organization. Life in rural areas is one of economic "underdevelopment" where family organization still is semipatriarchal, with all its implied legal and social subordination of women. There is a dichotomy in that the female's basic functions in family and society assign her a primary role in the general economic and social milieu. Nonetheless, she suffers all the burdens of the downtrodden, poor, rural classes—illiteracy, poor health, lack of communications due to distance from transport centers, as well as the inability to read, hunger, and disease. This is a prevalent pattern of rural life for Indians and mestizos in large sections of almost all Hispanic-American mainland nations.

In the cities, however, there are more opportunities to change the social system, as well as more and varied ways by which people can fall into dire health and welfare straits. In urban areas, industries provided more opportunities for labor and more types of occupations in which women could be employed. It provided also a freer atmosphere for contact between the sexes, which has seen the gradual weakening of traditional sexual attitudes and relationships. Separation of the sexes has broken down in elementary and secondary schools, young girls now move into their own or share an apartment away from parental tutelage, and unchaperoned dating has become a more acceptable form of social behavior.

The bastion of traditional mores remains the growing middle class. But even here there is an increase in extramarital relations by females and occasional disruptions in the sexual double standard by which males bear no guilt for discrepancies in social behavior but females lose "face" and dignity if involved in illicit romantic liaisons.

Women who know the rules of sexual relationships for their respective classes and who play by the rules usually fit into the scheme for the "modern" Latin woman. Those who are apt to get caught between custom and fancy are young rural girls who exchange the monotony of village life for the tedium of urban anonymity and often find themselves in illegitimate relationships and maternity clothes. For these legally and socially defenseless women, the "modern" world is cruel. Rarely do girls wish to return home. Generally they dispose of their babies, and because of the lack of facilities for social "rehabilitation" these women often turn to prostitution. Ironically, one of the positive values of the rural tradition-bound environment from which they try to escape is that should a wayward daughter wish to return home she could count on aid from her mother and family in caring for her child.

Birth control and illegitimate pregnancies are creeping more into the awareness of Latin American women. Recent surveys of CELADE indicate some changes. First, delayed marriages seem to be more common, although more than half of today's latinas have been married by the age of twenty to twenty-four, with the exception of women in Chile and Argentina, where only about 40 percent in that category are married. Second, more women of the upper classes and fewer women of the lower classes marry, with a high degree of consensual unions and widespread illegitimacy, especially among the lower classes, seemingly more frequent. Third, surveys in the Caribbean, Peru, Chile, Colombia, Venezuela, and Brazil show that most women, across all classes, do not regard a large family as ideal, but in reality the lower classes, who want the least, have the most. Fourth, Latin America has a high incidence of abortions, Chile and Argentina with the highest rates, the city of Lima, Peru, the lowest. Although some contraceptive methods have been utilized in most cultures in history, they are not widespread in Latin America because of cost and ignorance. The major method, among all classes of women, is provoked abortion, which is rising in Latin America and is becoming a critical social, cultural, public health, and economic problem (Stycos, 1958: 291-312, 295-8).

It is not possible to follow the social routine of females in all Latin American countries, so I have chosen Mexico and some Andean countries to demonstrate some characteristics of and some contrasts in nations whose fixed institutions and ideas bear the imprint of Iberia yet which are constantly exposed to North American social standards. The Mexican family follows certain ideals dictated by the Roman Catholic Church and reflects also a traditional view that regards children as economically valuable for labor and as socially prestigious. Children perform many intra- and extra-household chores. Girls' chores usually are more time-consuming than are those of boys, and girls are expected to be more responsible (Minturn, 1964: 200-8).

Demographic growth has been a problem the Mexican government has had to deal with, and in so doing has appealed to its women. However, social tradition has been reflected in female response to family and birth control. Most women admitted they had little influence in limiting the number of children, that "a man can make a woman pregnant *cuando quiera* [whenever he wishes]," they explain that "men have their physical needs. That's how you please them" (Corwin, 1963: 21).

Among working classes the societal image of the sexual relationship is of a passive female and an aggressive male and had sometimes been described as a sadomasochistic relationship. Oscar Lewis' thesis, subject to rigorous criticism, applies here in that poverty's own subculture, cutting across regional, rural-urban, and national boundaries, shows the despotic power of the male as an assertion of superior physical force, which the female must fear and respect (Lewis, 1951, 1959, 1961, and Stycos, 1958, for Mexico and Puerto Rico). Bermudez (1955) argues that regional differences do not matter; McGinn (1966) says that they do. Even men who outgrow their subculture, like David Castro in Lewis' *Five Families,* "possess" two or more women and, culturally and psychologically, the middle- and upper-class woman appears as a passive wife. In fact, middle- and upper-class women are influenced by the Church, obtain an exaggerated idea of what "decent" behavior is, and harbor an increased resistance to birth control since a "decent woman" should not know about such measures.

Mexican culture's placement of high value on manliness is more exaggerated in the middle class, since having a working wife is somewhat frowned upon. Middle- and upper-class unmarried girls are chaperoned up to the ages of twenty-five or thirty and are required to be chaste and dignified at marriage; although treated as a queen before marriage, after she becomes her husband's slave (McGinn, 1966: 307).

Mexican males tend to be concerned with the ego concept of *machismo,* or the chauvinistic need to populate their lands, or the cultural "cop-out" that large families are happier. But they do not consider the physically, emotionally, and psychologically damaging effects of this on the female, on the enforcement of her inabilty to view herself as other than an inferior animal to be used for whatever tasks or pleasures should suit her male masters. In some surveys, for example in one taken in Guadalajara, of 100 middle-class housewives sampled, 52 percent said that the majority of men believe women are inferior and 13 percent said that women are "only useful for housework" (McGinn, 1966: 307).

Mothers in Mexico, more than in other Latin cultures, seem to have surrounded themselves by an emotional veneration that enforces attitudes about the "Mexican way of life," a "cult of motherhood" fed by literate middle- and upper-class males and the Church. In fact, this mother cult and mystique of the family have been a major reason why Mexico never has sustained a feminist movement, and public advertisements of Mother's Day in Mexico center on the themes of the self-renounced woman, *La mujer abnegada,* who is a combination of the Virgin of Guadalupe, the Virgin Morena, the Virgin of Sorrows, and the Indian Guadalupe-Tonantzin.

Theoretically, and in some areas practically, women have achieved some stature. In return for their rostrum and battlefield participation in the revolution, women were given the right to divorce, the right to choose their own place of residence, and equal legal status with men (since 1917)

(Carranza, 1917: 3-71; Consentini, 1930: articles 1, 3, 16, 17, 19-22, 24, 27-31, 33, 63, 69, 93; and *México codigo civil*, article 2). Despite these legal social securities, very few women have been allowed to take advantage of the new measures because of the Church, family, and other pressures.

In contrast to the believed "progressiveness" of such Hispanic nations as Chile and Argentina vis à vis women, the nations of Peru and Colombia are examples of the most "conservative" and "traditional" of Latin countries in America. There are in these two nations several stereotypical images of the female that encourage construction of a pattern of female existence deemed repressive and exploitative by North Americans. There are varying interpretations as to just how repressive these attitudes are. Some would argue on the basis of recent research that contrary to accepted views Latin American women use their "passive image" to exert de facto power within their spheres (Jacquette, 1973: passim; Stevens, 1965, 1973: passim).

It can be said that the prevalence of the extended family of compadrazgo and a relative lack of geographical mobility all offer instruments of social regulation that allow women to dominate their families and to exert a considerable degree of power and influence from within the family about external matters. As the "saint-mother," woman is the focal point of reverence for her family and preserver of a sacred institution—the family. Through her sons she can arbitrarily intervene in both personal and public matters. Jacquette and Stevens have suggested strongly that women retain respect as wives and mothers partly by maintaining a virginal image, by favorably comparing themselves in that light with their husband's "other woman" (of whom the wife would approve, if not accept, for that reason), all of which is filtered through machismo by which the wife and mother acquires an emotional lever over husband and sons through her "moral superiority."

The "other women" not only is exploited by the husband but, perhaps even more so, by the wife since it is to the latter's benefit to have her husband (and sons) maintain another woman against whom she can measure her moral superiority. Usually the "other woman" is of a lower class than the family of the man with whom she is having an affair or being kept in the accepted *casa chica*. The end result is perpetuation of exploitation of the lower classes in these Hispanic societies. It is a crass practice of "bourgeois" elements in Hispanic societies, and the lower-class woman remains socially powerless in this context.

Two recent studies on machismo and other related factors in male-female relationships determined that adherence to concepts of life related to the virginity complex, machismo-marianismo, and the like, were not found among pure Indian cultures of Peru and Mexico but, rather, were common to the Peruvian mestizo culture of the coast and among the mixed-blood populations of Mexico. "Latin American mestizo cultures—from the Rio Grande to the Tierra del Fuego—exhibit a well-defined pattern of

beliefs and behavior centered on popular acceptance of a stereotype of
the ideal woman . . . like its *macho* counterpart, [it] is ubiquitous in
every social class" (Stevens, 1973: 10-11).

Middle- and especially upper-class Colombian and Peruvian women,
while economically more mobile than many middle-class and most upper-
class women, still adhere to traditional concepts of what a woman should
actually do with her life. In one study, most working-class, lower-stratum
women of the Colombian and Peruvian *barrios* (neighborhoods) felt social
insecurity and relative deprivation, sought status among their peers, nurtured ideals of womanhood based on "passivity," and since they realized
that they would not be able to achieve those ideals because they must work
in a man's world, they transferred those ideals to their daughters (Harkess,
1973: passim).

Another recent study has pointed to the existence of cross-cultural
characteristics among lower-class, and especially some lower-middle and middle-class, women in Peru, Ecuador, Colombia, Bolivia, and Mexico (Flora,
1971, 1973: passim; Smith, 1971, 1973: passim). Among women of the two
"class groups" in all these societies, the image of passive behavior as an
ideal characteristic of women was stronger among the middle groups than
among lower-class women. Studies equating the use of the written word
(newspapers, magazines, and other popular journals) and the visual media
(television, films, and the like have shown reinforcement of images of
passivity among classes to be a major factor in women's views of themselves. Since literacy and availability of and accessibility to the media is
more likely among middle classes, it is, perhaps, a basic reason why "traditionalism" in female behavior and attitudes still persists. These studies
were conducted and observations were made partly from the viewpoint
of possibilities of exporting United States-style "woman's liberation" to
peasant, proletariat, and middle sectors of society, with the conclusion
reached that passivity and traditionalism still are too engrained to allow
wholesale receptivity of either North American or Cuban (see below) programs for enhancement of the life and labor of these women.

In other areas of Spanish America there are variations on these patterns.
Paraguay's 1971 population of 2.5 million included a slightly higher number
of women (although the margin has been diminishing since the 1960s) who
tend to live longer than the male population, with a life expectancy four
years longer than men (AHPg, 1972: 21). Rural and less educated women
tend to produce more children but, in general, Paraguayans prize children
and a barren woman is regarded somewhat as an outcaste (AHPg, 1972:
22). Despite a heritage somewhat different from her Hispanic sisters, urban
and upper-class *Paraguayanas* remain guided by a patina of Iberian values.
They are expected to be submissive and dependent, no matter how involved
in professions or how educated. Among the rural population and urban
lower classes, however, there is relatively less moralizing. Common-law
marriage remains commonplace as does informal family life and structure.

In 1970 Uruguay's population of 3 million included about equal numbers of men and women although women slightly outnumbered males in urban areas and were slightly fewer in rural sectors. Uruguay is a good example of the worldwide trend of urbanization of women at a faster rate than men and for which the entire area of Latin America is a prime example for the rest of the world. In primarily agrarian or pastoral areas, of which Uruguay is one but to a lesser extent than some other Hispanic countries, females become less useful than males when agricultural and pastoral activities are mechanized. Women are surplus mouths for families; thus their answer is migration to urban areas (AHU, 19771: 38).

In general, Hispanic attitudes, characterized by the oft-used expression "pattern of male dominance," exist although Uruguayan women at upper levels are very active in cultural, commercial, and other public enterprises. Husbands' mistresses are accepted more readily by Uruguayan society than are misalliances by wives. This is particularly so among upper- and middle-class families where amorous dalliances can affect the strong ties of compadrazgo relationships. Uruguayan boys and girls apparently are taught sex roles at an early age, with boys expected to be dominant and girls to be deferential, their major future task to be competent wives and mothers.

Ecuador represents more traditional values that reflect the dominance of males that is basic to the traditions of both Hispanic peoples and highland Indians. In this geographic microcosm of Latin America, woman's activities, especially those of the upper classes, are circumscribed within her home's boundaries, and she manages households that contain numerous relatives and servants to carry out her commands. Ecuador is a nation that reflects notions of sentimentality toward motherhood and allows wives and mothers of upper classes only limited options in public activities.

For lower classes, there is more male-female interaction because of economic necessity. This also is so in Andean Indian communities where economic activities and social customs allow women a substantial amount of power in reality, while at the same time encourage females to act out stereotypical patterns of deferential behavior to male authority. Whether Indian or Spanish in ancestry peasant and proletariat women portray a life-style different from their upper-class counterparts. Most Ecuadorian lower classes are Indian, African, or of mixed ancestry, and much the same flexibility and extensive mobility exists among black and mulatta peasant and proletariat as exists among their white counterparts. Common-law marriages are the rule among lower classes in the sierra and on the coast, but among upper-class Ecuadorians formal church weddings remain the rule. Among urban and coastal poor, a common household consists of one woman and her illegitimate children, a pattern found in many areas where Afro-Americans live (Whitten, PC; Stutzman, PC).

As is now obvious, certain carryovers from Iberian, and to a lesser extent Amerindian, African, and more recent European immigrant groups, have influenced patterns of educational, civil, political, economic, and social changes and continuities, so that while it is possible to make some generalizations about Latin American females, it is also true that there are vast differences that reflect variations in culture of South American nations and Mexico.

THE SPANISH AMERICAN MAIN

The Caribbean contains more than 30 million women who, despite a great deal of change, are perhaps the most underutilized and overexploited human resource in this area. Our discussion centers on the six Central American and three island republics of the Spanish Caribbean: Costa Rica, El Salvador, Guatemala, Honduras, Nicaragua, Panamá, Cuba, the Dominican Republic, and (not discussed here) Haiti (after Macaya, 1967). The waste of manpower in these regions is familiar throughout all Latin America, for, as I noted earlier, there are fewer economically active females here than in any other world area (Macaya, 1967: 108-9).

Panamá offers an example of the fact that only a fifth of one-half of the Caribbean and Latin America's human resources are making an economic contribution (Tejeira, 1963: 133). In 1904 the Panamanian Constitution guaranteed equality of opportunity for all *educarnos* (educated). According to the 1950 Panamanian census only 45,130 women worked; a decade later still only 45,130 women worked; a decade later still only 59,435 women or 16.5 percent of the labor force worked. Reasons for this are basically that attitudes and customs of varying Caribbean cultures see the female as one who should not work outside of the home, either for moral reasons or because she might deprive a man of a job. Relatively few women have been integrated into economic processes, and that does not bode well for the Caribbean and Middle America, whose population growth rate of 2.8 percent to 3.8 percent is one of the highest in the world (Population Reference Bureau: passim).

Economic, educational, social, civic, and political problems of women and family in the Spanish Caribbean are similar to those of the mainland and also are inextricably linked to social mobility and opportunity (Lavalle Urbina, 1964). The Declaration of Cundinamarca stressed the need for participation of women in labor, and a free labor movement has been recognized by the OAS. Seven of the nine Caribbean states have subscribed to the International Convention 100 on equal pay for equal work, and other efforts are in force, such as the establishment of women's bureaus in the ministry of labor and seminars of ORIT, the inter-American affiliate of the AFL-CIO. (The declaration was issued at the first Inter-American Conference of Ministers of Labor, Bogotá, 1963; ORIT is the Inter-American Regional Organization of the International Confederation of Trade Unions.)

In the island republics and Central America, about half of the adult population is illiterate. Only a small minority are normal school and university graduates, and of these a fraction go into teaching. While the bulk of teachers are women, their struggle has been long and hard. It appears that more girls than boys enter primary grades but at the secondary level, enrollment among females drops steeply, and ultimately only about a fourth of all students graduate (Macaya, 1967: 111). Only about 1 percent of the entire Latin American population enrolls in universities, a small fraction of that 1 percent graduate, and a miniscule fraction of graduates are women. In Panama, for example, figures suggest that some 6.2 percent of the urban population and some 35.4 percent of the rural citizenry are illiterate (Tejeira, 1963: 154-5).

Among Central American nations Costa Rica is a leader. In that tiny country women and men have about equal literacy rates comparable to the nation's 85.7 percent. Primary education is free and compulsory and secondary education is free. In the university (only one exists) study, women comprise about 30 percent of the student body (AHCR, 1970: 155-61).

In the Spanish Caribbean sex relations are complicated by class and color. All women are considered inferior to men, but a wealthy mulatta of good family has a much better opportunity to overcome her inferior position than if she were a poor black.

Among the lower classes social and economic considerations are tied. Economic support is channeled through the woman both in agriculture and domestic duties. Adult females usually provide domestic services for entire households. Young women might provide the men of that household with sexual services, in return for a measure of economic support, but not domestic support, unless they live together.

Child care is an almost universal activity of Caribbean household groups. It is normally under the control of a woman whose status is "mother" although she might not necessarily be the biological mother (Smith, 1965: 67-8). As has been emphasized for the Caribbean, there is a "priority of emphasis placed upon the mother-child and sibling relationship, while the conjugal relationship is expected to be less solidary and less affectively intense," as in West African societies (Smith, 1973: 140-1).

Central American patterns fluctuate. In Costa Rica marriage is an important institution, but changes in it revolve around the changing role of upper- or middle-class females, often educated, and working in paying activities. Courtship has replaced fixed marriages. Nuclear families are the essential social unit in Costa Rica with husbands the absolute head of the family. Again, differences exist between classes in rural and urban areas.

This pattern is the same in Nicaragua and Honduras where males predominate in familial and societal activities despite an increasing participation of upper- and middle-class women. Nicaraguan and Honduran families are patriarchal, with wives the autonomous adminstrators of households and motherhood revered in traditional, sentimental fashion.

El Salvador is somewhat different from its Central American neighbors. Birth control programs were instituted in the late 1960s without Catholic opposition. Only about half of the married couples in a population predominantly white and mestizo have had civil or religious marital ceremonies. One of the reasons for this could be found in urbanization in Salvador's cities where there are many more women than men, especially among the lower classes. It is suggested that a majority of lower-class couples live in consensual unions as opposed to the upper classes, whose marriages by tradition enjoy official sanction (AHELS, 1971: 72-3). In areas of Panamá and San José, the majority of Catholic church-going married women use contraceptives (Clarke, 1971: 83-4).

Regarding civic and political matters there are differences among Central American nations. Costa Rica's laws promulgated in the last twenty-five years allow wives to retain control of their property after marriage and to engage in legal contracts without their husband's authorization. Costa Rican women were enfranchised in 1949, and voting for all citizens twenty years of older was made compulsory in 1959 (AHCR, 1970: 138). Nicaragua has had a small but strong feminist organization, A la Femenina Liberal, a branch of the Liberal party. Its functions are to promote civic awareness and to stimulate pride and loyalty by educating women and integrating them into the national life. Since the 1950s Salvadorean women's civic role has been changing rapidly in increased civic and political rights. In 1970 El Salvador boasted women in the governorship of San Salvador department, the secretariat of education, and in the legislative assembly.

A key political organization for Latin American women has been the Inter-American Commission of Women (IACW) of the OAS, which has worked more than forty years to help females secure political as well as social, civil, cultural, and economic rights. Aided by women's organizations in the United States, it has trained females to use their rights and to exert political leadership. Although the IACW was begun in 1928, it was not until the 1940s and 1950s that the greatest activity in granting of political rights to women in the Caribbean occurred, an effort successfully completed in 1955 by female enfranchisement in Honduras and Nicaragua.

The achievement of voting rights guaranteed females neither full participation in the political life of their country, nor wise and intelligent exercise of the franchise. Thus in 1959 the IACW began to focus on working directly with women. It established guidelines of a continuing educational program and an Inter-American Training Program for Women Leaders to rectify the dearth of leadership for any civic ventures that were begun. Despite barriers to growth a few Caribbean women have thus far attained success in international and national administrative and political positions. These exceptions are party heads (Costa Rica), ambassadors (Guatemala), OAS commissioners (Costa Rica and Nicaragua), and governors (Dominican Republic).

Civil as well as political rights for women now are broadly protected by constitutional guarantees in Caribbean nations, but great inequities still persist in internal civil codes especially as they relate actually and psychologically to interpretation of Latin American family law. The civil codes of participating nations maintain many outmoded and conflicting laws that create jurisdictional problems and are open to ambiguous interpretations on such fundamental matters as marriage, separation, divorce, remarriage, and paternity.

Let us examine two specific cultures, one prerevolutionary and one revolutionary or postrevolutionary: the Dominican Republic and Cuba. The former is a nation that has suffered decades of political and dictatorial stability; its skeletal socio-economic infrastructure has allowed a select distribution of wealth to the elite few at the expense of the masses. About two-thirds of the population of the Dominican Republic exists outside the market economy and are mainly subsistence farmers trying to eke out a living that is anything but satisfactory unless they live in the rich central plateau, the *Cibao*.

In the world of peasant and proletariat man leaves the work to his woman or women, as the case may be. Few males are wealthy enough to support more than one household; therefore they engage in serial marriages— arrangements whereby a loose relationship exists between man and woman, in which the man will agree to "support" any resulting children until he moves on to another relationship. Once this happens the woman, who generally is responsible for support in any case, is totally responsible for the care of her children and also assumes the burden of agricultural labor that had been undertaken by the man (Ornes, 1958: passim). Furthermore, if she relies on the aid of her family she also must assume some of the burdens of family work.

The rural, lower-class woman in fact has more real economic and familial power than she is in theory allotted. By reason of the anomie of lower-class existence as well as by necessity to fight for herself and her children, she has assumed roles not only of homemaker but also of earner.

The urban slum dweller has a somewhat different mode of existence. Here the man, less of his own volition and more from the results of social pressures, often is unable to support his woman and children, and in many urban circumstances it is the female who is the main earner.

Sociofamilial relationships respond more to economic necessity. Many urban lower-class women in the Dominican Republic perform domestic services and are "live-in" servants. This means that they are away from their husbands and also their children six days and nights each week.

Education is, as would be expected, considered less necessary for girls than for boys, and this is even more so in rural than in urban areas. There are, however, two types of schools for the lower-class girl. One is for training in the domestic arts and the other is an industrial school of domestic sciences (Hicks, 1946: 94; Ornes, 1958: 155; *América en Cifras* [OAS], 1964: V, 9; Pacheco, 1955: 85). As one would expect, the former trains young girls in basic arts of cookery and other talents for her own home while the other is concerned to train her for paying jobs. For the growing but slightly amorphous middle classes, women train and are educated for professions in teaching, secretarial services, and other white-collar professions, although not nursing. Elite females are either educated in universities abroad or are pampered by "finishing school" ecucations; they are prepared for perpetuation of a particular style of life.

Dominican women have had political and civil rights for the past three decades, and under Trujillo's regime certain laws were enacted that gave special benefits, social and economic, to laboring-class women. Nonetheless there have been no major changes in the status of women since they received the vote, and recent observers note that this inability to parlay political and civic gains into firm social and economic changes may be causing dissension, particularly among middle-rank females. Until such time as social and economic conditions improve women will continue to fulfill duties of wife, mother, and daughter in accordance with Dominican tradition (Tancer, PC, and 1973: passim).

Although they share space in the Caribbean Sea, more than a world of difference separates the cultures of the Dominican Republic and Cuba. Even before the revolution Cuba differed from other Spanish American countries in important ways although not consistently in its attitudes toward or treatment of women. The Cuban woman shared similar conditions with her Hispanic sisters in being simultaneously revered and reviled, in being kept at home, sheltered from social influences, and prevented from enjoying premarital intercourse.

But there were several ameliorating factors in Cuban historical development. For one thing, the Roman Catholic Church, which had much influence in other Hispanicized nations, was relatively weaker in Cuba and, consequently, weaker in influence on Cuban women. Also, Cuba had developed no extensive hacienda system but rather a "modern" plantation economy and society and rural proletariat. In addition, geographically Cuba was closer to the United States and reflected its social mores and patina of sexual equality, especially in the cities. Furthermore, Cuban laws regarding women were among the most advanced; the constitution of 1940 was perhaps the most progressive in Latin America in its concern for women; Article 20 forbade sexual discrimination and Article 62 mandated equal pay for equal work.

Yet, despite these favorable factors and despite differences in class that accounted for variations between theory and practice of the feminine ideal, Cuban women

> of all classes were defined, and defined themselves, in terms of their relationships to men. Women were taught to value above all the institutions of marriage, nuclear family, female chastity and monogamy. They were owned, privatized, ensconced in the home, isolated from each other, from the means of production and from the mainstream of society. (Camarano, 1971: 50.)

In 1953, only 17 percent of the total work force were women and the vast majority were employed in fields traditionally acceptable for women; 89 percent of all domestic workers were women, 82 percent of all teachers were women, 45 percent of all social workers, 34 percent of all pharmacists, and among critical industries, 24 percent were in food and tobacco, and 45 percent in clothing (MacGaffrey and Barnett, 1962: 142). This applies, of course, to the over-fourteen economically active population.

Yet the 1953 census also showed that 78.8 percent of the Cuban population was literate; there were fewer female illiterates (21 percent) than male (26 percent) and more females after the age of ten (77 percent compared to 73 percent for boys) received education.

All Cubans were privy to the same consistencies in schooling; in fact, 72 percent of the female population and 67 percent of the male population were educated in primary schools in a country that boasted one of the highest literacy rates of Spanish America (Jolly, 1964: 166-7).

Political and civic rights for women in prerevolutionary Cuba also came more quickly than for most other Spanish American nations. Women received the right to vote in 1934. In the past it was common for Cubans to elect several women to the house of representatives and the senate, and many females served as justices, ministers, and in other high-ranking positions. After 1940, Cuban women could legally own property.

Since the Cuban revolution was committed to the establishment of a classless, egalitarian society, any inequality between the sexes was an unacceptable and incompatible fact, and Castro declared priorities of change when he claimed that "women have of necessity to be revolutionary. Why must they be revolutionary? Because women, an essential part of each people, are simultaneously exploited as workers and discriminated against as women" (Castro, 15 January 1963: 7). According to both the needs and philosophy of the Cuban revolution, traditional attitudes that stressed woman's place at home and her avoidance of work in public were dysfunctional as was the low level of aspiration of women and discrimination against them, as well as sex typing of occupations. The aim of the revolution became to mobilize and resocialize females, to alter attitudes toward them, and to raise their level of education and training, even in fields that traditionally had been the purview of males.

In 1960 Castro created the Federation of Cuban Women (FMC) from small and diverse revolutionary groups. Raul Castro's wife Vilma Espin was appointed leader, and within one decade membership rose from 100,000 women in 1960 to 1,343,098 in 1970 (*Bohemia,* 6 December 1968: 70-1). It seems to have been extremely successful in attainment of its two goals: incorporating women into the work force and raising the level of consciousness of its members. Women have increased to be, as of 1966, some 32 percent of the work force, as workers, teachers, administrators, bureaucrats, and the like (Olesen, 1971: 549). Furthermore, they have moved into occupational areas previously unopened to them. They now work for the military in technical and communication services, as chauffeurs and tractor drivers, as farm managers or labor brigade leaders, as operators of heavy machinery, and even in cane harvesting (Olesen, 1971: 550).

One area of education involvement is in domestic service schools similar to those in the Dominican Republic, although the Cuban ones seem also to have added goals of raising the cultural level of domestics and of helping them to identify with the nation's political life (Purcell, 1973: passim, and PC, for excellent information on changes in roles and attitudes toward women). The results of various educational programs in Cuban education have produced more women for the labor force and, even more importantly, have aided them in working at tasks that traditionally had been performed by men: "Women were visible everywhere. . . . The landscape of Revolutionary Cuba was not a man's world. No longer were women the janitors, caretakers, and consumers of the society, but its producers and organizers" (Sutherland, 1969: 174-5).

There is some disagreement as to how rapidly the changes are occurring and how much they are consistent with the goals of the revolution. Some say that despite tremendous changes, where the incorporation of women into Cuba's economy and society is incongruent with revolutionary goals, the incorporation is met with resistance (Purcell, 1973: 16-20). Women still are expected to perform traditional roles as wife and mother, and there has been little effort to change prevailing occupational stereotypes. Further, the regime has made little effort to combat prejudice against women as supervisors of men, although many highly placed women are supervising other women.

On the other hand, prostitution was abolished and Castro noted that no longer did a father have to send his daughter away to work as a maid or in a brothel (*Granma,* 18 December 1966). Also, marriage and divorce laws were changed in 1959, making it easier for women to divorce and encouraging legalization of common-law relationships. Family planning is encouraged and contraceptives are available to release "woman from the drudgery of household chores, . . . for more productive service to the society . . . [and] from abortions," for the death rate from illegal operations was high (*Granma,* 9 July 1967).

Cuba stands apart from other Hispanic nations in both socio-economic-political aspirations for change in the nation and in traditional roles and attitudes toward women. A new dignity and status has accrued to the woman within society, and she now is being looked to as a model for change in other Hispanic nations. Anywhere on the scale between the traditionalism of the Dominican Republic and the "modernization" of Castro's Cuba, the observer of Hispanic America can find degrees of "what always has been," "what might have been," "what we shall overcome," and "what we have overcome."

⑨ THE TWENTIETH-CENTURY BRASILEIRA

Women in the twentieth-century United States tend to be actively involved in their communities in informal and organizational senses more than most other women in the world, and especially more than Latin American women. According to a number of studies, Latin American women are neither as knowledgeable nor as participatory as their international sisters in social interaction and political affairs. When discussing twentieth-century women we must view them within the context of "democracy" and treat the sex differential differently than we would other demographic criteria such as income, education, occupation, and the like. These women are married, raise families, "socialize" children, and hence affect the family as a unit and the way the family is "socialized" in the political system, all within the Iberian tradition. Latins generally regard woman as a mental minor, accepting paternalistic guidance and male mediation in the political world, and Latin women are forced, for the most part, to live "outside" the polity by virtue of the limited roles assigned them (Almond and Verba, 1963: 426-8).

The above description certainly reflects problems of various "classes" of women in Brazil today since their position is linked directly to the complexities of family relationships, which, in turn, reflect changes inherent in the transference of life styles from the rural casa grande to urban mansions and shanties (Freyre, 1963; 1964). There remains in today's Brazil a dichotomy between the patriarchal, poor, rural areas and the more permissive, "bourgeois," suburbs and cities, which have their own species of poverty. Even considering changes from one area to another, Brazil is more rural than urban, not so much in percentage of population as in attitudes and values, although these, too, differ from area to area. In many states, particularly Minas Gerais and those of the northeast, the patriarchal family, dominated by the Portuguese *pai* (father) is still the dominant social force in a subsistence economy subculture in which there is a preoccupation with marrying daughters at as early an age as possible, thirteen or less (Muraro, 1967: 122). In other rural areas of Brazil, especially in predominantly immigrant colony southern states of Paraná, Santa Catarina, and Rio Grande do Sul, the situation is somewhat different, not so much directly in regards to changed attitudes to and by females, as indirectly in the styles of patriarchy that were transferred to Brazil from various European cultures.

The dichotomy is not merely geographical or ethnic based but also is reflected in different social classes. Among the working classes more responsibility seems to be in the hands of women and, consequently they assume more prerogatives within the "family." The "family" in these classes is most likely a loose and transitory relationship between a woman and her "man" of the moment. This is true especially of *favela* (Brazilian urban slum sectors) dwellers in the cities who have a more informalized attitude regarding children and mates.

It has been said that Brazil's middle classes, especially those in the cities, reflect the nineteenth-century European bourgeois culture in which females are divided into two groups: respectable and nonrespectable (Muraro, 1967:123). Respectable women are protected by their fathers, husbands, or brothers who tend to use the possessive pronoun "my" with mother, wife, and daughters, with a heavy personal proprietary meaning. As in Spanish America, the middle class remains a bastion of petit bourgeois morality although these virtues are being subjected to stresses and strains of a turbulent society.

Brazilian upper classes reflect yet another dichotomy since within this group are found the most traditional attitudes regarding women and also the most "liberal" in the sense that the money, power, and position of a family afford some women the opportunity to move within the mores of the international jet set. Some of these young women become society leaders, while others turn to the professions, particularly university teaching. It is in this category that Brazilian women have achieved fame for their country's being a flexible society.

EDUCATION

Education presumably offers an important avenue for social mobility, but it was not until the end of the nineteenth century that women in sizable

numbers were matriculating. The first normal schools were founded in
the 1830s and 1840s, but girls had a difficult time attending them due
to attitudes about women. One study suggests that once "schools became
known as *colégios* for girls, rather than as centers for teacher training"
enrollments picked up (Havighurst and Moreira, 1965: 75). In 1898 the
first female graduated from the São Paulo law school, while in 1907 the
first two women graduated (baccalaureate) from fine arts courses (Morse,
1958: 215; Cruz, 1967: 211; Azevedo, 1971: 435 n19). Very few females
matriculated in high schools, and almost none entered college prior to
the Vargas era (1930-1954), but thereafter female attendance in upper
schools gradually grew. Increased social mobility and protoindustrial
economy encouraged the growth, which took place almost entirely in the
cities since traditional attitudes persisted among the rural citizenry regarding female roles in education and society.

It would be unfair to give the impression that education, including
female education, in Brazil has reached high proportions in quantity or
quality since 1930, for the fact is that Brazil retains one of the highest
illiteracy rates among American nations. In 1950 that rate was 57.2 percent
for the general populace; 60.67 percent of the women and 46.04 percent
of the men were illiterate; and rural areas showed a much higher illiteracy
rate than did the cities, both in general and among women (Cruz, 1967:
213). Paradoxically, since the 1930s although more boys have been admitted to elementary schools, more girls have graduated (Cruz, 1967: 213).
In secondary education, as of 1950, Brazil had 554,089 girl students and
623,333 boys, or 88.9 girls for each 100 boys, although it should be noted
that the numbers of girls and boys enrolled depended on the types of
education. For example, for every 100 boys, teacher-training schools had
147.7 girls, commercial schools 44.4, regular high schools 88.8, industrial
schools 27.2, and agricultural schools 5.5 (Cruz, 1967).

Not until 1920 was Brazil's first university founded (in Rio de Janeiro),
joined in 1934 by the University of São Paulo, both attempts at consolidation of faculties into formalized university structures. By the end of the
1950s Brazil possessed more than thirty universities, at least one in every
state, and its enrollments increased radically. For example, in 1957 Brazil's
universities showed 4,792 female and 10,173 male graduates, with women
choosing fine arts over social science.

In Brazil as a whole in 1960, among a population of more than 70
million, 4,895,313 girls from seven to ten years of age were in primary
schools, or an equivalent of 54 percent of the population in that age
group (Thomé, 1967: 46). This proportion was not so for the entire
country, for out of every 100 girls in school, 72 were from the southeast,
only 19 from the northeast, and 8 from the north, making a proportion
of 81 percent in the northeast and 92 percent in the north receiving no
schooling (Thomé, 1967: 46). Further, 38 out of every   ) girl: never

went to school. It also is significant that of the 4,895,313 students in the primary course between ages seven and ten, only 218,522 continued into secondary (Thomé, 1967: 47).

Education in Brazil for females—and for the population as a whole— continued to expand at the gradual pace expected of a country in which extremes of tradition and progress are greater, perhaps, than in any other American nation. The latest school census (1967) indicated more than 11 million children in elementary schools, of whom 5,562,126 were girls; nearly 3 million were in secondary school, of whom 1,411,582 were girls. In 1968, Brazil's forty-eight universities numbered 278,300 students; fewer than half were women. The southern industrial states of Guanabara (greater Rio), São Paulo, Minas Gerais, and Rio Grande do Sul alone had 50 percent of the elementary, 60 percent of the secondary, and 66.667 percent of the university enrollment (Poppino, 1968: 310; AEB, 1968: 511-20).

Education, especially secondary school, and university expansion education is intricately bound to the urbanization process and thus, although the southern industrial-urban triangle of Brazil shows healthy school enrollment, in fact only 12 percent of Brazil's school-age population was in secondary schools in 1960. Also, because of her population explosion Brazil's number of illiterates rose to 15.3 million while the proportion fell to 50.49 percent from 1900 figures of 6.3 million and 65.11 percent (Solari, 1967:459; Ribeiro, 1967:381 n. 6). Whatever its vices the military government of Brazil has recognized the relationship between population explosion, poor education, and industrial-urban growth in its $40 billion, four-year plan, and has stressed requirements of education. What this means for females remains to be seen.

ECONOMICS

Brazil's modernization has depended significantly on the growth of its industry, which has passed through cycles of development, dormancy, and revival since mid-nineteenth century (Graham. 1968; Dean, 1969; Wirth, 1970; Furtado, 1965; Stein, 1957; Vilela Luz, 1961). The progress of Brazil's industrial economy passed from a euphoric expansion during World War I, to revival of foreign competition in the 1920s and the world depression, to the commitment of Vargas from the 1930s for industry to form a keystone of a new and proud Brazilian nation. Since the end of World War I Brazil's plants have increased tenfold to nearly 150,000, while its industrial labor force also has increased ten times to 2.5 million, in a population that has more than doubled. The combination of industrial development, increased social mobility, modernization of the economy, urban growth, and their resultant abrasions on traditional modes of behavior, values, and attitudes created not only the opportunity for women to work but also generated a female labor force that had to be reckoned

with. Furthermore, the participation of working women in production
has been conditioned by these changes and modifications induced by
industrialization.

Even though the spurt in industrialization and modernization encouraged expansion of the labor force, particularly of females, and changes
in the types of work in which they engaged, another factor had been
responsible for the increment in the labor force between the abolition of
slavery (1888) and the start of World War I. Immigration had brought to
Brazil millions of Italians, Portuguese, Spanish, Syro-Lebanese, and other
European and Middle Eastern peoples (Pescatello, 1970/1971: passim).
Some engaged in retail trades, a substantial number worked coffee fazendas, and many went to the cities and there joined the labor force in
factories and other industrial concerns.

A large proportion of the industrial work force prior to 1914 consisted
of women and children. This was so partially because they were difficult
to organize into labor unions and therefore were less of a threat than male
workers were to factory owners. Also, they were easily replaceable because
they worked for lower wages and could be coerced into accepting a lower
salary or lose their jobs to others as eager to work.

The textile industry was the leading factory employer of the period
and relied on child and female labor. A government report on conditions
in São Paulo's textile in 1912 showed that 67 percent of the workers were
females and that more than 30 percent of all workers employed there
were under sixteen years of age (Martins Rodrigues, 1966: 116).

Despite this early participation in the work force the position of women
(and all) workers did not began to change until after 1914. For women
part of the change was in the reinforcement of woman's participation in
the public economy. No longer as valid was the stereotype of a woman's
place in the home, since economic pressures during World War I obliged
women to make a financial contribution to the family and a working contribution to the nation. Women working outside the home were less frowned
upon. This applied most to urban, middle-sector women who, in increasing numbers, joined working-class women in public activities. In 1920
women comprised 55 percent of the textile workers in São Paulo state and
44 percent in Rio de Janeiro state, Brazil's two most industrialized states.
In Brazil's four leading industries in 1920—textiles, food processing,
apparel, and chemical products which, together, comprised 75 percent
of the industrial labor force—the proportion of females and workers under
fourteen years of age ranged from about one-third in food processing to
more than one-half in textiles (*Recenseamento . . . do Brazil*, 1920).

Especially after Gétulio Vargas came to power in 1930, women were
able to obtain perquisites in the labor field through Vargas's wife's participation in feminist organizations and through his own legislative measures. In 1932, the year Brazilian women first won the right to vote (it

was later rescinded), laws were promulgated regulating the employment of women and adopting protective measures and rights of the International Labor Organization's decree of 1919. A partial inquiry by the Brazilian government showed that from 1918 until 1937, of some 569,900 industrial workers, 31 percent or 180,400 were women (Suggs, 1947: 62). A United States Department of Labor survey for the mid-1940s noted that a third of the 350,000 commercial employees registered by the Brazilian Social Security Institute were women (Cannon, ms. survey, in Suggs, 1947: 63). In 1946-1947, women workers in commerce and industry in Brazil earned from 240 to 1,000 cruzeiros or from $14.40 to $60.00 per month (1 cruzeiro = 6¢ U.S.)

Brazil's federal civil-service system (DASP) theoretically gives women equal opportunity with men for obtaining jobs in civil service, so that tens of thousands of women work for the government. However, discriminatory practices exist. For example, there are laws against admitting women to certain types of careers, against certain promotions, and against certain pensions, and, frequently, women are consigned to secondary posts in government and administration (Muraro, 1967: 33). According to the IGBE (Instituto Brasileiro Geografico e Economico) in 1960 fewer than 20 percent of the female population were economically active; of these 80 percent were field and farm workers while the remainder were employed primarily in domestic service (Muraro, 1967: 119; AHB, 1971: 69, 79, 81). It should be noted that females are a majority in all age groups except one to nine years and thirty to thirty-four years.

Prostitution is almost an adjunct of domestic service in some parts of Brazil, as some studies indicate. For example, a survey by the Escola de Serviço Social in Natal state in 1950 showed that 90 percent of that city's prostitutes also were domestic servants (Thomé, 1967: 61).

The 1943 labor laws prohibited night work (10 P.M. to 5 A.M.), provided at least eleven hours between two working periods, and prevented employment for those in poor health. Pregnant women were forbidden to work six weeks prior to and after childbirth, and other measures of consideration for breast-feeding time were provided. Yet, despite improvements vis à vis legislation for females, wide gaps remain; in 1966 in Brazil, most working women from the ages of twelve to seventy years still labored through a fourteen-hour day (Thomé, 1967: 61).

Economic power and burdens are still unevenly distributed between males and females, especially in families, for young Brazilian males still insist that their wives must not work, not only to preserve their social dignity but also because morally it is safer (OHI, 1968; 1970). However, these barriers, too, are breaking down. There is constant and increasing economic pressure from Brazil's inflationary economy to induce, however reluctantly, husbands of all classes, although primarily the middle class, to allow their wives or unmarried daughters to work. Traditionally acceptable work for middle- and upper-class women has been teaching, particularly in elementary schools, but more and more they have assumed positions both in high schools and universities, and a number of Brazil's best scholars are women. Other than agricultural and domestic services among the lower classes and teaching among other classes, women are engaging in other services such as national defense, banking, public security, business, and clerical professions.

Social services are almost exclusively in the hands of women, and since the majority of experienced social workers are women and since the law provides that principals' positions in social service schools be held only by experienced workers, women hold most of those positions as well as comparable ones in teaching and nursing. On the other·hand, men hold most top administrative posts in national or regional social services, teaching, and medicine. Women also are an active element in libraries, archives, and social sciences, especially sociology, although the latter sphere has been dominated by the São Paulo schools. (Madeira and Singer have recently completed a superb statistical analysis and excellent elaboration of women and economics [1973] excerpted in Pescatello, (1975a.)

Overall, the percentage and number of women working relative to the general population and to the national labor force is much less than that of female populations in most Spanish American nations. The least involvement of women in economic activities occurs still in the vast hinterland of the Brazilian center and west whereas, characteristically, the heaviest commitment is in the south-southeastern boom area. A statistical survey in 1968 indicated that in the eight states of that area, which contains 80 percent of Brazil's population, nearly 30 percent of the labor force was female (AHB, 1971: 81). Women are in jobs and regions where ten years ago their presence was practically nil. For example, in São Paulo in 1964, some 20 percent of the industrial employees were female in occupations and in a place that hitherto had offered them few opportunities (AHB, 1971: 81). Relatively few females are in trade, an area of substantial female employment in Spanish America, and despite their growing and needed involvement usually females are in lower paying and less productive occupations and usually have a third to a fourth higher unemployment rate than males, except in education where nearly all of the 370,654 elementary and about 45,796 (or nearly half) of the secondary teachers in 1967 were female (OHI, 1967; AHB, 1971: 82, 128, 180, 471).

POLITICAL AND CIVIL RIGHTS

The legal age for both sexes in Brazil is twenty-one, but that is where equality of status ends. The minimum age for legal matrimony for girls is sixteen while for boys it is eighteen. Once married, the civil rights of women are subject to male authority. A woman must have her husband's consent to work, to travel and reside away from her home, or to contest her husband's authority on certain civil matters. However, there is a contradiction to the civil code that specifies that "by marriage a woman assumes . . . the conditions of a man's companion, consort and helper with the family's burdens" but she cannot "carry out, without her husband's consent, the same acts which he cannot carry out without his wife's consent" (Cruz, 1967: 212).

From 1932 Brazilian governments played the political game of musical chairs, giving and rescinding female suffrage. Finally, in 1950 it was reconfirmed that women over eighteen had the franchise, although voting was not compulsory for any nongainfully employed female. Yet, Brazil does not extend the franchise to the illiterate, and this, combined with an illiteracy rate of 55 to 60 percent for females, effectively removes most women from political participation in "democracy."

Women's political groups were active in the 1960s, however. Several supported Goulart and prior to the "revolution of 1964" there was an active opposition to that group, especially from Lacerda's Women's Democratic Crusade.

Brazil has had its League for Women's Emancipation, the Brazilian National League, and numerous male supporters of the feminist cause such as Antonio Leão Veloso in "Aspirações feminanas," a tract to the treasury ministry, Alves de Sousa in *O Pais, A mulher e o trabalho,* for the agricultural congress, and deputy Andrade Bezerra in "O feminismo e a guestão social," in the newspaper *Correio da Manha* (Austrégeliso, 1923:128-9).

Labor protection legislation enacted in August 1969 amended the Consolidation of Labor Laws to allow women to work at night in many activities. But women still cannot work overtime unless authorized by a physician and cannot work more than forty-eight hours a week. Furthermore, husbands and fathers can bring action to terminate the employment of wives and daughters under twenty-one on grounds of family disruption (AHB, 1971: 460-1).

In other areas Brazil has been working to achieve equilibrium in civil action for females. It provides, better than most of its Hispanic neighbors, for female criminals. Most penal institutions for female offenders are run by nuns, they try to avoid use of the term "prison," and theoretically females have decent treatment in these institutions. However, most of Brazil's criminals are male; in 1966 of the total of some 50,000, most were males, and that year provides a relatively good sample for criminal composition since most women either are not in criminal activities or there is an unwritten code for not processing criminal action against females (AHB, 1971: 557-9).

Under Goulart, Law 4.121 of 27 August 1962 was a sweeping revision of the juridical situation of married women to grant them rights regarding working, and earning for themselves, and to bring about more cooperation between husbands and wives on family and societal matters (see Codigo Civil, 27 August 1962: Articles 1-6; 233, 240, 242, 248, 263, 269, 273, 326, 380, 393; 1,579 and 1,611; Codigo do Processo Civil, 469; Thomé, 1967: 96-102). This was followed in 1966 by the Reform Project of the Brazilian Civil Code, transacted by the chamber of deputies, which has such equality corollaries as husband-wife direction of the family, administrative power over the well-being of children, and general equality between husbands and wives (Anteprojecto de Reforma do Código Civil, in Muraro, 179-82). In 1970, Brazil finally passed a law legitimizing divorce, and thus gave some legal substance to the separation of undesired relationships.

Still, relatively few women participate in political activities, and consequently only a few hold elective office, these being primarily municipal councils. There have been very few state or federal congresswomen and no female yet has been elected to the national senate. In executive posts, Brazil boasts only a few women mayors, mostly in small interior towns, and no state governors, and only in the last decade or so have women held state cabinet posts, Guanabara and Pernambuco being two examples. In all other areas of community and citizen leadership, female participation is nearly negligible and, both in rural and urban areas, polity and civic concern remain male preserves (Cruz, 1967: 220).

SOCIAL

The position of Brazilian females in the 1970s, economically, educationally, and politically, is woven inherently into the fabric of a society that fundamentally adheres to tradition and male prerogatives. In the twentieth century that society has been battered by such forces of change as population growth, due to high birth rates and migration; mobility, characterized by transportation and communications developments; new ideologies; and the search for national identity. In the last hundred years Brazil's population has grown from 10 million to more than 100 million, and its birthrate of 3.5 percent is one of the world's highest. About 50 percent of Brazil's population is bound both to land and to rural traditional social structure, but rapid and persistent migration from the countryside to the cities has created a new subculture of poor, socially transitory slum dwellers. Furthermore, by 1960 nearly 70 percent of Brazil's population was under thirty and well over half were nineteen and younger, thus creating stresses on both educational structure and labor markets, and also on class behavioral patterns.

In Brazil, where does the female fit in this complex society? The position of the female is linked directly to the configuration of family, which, itself, is quite complex. One might observe that family, hence female, is a privilege of class for it is difficult for a worker at subsistence level—60 percent of Brazil's population—to maintain a family, as we think of it; hence the female's position is compromised. As there are further contrasts between the Brazilian rural situation (medieval patriarchalism) and the urban bourgeoisie, the positions of women are diverse. In many rural Brazilian states, primarily Minas and in the northeast, the family is dominated by the absolute authority of the man, and in this type of family the woman finds few opportunities to change her life style. Within this structure female members of the family labor within the house and often in the fields as well, as expected.

The family, the most common living unit which comprises husband, wife, and children, still exists as Brazil's predominant institution. In its extended form, especially, it serves the "premodern" functions of training and socializing children, providing health and welfare services, controlling economic and political loyalties, and affording a center for social life. This is so among middle- and especially among upper-class families and, in variation, among poorer peoples in urban slums. In the cities, in particular, the "blood" kin group is extended to include friends and associates. However, trends of modernization and urbanization are eroding this institution in Brazil as they are elsewhere in Latin America. The "modern" family is yielding many of its functions to public agencies, and parents have a great deal less influence over their children's marital situations than in the past.

It seems that the process of migration from country to city has had much to do with rearrangement of living patterns and social relationships, especially among the lower classes and, to a lesser extent, among the middle classes as well. Also, economic considerations have made it extremely difficult for middle- and upper-class Brazilian families to carry on ideals fostered by the heritage of plantation patriarchies, ideals such as family being the focus of all functions, of arranging marriages, of male domination, and such. Still, middle- and upper-class families in cities generally try to maintain a household of five to seven members—a nuclear unit—that shares incomes and domestic duties, and to have substantial numbers of kinsmen within the vicinity with whom they can exchange mutual assistance. This pattern is also true of farming communities among all classes, which are more stable and yet still rely on extensive kinship systems (*parentelas*), though the parentela is more characteristic of rural and urban upper and middle classes than of the lower classes in general.

Lower-class families generally lack a parentela and are unstable because of that lack and also from other societal stresses. Many are migrant and since most migrants are a large part of the illiterate population of Brazil, this makes it more difficult for them to maintain ties with their families. About half of Brazil's population now is urban and a majority of these are poor migrants who usually go to the cities without wives or family. By the late 1960s there were slightly more female migrants than males in urban areas, and this contributed substantially to the high number of temporary and informal relationships accounted for in Brazil. Brazilians may not shun formal marriage to the same extent as their Colombian, Venezuelan, and other Spanish American kin, but, nevertheless,

the Brazilian woman is almost twice as likely to live out her entire life
without contracting matrimony as is her sister in the United States.
No such differential prevails between the male populations . . .
[perhaps] due in part to the fact that the higher death rates in Brazil
give the old bachelors greater opportunities for marrying widows than
are present in the United States. (Smith, 1971: 63.)

In families of European immigrants in the south—Paraná, Santa Catarina,
and Rio Grande do Sul—the situation is different, reflecting more non-
Iberian European customs (see Cabral, 1937; Schapelle, 1917; Price, 1950).
The economic position of a woman is better here among even less favored
classes than in the rest of Brazil, although she is still in a dominated position
and consigned to traditional field and house tasks.

Among another segment of the rural population of Brazil, especially
itinerant workers in other parts of the south and the northeast, a female
is likely to be the woman of one of at least two "families" that her "man"
maintains (OHI, 1962, 1967, 1968, 1970). These "men" are field hands,
part-time industry workers, and, more often than not these days, truck
and bus drivers on the trunk highways that ribbon the country. If one
travels by bus along coasts or through the interior, one observes this
life-style among the drivers.

Illegitimacy is common. In the basically agricultural state of Maranhão,
nearly 60 percent of the unmarried women twenty years of age and older
have had babies, at an average of four children per woman (Cruz, 1967:
211). Lower-class female-family relations in cities maintain their rural
patterns. In cities the female also is subject to pressures of "domestic
service," a category of labor wrought with all the dangers of male employer
attitudes toward a working girl and lacking social or worker security
(Muraro, 1967: 123). On several excursions in Bahia and Pernambuco I have
observed many such situations.

In the Amazon, as in almost every other area, there is tremendous difference between theory and practice. In Amazon communities, in fact,
women and men share in business decisions. Men might carry the pocket-
book, but women tell them what to buy. In rural neighborhoods and in
towns, women help their husbands in almost every conceivable job. Females
take over tasks traditionally ascribed to men but men cannot usually take
over tasks traditionally ascribed to women. This aspect of spheres of influence seems general in Iberian, African, Asian, and Amerindian cultures
that we have observed. Women, in fact, are not merely central figures in
the household but must share a great portion of the responsibility and
authority in family and in society (Wagley, 1964: 159-76).

Middle classes reflect characteristics of nineteenth-century liberal,
bourgeois civilization in which woman is looked upon either as respectable
or not respectable. The same man who speaks possessively of his women is
likely to keep another on the side but it is not acceptable for the reverse

to occur. One of many travelers noted in 1932 in Goias state that "the women sit the entire day at the windows and gaze at the empty street in an ardent and provocative manner. The men sit the entire day in chairs on the street" (Fleming, 1957: 86-7). The middle-class Brazilian woman, whatever her color, but usually white, until recently was a recluse and not accorded the rights of sexual freedom that her man enjoyed. It seems, however, that the "middle class" is the transition, the social medium that acts as a catharsis for the female: she has moved from a "freeness" in lower-class lifeways to a reclusive state in the middle class and then, in entering the professions or other public areas, acquires more mobility and freedom—until she marries!

It is the assumption of some Brazilians that the initiation of Brazilian men to sexual activity, first with Amerindian and African women, and later with prostitutes or domestic servants, has been one of the chief factors of the degradation of love and of the women in Brazilian society (Morais, 1968: 152). But this is deeper than a racial factor and has many reasons. Its roots lie in part in Iberian ideas from the reconquest by which non-Christian Moorish slave or black servant girls could be used sexually. It also reflects earlier practices of rights of feudal lords over women of lower station, such as wedding night rights. Religion, class, slavery, and race also have been important factors. What also is important is that the female always has been regarded as a lesser, as property to be disposed of at the whim of male dictates, and to be used almost as an animal, and this overall has been a consistent them in Brazilian society. Freyre's designation of Brazilian "syphilization" (by this he means the seemingly free-wheeling sexual intercourse between the races and, concomitantly, the use of women, by any man, regardless of race) is as crowning a judgment on sexism as one of the most crucial problems of Brazilian culture.

One Brazilian laid out a matrix for comparison and contrast of "corrupt" Latin societies (including Greek and Arab) with those of the north. He sees Latins, as influenced by Arabs, Catholicism, subservience of women in the Church, a permissibility toward boys in a patriarchal society, a double code of conduct with the persistence of virginity for girls and even chaperonage, the domination of the image of masculinity, little birth control, segregation of the sexes, and discouragement of female participation in public life. In north European cultures he sees Germanic influence, Protestantism and married clergy, strong discipline but an accent on "liberty," more permissive sexual activity and decline of the virginity taboo, a tendency to equality in marriage, smaller families, less segregation, more public activity (Morais, 1968: 178-81). I present this to show how a person overly-influenced by Anglo-American values cannot grasp, in light of his own cultural heritage, basic problems of his society.

The contrast of the "repulsiveness" of Latin with the "beauty" of north European culture is all part of three disparate and incompatible complexes: virility, virginity, and matrimonial fidelity (Cruz, 1967: 215). The

first seeks sexual relations as early as possible for young boys since male
virginity is ridiculed in Brazilian culture. The second imposes prohibitive
measures to premarital sexual relations for women, frowned more upon
upper classes, especially in rural upper-class areas. The last implies that no
woman will be unfaithful to her husband, not so much for her sake but
more because it would be an insult to her husband's honor and a loss
of his status in society, an attitude that persists among all classes, although
there is somewhat greater freedom for some more cosmopolitan upper-
class women. These arguments represent stereotypes of ethnic characteristics. But in a larger sense they should better be seen as modes of living,
patterns of behavior tempered by particular historical experiences and
determined in part by environment, population, and geography. Characteristics applied to north Europeans would be applicable to Latins from
areas with characteristics similar to a north European environment, and
vice versa.

In September 1962 the Brazilian Society for Feminine Progress successfully pushed for reform of the Brazilian Code and fought for elimination of
such items as Article 6, which viewed wives as "relatively incapable" along
with minors and servants, Article 242, which forbade women to accept
a mandate "without authorization of the husband," Article 233, by which
the husband was not only the chief of conjugal society but also the exclusive
preserve of *patria poder* (i.e., legal authority over all family and which
power the woman could exercise only if he were not able to do so), and
others (*Código Civil,* 3 September 1962, in *Diario Oficial*). Law 4.212 of
27 August 1962 lessened some grievous aspects of masculine domination
in the code (full text in *Diario Oficial,* 3 September 1962).

In twentieth-century Brazil it has become less common for women to
marry before the age of twenty, and they have begun to free themselves
from humiliating patriarchal taboos of Portuguese propriety. They are
much more attuned to a career and now are looked upon as potential
extra breadwinners. On the other hand, working women are criticized
by their men for a decline in the quality of home life, sanitation, and the
like, and are accused of shirking their responsibility, while the security
syndrome operates to force them primarily into their traditional domestic
role. No one has yet undertaken any serious study in Brazil or other Latin
American nations to determine the stresses and strains on the female due
to her new social involvements and reorganization of her economic activities. Not only would it shed valuable insight into female problems but
also could tell us about societies in flux.

Attitudes toward labor in general and about working women in particular
have been pointed out in several case studies. Harris has observed that
occupational gradings in Minas Velhas are designated under the rubrics
menial, intellectual, or managerial, with varying degrees of influence. In
this society women occupy the bottom order as menials who work exclusively with their bodies—field workers, prostitutes, and the like; house-

hold skills are next in terms of prestige, and schoolteachers rate at the top. But women try to avoid being observed doing menial and domestic tasks, not because it is hard work but because it is shameful (Harris, 1956: 99-100).

Immigration, from northern to southern Brazil, has made women and children more important in local northern agriculture, a situation that means that females get the leavings once the men have gone. Yet emigration of single women from towns and rural areas from states bordering Rio de Janeiro and São Paulo into those southern industrial centers has greatly increased the female population there. The concentration of females from rural lower classes in search of jobs in industry, domestic service, bureaucracy, and business is a contributing factor to the institutions of "partial families" and *amaziados* (a type of common-law union) in urban areas. Barros (1954: 79) noted that in the 1950 census 930,000 people had migrated to Rio de Janeiro from the countryside; 437,000 were males and 493,000 were females.

An anthropologist who has studied Brazilian rural communities also has pointed out that socially women play specifically ascribed roles, as for example in the matter of morals. Women are the primary supporters of religious activities or comprise the choir but they cannot partake in the service. Similarly, the penitent role traditionally is the woman's in any illicit affair, while the male successfully is free of the stigma of errant sexual behavior (Harris, 1956: 212-3). For example, life in the community of Minas Velhas is one in which the sexes are separated and women relegated to back seats in churches; where women eat after males have finished and do not take coffee with visitors; where no females except widows have a source of income they can spend freely; and where "liberated" younger women are those who risk public exposure of their upper legs by learning to ride a bicycle, albeit after dark (Harris, 1956: 173-4, 147-78 passim). This is the case in this small country seat in the mountains of central Bahia. While it is not necessarily the case in larger urban areas, it does bespeak the possibility of a general national condition since Brazil is heavily rural, if not in population, then surely in values.

Prostitutes or the *moça perdida* (lost girl) often arise from premarital seductions since any girl who cannot prove rape has little opportunity for marriage. Divorce, or *desquite,* has contributed to prostitution since, according to moral codes, ex-husbands can establish a new home with a concubine but an ex-wife is expected to forego another man; thus her sexual outlet is through protitution. So cloying has the double standard been that the dignity of an ex-husband was intolerably tainted if he were betrayed by his ex-wife in any deviation from chastity, and she would be punished for such deviations (Azevedo, 1962: 27).

Since the Brazilian male is expected to have premarital heterosexual relations, prostitutes are available for the execution of this social requirement (Harris, 1956: 158-9). After marriage the urban Brazilian husband is expected to continue visiting prostitutes, and his wife is expected to tolerate it. Harris says that an "inflexible code for females" exists, which lumps as prostitutes all women who deviate in sexual behavior (1956: 167). Of thirty women in Minas Velhas only eight were real prostitutes while others were widowed concubines of married men or lived with a man in an informal relationship (Harris, 1956: 167ff.). In relation to pregnancy, childbirth, and the like, "There is no doubt that the majority of males fail to consider their wives' willingness to have sexual intercourse . . . they consider the woman's pleasure to be merely a by-product of their own" (Harris, 1956:169).

In the 1960s an extensive research project was undertaken involving 1,520 women of Rio de Janeiro (Cariocans) regarding sexual-social problems and activities. The results of that research yielded some tentative conclusions about the status of modern Brazilian women vis à vis sexual expectancies and accepted activities. Among other things the report determined that premarital pregnancy was lower among Cariocans than among similar groups in the United States and that religion and a father's and/or husband's position were the two most important factors determining the kinds of sexual activities with which females would allow themselves to become involved. Females from the lower strata of society were more likely to engage in premarital relations. Also, birth rates among lower groups were not likely to change despite movement from a rural, agricultural environment to an urban, industrial one. In sum, the results of the Rio and other surveys in Brazil indicate that since the behavior of lower-class groups is less of a threat to the total society than similar behavior by upper-class groups, it involves less of a commitment to such norms as chastity and legitimacy. Further, not only is such sexual-social deviance tolerated by society for lower-class groups, but also since premarital pregnancy has significance for social mobility through the avenue of mate selection, it is encouraged, in a sense, and acts as a considerable control valve by which upper-class groups maintain their hegemony over the masses (Bock and Iutaka, 1970: passim; Gendell and Rossell, 1967: 156; Goode, 1960: 21-30). The failure of fertility rates to change in transition from rural to urban refutes the hypothesis that one of the consequences of "development" is a reduction in fertility and therefore a decline in population. As an addendum, some experts see difference in fertility rates as reflective of contrasts between those working in industry and those working in agriculture and not between those living in urban or rural surroundings.

All these roles, activities, and views of woman in various Brazilian ambients have been substantiated in studies of other areas of Brazil (Hutchinson, 1957; Wagley, 1952; Pierson, 1939, 1966). The "virginity complex" retains strong moral and religious values that control the sexual behavior of women. In the most conservative of urban families a shamed daughter might be ensconced in a reformatory whereas among rural families bloody vengeance might be wreaked against the man, with the daughter driven to prostitution or thrown out of the home. In Brazil, prostitution is seen as part of a system of values and institutions that protect virginity in women as the essential prerequisite for marriage and for a role in the family (Azevedo, 1962: 13). Civil Code Articles 218 and 219 allow male repeals of their marriage if they discover their brides are not virgins (Willems, 1954: 333). Adultery by females is violently punished "alongside relative indulgence on the part of the male" (Candido, 1951: 310).

The taboo of virginity is less powerful among the lowest social strata where illiteracy is highest, economic conditions precarious, and the institutionalization of sexual unions less formal. In Brazil, as in the Caribbean islands, amaziado socially is tolerated as a result of tradition and custom rather than from the disorganization of slaves' families and is a relatively stable relationship that is most common in the poorest towns and rural areas where descendants of slaves are concentrated (Ribeiro, 1945: passim; Matthews, 1953: passim). In these unions primacy of the mother is the main ingredient for internal balance. She directs the household, the children are hers to praise or punish, and all monies earned by the children belong to their her (Hutchinson, 1957: 261ff.). Thus, among poorer and black groups, females tend to have a powerful role.

Another area in which the female enjoys a prerogative of social rights is the "partial family," which consists of households headed by women without the presence of husbands or lovers. In these households, most common among the lower strata of population in rural and urban sectors of old plantation areas in Brazil and the Caribbean, mothers are responsible for the sustenance of lifeways within (Hutchinson, 1957: 273; Cohen, 1956: 664; Solien, 1960: 103-5). The role and position of females in these "unions," "families," and "households" and as a decisive factor in the establishment of social relationships that emanate from these unions, is an enormous task but essential for future research and analysis. In this, a fundamental requirement is that a distinction between household and family, and between various types of households and families be made in any future studies of female, family, or household.

What, then, can we say about the female in contemporary Brazil where patriarchy is still omnipresent? We can say, with a reasonable amount of certainty, that this has been a changing society in which the role of female seems to have changed more in the past fifty to a hundred years than at any other comparable range of time. The patriarchal family, which was both the centrifugal and centripetal social force around which this Luso-civilization revolved and to which institutions or informal alliances such as church, school, and labor force adhered, is undergoing metamorphosis. Brazil has been a nation in which the image of man has been a suprahuman element and in which femaleness has operated in a culture in which the double standard has been more clearly defined than in any other Hispanic American nation.

How far away from past standards Brazilian women have moved is
suggested by the results of a poll commissioned and reported by
Manchete. The survey, based on 600 women of all social levels evenly
divided between residents of São Paulo and Rio de Janeiro, reportedly
confirms the existence of a "new Brazilian woman" who views beauty
as secondary to fair salaries and intellectual equality. Of those polled
39.2 percent would work regardless of family situation while others
indicated certain restrictive conditions such as marriage and children.
Only 7.4 percent upheld the traditional view that a woman's place is
in the home. As for training, 68.2 percent believed sex irrelevant and
another 28.5 percent stated that women were better prepared than
men. An insignificant 8.3 percent viewed themselves as inferior.
Significantly, 55.1 percent declared that they worked more to maintain
their sense of independence than to supplement the family income.
The survey also noted that 47.5 percent favored feminist groups.
(MacLachlan, 1973: 50-55.)

Iberian lifeways and the general Iberian civilization contextually
imposed itself and permeated Brazilian cultures. Very little of Amerindian
influence remains except in a few practices, some linguistic retentions,
and other scattered residue, but the impact of Africa was powerful and
has remained so, in whatever bastardized forms it has assumed. To the
extent that race and class and other elements that determine the amount
and extent of female power and authority dominate a particular group
within Brazilian culture, that is the extent to which Brazilian women are
either pawns of their menfolk or wielders of power, authority, and influence.

All these women have a master, and each master has a rifle. . . . And
even if they had not a master, you know already how many men there
are on the plantation. . . .

And that little girl leaning against the door?

That young girl is Lourenço's daughter. She's the one Agostinho wishes
to marry.

What? That girl? But she's still a child.

When a man can't get a woman. . . . (Ferreira da Castro, 1935: 167.)

EPILOGUE: IN THE MANNER OF SOME SUMMARY AND CONCLUDING REMARKS

At the beginning of this study I said that this work spoke to a dual interpretation of woman's place in history. One theory posits that the female has been the wellspring of power and influence in society. The other suggests that she has been a pawn in a world dominated by males and a member of an inferior caste within human society, as well as an outcaste from the mainstream of authority in human society. These theories are not merely schools of interpretation based on scholarly investigations. They also reflect the opinion of the ordinary citizenry. Obviously there is a dichotomy between what is real and what is ideal, and more than a paradox in that both these views can exist simultaneously in the minds of so many people. This so tantalized me as to seek answers to several questions that I posed in an effort to come to some conclusions about the historical world of women.

In order to do this I chose a rather large historical canvas. Yet, there are practicalities to that choice. I have a personal affinity for Iberian cultures and for culture areas outside of the western European-Anglo-American world. The world the Iberians "made" was the first and most enduring attempt to cross oceans and articulate and impose a way of life on cultures seemingly alien to their own. By my anti-imperial standards that was an unacceptable pattern of behavior. But at that time it

was an accepted mode of operation and thus has provided a unique opportunity to look at a specific value system but within a general multicul-
tural context.

Several points have been made about the place of the female in this
examination of the overall historical development of human societies. One
major thesis suggests that in society in general, and almost all spheres of
influence in particular, females held equal if not more power in agricultural
economies, in the riverine sedentary civilizations of several continents. In
some areas this real position was bolstered by a cult of feminine spiritual
superiority. Among nomadic and pastoral peoples the absence of sedentary
stability deprived woman of this power. She could not form permanent
homesteads, which were the seat of her influence, and there were few or
no agricultural products for her to control in production or distribution.
In areas of ecological imbalance, where population pressures and land
hunger drove people to war, victorious males acquired great wealth and
power. Hence the balance of power shifted from the locus of the female
in family and society to the locus of the male in society (on this
thesis of the shift from matriarchy to patriarchy see Bachofen, 1861;
Morgan, 1851, 1877; and others). This nineteenth-century evolutionary
theory implied a shift from chaos in a "prehistorical" stage of human
development organization by a principle of matriarchy in which women
publicly were recognized as more powerful and had more authority than
did men, to an advanced stage of social order in which males came to
dominate. Simply put, the female represented the world of the profane,
the uninitiated, the embodiment of childhood, of prehistory; the male
represented the world of the sacred, the initiated, adulthood, the historical world (Eliade, 1965:1-20 passim). The fatal flaw in this evolutionary concept of transition from female- to male-dominated worlds is
the implication that it is a transition from less advanced to more advanced, from "primitive" to "modern." While we could accept that the
shift occurred, we cannot accept the implications of inferiority and of
superiority that it implies.

With such shifts from matriarchal to patriarchal power appurtenances
such as bridegroom contributions of service degenerated into a bride
price, and female promiscuity became subject to penalties as a hedge
against lowering the value of a woman in these arrangements. The importance of kin and line further respricted the public purview of the female because it became necessary to guard against tainting the line. So,
too, did political, religious, and military turmoil contribute to seclusive
behavior and the development of an ideology to underwrite the legitimacy
of efforts to seclude and to remove women from positions of public influence.

Laws and attitudes developed and spread with the patriarchal family, as
did practices that seemed crucial to maintaining the external lines of
authority and patterns of behavior within a society. Yet, in practice, as

we have seen, the female retained, almost consistently throughout time and in almost every place, a power often of equal dispostion with the male. If in the old agricultural matriarchies she was the most important figure in family and society, in the patriarchies, although certain major practices changed and attitudes as well, in the figure of the mother and thus as "head" of the household, she has been the central figure in the family and thus in society.

How do we reconcile that discrepancy between theory and practice? The answer lies, perhaps, in the family. The family has been the major social unit, the primary institution in cultures. There are, as I have discussed, several types of family, the core of which seemed to be variations on the "nuclear" arrangements of mates, parents and children, and siblings. But in almost all instances these families in what we call "traditional" or more accurately "premodern westernized" societies, were extended, joint kinship groups, encompassing several generations, both biological and social in relationships. In some circumstances they formalized this in a household, which, in spatial terms, consisted of a central courtyard surrounded by homes of all members in the household-family. In other circumstances this was represented by homes of open rooms and lack of privacy. Among the masses who could barely manage a shack, ties were maintained through public events and social rites.

Furthermore, the family was the source of almost all economic, social, political, and other functions. Within all of these familial contexts, the female was a major figure. In the West, in particular in some areas of western Europe, during the late medieval times and Renaissance, and especially with the development of Reformation ideology, "modern" institutions, including the family, developed. The traditional communal, polygamous, and polymorphous unit of relatives, friends, servants began to change to one of smaller, more isolated, less public units. Of crucial importance seems to have been the emergence of the child as an individual, and with that change the role of the female changed to one primarily concerned with caring for the child. Since then, legal and particularly technological changes have done much to further shackle females to the home. And since the home is less the area of influence, having to share the purview of power with several other institutions, the influence of the female has declined disproportionately in "modern" societies. To be sure there are inconsistencies to this "model," variations due to demographic, ecological, economic, social, and other factors peculiar to the place at a particular time

In each of the chapters I have presented sets of summaries and conclusions about the various cultures and females in them; I shall not belabor those points here. But I shall make some general observations on the model. For Amerindians, Asians, Africans, and the Iberians, the general model extracted from general historical experience seems to have held up. To the extent to which societies acquire the ideas and the apparatus that we have associated with the post-Reformation, modern, industrial, capitalist, bourgeois culture is the extent to which the importance of the family, and thus of the female, declines in the public sphere. All of the functions that once had been the purview of the family have become subsumed by society's institutions. The personal control of the female has been eroded by the impersonal control of bureaucracies.

A further point can be made here regarding class or, rather, groups in society. It also seems that the masses of the peasants and proletariat are the people who continue to adhere to more "premodern" attitudes and patterns of behavior. An example of this is seen in frontier societies where women exhibit economic independence, social mobility, and political power. In "modern" societies women who belong to groups in power tend to be able to have some input into distribution of that power. Women who belong to groups on the periphery or totally outside the ken of power are as powerless as the groups to which they belong. The female cannot be separated from the group to which she belongs. Her influence or lack thereof lies in the socioeconomic differences between groups in society, their functions, their roles, the dimensions of the expression of behavior they are allowed.

In addition to some general conclusions about the female vis à vis family, society, class, and power some other points can be made. In terms of processes of assimilation and acculturation, the very simple analogy of "oil and water don't mix" can be applied. Cultures do not accept or reject each other on bases of racial, ethnic, religious, or superficial externalities. They do accept on the bases of patterns of belief and behavior with which they are familiar and comfortable, and they reject what does not fit into their own world view. In terms of religion, economy, politics, social arrangements, and other relationships this seems to have been the case with our cultures in particular.

This provides a means of generalizing about colonizers and colonized. At the elite levels, and in terms of laws and other theoretical constraints, colonization of one group by an alien group has some measured effects. So, too, does brutal aggressive action in colonization have its effects on the general society. But, again, for the masses who are peripheral to any avenues of power, colonial attitudes and behavior are a veneer affective primarily at the elite level. The people accept or reject on the basis of what is compatible with their world view. The people are exploited regardless, either by their own elites or by foreign colonizers.

I think that I have made some rather broad and general statements about the nature of human society—what is general to it and what is particular. I have drawn a general picture of patterns of belief and behavior regarding the female, her rights and responsibilities, her roles—social, economic, political, artistic, intellectual, religious, customary—that I think is applicable to all of the cultures under discussion in particular and to almost all in the historical development of human societies in general. Furthermore, I have suggested some important natural and social qualifiers to explain deviations in terms of peculiarities of geography, environment, and especially socioeconomic divisions that affect a culture. In terms of timing the natural qualifications are as often constant—the presence of rivers, mountains, and the like—as they are sudden—plagues, famines, and the like. But one constant qualifier is the division of cultures into socioeconomic strata in society.

I am a student of social groups in historical processes and the last general statement has suggestion for how I believe the study of the female in society should proceed. Historians and other scholars have drawn their own arbitrary and specialized areas for study. These, traditionally, have been a select and narrow range of institutions, such as political parties, military groups, diplomacy, and religion, areas dominated by men and, therefore, guaranteeing an exclusion of women from scholarly studies. So, too, when the "great men" have had their biographers, the great men invariably have been men by virtue of the arenas of influence studied. This approach has produced a unidimensional view of history. We must move away from the study of the narrow male elite groups and shift our attention to the heretofore inarticulate, the power *base* of history, as it were, rather than the power *manipulators.* To do this we must also shift our attention away from the small list of institutional arenas of power to dozens and hundreds of other groups that have yet to be studied, or studied with the same gusto as the "old boys' clubs." If we shift our attention in terms of who and what we study, probably the most important unit will be the family. And then the female will take on a new importance in the pages of written history. It is archaic to study the individual as an individual. Individuals must be studied within the context of the groups, societies, cultures to which they belong, in which they function, of whose structure they are a part. By analyzing the interaction of individual members of a particular group we shall have begun our approach to the multidimensional aspect of history. Men should not be studied exclusive of the groups to which they belong; rather, the larger human relationships should be the canvas.

It is my hope that this study will encourage that approach. I also hope that it has helped to explain why the dichotomous position of women can exist simultaneously in the ideas and institutions of cultures. The position of the female in history has depended less on race, ethnicity, religion, and more on the role and place of socioeconomic groups and units in history. In both matriarchal and patriarchal societies and families, the female has been the most important person, in the figure of the mother-matriarch, in the family household. In the sense that until recently in history, and in almost all "premodern" societies, the family has been the most important social unit and institution in any given society, the female has been the wielder of and has had access to the functions of power-broker. Attitudes and ideologies that have developed to legitimize the inferiority of females in theory are, perhaps, a mechanism by which those who do not have access to power in the family household can keep in balance and in perspective the functioning of rights and responsibilities in society. Among certain strata, males give more rights and their females acquire more rights and responsibilities than the males can, in fact, grant; among other strata of society, males grant more rights than they can, in fact, give and their females can, in fact, obtain. There has, indeed, been a consistency in patterns of belief and behavior in almost all cultures at comparable levels of development. So while, in theory, the female often has been an outcaste, a pawn, in practice, throughout history, she often has been the wellspring of power. The measure of the distance between her influence, her power, and her authority is the measure of the distance between her position as power or pawn.

BIBLIOGRAPHY

This bibliography was basic to the research and writing of this book and contains articles, books, newspapers, published primary and secondary sources, and archival and oral history collections—all of which I used in this study. There are many titles that do not bear directly on females. This is so primarily because I wished to use general sources, both old and new, reflective of the general milieux of the various cultures with which I was dealing. In particular, the sources reflect the preoccupation in this book with an Iberian and cross-cultural focus. They also reflect an implicit comparative approach. And further, they reflect my belief that sources on females, alone, are insufficient for putting females into the context of culture and society.

The sources reflect the often ad hoc and preferred multidisciplinary methodology and resources necessary for this study. By using the mix of written, oral, and other primary documentation and by synthesizing from secondary sources, I was able to tap underutilized and often—to the general researcher—unfamiliar resource lodes. The sources have been scattered and polemical, and the bulk of them have been so superficial or cursory in the information lent that my task often seemed akin to a chicken scratching on hard rock.

A note on orthography and morphology is in order. Especially with Spanish and Portuguese works, it is almost impossible to arrive at a uniform style; thus I have chosen to cite Spanish and Portuguese sources and names in the form in which they appeared in the resources and not revise them according to a set standard. I have done this primarily to avoid confusion in research materials, since often the change of spelling, grammar, and the like can cause great difficulty when one takes that to the archive and begins searching.

One other point should be made. This bibliography does not pretend to be exhaustive nor does it reflect by any means all of the materials that I examined in order to write this book. In the more than twelve years since I began the research for this project, the sources have fallen into several categories. One source has been a very impressionistic type of data gathering, simply from living in these cultures, talking with the local people, visiting their associations and clubs and festivals, appreciating and analyzing their artistic creations, and doing all of those things, among the people and among the elite, that we lump under the rubric oral history. That includes, I might add, something quite different from oral history in our contemporary sense; it includes oral tradition, which, in many societies, is and has served functions similar to our written history.

A second source has been all the media content in these cultures—newspaper, magazines, radio, television, and cinema—what they contained, about whom, and who collected it. Yet another source was the innumerable manuscript and printed collections of primary source materials not only in major archives and libraries, institutes and centers, but also in other, less utilized receptacles: church and other religious establishments; jails, morgues, hospitals, orphanages, and asylums; shipping companies; newspaper morgues; voluntary associations and mutual aid societies; businesses, banks, commercial, and industrial firms; family collections; memorabilia; and many, many more of the nuts-and-bolts type sources.

In light of that extensive collecting, perusing, browsing, examining, studying, and analyzing, the bibliography that follows might seem selective. It is—but only in the sense that each item represents, in most instances, the best or most usable or most accessible source of ten or twenty or more that say exactly the same thing. Also, I have tried to use and include sources in the bibliography that are more available and accessible to the general reader should he or she wish to expand on any point. Most all of the sources are in European languages (including English), although I consulted sources in non-European languages in bulk.

I have divided the bibliography into two sections. The first, and shorter, section includes the most common abbreviations, special collections, journals, archival collections, and the like. The second section includes general reference matter.

ABBREVIATIONS AND
SPECIAL CITATIONS

A de A	Arquivos de Angola.
AEB	Annuario Estatistica do Brasil.
AEP	Anuario Estadistico del Paraguay. Asunción. 1969.
AGI	Archivo General de Indias. Seville, Spain.
AGN	Archivo General de la Nación. Mexico City, Mexico.
AGS	Archivo General de Simancas. Simancas, Spain. A major source lode for materials on Portugal, especially for the 1580-1640 period.
AH	Area handbooks published by the American University Foreign Area Studies Program, Washington, D.C.
AHB	Area Handbook for Brazil. 1971.
AHCR	Area Handbook for Costa Rica. 1970.
AHEc	Area Handbook for Ecuador. 1971.
AHElS	Area Handbook for El Salvador. 1971.
AHI	Area Handbook for India. 1971.
AHMoz	Area Handbook for Mozambique. 1969.
AHPg	Area Handbook for Paraguay. 1972.
AHP	Area Handbook for the Philippines. 1969.
AHU	Area Handbook for Uruguay. 1970.
AHV	Area Handbook for Venezuela. 1971.
AHEI	Arquivo Historico de Estado da India.
AHN	Archivo Histórico Nacional. Madrid. Herein is housed the most important Philippine collection in Madrid, the Museo y Biblioteca del Ultramar, the most comprehensive for the nineteenth century.
AHN Libros	Archivo Histórico Nacional. Sala de Alcaldes de Casa y Corte. Libros de Gobierno, 1750-1808. Madrid.
AHR	American Historical Review.
AHU	Arquivo Historico Ultramarino. Lisboa.
AM	Arquivos de Macau. Publicação Oficial. Macao. Four volumes. Series 1: 3 volumes, 1929-1931; Series 2: 1 volume, 1941-1942.
AMC	Annaes Maritimos e Coloniaes. Lisboa, 1844-1846.

AN	Arquivo Nacional. Codice 952. Cartas regias, provisões, alvaras e avisos. Fifty volumes, 1662-1821.
ANTT	Arquivo Nacional Torre do Tombo. Lisboa.
APO	Arquivo Portuguez Oriental. Nova Goa, India.
ARSI	Archives of the Society of Jesus. Rome. This includes Jesuitica, documents of the AGI on microfilm, and the Fondo Gesuitico al Gesu di Roma. All are of great value for 1581-1767.
ASM	Arquivo Senado da Macao.
BAPP	Biblioteca e Arquivo Publico do Pará (Brazil).
BIT	Bureau International du Travail. Paris. Le statut légal des Travailleuses. 1938.
BM	British Museum. London.
BME	Boletin Mensual de Estadistica, DANE, Bogotá.
BNM	Biblioteca Nacional. Mexico.
Bol FUP	Boletim da Filmoteca Ultramarina Portuguesa. Lisboa.
Bohemia	Bohemia. Havana, 1960-1975.
	Brazil Codigo Civil.
Col de Doc	Collectión de Documentos.
Comisión Inter-americana	Comisión Interamericana de Mujeres. Union Panamericana: Documentos.
Correio Paulistano	Correio Paulistano. São Paulo, Brazil.
DM	Diario de Madrid.
D de Mx	Diario de Mexico. 1805-1807.
DO	Diario Oficial. Rio de Janeiro.
Documen-tos Históri-cos	Documentos Históricos da Cidade de Évora. Edited by Gabriel Pereira. Évora, 1885-1891.
Documen-tos Históri-cos	Documentos Históricos da Biblioteca Nacional do Rio de Janeiro. Rio de Janeiro, Brazil. 120 volumes. 1928-.
Ecuador	Ministerio de Economia Dirección General de Estadistica. Censo de Población, II. Quito, 1963.
El Censo EN	El Censo Educativo Nacional. Bogotá, 1968.
Estatuto... Timor	Estatuto de provincia de Timor, Dili.

Granma   Havana. Daily.

HAHR   Hispanic American Historical Review.

HMSO   His Majesty's Stationery Office. Great Britain Foreign
              Office, Historical Section. London. Macao: 1920; Portuguese
              Timor: 1920.

Hindustani The Hindustani Yearbook and Who's Who. Calcutta, 1970.
Yearbook

LARR   Latin American Research Review.

Memoria ... Memoria del Consejo Nacional de Educación. Buenos Aires,
Educación 1940-1941.

Memorial   Memorial literario. Madrid.
literario

MP   Mercurio Peruano, Lima, 1791-1793.

              México Código Civil.

              Moçambique Anuario Estatístico. Lourenço Marques, 1964.

MBU   Museo y Biblioteca Ultramar. Madrid.

NA   National Archives. Ibadan, Nigeria.

Nova   Novísima Recopilación de la Leyes de Espana. 6 vols.
Recop   Madrid, 1805-1807.

PHR   Pacific Historical Review.

PC   Personal Conversations-Personal Correspondence. PRB Pop-
              ulation Reference Bureau.

PRB   Population Reference Bureau.

OHI   Oral History Interviews. Ann M. Pescatello. 1960, 1962,
              1963-1966, 1967, 1968, 1969, 1970, 1973.

OAS   Organization of American States.

ORD   Ordinances of the Casa de Contratación and the Council of
              the Indies. Seville, Spain.

Oxford   Oxford Universal Dictionary. Oxford, 1955.
UD

PAB   Pan American Bulletin.

PAU   Pan American Union

RAH   Real Academia de Historia. Madrid.

RAPM   Revista do Arquivo Publico Mineiro.

Recop   Recopilación de leyes de los reynos de las Indias. 4 volumes.
             Madrid, 1681.

RG   Recenseamento geral. Lisboa, 1964.

RBPBA   Revista de la Biblioteca Pública de Buenos Aires.

RCNM   Revista del Consejo Nacional de Mujeres. Buenos Aires.

SALSETE   Archival collection housed in Goa, with data on seventeenth-
             through nineteenth-century local life.

SE   Seminario Economico. 1808-1810.

TM   Telegrafo Mercantil, político económico e historiógrafo del
             Rio de la Plata. Buenos Aires, 1801-1802, 1914-1915.

La Tribuna Agricultura. Argentina.

UN   United Nations.

UNESCO   United Nations Educational Social and Cultural Organization.

La Voz   La Voz de las Niñas. Buenos Aires.

REFERENCE MATERIALS

Abella de Ramirez, Maria. *Ensayos Feministas.* Montevideo, 1965.
Abraham, D. P. "Maramuca: An Exercise in the Combined Use of
    Portuguese Records and Oral Tradition." *Journal of African
    History* 2 (1961).
Abshire, David M., and Samuels, Michael. *Portuguese Africa: A Hand-
    book.* New York, 1969.
Accioli-Amaral. *Memorias Históricas e Politicas da Provincia de Bahia.*
    6 vols. Salvador, 1919-1940.
Acworth, Evelyn. *The New Matriarchy.* London, 1965.
Aggasiz, Louis, and Aggasiz, Elizabeth. *A Journey in Brazil.* Boston, 1868.
Aguirre Beltrán, Gonzalo. *La población negra de Mexico, 1519-1810:
    Estudio etnohistórico.* Mexico, 1946.
Aiyar, N. C. *Mayne's Treatise on Hindu Law and Usage.* 11th ed. Madras,
    1950.
Alden, Dauril, ed. *The Colonial Roots of Modern Brazil.* Berkeley and
    Los Angeles, 1973.
Allport, Gordon W. *The Nature of Prejudice.* Garden City, New York, 1958.
Almeida, António de. "Das ethóminias da Guiné Portuguesa do arquipélago
    de Cabo Verde e das ilhas de São Tomé e Principe." In *Cabo Verde,
    Guiné, Sao Tomé e Principe.* Lisboa, 1966.
Almeida de Eça, Filipe Gastão de. *Historia das guerras no Zambeze.* 2 vols.
Almeida Prado. *Primeiros Povoadores do Brasil, 1500-1530,* n.p., n.d.
Almond, Gabriel, and Verba, Sidney. *The Civic Culture.* Princeton, 1963.

Alsina, Juan, and Osuna, T. S. "Un ganadero Ingenuo." In *El Investigador*. Buenos Aires, 1880.

Altamira y Crevea, Rafael. *Historia de Espana y de la civilización española*. 4 vols. Barcelona, 1928-1930.

Altekar, A. S. *The Position of Women in Hindu Civilization*. Banaras, 1956.

Alvares, Francisco. *The Prester John of the Indies*. Translated by Stanley Alderman. 2 vols. London, 1961.

Amora, Paulo. *Rebelião das Mulheres em Minas Gerais*. Rio de Janeiro, 1968.

Amyot, Jacques. *The Chinese Community of Manila: A Study of Adaptation of Chinese Familism to the Philippine Environment*. Chicago, 1960.

Anderson, Lola. "Mexican Women Journalists," *PAB* 68 (May 1934): 315-20.

Angeles, Noli de los. "Marriage and Fertility Patterns in the Philippines." *Philippine Sociological Review* 13 (October 1965): 232-48.

Appleton-Century Crofts. *New Appleton Dictionary of the English and Portuguese Languages*. New York, 1964.

————. *Appleton's Revised Cuya's Spanish Dictionary*. New York, 1966.

Aráoz, de Lamadrid, Gregorio. *Memorias*, n.p., 1947.

Arciniegas, Germán. *Las mujeres y las Horas*. Buenos Aires, 1961.

Arenal, Concepción. *La igualdad social y política*. N.d.

————. *La mujer del porvenir*, n.p., n.d.

Argentina. Ministerio de Instrucción Pública. *Recopilación estadistica*. Buenos Aires, 1940-1941.

————. *Tercer Censo Nacional*. Buenos Aires, 1914.

Ariès, Philippe. *Centuries of Childhood: A Social History of Family Life*. New York, 1962.

Aristotle. *Opera Omnia*.

Arroyo, Anita. *Razón y Pasion de Sor Juana*. Mexico City, 1952.

d'Aulnoy, M. *Travels into Spain*. 1691. Reprint. Foulché-Delbosc edition, n.p., 1930.

Aurora Cáceres, Z. *Mujeres de Ayer de Hoy*. Paris, 1909.

Austregésilo, A. *Perfil da Mulher Brasileira*. Rio de Janeiro, 1923.

Avila de Azevedo. *O problema escolar de Angola*. Luanda, 1945.

Axelson, Eric, ed. *Documents on the Portuguese in Moçambique and Central Africa, 1497-1840*. 6 vols. Lisboa, 1962-.

Azevedo, Fernando. *Brazilian Culture*. New York, 1971.

Azevedo, Thales de. *Social Change in Brazil*. Monographs, School of Inter-American Studies, University of Florida. Gainesville, 1962; 22: 1-83.

Bachofen, J. J. *Das Mutterecht*. Stuttgart, 1861.

Bagú, Sergio. *Estructura social de la colonia*. Buenos Aires, 1952.

Baig, Tara Ali. *Women of India*. New Delhi, 1968.

Bamberger, Joan. "The Myth of Matriarchy: Why Men Rule in Primitive Society." In *Woman, Culture, and Society,* edited by Michelle Rosaldo and Louise Lamphere. Stanford, 1974.

Bamberger, Michael. "Causes and Consequ⌣ ⌣ces of the hanging Status of Women in Venezuela and Latin America." Mimeographed. AITEC, Caracas, November 1973b.

—————. "Changing Patterns of Female Labor Force Participation in Venezuela, 1950-1971." Mimeographed. AITEC, Caracas, September 1973a.

Banco Central del Ecuador. *Memoria del Gerente General: Correspondiente al Ejercicio de 1963.* Quito, 1963.

Bandelier, Adolph F. A. *The Islands of Titicaca and Coati.* New York, 1910.

Baquero Moreno, Humberto C. "Subsidios para o Estudo da Sociedade Medieval Portuguesa: Moralidades e Costumes." Ph.D. dissertation, Faculdade de Letras, Lisboa, 1961.

Barbinais, Le Gentil de la. *Nouveau voyage autour du monde.* 3 vols. Paris, 1728.

Barbot, James. *An Abstract of a Voyage to New Calabar River or Rio Real in the year 1699.* In John Churchill, *Collection of Voyages.* London, 1744-1746.

Bardis, Panos D. *Handbook on Marriage and the Family.* Chicago, 1964.

Barnes, B. H. "Relationships in Mashonaland." *MAN* 21 (1931).

Barros, E. Thimotheo de. "As migrações interioresno Brasil," *Revista de Estatística* 15 (Abril-Junho 1954). 58.

Barros Arana. *The History of Chile.* Santiago, n.d.

Basham, A. L. *The Wonder That Was India.* New York, 1959.

Beard, Mary. *Woman as Force in History.* New York,1962.

Beaumont, J. S. *Viajes por Buenos Aires, Entre Ríos y la Banda Oriental.* Buenos Aires, 1826-1827.

Beauvoir, Simone de. *The Second Sex.* New York, 1961.

Beccari, C., ed. *Rerum Aethiopicarum Scriptores Occidentales Inediti a Saeculo XVI ad XIX.* 15 vols. Rome, 1903-1917.

Beltrán, Juan Ramón. *Historia del protomedicato de Buenos Aires.* Buenos Aires, 1937.

Bennett, Wendell C. "The Andean Highlands: An Introduction." In *HSAI,* 2: 1-59, edited by Julian H. Steward, Washington, D.C., 1946.

Bermudez, Maria Elvira. *La Vida Familiar del Mexicano.* Mexico, 1955.

Bernard, Dr. Tomás Diego. *Mujeres en la epopeya San martiniana—un papel importantísimo en el espionaje de los indios y súbditos enemigos de la región de Cuyo.* Buenos Aires, 1941.

Beshah, Girma, and Aregay, Merid Wolde. *The Question of the Union of the Churches in Luso-Ethiopian Relations.* Lisbon, 1964.

Biesanz, John, and Biesanz, Mavis. *The People of Panama.* New York, 1955.

Bird, Junius. "The Alacaluf. In *HSAI,* 1:55-79, edited by Julian H. Steward. Washington, D.C., 1946.

Blachman, Morris J., "Eve in an Adamocracy: Women and Politics in Brazil," New York University: Occasional Papers, #5 (1973).

Blair, Emma H, and Robertson, James A. *The Philippine Islands, 1493-1803.* 55 vols. Cleveland, 1903-1909.

Blake, J. W. *Europeans in West Africa, 1450-1560.* 2 vols. London, 1942.

Blitz, Rudolph C. "The Role of High Level Manpower in Economic Development in Chile." In *Manpower and Education: Country Studies in Economic Development,* edited by Frederick H. Harbison. New York, 1965.

Blomberg, Héctor Pedro. *Mujeres de la Histórica Americana.* Buenos Aires, 1933.

Blough, William. "Political Attitudes of Mexican Women." *Journal of Interamerican Studies and World Affairs,* 14: 2 (May 1972), 201-24.

Boas, Franz. "Das Verwandtschaftsystem der Vandau." In *Zeitschrift Für Ethnologie.* Berlin 1923.

Boch, E. Wilbur, and Iutaka, Sugiyama. "Social Status, Mobility, and Premarital Pregnancy: A Case of Brazil." *Journal of Marriage and the Family* 32 (May 1970): 284-92.

Borah, Woodrow, and Cook, S.F. "La despoblacion del Mexico Central en el siglo XVI." *Historia Mexicana* 12 (1962) 1-12.

————. "Marriage and Legitimacy in Mexican Culture: Mexico and California." *California Law Review* 54 (1966).

————. "Race and Class in Mexico." *PHR* 23 (1954). 331-342.

————. *The Aboriginal Population of Central Mexico on the Eve of the Spanish Conquest.* Berkeley, 1963.

Bosman, Willem. *A New and Accurate Description of the Coast of Guinea Divided into the Gold, the Slave, and the Ivory Coasts.* London, 1705.

Botarro, Dr. Oswaldo L. *Sobre la divinación, curanderismo y el ejercicio ilegal de la medicina.* Buenos Aires, 1921.

Bourgoing, J. F. de. *Travels in Spain.* 3 vols. London, 1789.

Boxer, C. R. *Fidalgos in the Far East, 1550-1770.* The Hague, 1948.

———— "Fidalgos Portugueses e Bailadeiras Indianas. Séculos XVII e XVIII." *Revista de Historia, São Paulo* 56 (1961): 83-105.

————. *Four Centuries of Portuguese Expansion, 1415-1825: A Succinct Survey.* Berkeley and Los Angeles, 1969.

————. *Macao Three Hundred Years Ago,* n.p., 1942.

————. *Portuguese Society in the Tropics: The Municipal Councils of Goa, Macao, Bahia, and Luanda.* Madison, 1965.

————. *Race Relations in the Portuguese Colonial Empire, 1415-1825.* Oxford, 1963.

————. *The Topasses of Timor.* Pamphlet 24 (1947).

————. *The Dutch Seaborne Empire, 1600-1800.* London, 1965.

———— and de Azevedo, Carlos. *Fort Jesus and the Portuguese in Mombasa, 1593-1729.* London, 1960.

Boyle, Frederick. *A Ride Across a Continent: A Personal Narrative of Wanderings through Nicaragua and Costa Rica.* 2 vols. London, 868.

Boyd-Bowman, Peter, "The Regional Origins of the Earliest Spanish Colonists of America." *Publications of the Modern Language Association* 71 (1956): 1152-72.

Braga, Alberto V. *Dos Guimaraes: Tradiçoes e usancas populares.* Espozende, 1924.

Brasio, Antonío. *Monumenta Missionária Africana: Africa Ocidental.* Lisboa, 1952.

Braudel, Fernand. *The Mediterranean and the Mediterranean World in the Age of Philip II.* Translated by Sian Reynolds. 2 vols. New York, 1973, 1974.

Bravo, Mario. *Derechos políticos de la mujer.* N.d.

Brenner, Anita. *The Wind That Swept Mexico.* New York, 1943.

Briffault, Robert. *The Mothers.* 3 vols. London, 1927.

Brouwer, Hendrick. *Narración histórica del viaje ejecutado del este del estrecho de la Maire a las costas de Chile . . . en los años 1641 i 1643.* Reprint. Santiago, 1892.

Brown, Donald R. *The Role and Status of Women in the Soviet Union.* New York, 1968.

Bunge, Octavio. *Educación de la mujer,* n.d.

Burch, Thomas, and Gendell, Murray. "Extended Family Structure and Fertility: Some Conceptual and Methodological Issues." *Journal of Marriage and the Family* 32 (May 1970): 227-36.

Burgess, Ernest, and Locke, Harvey. *The Family: From Institution to Companionship.* New York, 1953.

Burn, Andrew R. "Hic Breve Vivitur." *Past and Present* 4 (1953).

Byron, John. *The Narrative of the Honorable John Byron (Commodore in a Late Expedition Around the World) containing an Account of the Great Distress Suffered by Himself and His Companions on the Coast of Patagonia, from the Year 1740, Till Their Arrival in England, 1746.* 2d ed. London, 1768.

Cabral, Oswaldo. *Santa Catarina.* São Paulo, 1937.

Cadete, X. *El campamento de 1878.* Buenos Aires, 1878.

Cadorenga, Antonio de Oliveira de. *História Geral das Guerras Angolanas.* 1681-1683. 3 vols. Reprint. Lisboa, 1940-1942.

Caillet-Bois, Horacio. *Sor Josefa Dias y Clucellas, Primera Pintora Santa Fesina en el Centenario de su Nacimineto.* Santa Fe, 1952.

Caldas, José Antonio. *Notícia geral de toda esta capitania da Bahia desde o seu descobrimiento até o presente anno de 1759.* Salvador, 1951.

Calderón de la Barca. *Frances: Life in Mexico.* New York, n.d.

Calmon, Pedro. *Historia Social do Brasil: Aspectos da Sociedade Colonial.* São Paulo, 1941.

————. *Historia Social do Brasil, 1500-1800.* 3 vols. Rio de Janeiro, 1939-1943.

Camarano, Chris. "On Cuban Women." *Science and Society* 35 (Spring 1971): 48-58.

Campbell, Alexander. *The Sequel to Bulkeley and Cummin's Voyage to the South Seas.* 1747. Reprint. London, 1947.

Campoalange, Maria La Fitte. *La Mujer en Espana: Cien Anos de su História, 1860-1860.* Madrid, 1964.

Campos, J. J. A. *History of the Portuguese in Bengal.* Calcutta, 1919.

Canals Frau, Salvador. "The Huarpe." In *HSAI,* 1: 169-75, edited by Julian H. Steward. Washington, D.C., 1946.

Candido, A. "The Brazilian Family." In *Brazil: Portrait of Half a Continent,* edited by T. Lynn Smith and Alexander Marchant. New York, 1951.

Cannarozzi, C. *Le prediche volgari.* Florence, 1968.

Cannon, Mary. "Women Workers in Argentina, Chile, and Uruguay." *PAB* 76 (March 1942): 148-54.

Capell, A. "Peoples and Languages of Timor." *Oceania* 14: 191-219, 311-37; 15: 19-49.

Capellanus, Andreas. *The Book of Courtly Love.* New York, 1941.

Capezzuoli, L., and Cappabianca, G. *História de la Emancipación Femenina.* Buenos Aires, 1966.

Careaga, Mercedes Formica de. "Spain." In *Women in the Modern World,* edited by Raphael Patai. New York, 1967.

Carlos, Manuel L. and Sellers, Lois, "Family, Kinship, Structure and Modernization in Latin America," *LARR* 7:2 (Summer 1972), 95-124.

Caro Baroja, Julio. *Estudios sobre la vida tradicional espanola.* Barcelona, 1968.

Carranza, Adolfo P. *Patricias Argentinas.* Buenos Aires, 1910.

Carranza, Venustiano. *Ley sobre relaciones familiares.* Mexico, 1917.

Carrasco, Pedro. "Family Structure of Sixteenth Century Tepotzlan." In *Process and Pattern of Culture,* edited by Robert Alan Manners. Chicago, 1964.

Carroll, Berenice. *Liberating Women's History.* Urbana, 1975.

Carroll, John J. *The Filipino Manufacturing Entrepreneur: Agent and Product of Change.* Ithaca, 1965.

Casas, Bartolomé de Las. *Apologética historia de las Indias.* Madrid. 1909.
———. *Historia de las Indias, 1520-1561.* Madrid, 1875-1876.

Castán Tobenas, José. *La condición social y juridica de la mujer.* N.d.

Castilla del Pino, Carlos. *La alienación de la mujer.* Madrid, 1970.

Castro, Modesto de. *Urbana et Felisa.* Manila, n.d.

CEDE. *Empleo y Desempleo en Colombia.* Bogotá, 1968.

Cenival, M. and Ricard, R., *Sources inédites de l'histoire du Maroc. Portugal.* 5 vols. Paris, 1934-1953.

CDFS. *Colección de documentos para la Formación social de Hispano-américa, 1493-1810,* I-III: 2. Madrid, 1953-1962.

Centurión, Carlos R. "Mujeres europeas en la conquista del Paraguay y Rio de la Plata." *La Prensa* (August 9, 1963).

Céspedes del Castillo, Guillermo. "La sociedad colonial americana en los siglos XVI y XVII." In Jaime Vicens Vives, ed., *Historia social y economica de España y América,* III. Barcelona, 1957.

Chadwick, D. *Social Life in the Days of Piers Plowman.* London, n.d.

Chaney, Elsa. "Supermadre: Women in Politics in Latin America." In Pescatello, 1973.

Chinas, Betty. *The Zapotec Woman.* New York, 1973.

Cieza de León, Pedro de. *La Chrónica general del Perú,* edited by H. H. Urteaga. Lima, 1924, 1945.

Clarke, A. *Working Life of Women in the Seventeenth Century.* London, n.d.

Clarke, E. *Letters concerning the Spanish Nation.* London, 1763.

Clarke, John J. *Population Geography and the Developing Countries.* Oxford, 1971.

Cocca, Aldo Armando. *Ley de Sufragio Feminino.* Buenos Aires, 1948.

Codigo Civil Brasileiro. Article 6; 240-255, promulgated on 1 January 1916. See *Diario Oficial,* 3 September 1962.

Codigo Civil Español. *Legislaciones forales o especiales y leyes complementarias.* Madrid, 1966.

Cohen, Lucy M. *Las Colombian ante de Renovación Universitaria.* Bogotá, 1971.

Cohen, Yehudi. "Structure and Function: Family Organization and Socialization in a Jamaican Community." *American Anthropologist* 53 (1956):4.

Cohn, Bernard. "Chamar Family in a North Indian Village," *Economic Weekly* 13 (1961):1051-1055.

⸻. *India: The Social Anthropology of a Civilization.* Englewood Cliffs, N. J., 1971.

Colección de Documentos inéditos relativos al descubrimiento, conquista, y organización de las antigas posesiones españolas de ultramar. 13 volumes. Madrid, 1885-1900.

Comhaire-Sylvain, Suzanne. *Femmes de Kinshasa hier et aujourd 'hui.* La Haye, 1968.

Concepción, Juan de la. *História general de Philipinas.* 14 vols. Manila, 1788-1792.

Condorcet, Jean Antoine. *Outlines of an Historical View of the Progress of the Human Mind.* London, 1795.

Congreso. Primer. Feminino Internacional de la República. Argentina. Reports in pamphlet. n.d. mimeo.

Connor, Jeanette T. *Pedro Menéndez de Avilés: Memorial by Gonzalo Solis de Merás.* Gainesville, 1964.

Cook, S. F. and Simpson, L. B., *The Population of Mexico in the Sixteenth Century*. Berkeley, 1948.

Cooper, John M. "The Araucanians." In *HSAI*, 2:687-760, edited by Julian H. Steward. Washington, D.C., 1946d.

————. "The Chono." In *HSAI*, 1:47-54., 1946.

————. "The Ona." In *HSAI*, 1:107-25., 1946b.

————. "The Patagonian and Pampean Hunters." In *HSAI*, 1:127-68, 1946.

————. *Temporal Sequence and the Marginal Cultures*. Anthropological Series, Catholic University of America, no. 10. Washington, D.C., 1941.

————. "The Yahgan." In *HSAI*, 1:81-106. 1946a.

Cormack, Margaret. *The Hindu Woman*. New York, 1953.

————. *She Who Rides a Peacock*. New York, 1961.

Correa de Azevedo. "Concorrera o modo porque Sao dirigidos entre nos a Educação e Instrucção da mocidade para o Benefico Desenvolvimiento Fisico e Moral do Homen?" *Annaes Brasilenses Medicina* 23 (April 1872) 416-40.

Correas, Gonzalo de. *Vocabularia de Refranes y Frases Proverbiales y otras Fórmulas Comunes de la Lengua Castellano*. Madrid. 1924.

Corwin, Arthur. *Contemporary Mexican Attitudes Toward Population, Poverty, and Public Opinion*. Monographs, School of Inter-American Studies, University of Florida, no. 25. Gainesville.

Cosentini, Francisco. *Declaración de los derechos i obligaciones civiles de la mujer y del hogar*. Mexico, 1930.

Couty, Louis. *L'esclavage au Brésil*. Paris, 1881.

Crawford, W. Rex. *A Century of Latin American Thought*. New York, 1966.

Crowder, Michael. *A Short History of Nigeria*. New York, 1966.

Cruz, Eloida. *Los politicos de la mujer en México*. Mexico, 1937.

Cruz, Josefina. *Dona Mencia la Adelantada*. Buenos Aires, 1960.

Cruz, Levy. "Brazil." In *Women in the Modern World*, edited by Raphael Patai. New York, 1967.

Cruz, Ramón de la. *El cortejo escarmentado*. Madrid, 1773.

————. *El Espejo de los padres*. Madrid, n.d.

————. *Los maridos engañados y desengañados*. Madrid, 1779.

————. *Las mujeres defendidas*. Madrid, 1764.

————. *La niñeria*. Madrid, n.d.

————. *El payo ingenuo*. Madrid, 1772.

————. *El picapedrero*. Madrid, 1767.

————. *Sainetes*. Madrid, n.d.

————. *El Sastre y el pelequero*. Madrid, n.d.

————. *Soltera, casada y viuda*. Madrid, 1775.

————. *El Prado por la noche*. Madrid, 1765.

Cunha Gonçalves, Luis da. *A vida rural do Alentejo*. Coimbra, 1922.

Curtin, Philip D. *The Atlantic Slave Trade: A Census.* Madison, 1969.

————. "The Slave Trade and the Atlantic Basin: Intercontinental Perspectives." In *Key Issues in the Afro-American Experience,* edited by Nathan I. Huggens, Martin Kilson, and Daniel M. Fox. 2 vols. New York, 1971.

Cutileiro, José. *A Portuguese Rural Society.* Oxford, 1971.

Daedalus 93 (1964). Entire issue.

————. 97 (1968). Entire issue.

Dalgado, R. *Glossario Luso-Asiático.* 2 vols. Coimbra, 1919-1921.

Dalrymple, F. *Travels Through Spain and Portugal in 1774.* London, 1777.

Danielou, Jean, and Marrou; Henri. *The Christian Centuries: A New History of the Catholic Church.* New York, 1964.

Danver, F. C. *The Portuguese in India, 1481-1894.* 2 vols. London, 1894.

Dean, Warren. *The Industrialization of São Paulo, 1880-1945.* Austin, Texas, 1969.

Degler, Carl. "Woman as Force in History, by Mary Beard. A Review." *Daedalus* 103 (1974):67-73.

Dellepiane, Antonio. *Dos Patricias Ilustres: Maria Sanchez de Mendeville y Carmen Nobrega de Avellaneda.* Buenos Aires, 1923.

Dellepiane, Elvira Rawson de. "La campana Feminista en la Argentina." In *La Mujer,* edited by Miguel Font. Buenos Aires, 1921.

Desai, Neera C. *Report on the Hindu Joint-Family System.* Bombay, 1936.

Deschamps, Paul. *Le Portugal: La vie social actuelle.* Paris, 1935.

Dias, Jorge. *Rio de Onor: Comunitarismo agro-pastoria.* Porto, 1953.

————. *Vilarinha da Furna: Uma aldeia comunitária.* Porto, 1948.

Diaz del Castillo, Bernal. *The True History of the Conquest of New Spain.* Edited by Genaro García and translated by A. P. Maudsley. 5 vols. London, 1908-1916.

Dickman, Enrique. *Emancipación Civil, Politica, y Social de la Mujer.* Buenos Aires, 1935.

Diffie, Bailey. *Prelude to Empire.* Lincoln, Nebraska, 1963.

Dobyns, Henry F. "Estimating Aboriginal American Population." *Current Anthropology* (October 1966); 395-416.

Domínguez Ortiz, Antonio. *The Golden Age of Spain, 1516-1659.* New York, 1971.

Dube, S. C. *Indian Villages.* London, 1955.

Duby, Georges. *La société aux XIᵉ et XIIᵉ siècles dans la region maconnaise.* Paris, 1953.

Duffy, James. *Portuguese Africa.* Cambridge, Mass., 1959.

DuMont, Louis. *Homo Hierarchicus: The Caste System and Its Implications,* Chicago, 1970.

Duncan, T. Bentley. *Atlantic Islands.* Chicago, 1972.

Dussen, Adriaen van der. *Relatório sôbre as capitanias conquistadas no Brasil pelos holandeses.* 1639. Reprint. Rio de Janeiro, 1947.

Dutra, Francis A. "Centralization vs. Donatorial Privilege: Pernambuco, 1602-1630." In *Colonial Roots of Modern Brazil*. Edited by Dauril Alden. Berkeley and Los Angeles, 1973.

————— Private conversations. 1973, 1974.

Earthy, E. Dora. *Valenge Woman*, n.p., 1935.

Economic Journal. "Women Traders in Medieval London." 1916.

Edwards, Adrian C. *The Ovimbundu Under Two Sovereignties*. London, 1962.

Eliade, Mircea. *Rites and Symbols of Initiation*. New York, 1965.

Elliott, J. H. *Imperial Spain, 1469-1716*. New York, 1966.

—————. *The Revolt of the Catalans: A Study in the Decline of Spain* (1598-1640). Cambridge, 1963.

Elmendorf, Mary Lindsay. *The Mayan Woman and Change*. Cuernavaca, 1972.

Elu de Lenero, Carmen. *¿Hacia donde va la mujer mexicana?* Mexico, 1969.

Encinas, Diego de, comp. *Provisiones, cédulas, capitulos de ordenanzas, instruciones [sic] y cartas . . . tocantes al buengovierno de las Indias*. 4 vols. Madrid, 1596.

Ennes, Ernesto. *Estudos sobre História do Brasil*, n.p., 1947.

Escobedo, Raquel. *Galeria de Mujeres Ilustres (de Mexico)*. Mexico, 1967.

Evans-Pritchard, E. E. *The Nuer: A Description of the Modes of Livelihood and Political Institutions of a Nilotic People*. Oxford, 1940.

Expilly, Charles. *Les femmes et les moeurs du Brésil*. Paris, 1963.

Ezquerra Del Bayo. *Retratos de mujeres espanolas del siglo XIX*, n.p., n.d.

Fanshawe, Ann. *The Memoirs of Ann Lady Fanshawe, . . . 1600-1672*. London, 1907.

Feijoó y Montenegro, Benito Jerónomi. *Three Essays or Discourses on the Following Subjects—a Defense or Vindication of Women*. London, 1778.

Felgas, Helio A. *Timor português*. Lisboa, 1956.

Fenelon, Archibishop. *Telemaque*. Paris, 1699.

—————. *Traité de l'education de filles*. N.d.

Fernandes, Florestan. *A organização Social dos Tupinamba*. São Paulo, 1948.

—————. *A função Social da Guerra na Sociedade Tupinamba*. 1948.

Fernández, Diego. "Historia del Perú." In *Crónicas del Peru*, edited by Sr. Tudela. Madrid, 1963-1965.

Fernández de Lizardi, José Joaquín. *La Quijotita y su prima*. Mexico, 1967.

Fernández Duró, Cesareo. *La mujer española en Indias: Disertación leida ante la Real Academia de la Historia*. Madrid, 1902.

Ferreira da Costa. *A Selva*. Translated by Charles Duff. New York, 1935.

First Conference of the American Commission of Women. Report as *Pan-American Union Bulletin* 63 (July 1929).

Fisher, Lillian E. "The Influence of the Present Mexican Revolution Upon the Status of Mexican Women." *HAHR* 22 (1942):211-28.

Fleming, Peter. *Brazilian Adventure*. Harmondsworth, 1957.

Flora, Cornelia. "The Passive Female and Social Change: A Cross-Cultural Comparison by Class of Women's Magazine Fiction in the United States and Colombia and Mexico." In *Female and Male in Latin America,* edited by Ann Pescatello. Pittsburgh, 1973.

————. "The Passive Female: Her Comparative Image by Class and Culture in Women's Magazine Fiction." *Journal of Marriage and the Family* (1971), 435-44.

Flores, Maria. *The Woman With the Whip: Eva Peron.* Garden City, New York, 1952.

Font, Miguel. *La mujer.* Buenos Aires, 1921.

Forde, Daryll. *The Yoruba-Speaking People of South-Western Nigeria.* London, 1951.

————, and Kaberry, P. M. *West African Kingdoms in the Nineteenth Century.* Oxford, 1969.

Fox, Frederick, S. J. "One Hundred Years of Philippine Education: 1860-1960." unpublished manuscript, 1963.

Fox, Robert B. "Social Organization." In *Area Handbook of the Philippines,* 1. Chicago, 1956.

Franco, Bento. *Macau eosseus Habitantes.* Lisboa, 1897.

Franco, Luis. *La Hembra Humana.* Buenos Aires, 1962.

Franco Rodríguez, José. *La mujer y la politica españolas.* Madrid, 1920.

Frazier, E. Franklin. "The Negro Family in Bahia, Brazil." *In Latin America Social Organization and Institutions,* edited by Olen E. Leonard and Charles P. Loomis. East Lansing, 1953.

Freeman, Susan Tax. *Neighbors: The Social Contract in a Castilian Hamlet.* Chicago, 1970.

Freyre, Gilberto. *The Mansions and the Shanties.* New York, 1963.

————. *The Masters and·the Slaves.* New York, 1964.

Frías, Bernardo. *Historia de Güemes y de la Provincia de Salta, I-III.* Buenos Aires, 1907-1911.

Friede, Juan. "The catálogo de pasajeros and Spanish Emigration to America to 1550." *HAHR* 31 (May 1951): 333-48.

————. *Los Welser en la conquista de Venezuela.* Caracas, 1961.

Frugoni, Emilio. *La mujer ante el derecho,* n.p., n.d.

Furlong, Guillermo. *La cultura femenina en la época colonial.* Buenos Aires, 1945.

Furtado, Celso. *The Economic Growth of Brazil.* Berkeley, 1965.

Gallagher, Ann Miriam. *The Family Backgrounds of the Nuns of Two Monasteries in Colonial Mexico: Santa Clara, Queretaro and Corpus Christi, Mexico City (1724-1822),* unpublished Ph.D. dissertation, Catholic University, Washington, D.C., 1971.

Galván Moreno, C. *Rivadavia, el Estadista Genial.* Buenos Aires, 1940.

Gamio de Alba, Margarita. *La Mujer Indigena de Centro America.* Mexico, 1957.

Garcia v. Bravo. AGI, Sevilla. 1570-1571. Antón García contra Feliciano

Bravo . . . 1570-71. Justicia, leg. 250 ff 1885-2255v. An *expediente,* part of the first *legajo* of the residencia of Gov Luis Céspedes de Oviedo, in France V. Scholes and Ralph L. Roys, *The Maya Chotal Indians of Acalan-Tixchel.* Norman, 1968.

García y García, Elvira. *Actividad Femenina.* Lima, 1928.

————. *La Mujer Peruana através de los siglos.* 2 vols. Lima, n.d.

García, José. "Diarío del viaje i navegación hechos por el padre José García." in AN. Hidr, Mar. Chile (1889: 14), 3-47.

García, Juan Agustin. *La Ciudad Indiana.* N.d.

García Pimental, Luis, ed. *Descripcion del arzobispado de Mexico hecha en 1570 y otras documentos.* Mexico, 1897.

Garran-Coulou, J. *Rapport sur les Troubles de St. Domingue Fait au nom de la Comission des Colonies des Comités.* 4 vols. Paris, 1798.

Geertz, Clifford. *The Interpretation of Cultures.* New York, 1973.

Gendell, Murray, and Rossell, Guillermo, *The Economic Activity of Women in Latin America.* Washington, D.C., 1967.

Germani, Gino. *Estructura social de la Argentina.* Buenos Aires, 1955.

Ghurye, G.S. *Caste and Class in India,* Bombay, 1957.

Gianello de Güller, María Zorayda. *Guerrilera.* Paraná, East Rios, 1966.

Gibson, Charles. *The Aztecs Under Spanish Rule.* Stanford, 1964.

———— *The Inca Concept of Sovereignty and the Spanish Administration in Peru.* Austin, 1948.

————. *Spain in America.* New York, 1966.

————. *Tlaxcala in the Sixteenth Century.* New Haven, 1952.

Gillin, John. "Tribes of the Guianas." In *HSAI* 2:799-858, edited by Julian H. Steward. Washington, D.C., 1948.

Glass, D. V. and Eversley, D. E. C. *Population in History,* Chicago, 1965.

Glauert, Earl. ms sources on Feijoó and the Enlightenment.

Goes Bettencourt, Anna. *Almanack de Lembranças Brasileiro.* N.p., 1885.

Gómara, Francisco López. *Cortes: The Life of the Conqueror.* Translated and edited by Lesley Bird Simpson. Berkeley and Los Angeles, 1964.

Gómez Morán, Luis. *Le Mujer en la historia y en la legislación.* N.d.

González, E. *El feminismo en las sociedades modernas.* N.d.

González, Arrili, Bernardo. *Mujeres de Nuestra Tierra.* Buenos Aires, 1950.

Goode, William. "Illegitimacy in the Caribbean Social Structure." *American Sociological Review* 25 (February 1960): 21-30.

————. *World Revolution and Family Patterns.* Glencoe, 1963.

Goody, Jack, ed. *The Character of Kinship.* Cambridge, Mass., 1973.

Gough, Kathleen. "Brahmin Kinship in a Tamil Village." *American Anthropologist* 58 (1956): 834-853.

Graham, Maria. *Journal of a Voyage to Brazil.* London, 1824.

Graham, Richard. *Britain and the Onset of Modernization in Brazil, 1850-1914.* Cambridge, Mass., 1968.

————. *Independence in Latin America.* New York, 1972.

Granada, Daniel. *Resena histórica-descriptiva de antiguos y modernas supersticiones en el Rio de la Plata.* Montevideo, 1896.

Gray, John Milner. "Early Portuguese Visitors to Kilwa." *Tanganyika Notes and Records* 52 (1959).

————. "Rezende's Description of East Africa in 1634." *Tanganyika Notes and Records* 23 (1947).

Green, M.M. *Ibo Village Affairs.* New York, 1964.

Greenberg, Joseph H. *The Languages of Africa.* Bloomington, 1966.

Gregorio Lavié, Lucila de. *Trayectoria de la condición social de las mujeres Argentina.* Santa Fe, 1947.

Grenan, P., S.J. *Literatura Feminina.* Buenos Aires, n.d.

Grey, Vicente. *La mujer de la independencia.* Santiago, Chile, 1910.

Guerrero, César H. *Mujeres de Sarmiento.* Buenos Aires, 1960.

Guerrero, Sylvia H. "An Analysis of Husband-Wife Roles among Filipino Professionals at U.P. Los Baños Campus." *Philippine Sociological Review* 13 (October 1965): 275-81.

Guimarães, Ruth. *As Mães na lenda e na historia.* São Paulo, 1960.

Gunawardena, K. W. A New Netherlands in Ceylon. Colombo, n.d.

Gusinde, Martin. *Die Feuerland–Indianer.* 2Band. Wien, 1937.

Guthrie, George M. *The Filipino Child and Philippine Society.* Manila, 1961.

Gutiérrez de Pineda, Virginia. *La Familia en Colombia.* 2 vols. Bogotá, 1963; 1968.

Gutiérrez de Santa Clara, Pedro. *Quinquenarios o historia de las guerras civiles del Perú, Crónicas del Perú.* Edited by Sr. Tudela. 5 vols. Madrid, 1963-1965.

Guy, Henry A., ed. *Women in the Caribbean.* Jamaica, 1968.

von Hagen, Victor W. *The Four Seasons of Manuela: A Biography.* New York, 1952.

————. *The World of the Maya.* New York, 1960.

Hajnal, John. "European Marriage Patterns in Perspective." In *Population in History,* edited by D.V. Glass and D.E.C. Eversley. Chicago, 1965.

Hammond, R. J. *Portugal and Africa, 1815-1910.* Stanford, 1966.

Hamy, Jules Theodore. *Documents pour servir al'anthropologie de l'ile de Timor.* Paris, n.d.

Hanke, Lewis. *Mexico and the Caribbean.* New York, 1967.

Haring, Clarence. *Trade and Navigation Between Spain and the Indies.* Gloucester, 1964.

Harkess, Shirley. "The Pursuit of an Ideal. Migration, Social Class, and Women's Roles in Bogotá, Colombia." In *Female and Male in Latin America,* edited by Ann Pescatello. Pittsburgh, 1973.

Harris, C. C. *The Family: An Introduction.* New York, 1969.

Harris, Jack. "The Position of Women in a Nigerian Society." *Transactions of the New York Academy of Sciences,* 2d ser., no. 5.

Harris, Marvin. *Town and Country in Brazil.* New York, 1956.

Havel, J. E. *La condición de la mujer.* Eudeba, 1965.

Havighurst, Robert, and Moreira, J. Robert. *Society and Education in Brazil.* Pittsburgh, 1965.

Helblom, Anna-Britta. *La participación cultural de las mujeres: Indias y mestizas en el Mexico precortesiano y post revolucionario.* Stockholm, 1967.

Henriques, Fernando. *Prostitution in Europe and the New World.* Prostitution and Society, vol. 2. London, 1963.

Herculano, Alexandre. *Casamento civil.* Lisboa, 1907.

Herlihy, David. "Land, Family, and Women in Continental Europe, 701-1200." *Tradito* 18 (1962): 89-120.

————. *Medieval and Renaissance Pistoia: The Social History of an Italian Town, 1200-1430.* New Haven, 1967.

Hernandez de Alba, Gregorio. "The Highland Tribes of Southern Colombia." In *HSAI*, 2:915-60, edited by Julian H. Steward. Washington, D. C., 1946.

————."Sub-Andean Tribes of the Cauca Valley." In *HSAI*, 4:297-327. 1948.

————. "The Tribes of Northwestern Venezuela." In *HSAI*, 4:467-79. 1948a.

Herrera, Ataliva. *La Ilumindad: Madre María de la Paz y Figueria.* 1934.

Herrera y Tordesillas, Antonio de. *Historia general de los hechos de los castellaños, en las islas, y tierra firme de el Mar Oceano.* 4 vols. 1601-1615. Reprint (4 vols. in 12). Madrid, 1934.

Herskovits, Melville. *Dahomey, an Ancient West African Kingdom.* 2 vols. New York, 1938.

————. *Life in a Haitian Valley.* New York, 1971.

Hicks, Albert C. *Blood in the Street: The Life and Rule of Trujillo.* New York, 1946.

d'Holbach, Paul Henri. *Common Sense.* Paris, 1772.

Holmberg, Allan. "The Sirionó. In *HSAI*, 2:455-63, edited by Julian H. Steward. Washington, D. C., 1948.

Hopper, Janice H., ed. and trans. *Indians of Brazil in the Twentieth Century.* Washington, D. C., 1967.

Hsu, Francis L. K. *Clan, Caste, Club.* Princeton, 1963.

International Labour Review. "Agricultural Labour in India." 1962: 148-62.

————. "The Apprenticeship of Women and Girls." 1952.

————. "Women's Employment in Latin America." 1956.

————. "Youth and Work in Latin America." 1964: 1-23, 150-79.

Isaacman, Alan. "The Prazos da Coroa, 1752-1830: A Functional Analysis of the Political System." *Studia* (1969).

————. *Mozambique, The Africanization of a European Institution: the Zambesi Prazos, 1750-1902.* Madison, 1972.

Jacobs, Sue Ellen. *Women in Perspective.* Urbana, 1974.

Jaquette, Jane. "Literary Images and Female Role Stereotypes: The Woman and the Novel in Latin America." In *Female and Male in Latin America,* ed. Ann Pescatello. Pittsburgh, 1973.

————. *Women in Politics.* New York, 1974.

James, Edwin Oliver. *The Cult of the Mother Goddess.* London, 1965.

Jara, Alvaro. *Legislación indigenista de Chile,* Mexico, 1956/1960.

Jaramillo Uribe, Jaime. "La población indígena de Colombia en el momento de la conquista y sus transformaciones posteriores." *Annuario Colombiano de Historia Social y de la Cultura* 7:2 (1964).

Jocano, F. Landa. *Growing Up in a Philippine Barrio.* New York, 1969.

Johnson, Frederick. "Central American Cultures: An Introduction." In *HSAI,* 4:43-67, edited by Julian H. Steward. Washington, D.C., 1948.

Johnson, Hal B. "The Donatary Captaincy in Perspective: Portuguese Backgrounds to the Settlement of Brazil." *HAHR* (1972): 203-14.

————. *From Reconquest to Empire.* New York, 1970.

Jolly, Richard. "Education." In *Cuba, the Economic and Social Revolution,* edited by Dudley Seers. Chapel Hill, 1964.

Jones, G. I. "Native and Trade Currencies in Southern Nigeria during the Eighteenth and Nineteenth Centuries." *Africa* 28 (1958).

Jones, Thomas Jesse. *Education in Africa.* New York, 1922.

————. *Education in East Africa.* New York, 1926.

Juan, Jorge, and Ulloa, Antonio de. *Noticias secretas de América.* Buenos Aires, 1953/1964.

Junod, Henri. *The Life of a South African Tribe.* N.p., 1913.

Kahy, Charles E. *Life and Manners in Madrid, 1750-1800.* Berkeley and Los Angeles, 1932.

Kamen, Henry. *The Iron Century: Social Change in Europe.* New York, 1971.

Kanowitz, Leo. *Women and the Law.* Albuquerque, 1969.

Kapadia, K. M. *Marriage and the Family in India.* Oxford, 1966.

Karasch, Mary. Mimeo materials. 1972.

Karve, Irawati. *Kinship Organization in India.* Poona, 1953.

Kavanagh, Julia. *Woman in France.* London, 1864.

Kaye, Barrington. *Bringing Up Children in Ghana.* London, 1962.

Kelly, John Eoghan. *Pedro de Alvarado, Conquistador.* Princeton, n.d.

Kenny, Michael. *A Spanish Tapestry: Town and Country in Castile.* New York, 1966.

King, Margaret. *Eden to Paradise.* London, 1963.

Kingsley, Mary H. *West African Studies.* London, 1899.

Kirchoff, Paul. "Food-gathering Tribes of the Venezuelan Llanos." In *HSAI,* 4:445-68, edited by Julian H. Steward. Washington, D.C., 1948.

Klein, A. Norman. "West African Unfree Labor Before and After the Rise of the Atlantic Slave Trade." In *Slavery in the New World,* edited by Eugene Genovese and Laura Foner, New Jersey, 1969.

Klein, Julius. *The Mesta: A Study in Spanish Economic History, 1273-1836.* Cambridge, Mass., 1920.

Klimpel Alvarado, Felicitas. *La mujer chilena. Al porte feminino al progreso de Chile, 1910-1960.* Santiago, 1962.

Konetzke, Richard. "La emigración de las mujeres españolas a América durante la época colonial." *Revista Internacional de la Sociologia* 3 (1945): 123-50.

————— "La esclavitud de los indios como elemento de la estructuración Social de Hispanoamerica." *Estudios de Historia Social de Espana* 7 (1949).

Kroeber, A.L. "The Chibcha." In *HSAI,* 2:887-909, edited by Julian H. Steward. Washington, D.C., 1946.

—————. *Cultural and Natural Areas of Native South America.* Berkeley, 1939.

Kubler, George. "The Quechua in the Colonial World," in *HSAI,* 2:331-410 edited by Julian H. Steward. Washington, D.C., 1946.

Kuczynski, Robert R. *Population Movements.* Oxford, 1936.

LaBarca Hubertson, Amanda. *¿A donde va la mujer?* 1952.

LaBarre, Weston, "The Uru Chipaya." In *HSAI,* 2:575-85, edited by Julian H. Steward. Washington, D.C., 1946.

Lach, Donald F. *India in the Eyes of Europe.* Chicago, 1968.

Laigle, Mathilde. *Le Livre des trois vertus de Christine de Pison et son milieu historique et litteraire.* Paris, 1912.

Lamphere, Louise. "Strategies, Cooperation, and Conflict Among Women in Domestic Groups." In *Woman, Culture, and Society,* edited by Michelle Z. Rosaldo and Louise Lamphere. Stanford, 1974.

Landa, Fray Diego de. *Relacion de las cosas de Yucatán.* Mérida, 1938.

Landes, Ruth. *A Cidade das Mulheres.* N.d.

Langer, Thomas S. "Psycho-physiological Symptoms and the Status of Women in Two Mexican Communities." In *Approaches to Cross-Cultural Psychiatry,* edited by Jane M. Murphy. Ithaca. 1965.

Larco Hoyle, Rafael. "A Culture Sequence for the North Coast of Perú." In *HSAI,* 2:149-75, edited by Julian H. Steward. Washington, D.C., 1946.

Larruga, E. *Memorias políticas y económicas sobre los frutos, commercio, fabricas y minas de España.* 45 vols. Madrid, 1793.

Las Casas, Bartolomé de. *Colección de tratados; Apologetica historia de las Indias; Historia de las Indias.* Madrid/Barcelona, 1908-1916.

Laslett, Peter. *The World We Have Lost.* Cambridge, Mass., 1965.

Lavalle Urbina, M. *Situación de la mujer en el derecho de familia latino americano: Documento de Trabajo B/P/B and Add.L, Seminario de 1963 sobre la condicion de la mujer en el derecho de familia.* Bogotá, 1964.

Lavrin, Asunción. "The Role of the Nunneries in the Economy of New Spain in the Eighteenth Century." *HAHR* (November 1966): 371-93.

───────. " Values and Meaning of Monastic Life for Nuns in Colonial Mexico." *Catholic Historical Review* 58:3 (October 1972) 367-87.

───────. "La riqueza de los conventos de monjas en Nueva España: estruturay evolucion durante el síglo XVIII." *Cahiers des Ameriques Latines,* 8 (1973), 91-122.

───────. *Religious Life of Mexican Women in the Eighteenth Century.* Unpub. Ph.D. dissertation, Harvard University, 1963.

Lenero Otero, Luis. *Investigacion de la familia en Mexico.* Mexico, 1968.

Leitao, Humberto. *Os Portugueses em Solor e Timor de 1515 a 1702.* Lisboa, 1948.

─────── *Vinte-Oito Anos de Historia de Timor, 1698-1725.* Lisboa, n.d.

Leroy, James. *Philippine Life in Town and Country.* New York, 1906.

Levene, Ricardo. *La cultura histórica y el sentimiento de la nacionalidade.* Buenos Aires, 1942.

Lévi-Strauss, Claude. "Tribes of the Upper Xingu River." In *HSAI* 2:321-48, edited by Julian H. Steward. Washington, D.C., 1948.

Lewis, Oscar. *The Children of Sánchez.* New York, 1961.

───────. *Five Families.* New York, 1959.

───────. "Husbands and Wives in a Mexican Village: A Study of Role Conflict." In *Latin American Social Organization and Institutions,* edited by Olen E. Leonard and Charles P. Loomis. East Lansing, 1953.

─────── *Life in a Mexican Village.* Urbana, 1951.

Lillo Catalan, V. *La influencia de la Mujer.* Buenos Aires, 1940.

Linschoten, J. *Discours de Voyages.* London, 1622.

Lipkind, William. "The Caraja." In *HSAI,* 2:179-91, edited by Julian H. Steward. Washington, D.C., 1948.

Lobato, Alexandre. *Evolução administrativa e econômica de Moçambique, 1752-1763.* Lisboa, 1957.

Lipset, Seymour, and Solari, Also. *Elites in Latin America.* London, 1967.

Lison-Tolosana, Carmelo. *Belmonte de los Caballeros: A Sociological Study of a Spanish Town.* Oxford, 1966.

Livi-Bacci, Massimo. "Fertility and Population Growth in Spain in the Eighteenth and Nineteenth Centuries." *Daedalus* 97 (1968) 523-35.

Livros de Linhagens. *Portugalia Monumenta Historica Scriptores.* Lisboa, 1856.

Lloyd, P. C. *Africa in Social Change: West African Societies in Transition.* New York, 1968.

Lobato, Alexandre. "Colonização Senhorial de Zambézia." In *Colonização Senhorial da Zambezia e Outros Estudos.* Lisboa, 1962.

Locher, A. *Area Study of Dutch Timor, Terrain Study 70 of the Allied Geographical Section, on Timor's Social Structure.* N.p., 1943.

Locke, John. *Some Thoughts Concerning Education.* London, 1693.

Lockhart, James. *Spanish Peru, 1532-1560.* Madison, 1968.
Lopes, D. *História de Arzila durante o dominio portugues.* Coimbra, 1924.
López, Vicente Fidel. *Historia de la Republica Argentina.* Buenos Aires, 1939/1957.
López Morán, E. "Leon." In *Derecho con su etudinario y economía popular de Espana,* edited by Sr. Costa, 2 vols. Barcelona, 1902.
Loreto Hernández, Margarita. *Personalidad de la mujer mexicana.* Mexico, 1961.
Lothrop, S. K. "Indians of the Paraná Delta and La Plata Littoral." In *HSAI,* 1:179-90, edited by Julian H. Steward. Washington, D.C., 1946.
Love, Edgar F. "Marriage Patterns of Persons of African Descent in a Colonial Mexico City Parish." *HAHR* 51 (February 1971): 79-91.
Lowie, Robert. "The Bororo. In *HSAI,* 1:419-34, edited by Julian H. Steward, Washington, D.C., 1946a.
─────. "Eastern Brazil." In *HSAI,* I, 1:381-97. 1946.
─────. "The Northwestern and Central Ge." In *HSAI* 1:477-517. 1946b.
─────."The Southern Cayapó." In *HSAI,* 1:519-520. 1946c.
─────. "The Tapuya," "The Cariri," "The Pancararú," "The Tarairiu," "The Jeico," "The Guck." In *HSAI,* 1:553-69. 1946d.
Ludwig, Emil. *Bolívar, the Life of an Idealist.* New York, 1942.
Luna Arroyo, Antonio. *La mujer mexicana en la lucha social.* Mexico, 1936.
Luna Morales, Clara. *El sufragio Feminino en Mexico.* Mexico, 1947.
Luna de Oliveira. *Timor in Portuguese History.* 3 vols. Lisboa, n.d.
Lynch, Frank. "The Conjugal Bond Where the Philippines Changes." *Philippine Sociological Review* 7 (July-October, n.d., 7): 3-4.
─────. *Social Class in a Bikol Town.* Chicago, 1959.
Mabragana, N. *Los Mensajes, 1810-1910.* Buenos Aires, 1910.
Macaya, Margarita. "Women—Their Role, Present and Potential, in the Caribbean." In *The Caribbean: Its Hemispheric Role,* edited by A. Wilgus. Gainesville, 1967.
MacFarlane, Alan. *The Family Life of Ralph Josselin. A Seventeenth Century Clergyman.* Cambridge, England, 1970.
Machado de Arnao, Lus. "Teresa Carreno." *Revista Nacional de Cultura* (July-August 1965).
MacGaffrey, Wyatt, and Barnett, Clifford R. *Cuba, Its People, Its Society, Its Culture.* New Haven, 1962.
MacLachlan, Colin. "The Feminine Mystique in Brazil: The Middle Class Image." Paper presented at PICLAS, Monterrey, Autumn 1972.
Madeira, Felicia R., and Singer, Paul I. "Estrutura do Emprego e Trabalho feminino no Brasil, 1920-1970." Caderno 13, CEBRAP, Sao Paulo, 1973.
Mafud, Julio. *La Revolución Sexual Argentina.* Buenos Aires, 1966.
Mandelbaum, David G. "The Family in India." *Southwestern Journal of Anthropology* 4 (1948) 123-39.
─────. *Society in India.* 2 vols. Berkeley and Los Angeles, 1972.

Mansilla, General Lucio V. Excursion a los indios ranqueles. *Edit. Biblioteca de "La Nacion,"* n.p. (1907: vols. 197, 198).

————. *Rosas.* Buenos Aires, 1933.

Mantegazza, Pedro. *Cartas Médicas sobre la América Meriodional.* Tucumán, 1949.

Manusamhita. Translated by G. Bühler. N.p., 1933.

Marañon, Gregorio. *Maternidad y Femenismo.* N.d.

Maria de Jesus, Carolina. *Child of the Dark.* New York, 1962.

Marino de Lovera, Pedro. *Crónica del reino de Chile.* Santiago, 1865.

Marques Pereira, Nuno. *Compendio Narrativo do Peregrino da America, em que se tratam de varios discursos.* 2 vols. n.p., 1939.

Marriott, McKim. *Caste Ranking and Community Structure in Five Regions of India and Pakistan.* Poona, 1955-1960.

————. *Village India.* Chicago, 1955.

Marris, Peter. *Family and Social Change in an African City, A Study in Rehousing in Lagos.* Evanston, 1962.

Marshall, C. E. "The Birth of the Mestizo in New Spain." *HAHR* 19 (1939): 161-84.

Marti, Rosa Signorelli de. "Spanish America." In *Women in the Modern World,* edited by Raphael Patao. New York, 1967.

Martins Rodrigues, Leônicio. *Conflito Industriel e Sindicalismo no Brasil.* N.p., 1966.

Martinez-Alier, Verena. "Elopement and Seduction in Nineteenth-Century Cuba." *Past and Present,* 55 (May 1972), 91-129.

————. *Marriage, Class and Color in Nineteenth-Century Cuba: A Study of Racial Attitudes and Sexual Values in a Slave Society,* Cambridge, 1975.

Martinez Sierra, Maria. *La Mujer Española Ante la República.* Madrid, 1931.

Marx, Karl. *Morceaus choisies.* Paris, n.d.

Matthews, Dom Basil. *Crisis of the West Indian Family.* 1953.

Maxwell, Kenneth. Ms. materials on the Luso-Enlightenment.

Maybury-Lewis, David. *Akwe-Shavante Society.* Oxford, 1967.

————. *The Savage and the Innocent.* London, 1965.

Mayer, Adrian C. *Land and Society in Malabar.* Bombay, 1952.

Mayer, Kurt B. *Class and Society.* New York, 1955.

McAlister, Lyle. "Social Structure in New Spain." *HAHR* 53 (1963) 349-70.

McGuinn, Noel F. "Marriage and Family in Middle-Class Mexico." *Journal of Marriage and the Family* 28 (August 1966): 305-13.

McLennan, J. F. *The Patriarchal Theory.* London, 1885.

————. *Primitive Marriage.* Edinburgh, 1865.

MacLeod, Murdo J. *Spanish Central America. A Socioeconomic History, 1520-1720.* Berkeley and Los Angeles, 1973.

McLennan, L. H. *Studies in Ancient History.* New York, 1886.

Means, P. A. *Ancient Civilizations of the Andes.* London, 1931.

Melo Lancheros, Livia Stella. *Valores Femininos de Colombia.* Bogotá, 1966.

Mello Leitão, C. de. *Visitantes do Primeiro Imperio*. São Paulo, 1934.
Mendo Trigoso, S. F. de, ed. *Viagem de Lisboa à ilha de Sao Tomè escrita por hum piloto portugues*. Lisboa, n.d.
Menezes, Fernando de. *História de Tangere*. Lisboa, 1732.
Métraux, Alfred. "The Botocudo. In *HSAI*, 1:531-40, edited by Julian H. Steward. Washington, D.C., 1946e.
————. "The Caingang." In *HSAI*, 1: 445-75. 1946b.
————. "Ethnography of the Chaco." In *HSAI*, 1: 197-38. 1946.
————. "The Fulvio," "The Terembé." In *HSAI*, 1:571-4. 1946f.
————. "The Guaitacá." In *HSAI*, 1:521-2. 1946c.
————. "The Guató." In *HSAI*, 1:409-18. 1946a.
————. "The Guarani." In *HSAI*, 1:69-94. 1948.
————. "The Purí-Coroado Linguistic Family." In *HSAI*, 1:523-30. 1948d.
———— "Tribes of Eastern Bolivia and the Madeira Headwaters." In *HSAI*, 2:381-454. 1948b.
————. "Tribes of the Eastern Slopes of the Bolivian Andes." In *HSAI*, 2:465-506. 1948c.
————. "Tribes of the Juruá-Burus Basin." In *HSAI*, 2:657-86. 1948d.
————. "Tribes of the Middle and Upper Amazon River." In *HSAI*, 2:687-712. 1948e.
————. "The Tupinambá." In *HSAI*, 2:95-133. 1948a.
————, and Baldus, Herbert. "The Guayaki." In *HSAI*, 1:435-44. 1946.
————, and Kirchoff, Paul. "The Northwestern Extension of Andean Culture." In *HSAI*, 4:349-68. 1948.
————, and Nimuendaju, Curt. "The Camacan Linguistic Family." In *HSAI*, 1:547-62. 1946a.
————. "The Mashacali, Patasho, and Malali Linguistic Families." In *HSAI*, 1:541-45. 1946.
Meyer, Johan Jakob. *Sexual Life in Ancient India*. London, 1953.
Meyer Arana, Alberto. *Las Beneméritas de 1828*. Buenos Aires, 1923.
————. *Matronas y Maestras*. Buenos Aires, 1923.
Meyerowitz, Eva L. R. *Akan Traditions of Origin*. London, 1952.
Midelfort, H. C. Erik. *Witch-Hunting in Southwestern Germany, 1562-1684*. Stanford, 1972.
Minturn, Leigh. *Mothers of Six Cultures*. New York, 1964.
————. *The Rajputs of Khalapur, India*. New York, 1966.
Mintz, Sidney. "Men, Women and Trade." *Comparative Studies in Society and History*, 13 (1971), 247-69.
Moçambique. Direcção Provincial dos Servicos de Estatistica Geral. *Anuário Estatístico*. Moçambique, 1964.
Moigenie, Victor de. *A mulher em Portugal*. Porto, 1924.
Mondlane, Eduardo. *The Struggle for Mozambique*. London, 1969.
Montanari, Paolo. *Documenti su la popolazione di Bologne*. Bologna, 1966.

Montejo, Esteban. *The Autobiography of a Runaway Slave.* New York, 1973.

Morais, Vamberto. *A Emancipação da Mulher.* 1968.

Moreau de Justo. *La Mujer en la Democracia.* Buenos Aires, 1945.

Morgan, Edmund. *Virginians at Home.* Williamsburg, 1952.

————. *The Puritan Family.* Boston, 1944.

Morgan, L. H. *Ancient Society.* New York, 1877.

————. *Systems of Consanguinity and Affinity in Human Family.* Washington, D.C., 1971.

Morley, Sylvanus G. *The Ancient Maya.* Stanford, 1946.

Mörner, Magnus. *Race Mixture in the History of Latin America.* Boston, 1967.

Morse, Richard M. *From Community to Metropolis: A Biography of São Paulo, Brazil.* Gainesville, 1958.

Morton, Ward M. *Woman Suffrage in Mexico.* Gainesville, 1962.

Motolinia, Toribio. *History of the Indians of New Spain.* Translated and edited by F. B. Steck. Washington, D.C., 1951.

Mousinho de Albuquerque, Joaquim. *Moçambique.* 2 vols. Lisboa, 1934.

Muraro, Rose Marie. *A Mulher na Construção do Mundo Future.* Petropolis, 1967.

Murias, Manuel, ed. *Instrução para o Bispo de Pequim (1784) e outros documentos para a historia de Macau.* Lisboa, 1943.

Muriel, Josefina. *Conventos de monjas en la Nueva Espana.* Mexico, 1946.

Murra, John. "The Historic Tribes of Ecuador." In *HSAI,* 2:785-82, edited by Julian H. Steward. Washington, D.C., 1946.

El Nacional. "La mujer en la política. Por que no ha llegado a desempenar los mas altos cargos." *Caracas* (17 January 1966).

Nadal, J., and Giralt, E. *La Population Catalane de 1553 a 1717.* Paris, 1960.

Nash, June. "A Critique of Social Science Models of Contemporary Latin American Society." Paper read at the Conference on Feminine Perspectives on Social Science Research in Latin America. Buenos Aires, (March 19-24, 1974).

————. *In the Eyes of the Ancestors: Beliefs and Behavior in a Maya Community.* New Haven, 1967.

Navarrete, Martin Fernandez de. *Colección de los viages y descubrimientos que hicieron por mar los espanoles.* 5 vols. Madrid, 1825-1837.

Neasham, V. Aubrey. "Spain's Emigrants to the New World, 1492-1592." *HAHR* 19 (1939): 147-60.

Nelken, Margarita. *La condición social de la mujer en Espana.* N.d.

Nett, Emily. "The Servant Class in a Developing Country: Ecuador." *Journal of Inter-American Studies* (1966): 437-52.

Neumann, Erich. *The Great Mother: An Analysis of the Archetype.* New York, 1955.

Nimuendajú, Curt. "The Cawahib, Parintintin, and their neighbors." In *HSAI,* 2:283-97, edited by Julian H. Steward. Washington, D.C., 1948b.

————. "Little Known Tribes of the Lower Tocantins," "Little Known Tribes of the Lower Amazon," "Tribes of the Lower and Middle Xingú River." In *HSAI*, 2:203-43. 1948a.

————. "The Turiwara and Arua." In *HSAI*, 2:193-8. 1948.

Noonan, John. "Intellectual and Demographic History." *Daedalus* 97 (1968): 463-85.

Nova Santos. *La mujer, nuestro sexto sentido y otros esposos*, n.d.

Nunes Pereira Neto, João Baptista. "A Evolução Social em Portugal depois de 1945." Ms. 1968.

Nuñez de Pineda y Bascuñan Francisco. *Cautiverio feliz.* 1673. Reprint. Santiago, 1863.

Nye, F. Ivan, and Berardo, Felix M. *Emerging Conceptual Framework in Family Analysis.* New York, 1968.

Ocampo, Victoria, "Pasado y Presente de la Mujer." *La Nación* (9 January 1966).

Olesen, Virginia. "Context and Posture: Notes on Socio-Cultural Aspects of Women's Roles and Family Policy in Contemporary Cuba." *Journal of Marriage and the Family* (August 1971): 548-60.

Oliveira Marques, A. H. *Daily Life in Portugal in the late Middle Ages.* Madison, 1971.

————. *History of Portugal.* 2 vols. New York, 1972.

Omari, T. Peter. "Changing Attitudes of Students in West African Society Towards Marriage and Family Relationships." *British Journal of Sociology* 11 (September 1960): 3.

Oñate, Maria del Pilar. *El feminismo en la literatur española.* N.d.

d'Orbigny, Alcide. *Voyage dans l'Amerique Meridionale.* 9 vols. Paris, 1835-1847.

Orenstein, Henry. *Conflict and Cohesion in an Indian Village.* Princeton, 1965.

Organization of America States. *Informe presentado por la Comisión Interamericana de mujeres sobre la condición económica de la mujer trabajadora en las Republicas Americanas.* Washington, D.C., 1959.

————. *América en Cífras: situación social.* Washington, D.C., 1969.

————. *Important Women in Public and Professional Life in Latin America.* Washington, D.C., 1969.

Orientación Revolutionaria. *Orientación Revolutionaria de Union de Mujeres de Bolivia.* 1966.

Ormeling, Ferdinand Jan. *The Timor Problem.* The Hague, 1956/1957.

Ornes, German E. *Trujillo, Little Caesar of the Caribbean.* New York, 1958.

Ossorio, Angel. *A legato en defensa del sufragio feminino.* N.d.

————. *Cartas a las mujeres sobre derecho político*, n.p., n.d.

Otero Muñoz, Gustavo. "Figuras Femininas de la colonia." *Academia Colombiana de historia, Bogotá, Conferencias* (1936): 79-111.

Ots Capdequi, Josep María. "Bosquejo histórico de los derechos de la mujer casade en la legislación de Indias." *Revista general de legislación y jurisprudencia, Madrid* (1920): 23.

―――. *Instituciones sociales de la América española en el período colonial.* La Plata, Argentina, 1934.

Oviedo y Valdés, Gonzalo Fernández de. *Sumario de la natural historia de las Indias, 1526.* Mexico, 1950.

Pacheco, Armando O. *La Obra Educativa de Trujillo.* La Era de Trujillo, vol. 5. Ciudad Trujillo, 1955.

Pagés Larraya, Antonio. *Gabriela de Coni y sus Ficciones precursoras.* Buenos Aires, 1965.

Palmério, Mário. *Chapado do Bugre.* Rio de Janeiro, 1965.

Panikkar, K. M. *Malabar and the Portuguese.* Bombay, 1929.

Paredes de Salazar, Elssa. *Diccionario Biografica de la Mujer Boliviana.* La Paz, 1965.

Park, Willard Z., "Tribes of the Sierra Nevada de Santa Marta, Colombia." In *HSAI,* 2:865-86, edited by Julian H. Steward. Washington, D.C., 1946.

Parra, Teresa de la. *Tres Conferencias Inéditas.* Caracas, 1961.

Parry, J. H. *The Age of Reconnaissance.* New York, 1963.

―――. *The Sale of Public Offices in the Spanish Indies.* 1953.

Parsons, Talcott. "The American Family: Its Relation to Personality and the Social Structure." In *Family, Socialization, and Interaction Process,* edited by Talcott Parsons, et al. New York, 1955.

Parsons, Talcott, "On the Concept of Influence." *Public Opinion Quarterly* 27 (1963b): 37-62.

―――. "On the Concept of Influence." *Public Opinion Quarterly Philosophical Society* 107 (1963a): 232-62.

Pasajeros a Indias. Cristóbal Bermúdez Plata, ed., *Catálogo de pasajeros a Indias.* 3 vols. Seville, 1940-1946.

Pastells, Pablo, S.J. *Catálogo de los documentos relativos a las Islas Filipinas.* 9 vols. Barcelona, 1925-1938.

Patai, Raphael. *Women in the Modern World.* New York, 1967.

Patricias cordobesas. Sección patrítica. n.p., n.d.

Paulo Merea, M. *Evolução dos regimes matrimoniais: Contribuções para a História do Direito Portugues.* vol. II. Coimbra, 1913.

Paulme, Denise, *Women of Tropical Africa.* London, 1963.

Payne, Stanley. *A History of Spain and Portugal.* 2 vols. Madison, 1973.

Paz, José Maria. *Memorias Póstumas.* Buenos Aires. 1935.

Pellington, Frank. "Los Escritos de Frank Pellington." In *Annuario de la Sociedade de Historia.* Argentina, 1939.

Penalosa, Fernando. "Mexican Family Roles." *Journal of Marriage and the Family* 30 (November 1968): 680-8.

Pereira, Gabriel. *Documentos Historicos da Cidade de Évora.* Évora, 1885-1891.

Perera, Hilda. "Women in a New Social Context in Cuba." *International Journal of Adult and Youth Education* 3 (1962).

Pereyra, Carlos. *Historia de la America española.* 8 vols. Madrid, 1920-1926.

Pérez Botija, Margarita. *El trabajo feminino en España,* n.d.

Pérez Bustamante, C. "Las regiones españolas y la población de América, 1509-1534." *Revista de Indias* 2 (1941): 81-120.

Pérez Godoy, Manuel. "Juana Azurouy." In *Mujeres de América.* México, n.d.

Peristiany, J. *Honor and Shame: The Values of a Mediterranean Society.* Chicago, 1966.

Perón, Eva. *Discurso: En la sesion de Clausura de la Asamblea a Extraordinaris de la Comision Interamericana de Mujeres.* Buenos Aires, 1952.

Pertile, Antonio. *Storia del diritto italiano dalla caduta dell'impero romano alla codificazione.* Turin, 1894.

Pescatello, Ann M. *The African in Latin America.* New York, 1975.

————. *The African Diaspora: Historical and Anthropological Essay on Nineteenth and Twentieth Century Black Experiences in the Americas.* Forthcoming.

————. *Both Ends of the Journey: An Historical Study of Migration and Change in Brazil and Portugal, 1889-1914.* Ann Arbor, 1971.

————. *The Changing Role of the Latin American Woman in a Changing Latin America.* Special Issue. *Journal of Inter-American Studies and World Affairs* (November 1975a).

————. *Female and Male in Latin America: Essays.* Pittsburgh, 1973.

————. "The Female in Ibero-America: Research Directions and Research Opportunities." *LARR* (Summer 1972): 126-41.

————. *The Hispanic Caribbean Woman and the Literary Media.* Special Issue of the Revista/Review Interamerican (Summer 1974).

Phelan, John Leddy. *The Hispanization of the Philippines. Spanish Aims and Filipino Responses, 1565-1700.* Madison, 1967.

————. "Administrative Authority and Flexibility in the Spanish Imperial Bureaucracy." *Administrative Science Quarterly* (1960).

————. "The Philippine Collection in the Newberry Library." *The Newberry Library Bulletin* 3 (March 1955): 229-36.

Philippine Islands. Census Office. *Census of the Philippine Islands, 1903.* 4 vols., Washington, D.C., 1905.

Philips, Carla Rahn. "Seventeenth-Century Ciudad Real: A Demographic Study." Paper for the Society for Spanish and Portuguese Historical Studies. Rutgers University, April 1972.

Piçao, José da Silva. *Através dos campos usos e costumes agriculo-alentejanos.* Lisboa, 1947.

Pichel, Vera. *Mi Pais y sus mujeres.* Buenos Aires, 1968.

Pieris, P. E. *Ceylon: The Portuguese Era.* 2 vols. Colombo, 1923-1924.

Pierson, Donald. *Negroes in Brazil: A Study of Race Contact at Bahia.* Carbondale, 1966.

Pike, Ruth. *Aristocrats and Traders: Sevillian Society in the Sixteenth Century.* Ithaca, 1972.

————. "Sevillian Society in the Sixteenth Century: Slaves and Freedman." *HAHR* 47 (1967): 344-59.

Pinho, Wanderley. *Salões e damas do Segundo Reinado.* São Paulo, 1942.

Pissurlencar, P. *Assentos do Conselho do Estado da India, 1618-1750.* Pangim (Goa) 1957.

Pistone de Dagatti, Catalina. *Primeras Escritoras de Santa Fe.* Santa Fe, 1965.

Pitt-Rivers, Julian. *Mediterranean Countrymen: Essays in the Social Anthropology of the Mediterranean.* Paris, 1963.

————. *The People of the Sierra.* Chicago, 1961.

Polanyi, Karl. *Dahomey and the Slave Trade.* Seattle, 1966.

Poppino, Rollie. *Brazil: The Land and People.* New York, 1968.

Portal, Magda. *La Trampa.* Lima, 1956.

Portugal. Província de Angola. *Repartição de Estatistica Geral 3º. Recenseamento geral da população 1960.* Luanda, 1964.

Posada, Adolfo. *Feminismo.* 1963.

Prado, Javier. *Estado social del Perú durante la dominación española.* CLD Perú, Series 3. Lima, 1941.

Price, Paul H. "The Polish Immigrant in Brazil." Ph.D. dissertation, Vanderbilt University, 1950.

Purcell, Susan Kaufman. "Modernizing Women for a Modern Society: The Cuban Case." In *Female and Male in Latin America,* edited by Ann Pescatello. Pittsburgh, 1973.

Purifição, Miguel de. *Relacão defensive dos Filhos da India Oriental e da Provincia do Apostolo S. Thome dos Frades menores da regular observancia da mesma India.* Barcelona, 1640.

Queiroz, Bishop João de São José. *Visitas Pastorais: Memorias (1761 e 1762-1763).* Rio de Janeiro, 1961.

Quesada, Ginés. *Exemplo de todas las virtudes y vida milagrosa de la venerable madre Geronima de la Assumpción.* Madrid, 1717.

Quijano, G. *Vicios de la tertulias y concurrencias del tiempo.* Barcelona, 1785.

Raday Delgado, Juan de Dios de la. *Mujeres Célebres de España y Portugal,* Buenos Aires, 1942.

Radcliffe-Brown, A. R., and Forde, Daryll. *African Systems of Kinship and Marriage.* London, 1964.

Ramayón, Eduardo. *Ejercito guerrero, poblador y civilizador.* Buenos Aires, 1921.

Ramón y Cajal, Santiago. *La mujer,* n.d.

Ramos, Maria. *Mulheres da America.* Rio de Janeiro, 1964.

Rattray, R. S. *Ashanti.* London, 1927.

Recenseamento do Brasil. *Recenseamento do Brasil. Industria (y otros secções).* 1920.

Recop. Estadistica. *Recopilación estadistica, 1940-41.* Buenos Aires, 1941.

Redfield, Robert. *Peasant Society and Culture.* Chicago, 1956.

Regimento do Conselho do Império Colonial. Macau, 1943.

Rego Quirino, Tarcizio do. *Os Habitantes do Brasil no Fim do Século XVI,* n.p., 1966.

Reiner, Silvain. *Eva Perón.* Paris, 1960.

Relacion de mando del Virrey Antonio Caballero y Góngora. In Biblioteca de Historia nacional. Bogotá, 1789.

Relación del Virrey José de Espleta. In Biblioteca de Historia nacional. Bogotá, 1796.

Relatório da commicão encarregada de estudar as reformas a introduzir no sistema dos prazos de Moçambique. Lisboa, 1889.

Repartição Provincial dos Serviços de Economia e Estatistica Geral. Anuário estatistico de Macau, Ano de 1967. Macau, 1968.

Reports. Congress of the International Woman Suffrage Alliance.

Ribeiro, Darcy. "Universities and Social Development." In *Elites in Latin America,* edited by Seymour Lipset and Solari Also. London, 1967.

Ribeiro, João. *Fatalida de Historica de Ilha de Ceilão.* 1685.

Ribeiro, Orlando. "Cidade." In *Dicionario Historia de Portugal.* Lisboa, n.d.

Ribeiro, R. "The Amaziado Relationship and Other Aspects of the Family in Recife (Brazil)." *American Sociological Review* 10 (1945).

Ricard, Robert. *La Conquête spirituelle du Méxique . . . 1523 à 1572.* Paris, 1933.

————. *Etudes sur l'histoire des Portugais au Maroc.* Coimbra, 1955.

Riegelhaupt, Joyce. "Saloie Women: An Analysis of Informal and Formal Political and Economic Roles of Portuguese Peasant Women." *Anthropological Quarterly* 40:3 (July 1967), 95-126.

Rivera, Generoso F., and McMillan, Robert T. *The Rural Philippines.* Manila, 1952.

Robles de Mendoza, Margarita. *La evolución de la mujer en Mexico.* México, 1931.

Rodó de Villagran, Lucila. *Desarollo histórico de la educación de la mujer y su situación actual.* Guatemala, 1965.

Rodrigues, Lêda Maria Pereira. "A instrucao Feminina em São Paulo." São Paulo, 1962.

Rogers, Kenneth. *Reports on Education in Latin America.* Mimeographed. St. Louis, 1970, 1971.

Rojas, Ricardo. *La literature Argentina.* Buenos Aires, 1925.

Rosaldo, Michelle Z., and Lamphere, Louise, eds. *Woman, Culture, and Society.* Stanford, 1974. The entire collection and sources cited therein.

Rosen, Bernard C. "Socialization and Achievement Motivation in Brazil."
    American Sociological Review 27 (October 1962): 612-24.
————, and Anita LaRaia, "Modernity in Women: An Index of Social
    Change in Brazil," *Journal of Marriage and the Family*, 34:2 (May 1972),
    353-60.
Rosenblatt, Angel. *La poblacion indigena de America desde 1492 hasta la
    actualidad*. Buenos Aires, 1945.
————. *La población indigena y el mestizaje en América*. 2 vols. Buenos
    Aires, 1954.
Rosés Lacoigne, Zulema. *Mujeres Compositoras*. Buenos Aires, 1950.
Rotberg, Robert I. *A Political History of Tropical Africa*. New York, 1965.
Rothfeld, Otto. *Women of India*. Bombay, 1928.
Rouse, Irving. "The Arawak. In *HSAI*, 4:507-46, edited by Julian H.
    Steward. Washington, D.C., 1948.
————. "The Carib." In *HSAI*, 4:547-65. 1948a.
Rowe, John Howland. "Inca Culture at the Time of the Spanish Conquest."
    In *HSAI*, 2:183-330, edited by Julian H. Steward. Washington, D.C., 1946.
Royer, Fanchón. "Working Women of Mexico." *The Americas* 6 (October
    1949): 167-72.
————. *The Tenth Muse: Sor Juana de la Cruz*. Paterson, New Jersey, 1952.
Roys, Ralph L. "Yucatec Maya Socio-Political Organization at the Conquest."
    In *The Indian Background of Latin American History*, edited by Robert
    Wauchope. New York, 1970, 113-23.
Ruiz Almansa, Javier. "La poplación española en el siglo XVI." *Revista
    Internacional de Sociologia* 3 (1943): 4.
Russell, Jeffrey. *Witchcraft in the Middle Ages*. 1971.
Russell, P. E. *The English Intervention in Spain and Portugal in the Time
    of Edward III and Richard II*. Oxford, 1955.
Russell-Wood, A. J. R. *Fidalgos and Philanthropists: The Santa Casa da
    Misericordia of Bahia, 1550-1755*. Berkeley and Los Angeles, 1968.
Ryder, A. F. C. "An Early Portuguese Trading Voyage to the Forcados
    River." *Journal of the Historical Society of Nigeria* 1 (1959): 294-321.
————. "The Re-establishment of Portuguese Factories on the Costa
    da Mina to the Mid-Eighteenth Century." *Journal of the Historical
    Society of Nigeria* 1 (1958): 157-83.
Saffioti, Heleith Iara B. *A mulher na sociedade de classe: Mito e realidade*.
    São Paulo, 1969.
Saint-Hilarie, Auguste de. *Voyages dans l'Interieur du Brésil*. Paris, 1830.
Salinas y Cordoba, Buenaventura da. *Memorial de las historias del nuevo
    mundo Perú*. N.p., 1957.
Salt, Henry. *A Voyage to Abyssinia . . . and an Account of the Portuguese
    on the East Coast of Africa*. Philadelphia, 1916.
Sánchez, Luis A. *Una mujer sola contra el mundo*, n.d.

Sanders, William T. "Pre-Conquest Settlement Patterns: Sources." in *Indian Background of Latin American History,* edited by Robert Wauchope. New York, 1970, 85-90.

Santa Ines, Francisco de. *Crónica de la provincia de San Gregorio Magno . . . en la islas Filipinas, China, Japón, etcetera.* 2 vols. Manila, 1892.

Santa Maria, Agostinho de. *Historia do Real Convento de Santa Monica da Cidade de Goa,* n.p., n.d.

Santos Cruz, Francisco Inacio dos. *Da Prostituçāo na cidade de Lisboa.* Lisboa, 1841.

Santos Vilhena, Luiz dos. *Cartas Soteropolitanas e Brasilicas.* Bahia, 1922.

Sapper, Karl. "Die Zahl und die Volksdichte der indianischen Bevölkerung in Amerika." *Proceedings of the Twenty-First International Congress of Americanists.* The Hague, 1924.

Sarfatti, Margali (Larson). *Spanish Bureaucratic-Patrimonialism in America.* Berkeley, 1966.

Sarmiento, Domingo. *Recuerdos de Provincia.* Buenos Aires, 1911/1916.

Sartin, Pierette. *La promoción de la mujer.* Barcelona, n.d.

Sauer, Carl O. *The Early Spanish Main.* Berkeley and Los Angeles, 1966.

Schaden, Egon. *Aspectos Fundamentais da Cultura Guarani.* São Paulo, 1960.

Schapelle, Benjamin. *The German Element in Brazil.* Philadelphia, 1917.

Schipske, Evelyn G. "Analysis of the Consejo Nacional de Mujeres del Peru." In *The Changing Latin American Woman . . .* edited by Ann Pescatello, 1975.

Schmidel, U. *Derrotero y viaje a Espana y las Indias.* Santa Fe, 1938.

Schmidt, Peter. *The Historical Archaeology of African Culture.* In ms.

Schneider, David M., and Gough, Lathleen. *Matrilineal Kinship.* Berkeley and Los Angeles, 1961.

Schneider, David M., and Gough, Kathleen. *Matrilineal Kinship.* Berkeley Resources in Mediterranean Societies." *Ethnology* 10:1 (January 1971), 2.

Scholes, France V., and Roys, Ralph L. *The Maya Chotal Indians of Acalan-Tixchel.* Norman, 1968.

Schulte Nordholt, H.G. *The Political System of the Atoni of Timor.* The Hague, 1971.

Schultz de Mantovani, Fryda. *La Mujer en la Vida Nacional.* Buenos Aires, 1960.

Schurz, William. *The Manila Galleon.* New York, 1959.

Schwartz, Stuart B. "Free Farmers in a Slave Economy: The *Lavradores de Cana* of Bahia, 1550-1750." In *Colonial Roots of Modern Brazil,* edited by Dauril Alden. Berkeley and Los Angeles, 1973.

————. *Sovereignty and Society in Colonial Brazil.* Berkeley and Los Angeles, 1973a.

Scobie, James R. *Argentina, A City and Nation.* New York, 1964.

Seltman, Charles. *La Mujer en la Antigüedad.* Buenos Aires, 1965.

Senet, Rodolfo. *Es superior el hombre a la mujer,* n.p., n.d.

Serrano, Antonio. "The Charrua. In *HSAI,* 1:191-6, edited by Julian H. Steward. Washington, D.C., 1946.

Serrano y Sanz, M. *Origenes de la dominación española en America.* Madrid, 1918.

Service, Helen, and Service, Elman. *Tobati, a Paraguayan Village.* Chicago, 1954.

Sierra Martinez, G. *Cartas a las mujeres de Espana,* n.p., n.d.

————. *Feminismo, feminidad, espanolismo,* n.p., n.d.

Silva, Carmen da. *A Arte de Ser Mulher.* Rio de Janeiro, N.d.

Silva Correia, Germano da. *História da colonizaçao portuguesa na India.* 6 vols. Lisboa, 1943-1958.

Silva Rego, Antonio da. *Documentação para a historia das missoes do padroado portugês do Oriente, India.* Lisboa, 1947-.

Silva Valdés, Hernán. "El romance de la peona de estancia." In *Surestada,* 25 October 1952.

Silvert, Kalman. "The University Student." In *Continuity and Change in Latin America,* edited by John Johnson. Stanford, 1967.

Simón, Pedro. *Noticias historiales da las conquistas de Tierra Firme en las Indias Occidentales.* Bogotá, 1882-1892.

Singer, Milton. *When a Great Tradition Modernizes: An Anthropological Approach to Indian Civilization.* New York, 1972.

Smelser, Neil. *Social Change in the Industrial Revolution: An Application of Theory to the British Cotton Industry.* Chicago, 1959.

Smith, Daniel Scott. "Lectures in Demography," Newberry Library, Family History Institute. Chicago, 1974.

Smith, Hubert H. *Brazil: The Amazons and the Coast.* New York, 1879.

Smith, Margo. "Domestic Service as a Channel of Upward Mobility for the Lower Class Woman: The Lima Case." In *Female and Male in Latin America,* edited by Ann Pesatello. Pittsburgh, 1973.

Smith, M. G. *Government in Zazzau.* London, 1960.

————. "Social and Cultural Pluralism." In *Africa: Social Problems of Change and Conflict,* edited by Pierre vanden Berghe. San Francisco, 1965.

Smith, Raymond T. "The Matriarchal Family." In *The Character of Kinship,* edited by Jack Goody. Cambridge, England, 1973.

Smith, T. Lynn. "The People of Brazil and Their Characteristics." in *Modern Brazil,* edited by John Saunders. Gainesville, 1971.

Soares, José C. *Macau e a Assistência: Panorama médico-social.* Lisboa, 1950.

Soares de Sousa, Gabriel. *Noticia do Brasil.* São Paulo, 1940.

Soeiro, Susan. "The Social and Economic Role of the Convent: Women and Nuns in Colonial Bahia, 1677-1800. *HAHR* 54 (1974) 209-32.

Solari, Also. "Secondary Education and the Development of Elites." In *Elites in Latin America*, edited by Seymour Lipset and Also Solari. London, 1967.

Solberg, Carl. *Immigration and Nationalism: Argentina and Chile, 1890-1914*. Austin, 1971.

Solien, Nancy. *Black Carib Household Structure: A Study of Migration and Modernization*. Seattle, 1969.

Sors, Antonio. *Historia del Reino de Chile, situado en la América Meridional*. Santiago, 1921.

Sosa de Newton, Lily. *Las Argentinas de Ayer a Hoy*. Buenos Aires, 1967.

Sousa, Francisco de. *Oreinte Conquistado a Jesu Christo pelos Padres da Companhia de Jesus da Provincia de Goa*. 2 vols. Lisboa, 1710.

Souza e Silva, J. Norberto. *Brasileiras célebres*. Rio de Janeiro, 1892.

Southern, Richard. *Medieval Humanism and Other Studies*. Oxford, 1970.

————. *Western Society and the Church in the Middle Ages*. Harmondsworth, 1970a.

Southey, Robert. *History of Brazil*. 3 vols. London, 1810-1819.

Spengler, Joseph. "Demographic Factors and Early Modern Economic Development." *Daedalus* 97 (1968) 433-46.

Spinden, H. J. "The Population of Ancient America." *Geographic Review* (1928) 18.

Srinivas, Mysore N. *Caste in Modern India and Other Essays*. New York, 1962.

————. *Social Change in Modern India*. Berkeley and Los Angeles, 1966.

Stabile, Blanca. *La Mujer en el Desarollo Nacional*. Buenos Aires, 1961.

————. "The Working Woman in the Argentine Economy." *International Labour Review* 85 (1962): 122-8.

Steggerda, Morris. "Mestizos of South America." In *HSAI*, 6:105-9, edited by Julian H. Steward. Washington, D.C., 1950.

Stein, Stanley. *The Brazilian Cotton Manufacture Textile Enterprise in an Underdeveloped Area, 1850-1950*. Cambridge, Mass., 1957.

————. *Vassouras: A Brazilian Coffee County, 1850-1900*. Cambridge, Mass., 1957a.

Steinen, Karl von den. *Unter den Naturvölken Zentral-Brasiliens*. Berlin, 1894.

Stevens, Evelyn. "Marianismo: The Other Face of Machismo in Latin America." In *Female and Male in Latin America*, edited by Ann Pescatello. Pittsburgh, 1973.

————. "Mexican Machismo: Politics and Value Orientations." *Western Political Quarterly* (1965).

Steward, Julian H. "The Circum-Caribbean Tribes: An Introduction," in 4:1-41, edited by Julian H. Steward. Washington, D.C. 1948.

————, ed. *Handbook of South American Indians*. 7 vols. Washington, D.C., 1946-1959.

————, and Faron, Louis C. *Native Peoples of South America*. New York, 1959.

————, and Métraux, Alfred. "Tribes of the Peruvian and Ecuadorian
  Montana." In *HSAI*, 2:535-656. 1948.
Stewart, C. S. *Brazil and La Plata: The Personal Record of a Cruise.* New
  York, 1856.
Strandes, Justus. *The Portuguese Period in East Africa.* Nairobi, 1961.
Stutzman, Ronald. Private conversations, 1969-1971.
Stycos, J. Mayone. *Familia y fecundidad en Puerto Rico: Estudio del
  grupo de ingresos más bajos.* Mexico, 1958.
————. *History of the Family in Latin America.*
Suggs, Julia Flanigan. "Women Workers in Brazil." *Phylon* 8 (1947):
  60-7.
Sutherland, Elizabeth. *The Youngest Revolution.* New York, 1969.
Tagumpay-Castillo, Gelia, and Hilomen-Guerrero, Sylvia. "The Filipino
  Woman: A Study in Multiple Roles." *Journal of Asian and African Studies*
  4 (January 1969): 18-29.
Tancer, Shoshana. "La Quisqueyana:" The Dominican Woman, 1940-1970."
  In *Female and Male in Latin America,* edited by Anne Pescatello.
  Pittsburgh, 1973.
Tejeira, Otilia A. de. *La mujer en la vida panamena.* Panama, 1963.
Tenreiro, Francisco. *A ilha de São Tomé.* Lisboa, 1961.
Teixeira, Carlos. *A mulher portuguesa e os seu papel bio-sociológico.*
  Porto, 1940.
Texeira, Manuel. "O trajo feminino em Macau do século XVI ao século
  XVII." *Boletim Instituto Luis de Camoes, Macau* 3 (Spring 1969).
Texeira Botelho, J. J. *História militare política dos portugueses em
  Moçambique de 1833 aos nossos dias.* Lisboa, 1936.
Tercer Censo nacional. Buenos Aires, 1914.
Thirsk, Joan. "The Family." *Past and Present* 17 (1964) 116-22.
Thomas, Hugh. *The Spanish Civil War.* Harmondsworth, 1965.
Thomas, Keith. "History and Anthropology." *Past and Present* 24 (1963), 3-24.
————. "The Relevance of Social Anthropology to the Historical Study of
  English Witchcraft." In *Witchcraft Confessions and Accusations,* edited by
  Mary Douglas. London, 1970.
————. *Religion and the Decline of Magic.* New York, 1971.
Thomas, P. *Indian Women through the Ages.* London, 1964.
Thomé, Yolanda Bettencourt. *A mulher no mundo de Hoje.* Petrópolis, 1967.
Tiger, Lionel. *Men in Groups.* London, 1969.
The Times of India Directory and Yearbook including Who's Who. Bombay,
  1969.
Toro Godoy, Julia. *Presencia y Destino de la Mujer en Nuestro Pueblo.*
  Santiago, 1967.
Torre REvello, José. "Esclavos blancas en las Indias Occidentales." *Boletin
  del Investigaciones Historicas, Buenos Aires* 6 (September 1927): 263-71.

Torres Homem, J. V. *Elementos de Clinica Medica.* Rio de Janeiro, 1870.

Torres Texugo, F. *A Letter on the Slave Trade.* London, 1839.

Torres y Villaroel, D. de. *Suenos morales (Obras).* Madrid, 1794-1799.

Tovar, Beatriz. *Milheres Portuguêsas no Brasil.* Rio de Janeiro, n.d.

Trenti Rocamora, Luis. *Grandes Mujeres de America.* Huarpes, 1945.

Tschopik, Harry, Jr. "The Aymara. In *HSAI,* 2:501-73, edited by Julian H. Steward. Washington, D.C., 1946.

Ullman, Joan Connelly. *The Tragic Week: A Study of Anti-clericalism in Spain, 1875-1912.* Cambridge, Mass., 1968.

UNESCO. *Legal Status of Married Women.* New York, 1957.

United Nations. *The United Nations and the Status of Women.* 1964.

United States. Department of Labor. *The 1969 Handbook on Women Workers.* Washington, D.C., 1969.

——————. Publication Series. Bureau of Census. 1960-1975.

Uribe de Acosta, Ofelia. *Una voz insurgente.* Bogotá, 1963.

Ursins, P. des. *Lettres inédites de Mme. de Maintenon à Mme. la Princesse des Ursins.* 4 vols. Paris, 1826.

Vaillant, George. *The Aztecs of Mexico.* London, 1953.

Vansina, Jan. *Kingdoms of the Savanna.* Madison, 1968.

Van de Walle, Etienne. "Marriage and Marital Fertility." *Daedalus* 97 (1968) 486-501.

Varallanos, Jose. *El cholo y el Perú.* Buenos Aires, 1962.

Vasconcelos e Cirne, Manuel Joaquim M. *Memória sobre a provincia de Moçambique.* Lisboa, 1890.

Vaz Ferreyra, Carlos. *Sobre Feminismo.* Montevideo, 1933.

Vega, Garcilaso de la. *Royal Commentaries of the Incas and General History of Peru.* 2 vols. Austin, 1965.

Vega Díaz, Dardo de la. *La Rioja Heroica.* Mendoza, 1955.

Veitia Linaje, Joseph de. *Norte de la contratación de las Indias Occidentales.* 1672.

Velasco, Juan López de. *Geografía descripción universal de las Indias.* Madrid, 1894.

Vélez Sársfeld, Dalmacio. *Codigo civil de la Republica Argentina.* Buenos Aires, 1870.

Verlinden, Charles. "Le Probléme de la continuité en histoire coloniale." *Revista de Indias* 11 (1951): 219-36.

——————. *Précédents mediévaux de la colonisation en Amerique.* Mexico City, 1954.

Vertiz y Salcedo, Juan José de. Documentos ineditos. Microfilm.

Viajes. *Colección de los viajes y descubrimientos que hicieron por mar los Espanoles des de fines del siglo XV.* 5 vols. Madrid, 1825-1837.

Vilela Luz, Nicia. *A luta pela industrialização no Brasil, 1808-1930.* São Paulo, 1961.

Vilhena, Ernesto de. *O regime dos prazos de Zambézia.* Lisboa, 1916.
Villafane Casal, Maria Teresa. "La Mujer Española en la Counquista y
Colonización de America." *Cuadernos Hispanoamericanos,* no.
175-176 (n.d.).
————. *La mujer en la Pampa: Siglos XVII y XIX.* La Plata, 1958.
Villani, Giovanni. *Cronica de Giovanni Villani.* Florence, 1823.
Villasenor Martinez, Irene. "El Mexicano: La Familia." Ph.D. dissertation,
Guadalajara University. Guadalajara, 1964.
Vittone, Luis. *La mujer Paraguaya en la Vida Nacional.* Asunción, 1968.
Virey, Julio José. *La mujer,* n.d.
Voltaire. *Candide,* n.d.
Wafer, Lionel. *A New Voyage and Description of the Isthmus of America.*
London, 1729.
Wagley, Charles. *Race and Class in Rural Brazil.* Paris, 1952.
————. *Amazon Town: A Study of Man in the Tropics.* New York,
1964.
————, and Galvão, Eduardo. "The Tapirapé." In *HSAI,* 2:167-78,
edited by Julian H. Steward. Washington, D.C., 1948.
————. "The Tenetehara." In *HSAI,* 2:137-48. 1948a.
Wallis, Marie P. "Modern Poets of Brazil." Ph.D. dissertation, University of
New Mexico. New Mexico, 1947.
Ward, Barbara. *Women in the New Asia.* Paris, 1964.
Wauchope, Robert. *Handbook of Middle American Indians.* 10 vols. Austin,
1965-.
————. *The Indian Background of Latin American History.* New York, 1970.
Weber, Max. *The Theory of Social and Economic Organization.* New York, 196(
Wernstedt, Frederick L., and Spencer, J. E. *The Philippine Island World.*
Berkeley and Los Angeles, 1967.
Whiteway, R. S. *The Rise of Portuguese Power in India, 1497-1550.*
London, 1899.
Whitten, Norman P. Private conversations, 1971.
Wickberg, Edgar. *The Chinese in Philippine LIfe, 1850-1898.* New
Haven, 1965.
————. "The Chinese Mestizo in Philippine HIstory." *Journal of South-
eastern Asian History* (March 1964): 62-100.
————. "Spanish Records in the Philippine National Archives." *HAHR*
35 (February 1955), 77-89.
Wilde, Joseph. *Buenos Aires desde 70 anos Atrás.* Eudeba, 1961.
Willems, E. "A estrutura de familia brasileira." *Sociologia* (Sao Paulo)
16 (1954): 4.
————. "A familia portuguesa contemporânea." *Sociologia* (1955): 6-55.
————. "On Portuguese Family Structure." *International Journal of
Comparative Sociology* 3 (1962): 65-79.

———. "The Structure of the Brazilian Family." *Social Forces* 31 (1953): 339-46.

Wirth, John. *The Politics of Brazilian Development, 1930-1954.* Stanford, 1970.

Wolf, Eric. *Anthropology.* Englewood Cliffs, 1964.

———. "Kinship, Friendship and Patron-Client Relations in Complex Societies." In *The Social Anthropology of Complex Societies,* edited by Michael Banton. London, 1964.

———. *Sons of the Shaking Earth.* Chicago, 1959.

Wolf, Margery. "Chinese Women: Old Skills in a New Context." In *Women, Culture, and Society,* edited by Michelle Z. Rosaldo and Louise Lamphere. Stanford, 1974.

Woodsmall, Ruth. *Women in the Near East.* Washington, D.C., 1960.

Woortman, K. A. A. W. "A mulher en situação de Classe." *America Latina* 8:3 (1965), 62-83.

Wright, L. P. "The Military Orders in Sixteenth and Seventeenth Century Spanish Society." *Past and Present* (1968).

Wrigley, E. A. "Family Limitation in Preindustrial England." *Economic History Review* 19 (1966): 82-109.

Yearbook of Labor Statistics. Geneva, 1970.

Youssef, Nadia, "Cultural Ideals, Feminine Behavior and Family Control," *Comparative Studies in Society and History,* 15:3 (June 1973), 326-47.

Zinny, Antonio. *Historia de los Gobernadores de las Provincias Argentinas.* Buenos Aires, 1941.

INDEX